THE HOUGHTON MIFFLIN

RADIO BROADCASTING SERIES

Albert Crews
EDITOR

RADIO PRODUCTION DIRECTING

Albert Crews

PRODUCTION DIRECTOR
CENTRAL DIVISION
NATIONAL BROADCASTING COMPANY
AND FORMERLY
ASSISTANT PROFESSOR OF SPEECH AND
CHAIRMAN OF THE RADIO DEPARTMENT
SCHOOL OF SPEECH NORTHWESTERN UNIVERSITY

HOUGHTON MIFFLIN COMPANY
BOSTON · NEW YORK · CHICAGO · DALLAS · ATLANTA · SAN FRANCISCO
The Riverside Press Cambridge

The Riverside Press
CAMBRIDGE · MASSACHUSETTS
PRINTED IN THE U.S.A.

PREFACE

RADIO is a wonderful thing, not because it created the RCA Building, or Bing Crosby, or the soap industry. It is wonderful for a purely impersonal, scientific reason. It is an invention which allows one man in a single moment of time to be heard by millions of human beings. When the President of the United States speaks, he has an audience that often numbers more than sixty million people. Radio could make it possible for the president of the world to sit at a microphone and address an audience of every person in the world who could hear.

Radio, itself, is a neutral thing. It is merely a device for transporting noise from one place to many others. But its power lies in the fact that the noise it transmits can be heard anywhere in the world, by as many people as wish to listen.

A medium with such potentialities should be in good hands. The broadcasters to come must be men and women who are skilled in the use of their medium, and who have a deep sense of the power they hold and of the obligation to use it well. And from where will such people come?

The training of men and women to use the medium of radio is a thing too important to be left to chance. It is one of the most significant tasks confronting contemporary education. So far, our attemps at training people for radio have been fumbling and inept. The attempts have been honest and the efforts sincere, but the results have not been encouraging. Professional radio people have been too busy to do the job. Teachers, for the most part, have not been sufficiently well informed to do it. And there was mutual distrust between the two. Schools looked on broadcasters as crass commercialists; broadcasters looked on school teachers as ivory-tower inhabitants – too impractical to do the job. Meantime, young people with a serious interest in radio had no place to turn.

It seems obvious that schools know the problems of pedagogy; broadcasters know their subject matter. If the broadcasters could be made into teachers and the teachers into broadcasters, their combined efforts might result in training for radio that would be both academically sound and professionally practicable. It was this thought that was behind the formation, in the summer of 1942, of the Summer Radio Institute, jointly sponsored by Northwestern University and the National Broadcasting Company.

Had it not been for the vision and daring of Ralph Brownell Dennis, late dean of the School of Speech of Northwestern University, this Institute would never have come into being. When the idea was presented to him, he lent the full weight of his support to it at once. He was a great educator and a great man. It was his belief and that of Miss Judith Waller of NBC which made the first Institute possible. They believed firmly that a medium so important to so many people must be in the hands of the most competent and best-trained individuals it is possible to find. It was to this end that the Summer Radio Institute was dedicated.

It soon became evident that one of the greatest difficulties in teaching radio was the lack of textbooks in the field. To meet this need a series of such books was commissioned by the National Broadcasting Company. This volume is one of the first in this series. If it can help toward the end of professional radio training in any small way, it will have served its purpose.

This volume, as far as possible, represents the best thinking of some of the National Broadcasting Company's most capable people. Their help, criticism, and contributions have given it whatever authority it may have. However, this volume is not meant to be merely the exposition of NBC production methods, but rather of those basic concepts on which all sound production work is founded.

Miss Judith Waller, director of Public Service, Central Division, NBC, first suggested this series. It was her belief in the work which prompted NBC to sponsor it. Since the inception of the project she has been in constant contact with its progress. Her interest and help have done much to make it possible.

I am also grateful to Doctor James Rowland Angell, Public Service Counselor for the National Broadcasting Company, and to Mr. Harry Kopf, Vice-President in charge of the Central Division, for their approval of the project and their interest in its progress.

Much credit is due to Wynn Wright, National Production Manager, NBC, who conferred in detail on the first eight chapters. Many of the ideas and suggestions for organization are his.

My thanks go also to Jules Herbeveaux, Program Director, Central Division, and Arthur Jacobson, Production Manager, Central Division, for their help and criticism on the manuscript; to Beverly Fredendall, Transmission Engineer, Central Division, for his help on Chapter 3 and for permission to use one of his drawings; to Howard Wiley, Production Manager, Western Division, for his help on the music aspects of production; and to George Voutsas for permission to reprint parts of his lecture on music production.

I must express my thanks to Dean James McBurney, Dean of the School of Speech, Northwestern University, for his cooperation on the project while I was on the staff at Northwestern University.

Finally, my thanks go to all those students in the Summer Radio Institutes at Northwestern University, at the University of California, Los Angeles, and at Stanford University, who used and criticized the preliminary version of the present book during the summer of 1943. My particular thanks go to Jennings Pierce, Director of Public Service, Western Division, who was also director of the NBC-UCLA Institute, and to Miss Inez Richardson of Stanford University, for their comments and criticisms on the preliminary version of this book.

All these people gave unselfishly of their time and knowledge because they believed in the idea of sound professional radio training.

ALBERT CREWS

CHICAGO, ILLINOIS

CONTENTS

SECTION ONE
THE MEDIUM AND THE MAN

SECTION TWO
THE TOOLS OF RADIO PRODUCTION DIRECTING

SECTION THREE
GENERAL PROCEDURES

SECTION FOUR
APPLICATION OF PROCEDURE

APPENDIX

LIST OF PLATES

1

THE MEDIUM AND THE MAN

CHAPTER 1

THE MEDIUM

LISTENERS to "Vic and Sade" will remember that Uncle Fletcher frequently asks them if they know, "What and where Fiendish, Indiana, are." In embarking on a treatise on radio production, it is well to come to an understanding with the reader as to what and who a radio production director "are." Strangely enough, the job of describing the position and duties of a radio production director is not easy. One exasperated director, after half an hour of desperate effort to make clear his duties to an uninitiated outsider, had this summary handed back to him: "Oh, I see. You tell them when to start and when to stop!"

What is radio production, and what are the duties of a radio production director? To answer these questions it is necessary to define terms. People in radio, as in other branches of the theatrical business, use terms rather loosely. Many people use the term "producer" to indicate the man in charge of a radio program. Another common term is "production man." The theater has its theatrical managers, its producers, its directors. Hollywood has producers, directors, dialogue directors, dance directors, and music directors. All these terms are used indiscriminately by most people and the result is complete confusion.

The term "producer" is sometimes used to designate the overseer of a production, under whose direction several specialized directors may work. It is sometimes applied to radio directors who do all the work on a program. Since there is no definitely established terminology, some arbitrary assignment of meaning must be made. In the field of radio, we will call our executive in charge of a program a *production director.*

The term "production director" is not in general use (being more often supplanted by "producer" or "production man" at

CBS, Blue, and Mutual), but it is a more accurate term than any now in use and it is accepted at NBC. The term is applied to the person who completely supervises a program including the conducting of rehearsals.

The Production Director's Goal

It is the production director's goal to make people listen. That comes first. In addition, he may have to move people emotionally. He may have to move them to action. Perhaps he may have to instruct them. He may often have to amuse them. He must carry to them an emotion, an idea, an urge to act — and he must do all of this through the medium of sound alone. He must create such pointings, such overtones, must plant subtly such ideas as the program, the script, the station, or the sponsor may dictate.

Like most definitions, this one covers a multitude of tangible and intangible demands which are made on the person in the responsible position of a production director. His aim in producing a program may be to entertain or to amuse. Or it may be to transmit to a listening audience a piece of startling news. Again, his only purpose may be the creation of a pleasant background of music against which the listener can proceed with his normal daily routine. He may be enlisted to present a complex series of technical facts. He may be called upon to create a living drama. Or he may be asked to introduce the listening audience to the intricacies of Beethoven or boogie-woogie. Whatever the content of his program, whatever the specific tools with which he works, whatever the program idea may be, it is his job to make that content, that material, that idea, intelligible to a listening audience through the single medium of sound and the single perceiving sense of human hearing.

The Production Director's Position

These are the ends to be achieved; the next question is how these results may be obtained. The answer involves, among other things, the question of authority. Where does the production director stand in the hierarchy of radio? Where does his authority begin and where does it end? In all the complex matters of business, of policy, of artistic conception, of difficult interpretation, what are the boundaries within which he maintains control? Naturally the amount of authority given to a production director will vary from station to station and from network to network. In general, however, there are certain fairly definite areas which he may consider his own and there are limits in most organizations beyond which he may seldom go.

The production director rarely has voice in the matters of broadcast policy. Too often he has little voice in the kinds of programs he is asked to produce. In many cases he will have little or no authority over the script or content of the program which he is asked to direct. However, in a well-organized production unit, he may have some small voice in all of these matters. His least likely sphere of influence is in the field of broadcast policy, where decisions are usually made by higher executives. More often than not he will have little to do with the creation of a program or a program idea. He may, however, wield considerable influence over both the program and the basic idea after the matter has been placed in his hands. Suppose, for example, that a rather poor dramatic script is given to an excellent production director who has a fine sense of his duty to his audience. In many broadcast organizations the respect for the director is such that his recommendation might cause either a complete abandonment of the script or a rewrite so extensive as to make it practically a new script. On the other extreme, in another organization he might be allowed no voice at all in the revision of the script and would be forced to produce the program as originally handed to him. Somewhere between these extremes probably lies the usual procedure. It is reasonably safe to say that the production director's authority begins after the idea has been approved by the program board and a script written and accepted by the continuity department. From that time forward the responsibility is his. From that time, until the broadcast comes off the air, his word is absolute. Thereafter he is subject to dictation only in case he is doing an unacceptable job.

The production director obviously has the complete and final voice in casting most programs. His word is final regarding all matters of selection of sound and music and the manner in which the script is treated on the air. He is the final authority in the matter of interpretation, of the placing of microphones, of any of the myriad details which become important in the final execution of a program on the air.

There are exceptions and irregularities in the distribution of authority in various broadcasting organizations, but in general the lines described here are the most common. Within this framework the production director is responsible for the excellence of the program which is placed in his hands.

There are certain business limitations upon the will of the production director. There are limitations of budget, of station policy, of the availability of personnel, of the availability and caliber of talent. In some instances he will also be limited by the wishes of the sponsor or by the department originating the program within the station. All these things are obvious and they are the same kind of limitations which are placed on a man in any business. The production director, for example, obviously cannot have a forty-piece orchestra to furnish cue music for a dramatic show if the budget does not allow for so many musicians. Or he may not have his wish if there are not that many musicians available. All these things and dozens of others like them are limiting factors from a business point of view upon the production director both as an interpretive and as a creative artist.

On the creative and interpretive side of his work the production director has a free hand, subject only to business limitations. The choosing of a cast, the interpretation of the script, the use of sound, the pacing and timing of the show, the placing of parts, the arrangement of the studio, even the manner of engineering — all these things are in the hands of the production director and his decisions on them are final. How much of this responsibility he delegates to members of his company will be discussed in detail later, but the responsibility for the final result in all these fields belongs solely with him. He is the czar of the production from the artistic and interpretive point of view. What a broadcasting company pays a production director for is to have that innate sense of showmanship which creates the right effect with the given materials on a given audience.

A Basic Philosophy for Production Directors

Having defined terms, set up goals, and indicated the area within which the production director works, we should next express a working philosophy for the potential production director, conditioned by the medium in which he works. Every artist is bound by certain principles which are determined by the nature of the medium. The medium will determine his tools, his forms, his audience, his advantages, and his limitations. Since radio production is a job for an artist, we should begin by examining the condition of his art. Once having understood basic principles, then, and *only then*, may we proceed to the more prosaic matter of ways and means.

The radio production director is a painter who uses a loudspeaker for his canvas; actors, speakers, music, sound effects for his colors; and a mixing panel for his palette. He must consider himself a conductor as well as a partner-creator of a symphony in sound.

This basic idea of a conductor handling a sound symphony must be retained no matter what the form or content of the program may be. Whether it is a simple program of recorded music or an elaborate production involving complicated dramatic scenes and pickups from all over the world, the basic concept is still the same. It differs only in the complexity of detail!

A director's success in radio will depend almost completely upon his knowledge of his medium. He must have respect for his medium and pride in it. But more than that he must have a detailed knowledge of the vast possibilities which are his in the use of sound. Without a detailed and confident knowledge of the basic elements of his medium, no production director can do more than a pedestrian job.

The Medium

The production director's medium is sound. Since he is to work in the medium of sound, he must know what sound is, what its characteristics are, what its artistic potentials can be, what can be done with it. Just as a ballet dancer works with the medium of sight and uses line, form, color, mass, and kinesthetic impressions to create an idea or a story for an audience, so must the production director work with the tools made available to him in the field of sound.

What are the artistic potentials of sound? Can one measure the greatness of any art form? The answer is yes. *The greatness of any art can be measured in terms of the number of people it moves, the depth to which it moves them, and the length of time that its influence is effective. Likewise, any artistic medium may be measured in terms of its power over an audience, its flexibility, its intelligibility, and the length of time that its impression endures.*

If we apply this measuring rod to the medium of sound as it is used in radio, the results are most encouraging. Sound has always had the power – in all times and in all civilizations – to move people deeply. From the jungle drums of primitive man to the air-raid siren screaming over a continent, sound carries a tremendous power to give a message. Think back to the last successful movie you saw. (We must consider a movie as a visual medium even though it has the auxiliary power of sound.) Do you remember that the audience gave any physical demonstration of emotional response to that artistic performance? Of course not. Scattered applause was the most that was heard. Now think of the last moving symphony you heard, or the last piece of swing music beautifully executed. What a different response from the audience! Even dignified symphony audiences will cheer, cry "Bravo," stand on their seats and call the artists back for bow after bow. This is only a crude indication of the power that sound has to reach an audience. It could probably be argued that sound is the most powerful of all media with which to reach an audience. Londoners say that the sight of a Stuka dive-bomber coming in is a terrifying thing, but that it is only when the whine of a shell or a descending bomb reaches a shrieking crescendo that the ultimate in fear is generated. There can be no doubt of the power of sound.

Consider now the number of people that can be reached through the medium of sound. The language of sound knows no barriers of time, place, language, civilization, or creed. It is true that when sound is formalized into the symbols of a given language, it lacks universality of communication. But that limitation holds only for language. Other sounds have a message for all people in all times. It is interesting to know that the same sound has the same effect on a Russian peasant and a board chairman in the New York Stock Exchange. Both these men, at opposite poles in conditioning, in background, in language, in philosophy of government, have a common reaction to the sound pattern of a schottische or the scream of a woman in mortal agony. When one considers sound only as a phenomenon of radio and thinks of the number of people which sound can reach by the means of radio, it becomes one of the most important media of communication of all times. No other medium has the great audience which is given to it. A successful novel may have a sale of two million copies and be read by ten million people. It is not unusual for a radio broadcast to be heard by forty million people in the normal course of things. In times of stress, when the eyes of the entire world are on certain focal points in the crisis of history in the making, a single broadcast, translated into a dozen different languages, can be heard simultaneously by millions of people all over the world. The mind of man has never conceived a medium with such a vast audience. If, as we have said, one of the measures of greatness of a medium is the number of people it can reach, nothing like radio has ever been before.

When one considers the length of time which a sound impression will remain with an audience, one comes to the only chink in the armor of sound as an ideal medium. The ear's memory for sound is admittedly shorter than the eye's memory for visual impressions. Sounds are quickly forgotten. But because sound has such tremendous power to move man deeply, the impressions created by it last many years. The memory of a sound is an ephemeral thing. The memory of an emotion aroused by sound may last a lifetime. Can you close your eyes and call to mind the haunting, lonely sound of a freight train whistling from far off in the night? The actual memory of the sound may have left you, but the impression, the emotion aroused are probably still vivid, though you may not have heard it since childhood.

Because of the shortness of the ear's memory, radio often is an ephemeral thing. When it reaches true greatness, however, it creates an impression which an audience will carry with it for many years. Radio, like any other artistic endeavor which lies within the framework of time, must inevitably tend to be ephemeral. Even though a great play may be reduced to cold type on the pages of a book, it does not contain the essence of theater. A great play occurs when the united alchemies of writer, actor, director, scenic artist, and lighting man create the electric moment when there is a tremendous flow of ideas and emotions between a cast on a stage and an audience in a theater. This is an ephemeral thing occurring at a given place in a given moment of time. It cannot be written down and repeated at will. So it is with radio or with any other medium that works within the framework of time rather than of space. This is the one area in which the artist, the poet, the painter, have a decided advantage. Once created, their work can be absorbed by an audience at the will of the audience. It is a fixed thing which can be stored away and brought out at the pleasure of the audience. Radio and all other dynamic artistic media lack this permanence. It must be considered one of the limitations of the medium of radio and the production director working in this medium must be willing to accept this impermanence. He may console himself, however, with the assurance that if he does a great piece of work it will survive in the memory of his audience because of the power of his medium to reach them and the depth to which the impression can be embedded in the minds of his listeners.

We come now to the consideration of the flexibility of the medium of sound and its application in radio. On this count the production director has no cause for complaint. Several generations of production directors will probably fumble through the learning of their art before we even approach a complete exploration of the possibilities which sound offers to radio.

Hear in your mind's ear for a moment, if you can, the magnificent evolution of the theme in the last movement of Tschaikovsky's *Fourth Symphony.* A hundred men using thirty or forty different instruments, each one of them capable of producing an almost infinite variety of sound and sound combinations, all work together to create a tonal pattern which, in strength and beauty, has seldom been surpassed by the creative mind of man. Think of the tremendous number of sounds and sound combinations which Tschaikovsky has woven into these few measures of his great work! Here is no limiting medium on an ambitious artist! This is a whole world of sound in infinite variety with which to tell one's story. While this impression is still fresh, try to conjure up across the chasm of the years the rasping, mellow, deep, sad voice of Abraham Lincoln intoning the immortal words of his *Gettysburg Address.* What is that speech? It is a series of sounds arranged in meaningful symbols refined through centuries of experiment. Realize that this set of symbols which has meaning for all English-speaking peoples can be reproduced in dozens of other languages which would make it equally intelligible to any race of people on the face of the earth, and you have again some concept of the flexibility of the medium of sound as it is placed in the hands of a radio production director.

This analysis of the effectiveness of radio as an artistic medium should be encouraging to the prospective production director. By any yardstick one may wish to use to measure an artistic medium, radio is good. In many respects it is outstanding. Certainly it is a medium that offers tools and an audience to challenge any real artist.

An Evaluation of the Medium

Its Limitations

Any medium, no matter how ideal, must by its very nature have certain inherent drawbacks. These must be recognized by the artist and proper allowances made for them. Radio has such limitations. We must recognize these limitations and stay within them if we are to make radio the artistically sound thing it can be.

In the first place, radio is not an ideal medium for exposition of a kind that is inherently visual. When a station attempts to broadcast a parade, it is tackling a job for which the medium is unsuited. Such a spectacle is primarily visual and a spoken description can never re-create it with complete success for the listener. Anyone who does not know baseball rather well before he hears the broadcast will be completely bored with the play-by-play description. Baseball makes good listening only because the average listener brings such a tremendous amount of background and information that he can enjoy it without the visual cues.

A second limitation is the difficulty of making complex action clear to an audience over the air. Either in news or in drama this difficulty is a serious one.

The third limitation is the condition of the audience. It is shifting, uninhibited, easily bored, often distracted, and in no way obligated either to the production director or to his program. There are no social or economic pressures to keep him at his radio, and there are many factors which make listening difficult even if he wants to listen. The theater is designed for looking and listening. People pay good money to come there to look and listen. When they get there, all the lights are turned out except those on the stage. There is nothing to see but the play. Such is not the case in radio. There are literally dozens of possible distractions, many of which the listener cannot control, to say nothing of the director of the program.

For all these reasons, radio directors play to one of the most difficult audience situations known.

It must be recognized as a fourth limitation of the medium of radio that it can play to one sense only. Whereas the dance, the theater, the movies, and others can appeal to both sight and sound, radio is limited to sound alone.

There is, fifth, always the limitation of time. This has nothing to do with the qualities of the medium itself, but it has a great deal to do with its practical working. Because a station must stay on the air so many hours a day, the necessity of producing a large number of programs in a short time is always present. Because of the system of network broadcasting in effect in this country, time is not a matter to be played with. Programs must end punctually, and there is a final limitation beyond which they cannot, in any circumstances, go.

There is, finally, an economic limitation in radio. Whereas a Broadway producer may spend five weeks getting a single two-and-a-half-hour program ready and then play it to packed houses for the remainder of the season, radio must get five programs ready to fill the same amount of time and must do it day in and day out for every half-hour broadcast period in the day. This means that many, many more programs must be presented, and it inevitably follows that quality suffers in favor of quantity in such a medium. There is less money and less time to spend on each program "readied" for radio than that invested in either a play or a movie. It means hurried production and consequent carelessness with detail in many cases. Certainly it is an economic inhibition which is not ideal but with which the medium is saddled through necessity.

Its Advantages

One of the greatest advantages of radio is its emotional power. Because radio appeals more to the emotions than to the intellect, it commands a powerful appeal because of the psychological fact that emotional drives are stronger than intellectual ones.

Radio allows an artistic treatment that is not always available in other media. Archibald MacLeish, in his preface to *The Fall of the City,* says of radio, "Only the ear is engaged and the ear is already half poet." This, better than any lengthy discussion, sums up the advantages of radio as a poetic medium. The possible use of formal rhythms and organized sound patterns has been denied to writers in most other media The poet is no poet in print because poetry is written for sound, to be spoken, to be heard. In radio is a medium where the poet may speak out loud and clear in his own peculiar manner and with his own peculiar power.

Music comes into its own on radio, and this should certainly be listed as one of the advantages of the medium. No visual cues are needed for the enjoyment of music. There are even those who say that the sight of the gyrations of a first violinist distract from, rather than add to, the enjoyment of music, since these actions do not co-ordinate with or amplify the sound they initiate. It is certain that music appeals only to the ear and that this is radio's particular mode of expression.

While it is true that certain kinds of drama are restricted on radio, it is equally true that there are many kinds of drama that can be done more effectively on radio than in any other medium. Fantasy, for example, and expressionistic drama find a natural medium of outlet in radio.

By all odds, however, the most important advantage of the medium is the size of its audience. It is the production director's job to make clear to an audience certain ideas, happenings, people, places, music. No other artist in any medium has the privilege of making an idea clear to so many people.

As radio develops, it seems likely that its audience will grow even more and outstrip the movies, which now claim almost equality with radio. Moving pictures have been losing their audiences steadily for the last few years. The loss is slight, but it is perceptible. Radio already has a full-time audience of better than two thirds of the total population. For peak performances under extreme pressure this audience could be pushed to three fourths of the total population. Certain economic limitations may prevent it from expanding beyond that.

What is even more important than numbers in an audience is the frequency of their use of radio. Whereas movies have followers who go once or twice a week, radio audiences report for daily listening and do it several times during the day. Radio certainly offers more audience in shorter time and far more contacts than any other artistic medium known to man.

Well, there it is — the whole complex picture! We have talked about the job of the production director, we have talked about the limitations and extent of his authority. We have discussed in detail the medium in which he works. Out of all this, it may be possible to distill the essence of the job called production directing. Can some kind of goal or creed or point of view be established? Perhaps it could be summed up:

A production director is a conductor. He conducts a mighty symphony of music, of noise, of language — all of it sound, and all of it is ready to be controlled and molded into intelligible patterns. The materials are his. The audience is there. It remains only to make the material meaningful to the audience - through patterns of moving sound.

CHAPTER 2

THE MAN FOR THE JOB

THE JOB of the production director, and the medium in which the job must be done, have now been described. The next logical step is to consider the kind of man who can best do such a job. What are the tangible and intangible factors that go to make up a successful production director? What are the factors in terms of knowledge, experience, and factual information which one needs to acquire before one can approach the job of directing a radio program? The answer to these questions will be attempted in this chapter.

The answers cannot be absolute. The requirements for both an art and an artist are relative and few people will be the paragons described in this chapter. Many people who are today drawing good-sized salaries for directing radio programs would be the first to admit that they could not begin to meet the complete list of qualifications which are here endorsed. These are ideals toward which the beginning production director should strive. They are not goals which can be easily and offhandedly acquired by the taking of a course. They can be achieved only as a result of much experience and hard work and careful analytical thought.

Unfortunately, so many intangibles are inherent in the picture that any kind of objective tests to measure the aptitude of an individual for this work have not been developed. It is doubtful whether such tests could be developed. Psychologists have outlined tests which indicate certain character traits and these may have some usefulness in the present discussion. It is conceivable, however, that an individual entering the field of broadcasting might be able to comply with every demand made here of the prospective production director and still not be able to produce good radio programs. All that this chapter can do is to describe some of the specific requirements which it is certain must be present in a good production director.

The good production director is a combination of creative artist, interpretive artist, and executive. If radio writers were perfect and if their output was true radio writing in the strictest sense — completely written, realistically conceived, and entirely designed for execution in the medium of radio — there would be little need for the production director to do creative work. He could confine himself to the interpretation of the writer's script. Unfortunately, this is not always the case. Writers do not always write complete scripts. They do not always foresee production difficulties and details nor provide for them. They do not always take full advantage of the possibilities of the medium. Because of this lack, production directors often find themselves doing creative work which is properly in the writer's province. Perhaps it is better so. Good production directors have made real contributions to the conceptions of radio writers and the end result has often been better radio programs. The production director takes the script which the writer furnishes, filters it through the alchemy of his own mind, and turns out a finished product which is often a better program, the result of a union of two artistic efforts.

Radio, like its theatrical brethren, the theater and the movies, is a business. Its continued existence, like theirs, depends on box-office support. It is true that radio's box office is once-removed. Audiences listen, buy the sponsor's product; the sponsor in turn increases or decreases his advertising appropriation on the basis of sales; the appropriation is the box-office index of radio. Therefore, the basic business structure of radio is essentially the same as that of other theatrical enterprises. However, because the sponsor, who is the "angel" of radio, has a hand in the planning of a radio program *before* it gets its box-office tryout, the production director is in much more intimate contact with the business end of his art than directors in other media.

Since the radio production director works so closely with the sponsor, he must always straddle any gap between the artistic and the business sides of his job. These two are not always in harmony, and the necessity for meeting the demands of both sometimes tests the mettle of a director. Both aspects of the job have their special requirements and limitations. They are an inherent part of the medium in which the production director works.

The characteristics needed in the job of production director can be catalogued under two general headings. First are a man's personal qualifications. These will be almost entirely dependent on the kind of man he is himself and what he has made himself through practice, experience, and self-discipline. Secondly, there are the personal background, experiences, and education he brings to the task. Knowing a man's personal qualifications and his educational or experience qualifications, a guess may be made as to whether he will be useful in the field of production directing. Even with all these data it is quite possible to make many bad guesses. Production managers of networks, even with all the care they exercise in selecting personnel, freely admit they make mistakes frequently.

It is hoped that this chapter will serve as a check list against which the student approaching the field of production direction may check himself more or less objectively and give himself some kind of rating. If it shows where he measures up and where he falls short, the following material may be valuable in indicating those areas in which he needs to improve.

Personal Qualifications

Here is a list of eleven personal qualities which are highly desirable in a production director. Some of these may come to a person by inheritance or conditioning. Some of them may be absent or weak, but through a judicious planning of study and experience may be acquired or strengthened. However, the aspiring production director should be able to measure up at least to the basic qualifications.

Leadership

Paramount among the qualities which will make for success

in production directing is leadership. In a radio program there are many components which must be molded together under the strong-handed guidance of one individual. The myriad responsibilities of talent, music, engineering, sound, must all be amalgamated into a cohesive, unified whole. This can be possible only if the production director is a strong enough personality to do the job. Stations and networks give him authority to do the job, but if he lacks the essential quality of leadership, the authority will be of little use to him.

The ability to lead people results from a combination of many faculties, all of which are commonly recognizable. Leadership can come only to a man who has the respect of his coworkers. It presupposes the willingness of the man to do as much or more work than any of his subordinates and to submit himself to the same rigid discipline he asks of them. It involves high standards to which he holds himself as well as those under him. It involves the efficient use of all the man-power available to him with a minimum waste of time of any member of his group. It presupposes a human approach to personal relationships which makes understanding possible between two individuals. All these things put together give a quality of leadership which is necessary in the complex job of production director.

Executive Ability

The ability to organize work and to get it done promptly and with an economy of time and means is an important factor in the production of a radio program. This means that a production director must be an efficient executive. He must know how and when he can delegate work, and which work he must do himself. He must be able to supervise a half-dozen detailed procedures progressing simultaneously and keep his fingers on all of them. He must be able to supervise the work of all the members of his staff and still not do their work for them. Getting a great many people to do a number of different things all at the same time according to a prearranged design does not happen by accident. It is the result of painstaking planning, of careful organization, and of definite division of responsibility. This organizing and planning a production director must be able to do and do well.

Ability to Handle Details

Not only must the production director be able to handle details without becoming impatient, but he must also handle them without losing perspective. The power to see the whole and to work minutely with all its parts combines a dual ability which few people possess. The kind of person who works in a slapdash way has no business in the field of production directing. Successful programs are built by careful and patient attention to a multitude of details and by a careful co-ordination of these details into a predetermined pattern. Whether the prospective director likes detail work or not, he must be capable of doing it well.

Lester O'Keefe, former production manager of the Eastern Division of NBC, tells an amusing story which illustrates the case in point. Several years ago he was asked to direct a very complex program which was scheduled out of New York. It involved pickups of a dramatic nature from Hollywood and Chicago. Sonja Henie was to take part from Norway. Orchestral music was to be furnished to the program from New York. The broadcast was as complex as it was humanly possible to make it from a technical point of view. Imagine trying to conduct a rehearsal when your music was in New York, part of your cast in Hollywood and part in Norway! Mr. O'Keefe says that he tried to conceive of every possible emergency and plan for it. A double for Miss Henie was standing by in New York in case there was a program failure from Norway. Dual facilities across the ocean were planned in case of a failure on one line. Every possible detail that could have been conceived seemed to be planned for. Yet, when the program went on the air and the time came for the first switch to Hollywood, Hollywood didn't come in on cue! Switches to the West Coast had been done so often they were considered routine. There was no need for a special arrangement to be made for an ordinary land switch across this country. Such a thing was done every day without so much as turning a hair, and yet this simple operation, the simplest in the whole program, was the one that broke down and the one for which no provision had been made. Fortunately, the lapse of time was covered by the orchestra in New York and the program was soon back on schedule. This story illustrates, however, the care which must be taken with every detail without losing sight of the over-all end results to be achieved.

The Ability to Work Under Pressure

Always and forever the production director is running a race against time. There is never enough time to do all the things that need to be done. The amount of rehearsal scheduled for a program is almost never adequate to do the job in the way a first-class artist would like to see it done. The reasons for this have already been discussed. Radio does so many programs a day that only so much time can be spent on each one.

A production director must not only be able to handle men, organize work, and take care of various details, but he must do them always under the pressure of time and speed. Many people might ordinarily be able to conform to the three preceding requirements, but not under the arbitrary speed requirements of radio.

Although a production director's work may be planned in the quiet of his home or office, the actual execution of the work must go on in a hurly-burly of confusion, against the uncompromising advance of the minute hand on the clock. The time allowed for rehearsal is conditioned by budget, the pressure of studio space, and the cost of holding orchestras. The result is that the radio production director must be one of the most efficient men in theater business. He works on a time schedule that would stagger his colleague in the theater, doing in two hours what a stage director often has two weeks to accomplish.

The speed of radio production directing makes inevitable the lowering of standards. It also makes for efficiency in the production director himself. He cannot afford temperamental outbursts, lax attendance at rehearsals, time out for pacing up and down the center aisle while he makes up his mind, and all the other trappings of the business in which the theater director sometimes indulges. Efficiency, if nothing else, demands that he know what he wants before he steps into his control room.

And no matter what else happens to him, he dare not lose his head under the pressure of time. No matter how much there is to do, he must make instant decisions about which shall be done and which shall not, and how much time should be spent on each item. This ability to work under pressure must always be coupled with a certain attitude of detachment which will allow him, even in the white heat of a hundred production details, to stand off and evaluate the effect of these details in the finished production. He must be able to direct cues, check timing, listen to interpretation, direct the engineer, and still stand mentally apart from the turmoil to listen objectively to what is coming out of the loud-speaker. This ability to work under pressure is one of the most important personal characteristics which the production director must have.

Sense of Structure

The production director must have some inherent sense of proper structure if he is to be successful in his work. This presupposes a sense of the right material to be used and the proper use of it in attaining the ultimate structural form. The multiplicity of materials with which he must work means that he must have a considerable versatility in his sense of structure. On one program he may be working with a speaker. The next may necessitate his using a large orchestra. The third program may be an audience-participation show. In each case a completely different structure is required. In each case his materials are different and their use must therefore be different. And yet upon these varying materials and forms the director must impress a feeling of solid structure which rises from a broad foundation to an ultimate end and shows the sense of balance and proportion and allowance for stress which mark the good architect. But, whereas the architect works in steel and stone and bricks and mortar, the production director works with humans, with time, with sound, with technical equipment, all of which he must somehow weld into a meaningful structural pattern.

Accurate Hearing

A purely physical characteristic which ranks high among the personal qualifications a production director must have is an accurate and a wide-range sense of hearing. It may be possible to do successful production directing even with certain hearing anomalies, provided they are known and proper compensation is made for them. The range of frequencies which one can hear and the accuracy with which one hears them can easily be checked by an audiometer test. This will show the lowest point on one's threshold of pitch perception and the highest, with the percentage of hearing loss at various pitches throughout the range. It frequently happens that the hearing may be perfectly accurate up to a certain point in the pitch scale, then drop forty to seventy per cent in efficiency for a certain band of frequencies, and rise again to normal for the rest of the range. Frequently there occurs also a decided difference in effectiveness between the operation of the two ears. These matters are subject to scientific testing in the same way as the eyes, and no production director should attempt to do much work without first learning his own pattern of perception.

If the hearing is too defective, it might be unwise to attempt to work in this field. In most cases, however, slight anomalies can easily be compensated for, once the individual knows where his weaknesses lie. He can then learn automatically to compensate for lack of perception in that particular area.

A Good Memory

If this discussion concerned production directing at the British Broadcasting Corporation instead of in the United States, this item would not be so important. Every producer at the BBC is furnished with a secretary who sits with him at the control panel to take notes and make jottings of memoranda which the director has to remember. No such help is offered American production directors. Because of the multiplicity of detail and because most of this detail must be carried in the production director's head, he has great need of a good memory. This requirement goes on beyond the mundane "things to do" which must be taken care of. He must have a memory for sound. He must have a memory for facts. He must have a memory for music. And finally he must have a memory for details.

Since the whole business of directing in radio has to do with the handling of sound in all its various manifestations, it is quite obvious that the production director must be able to remember sound. Having heard a thing once, he should be able to recall it in his "mind's ear." He may have to pass on the authenticity of a sound effect. He may have to remember the acoustical quality of a sound he heard ten years before. He must remember special effects from one rehearsal to another to be able to compare progress. Both the immediate memory and the recall memory in the field of sound are important. The trick of remembering sound must be mastered.

To the production director who is not musical, to remember music may be one of the most difficult of all memory tasks, but it is still one of the most important. In a musical program, or in a dramatic program involving music, the production director often decides that all his cues and his handling of certain portions of the program are to come from certain figurations in a piece of music. He must therefore be able to memorize the music quickly, be able to recognize it at once in following rehearsals, and to know by context exactly when a certain cue is coming up. Only by this kind of anticipation can he manage even the simplest kinds of production work. Often he may have to do a dramatic show with one or two music rehearsals, in which he hears each cue only two or three times at the most. He must be able to recognize how each starts and at what exact point he wishes to end it or to fade it down for dialogue. All this involves quick memorization of music.

If you wish to see how you stand on this score, sit down and play a symphony through on recordings. See if you can, on the second hearing, anticipate the change in movements. See if you can remember which choir in the orchestra carries which particular section of the melody, of the harmony, of the rhythm. Is the second movement dominated by horns? Strings? Brasses? This practical testing can be most useful to tell you how facile you are at remembering music now and it will also improve your memory of music.

Observation

Much of what has been said before makes clear the necessity for constant and detailed observation on the part of the production director. Boleslavsky says that the art of observation is one of the first lessons which an actor must master. This holds true for the production director and for exactly the same reasons. In many kinds of programs the production director is "holding the mirror up to nature" just as an actor must. The only difference is that in all cases where acting is concerned, the production director is the final arbiter. His is the final decision even on the actor's observation. It therefore becomes essential for him to form the habit of keeping his eyes open and absorbing and remembering something of everything he sees. Sooner or later it will have direct and immediate application in some program which he is called upon to produce.

Good Taste

It is essential that a production director have an intuitive sense of good taste. This is one of those intangibles like Barrie's definition of charm: "It's a sort of bloom on a woman. If you have it, you don't need anything else; if you don't have it, it doesn't much matter what else you have." Good taste is the same sort of thing. It is most important because of its very intangibility. There are no courses in any university which set out to teach good taste. Perhaps taste can be developed by exposure to good things. It goes under many other equally vague names in the theater world. Sometimes it is called showmanship, sometimes theater sense, or a sense of the dramatic. But whatever it is, it usually boils down to a matter of theatrical good taste.

In general it may be defined as a sense of the rightness of material for an audience plus the rightness of the use of that material in the particular situation. Rules can be laid down, but they are of little use. It is one of those things which the director must feel. It comes from years of making decisions about things theatrical on the basis of some inner sense which says, "This is the right thing to do in this place." Almost certainly it is something which improves with use. It is a part of the intangible addition to a man which comes with experience. Possibly this very factor *is* experience boiled down to its final essence. Whatever it is, an intuitive sense of good taste in showmanship is a necessary faculty for the production director.

Self-Discipline

Because the production director is a virtual czar in his own realm, he must be a strong self-disciplinarian. In the course of the creation of a program there is no one to tell the director what to do. He must constantly be in the position of telling others what to do. This involves the rigid handling of his own actions.

There are many ways in which this fact has application to the production director. Many directors are disappointed actors, judging from the number who like to put on a show for their cast. The urge to show off before a company is certainly common enough among second-rate directors. Working under the press of time, a radio director cannot afford to display his own virtuosity. He cannot allow himself the luxury of a temper tantrum. He must hew to the line.

The director cannot call a rehearsal for two-thirty for his company and insist they be there on the dot when he himself fails to show up until a quarter of three. He cannot insist on preparation from the actors if he himself has not prepared. He cannot insist that actors take cues from him if he habitually forgets to give those cues. All these things come under the heading of self-discipline. It is the price one pays for holding a position of authority.

The Question of Men Versus Women

Whether or not production directing is a job which is suited only to the qualifications of the male of the species is a question which cannot be decided on the basis of present evidence. The fact is that at the moment production directing is a man's job. There are very, very few women production directors now actually earning their living in radio. Whether this is because they are physically and mentally unsuited to the work or whether men have somehow managed to retain a monopoly in this kind of work is hard to say. Increasingly, women are eyeing the field of production directing with a certain predatory glint. The dislocation of man-power due to the war has made the problem even more acute than it would otherwise have been in the normal course of events.

The only way the problem should be discussed is realistically. The fact now stands that it is a man's job. It remains only to ask why this is true. Certain reasons seem to be evident, although, so far as is known, no actual scientific tests have been made by personnel directors to determine the logic of these facts. However, here is the case for the male production director. Radio is greatly concerned with technical matters. Women tend to be more practical-minded than technical-minded, with the result that most women do not handle purely technical matters as well as men. A complicated control panel throws the average woman into a state of alarm by its very looks. A man sees only knobs and dials to be twisted so that a given result occurs. This mental hazard regarding equipment has been a serious drawback to the woman production director.

Few men like to take orders from women. If a woman is a production director, it means that all the men under her — and there will inevitably be many — have to do just that. A man will take orders from another man and a woman will take orders from a man, but for a woman to give orders to a group of men sometimes creates psychological difficulties and friction among personnel.

There is a tendency among women directors to be excellent at detail work, but to lose sight of over-all end results. More often than not they do a better job of detail work than the average male director. But they also more often fall into the error of losing the over-all view in the welter of detail.

As is true in all organizations where members of both sexes work together, staff difficulties often arise. Where a woman production director is working in day-to-day open competition and co-operation with men, there often tends to develop certain staff frictions which become an executive headache. Jealousy of men about the woman's job and vice versa lead to personnel difficulties which makes experimentation in this direction often undesirable.

There is also the matter of health and nervous stability to be considered. Normally a man can stand longer hours of rehearsal and more frustration from a company without losing his emotional and nervous balance than a woman can. It may be because he is less sensitive or because he is more stable, depending on who is making the definitions. Certainly it is true that physically he can better stand the gruelling hours of intensive work which are necessary in a heavy rehearsal schedule. He is less likely to crack under the strain of pressure. He is more likely to be able to stand long hours, split shifts, loss of sleep, and the other irregularities in the pattern of a working day to which a production director is often subjected. These last facts are probably the most admissible of the whole group. Many of the others may be open to question. So far as is known there is no major network or advertising agency which has an out-and-out policy of excluding women from the work of production directing. It is obvious, however, that there is a preference for men, as is shown by the number of men employed. It will be interesting to see how the problems of the man-power shortage affect this balance and how it influences the post-war personnel in the field.

Background and Experience

Up to this point we have been discussing personal traits. What follows is a list of backgrounds and experiences which it is possible for anyone to acquire. This is training, as opposed to inherent traits or ability. These are some of the steps in apprenticeship which the student must take if he hopes to become the kind of production director that radio needs. Some of these are simple and easily acquirable. Others may take years of careful observation and absorption to obtain; but all of them are, to a greater or lesser degree, necessary.

Stage Experience

Stage experience as a director or stage manager or as an actor (probably valuable in that order) is of great help to the production director in radio. There are certain deep-seated theater knowledges which radio has not yet been able to give to incoming directors. One of these is a knowledge of audiences – what they are like and how they react. And how does one learn about audiences? By reading about it in books? Of course not! Can it be learned by watching mobs on the street corners? Something might be learned here, but certainly not final answers. When one is releasing a drama or a program of any kind, one has a specific relationship to his audience. There is only one way to learn what that relationship is and that is to play before audiences.

It is a favorite device of certain stage comedians to insert what they call a "buffer scene" at the beginning of a stage revue. In the buffer scene there are usually some pretty girls and a comedian with a few gags, placed there for the specific purpose of testing the temper of the audience. There are always a few jokes in this opening scene – they may not be necessarily the best jokes in the show, but they are good. During the scene the well-trained comedian who knows his craft will classify the type of audience for which he must work, and shape his whole performance to meet the challenge it represents. He may classify them as a "show me" audience, in which case his entrance is much more forceful, his voice louder, his gestures broader than they might otherwise be. He simply browbeats the audience until he gets them coming his way. Or it may be an easy audience. If so he finds it out in the buffer scene and makes a correspondingly free entrance. This use of a trial scene at the beginning of a show tells an old-hand comedian a great deal about the nightly temper of the audience.

Obviously this kind of working with and on an audience is impossible in radio, where the audience is something nebulous that vaguely surrounds the station antenna. Often its only manifestation is in the form of crank letters. The theater is still the best school for learning something about audience psychology. It is the thing that Alexander Woollcott talked about in his book, *While Rome Burns*, when he said the audience is always referred to as "they," and "they" are always unpredictable. Sometimes they are in a holiday mood and must be handled accordingly. At other times they seem to come to the theater for the specific purpose of thinking over their own private woes, and this, too, presents problems to a director. The final development of "audience sense" can be possible only in a medium where the audience is present. The theater is the production director's best laboratory for learning audience psychology at first hand.

There is another thing which the director can learn only from stage experience, and that is timing. In radio the actor is seldom allowed much real physical action. He must remain fairly close to a stationary microphone regardless of the action indicated by the script itself. This means that the actor or director with only radio training seldom has as sure a sense of timing line to business, either real or imagined, as the individual with the benefit of stage experience. Work in the theater requires the actor or director, not only to handle the line and the interpretation, but to gear it to actual business. This sense of combining line and physical action, which is an essential part of the art of acting and directing on the stage, needs to be transplanted to radio. It becomes even more important because the action itself cannot be seen in radio. This means that the director must develop the ability to project action by the manner in which a line is handled. The stage is the best school for learning that lesson.

Stage experience has one other advantage which should be noted. Stage plays tend to run for a rather long period of time. This gives the beginner a chance to watch stars at work at close range over a considerable period. Watching an expert work is one of the best possible ways to learn one's own craft. It is quite possible to watch stars work in radio. But in radio, rehearsals are short, there is a constant procession of stars, and no chance for intensive observation over a long period.

For all these reasons and many more, background in the theater is helpful to the production director in radio. The experience can be in any job which will furnish an excuse for an eager student to spend time on the stage watching a play put together and watching it play to a succession of audiences.

Technical Background

It is helpful if the production director has enough technical background to understand the workings of the equipment with which he must deal. He should understand the theory of operation, the characteristics, and the uses of all the equipment involved in his work. It is true that many directors do capable work without this knowledge. These same directors, however, might be capable of better work if they had this background. It is hard to see how any artist can create anything worth while when he does not even know the basic rudiments of the tools out of which art is created.

It is not to be understood that a production director must be a graduate engineer. It is perfectly possible to drive an automobile without being able to build one. Many people operate automobiles every day who cannot fix them if the simplest thing goes wrong. But ignorance in these matters and ignorance of the basic tools with which one earns one's living are two different things. A production director who does not know the basic facts about amplifiers, microphones, filter circuits, and turntables is at the mercy of his staff. His decision of whether something can or cannot be done is not his own but his engineer's or his sound man's. No man can be a good executive when he must depend on others to tell him what he can or cannot do.

The critical question, then, is: How much technical information should the production director have? He should have the following information about every piece of equipment that is likely to be involved in his direct control:

1. Its principle of operation.
2. Its basic characteristics in terms of its capacity to handle sound.
3. Its limitations because of inherent mechanical or electrical construction.
4. Its normal uses in radio production.
5. Its particular function in relation to other instruments in the total production.

Nearly all these items can be explained either non-technically or within the terms of the technical knowledge of sound which the production director should have. No principle of operation of any instrument is so complex or so hard to understand that simple statements of it cannot be made. In succeeding chapters will be set forth in non-technical terms the basic principles of all the instruments which the production director will use.

This kind of background assures the director of a degree of control over his staff and his programs which is not otherwise possible. It is the only guarantee of control that a production director has over an inefficient or nonco-operative staff. This kind of sure knowledge is one of the shortest cuts to thoroughgoing, respectful co-operation by the members of a staff. The man who knows his business, down to the last detail, will not be hoodwinked.

Conversely, the informed director will not ask engineers or sound men or musicians to do impossible things. But there are circumstances under which a little knowledge is a dangerous thing. If you know enough to know that a certain effect cannot be achieved in a normal way, it may inhibit you from asking expert advice on how to do it some other way. There is a danger of the production director saying, "No, that can't be done." To a technician with imagination there are very few things which "cannot be done."

The technical background required for production directing can be acquired in a number of ways. Most of it can be gained by reading alone. If the reading can be coupled with a little first-hand investigation of actual studio and production equipment, it should be sufficient to equip the director in this area. The material which will be found in Chapter 3 should be sufficient to acquaint a production director with everything he needs to know about the technical backgrounds of his craft. Once these are understood, he may progress on firm ground.

Dramatic Literature

It goes without saying that the production director should have an intimate and catholic knowledge of the world's dramatic literature. He needs this for a number of reasons. First, and most obvious, he may be called upon to direct many plays out of this body of literature. If his acquaintance with them is of long standing, he can do better work.

A wide acquaintance with dramatic literature is one of the best possible ways to develop a sense of standards and a discriminating theater sense of proportion. Only after one has read many plays by the world's outstanding playwrights does one come to a consciousness of the manner in which great drama is made. This deep-rooted sense of the dramatic rightness of material can be carried over indirectly even to rather trashy material. Standards of taste develop only with exposure to different levels of work and with an opportunity for comparison between good work and bad.

Careful reading of good plays will, inevitably, bring to the director a strong sense of the technique of play writing. Since the radio production director some of his time will be dealing with the production of plays, this is essential information for him to have. It should not be the case, but unfortunately it is that the director is more often than not cast in the rôle of play doctor. This is because there are so many poor radio plays written. It is a sorry commentary on the profession that some production directors have little sense of the technique of play structure or play writing. They may look at a play and say, "This is no good!" Or they may say, "Something is wrong with this script." It is possible that they may be right. But such statements as that have absolutely no value to the playwright who is called upon to rewrite the script or it gives them no help at all if they have to do it themselves.

Such simple matters as introduction of characters, the handling of opening exposition, the placing of the inciting action, the subsequent building to sub-climaxes, and the ready recognition of major climactic spots are all simple, basic, play-writing principles which anyone who has studied a great number of plays knows by experience. When one is considering a play for production, it is not enough to be able to say, "This is a good (or bad) play." One must be able to say that on page 5, line 16, the speech which is planted there as inciting action for the main conflict in the play is too weak to do the job which needs to be done. One must be as specific as that to give one's best efforts to getting material ready for broadcast.

Music

Every production director needs a broad and catholic background of information in the field of music. The broader and the deeper this knowledge is, the better equipped is the man for his work. Network production directing is usually subject to a strict cleavage between dramatic and musical production. In many production staffs the separation is complete. Men are not asked to cross the line from one to the other, being assigned only to their specific kind of work. Obviously this can be true only in staffs large enough to allow specialization, such as are afforded on the larger networks. In all other situations production directors must be competent in both fields. Even on the networks there are certain kinds of shows which, by their very nature, involve both elements. This is true with a variety show, for instance. In such a case one man must be responsible for the two elements.

For the production director who is aiming for the specialized job of producing musical programs, it is obvious that his background must be deeper, broader, and more technical than that of the director who is heading for dramatic work primarily. Ideally, a man should be able to do both jobs. This is asking a great deal of a mere mortal, but let us for the moment forget practical matters and draw up an ideal background in the field of music which an ideal production director might have.

The man who specializes in dramatic production will have to use a great deal of music of two general kinds: theme or signature music, and "cue" or transitional music. Many dramas have music as a realistic part of the background of the scene being portrayed. Music is constantly used as a background for narration or as a "melodramatic" effect. And music is used more than any other single device as a transitional effect between scenes. The frequency of occurrence of these items alone is enough to establish the necessity for some kind of musical background for the director primarily interested in dramatic work.

How wide and how deep should that background extend? Certainly the "dramatic man" in the field of production directing should be familiar with the world's outstanding musical literature. He should be familiar enough with great music to recognize important themes and passages and have at least a good listening acquaintance with the best music, both classical and modern. This may sound like a big order, but there is a comparatively small number of so-called "world classics." This interesting fact was developed when the Music Appreciation Series of recordings was first issued. This group, which purported to represent the world's great symphonies, did not number as many records as might be supposed. The production director should have a knowledge of symphony, of opera, of light opera, of musical comedy, and of current popular music. All these groups, with the exception of the last, are more or less standard, and the best works in each have already been fairly well determined. Popular music is constantly shifting, and must be followed from week to week as it develops. The judgment of time acts even here fairly quickly and only a small percentage of popular music survives the first few weeks of national acceptance.

Knowing this much about music also includes of necessity knowing something about the composers, their typical styles, and the basic approach each has to the work of composition. One soon learns to detect the flavor of each composer and one finds that flavor over and over again in most of his work.

To learn this much may seem a mountainous task. As a matter of fact, it is possible to gain a reasonable knowledge of a great many composers and their style without spending undue time in the search. But regardless of the time it takes, the effort must be made, because it is an inevitable and completely necessary part of the background of every production director.

The director should be familiar with the basic tonal and emotional qualities of the various instruments in an orchestra. He must know the effect that can be obtained from a woodwind, a french horn, a banjo, or a "schmaltzie" violin. A study of the tonal quality and the emotional and mood quality of various instruments is one of the best and shortest paths to an understanding of how music can reinforce drama. An understanding of the use and application of various instruments and combinations of instruments is basic in the work of a dramatic production director.

For the person who aspires to become a musical production director, the requirements are much more stringent. He should be a musician himself. His musical training should be specific and thorough, preferably in a group of instruments. Ideally he should have had some experience as an orchestral director or conductor. Some of the best production directors in the field of music have been either choir directors or conductors of orchestras.

In addition to this training he should have a thorough musical knowledge, or what the profession calls "musicianship."

Any number of fine instrumentalists can perform if they see the notes in front of them; but to select music from memory or out of a library to build for specific needs and a specific program requires something more than that.

A production director of musical programs must be able to read a score. The score is to the musical director what the script is to the dramatic man, and he must be able to read it with ease. If, during the course of a rehearsal there is a sudden peak in volume, he must know his score so thoroughly that a quick glance will indicate the point where the peak occurs; he can then arrange for proper balance in the next run-through.

Ideally he should be able to compose, because he will frequently need original music. He must have an intimate and complete knowledge of the component parts of an orchestra, so that he can satisfactorily balance it. He should be able to listen to a composition and say, "This is wrong because the arrangement is bad. In this place the brasses are overwhelming the woodwinds and harmony is topping melody at this point." He should be able to be as specific as that. Finally, the musical production director should have a strong sense of routining and programming, and broad information about the musical preferences of his audience.

Voice and Diction

The production director should have a thorough knowledge of the problems of voice production and pronunciation. This information is used by the director a dozen times a day. It should be as much a part of his knowledge as the garageman's knowledge of the function of the spark plug. This is true for a quite obvious reason: of the total sound pattern of a radio program, more consists of words spoken by individuals than of sounds generated by any other source. It would be ideal if the production director could assume that everybody who steps into his studio had mastered the principles of good voice production and accurate diction. Unfortunately this is not the case.

There are at least four reasons why a sound knowledge of voice and diction is useful to the production director. For one, he may be faced with problems in voice hygiene. If members of his cast suddenly develop vocal troubles in the midst of a rehearsal, and do not themselves know how to take care of their voices, the production director must know. Simple matters may come up, such as helping an announcer or an actor work through a cold or a throat irritation without doing damage to the membranes. In his rôle of teacher the production director may have to correct certain bad voice tricks or habits of some of the people who work with him. He can do this only if he knows enough about voice work to give them specific suggestions and directions for making the desired changes.

Second, the most important use of a knowledge of voice and diction is in the directing of dramatic dialogue. The basic tool of an actor is his voice quality and the pattern of his diction. If these do not please the production director, he must change them. It is very difficult to ask for changes in voice quality and diction unless the director can describe exactly what he wishes. For example, the director may say to an actor, "That character isn't hard enough. He isn't hard-boiled enough. He's soft yet." An extremely capable actor might be able to correct the interpretation with no more direction than that. A less capable actor might have to have specific help. It is obvious that the actor has to "feel" harder, feel sterner inside himself, and make a complete new attack on his lines, but it will also help if the director can tell him specifically to retract his speech a little more, increase the intensity of intonation, and give other specific suggestions which will give the particular quality of characterization he wants.

Third, the same application can be made to diction. The problems of regional speech, of foreign dialect, of getting a character to sound as though he actually lived in Kansas, for example, can be greatly facilitated if the director has a basic knowledge of pronunciation habits in those parts of the world. Often little deviations from the norm in diction will do wonders in giving authenticity or reality to a character. The audience may not be able to put their fingers on it and say, "That man sounds as though he came from Oklahoma because in Oklahoma they use the nasalized ă." But they will recognize the smack of authenticity in the speech. This can only come with a production director who knows the patterns of regional speech and can direct the diction of his company.

For at least one other reason the matter of voice and diction is important. The production director is constantly called upon to be an arbiter of pronunciation. Like any good arbiter, if he is in doubt he will consult a dictionary – incidentally, that item is a useful one in any control room. It is a time-consuming job, however, and should not be indulged in too much during rehearsals. On all matters of standard diction and pronunciation the production director should know what is right and what is wrong without looking it up. Not only must he know what is right and what is wrong, but also when to vary from the norm in order to achieve a given result in characterization or dialogue.

For all these reasons and for many more, it is important that the production director know at least the basic rudiments of good voice production and the basic standards of good pronunciation, with a wide and reasonably accurate knowledge of regional and foreign dialect.

Acting Ability

The question now comes of whether experience in acting is important in the preparation for a production director. Let us grant at the outset that this is a debatable question. The answer seems to lie in this statement: Acting experience may be a help to the production director, but it is not a necessity. The advantages of an acting background can be fairly definitely stated. First, the man who must tell others what to do is better fortified for his job if he can do it himself. If he can do the job better than his actors, he is in a perfect position to command the respect and co-operation of his company. One who has done professional acting certainly brings a greater understanding to the handling of other actors than one who has not

Having spent some time on the studio side of the glass, the production director has some notion of how his cast looks at him in the control room, and can conduct himself accordingly. He is more likely to be a reasonable director for the experience.

But there are inherent dangers for the production director who has come from the field of acting. Being capable of reading a line himself, he may become guilty of dictating interpretation to an actor. He may direct by the purely imitative method, which most good directors agree is bad.

If the director is also a good actor, there is always the chance that he may wish to display his virtuosity — to become a show-off — for his company. Not only is this bad directing, but it is also a waste of good rehearsal time and the sponsor's money.

The director should know everything there is to know about acting. He need not be able to do it himself. But he must understand those techniques and processes — the business and the craftsmanship of the job — which make an actor an actor. He must have keen analytical powers of acting ability. He must be able to be constructive in his suggestions as well as destructive. He must know the limitations beyond which an actor cannot go in his art. Above all, he must be deadly conscious of the standards to which he holds his cast.

A Broad Cultural Background

One of the most necessary of all preparations for the production director is a broad general background in all the arts and sciences. It is possibly this background which most often distinguishes the great director artist from the "show-biz" man, however successful either may be. The polish, the sureness, the universality which the educated artist brings to a job will more than offset a surface facility which the uneducated but shrewd and practical show-business man may provide. It must be understood, of course, that this artist must have just as firm a grounding in show business from a hard-headed practical point of view as the uneducated man who may have grown up in the business. But with a broad background of the world's culture on which to draw, he is infinitely more fitted to do his job.

This is true for one primary reason. We think of the "self-made man" in show business as the one who has fought his way up by knowing all the tricks of the trade. But the emphasis with this kind of man tends to be on the tricks. He knows audiences, he knows actors, he knows music, and he knows what people like. His great lack may be that he himself has nothing important to say. After all, the most important thing about a book, or a play, or a radio program is what it has to say. The broader the background of the director who is handling the material, the more likely it is that the content of the book or play will reach its public without getting lost somewhere in production.

A good background in history is important. If one knows the long road that man has come in his struggle up through the ages and the trends of the times that have influenced our civilizations as they have evolved, one comes to a more intimate understanding of the world as it now exists. Directly coupled with history is political science. Art and philosophy have their place. So do the down-to-earth current social sciences like psychology and sociology, and the sciences of business such as economics and commerce. In these days of emphasis on vocational education, it is quite possible to overlook the benefits which are to be derived from a broad liberal arts education. These remarks are not a brief for that stodgy, stolid, inflexible classical education which was fashionable many years ago. But there is reason for hoping that our future production directors will have some knowledge of the world's cultures and the major trends in world thought from which spring much of what goes through his control room in terms of radio productions every day. The self-made man who has arrived at a position of eminence almost entirely through his own efforts and his own direct hand-to-hand struggle with the world is in some respects a dangerous individual. In spite of his success, however large it may be, he tends to assume that the rules by which the game is played are those which he himself knows from first-hand experience. He is without benefit of all the other rules of all the other games which have been played in the past by people who may have been more truly civilized.

Living Experience

Finally, in the long list of preparations which the production director must have for his work comes that rather vague term – experience in living. This is something which can be acquired only in time and by the application of eternal curiosity. This is the one place where the young production director cannot hope to compete with his elders in the business. Time and curiosity will help to gather the experience in living with people and in working with his art which gives to his work a final polish and surface possible through no other means. There is no substitute for having lived eagerly for ten years, and no substitute for having produced, always with an effort toward perfection, five hundred programs. These are part of the apprenticeship of the production director which time alone can give him. The mere passage of time does not guarantee this kind of experience. There are many people who, as Carl Sandburg has said, are "dead years before burial." A thoughtless, haphazard approach to life and work does not net those experiences from which the artist can prosper. It is only when he applies the eternal search for the better result, for more information and more understanding, that he eventually finds in his own soul the springs out of which come new artistic truth.

In the last few pages we have attempted to lay down the specifications and blueprints for an ideal production director. It will not be surprising if many production directors who now earn good-sized pay checks each week may read this chapter and get a chuckle from it. The specifications are, indeed, idealistic. It would be a rare individual who could measure up to all the standards here set forth. That does not in any way deter us from setting forth such standards. There is no assurance that the present group of production directors are the best that radio can develop. A considerable amount of improvement both in production itself and in the skill of individuals handling production still needs to be made.

The new generations of production directors coming on in a medium as important as radio should try to "shoot for the moon." The future excellence of radio depends on developing a class of production directors who will learn what they can from the present pioneers in the field, take what is good, and go on from there. We must develop men whose critical standards say, "This has to be better than it is!"

2

THE TOOLS OF RADIO PRODUCTION DIRECTING

CHAPTER 3

THE NATURE OF SOUND IN RADIO

UP TO THIS POINT in our discussion we have considered the job to be done, the medium in which it is done, and the man who must do the job. The next logical step is to consider the tools with which the artist works. We can begin this with some understanding of the medium of sound which we have already discussed. After learning the basic characteristics of sound, we need to know how sound is generated and how it is used by the production director in the execution of his work.

Sound, the medium of radio, comes up now for consideration. The medium is conditioned by three factors:

1. The physical characteristics of sound.
2. The conditions of the perception of sounds by the human ear.
3. The technical ability of the radio to transmit sound.

We have said that radio production is an art. It may seem a far cry from any artistic endeavor to the practical, physical, and psychological considerations listed above. In spite of the seeming divergence, the connection is direct and necessary. An artist must know the capability of his tools, the condition of their use, and the perceiving power and manner of the sense to which they are directed. Just as the painter must know his pigments, color values, and the tricks which the eye plays in perception, so must the radio production director know what he can do with sound and what happens to the individual in the hearing of it. It therefore becomes necessary to be technical and exact at this point.

PHYSICAL CHARACTERISTICS OF SOUND

Sound is a disturbance of the normal distribution of molecules in the air, caused by some vibrating object. For a simple illustration, suppose one plucks a harp string. The string gives in the direction in which it is plucked and, on release, snaps back in the opposite direction, and repeats this process very rapidly until the force of the motion dies out. As the harp string snaps outward, it pushes together the molecules of the air in its path, causing a condensation of molecules in its immediate vicinity. As it reverses its direction, it causes a corresponding condensation on the other side of its swing. This "bunching of molecules," pushed together by the vibrating strings, in turn travels outward from the vibrating source in a pattern of condensation and rarefactions of the molecules in the air. This is illustrated in Figure 1.

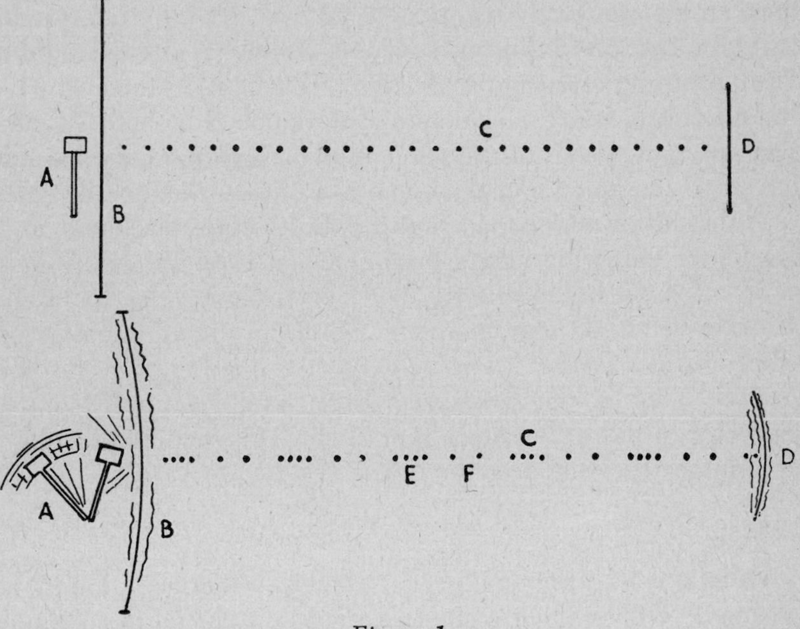

Figure 1

The foregoing is an objective description of how sound is created. Subjectively, sound is what the ear hears. These waves of condensation and rarefaction of molecules bombard the ear drum, causing it to vibrate. Thus, the sound created by the vibration of the harp string is transmitted through the molecules of the air to the ear drum and we "hear" sound.

Sound has four characteristics: pitch, volume, quality or timbre, and duration. All the differences between sounds, no matter how simple or complex, can be explained in terms of these four characteristics. These need to be examined and understood if one is to be able to work with them.

Pitch

Pitch is commonly designated as high or low, and it is a precisely definable characteristic. Pitch is determined by the number of complete vibrations per second which the vibrator makes in originating the sound. For example, if we pluck the harp string previously mentioned, we will get a certain pitch. If it vibrates 258.85 times per second, we say its pitch is middle C, an arbitrary assignment of name.[1] If it vibrates more slowly, the pitch is lower; if more rapidly, the pitch is higher. To certain different speeds of vibration, more or less regularly spaced, have been assigned names, the notes in the musical scale.

It should be understood that it is the length, thickness, and tension of the string (the vibrator) which actually determines at what speed it can vibrate, and hence determines its pitch. A cycle refers to one complete vibration. Thus, number of vibrations per second is equivalent to the number of cycles per second. Thus, a long thick harp string would naturally give a low pitch, a short thin one a high pitch. This fact, incidentally, determines the shape of the harp.

Volume

Volume is the common term applied to intensity or loudness of sound. Unlike pitch, volume cannot be reduced to accurate

[1] Historically, middle C, or, more commonly, A above middle C on the musical scale, which is considered by musicians as standard pitch, has had many different values. Out of the welter of values which have developed over the last two hundred years only two common ones remain: Concert Pitch and International Pitch. International Pitch places the value of A at 435 vibrations per second at 20° centigrade. Concert Pitch calls for 440 vibrations per second for A.

measurements as long as it remains within the realm of sound. However, as soon as sound is transformed into electrical energy by a microphone, it becomes a variable alternating voltage and the resulting power can be measured in terms of bels. Therefore, for all practical purposes, we can measure the intensity or loudness or volume of a sound in terms of its electrical equivalent. Intensity of sound is governed entirely by the amount of force in the vibrating body. Again, using our harp string as an example, if it is lightly plucked, it will still give "middle C" pitch, but the resultant sound will be low in volume or intensity. If it is plucked vigorously, the same pitch will result, but the sound will be louder or of higher intensity. This is because the harp string vibrates harder and the arc of its vibration is wider, but it does not change its number of vibrations per second. Both volume and pitch are fairly simple matters, since they are the result of two simple originating forces. They are both easily discernible even to an untrained ear and the average individual reacts constantly to stimuli of both pitch and volume.

Quality

The quality of a sound, sometimes called its timbre, is a definitely discernible characteristic, but one which results from a complex set of circumstances. Actually one hears few pure sounds in any form. Sounds generated electrically in a vacuum tube offer about the only means for the creation of sound of a given pure pitch. A tuning fork is another source. Almost any sound or noise we hear from nature or from musical instruments is not a single pitch but a complex pattern of pitches.

Suppose we examine what really happens when a harp string is plucked, instead of the theory of what happens as illustrated in Figure 1. This can best be shown by Figure 2. When the harp string, represented in Figure 2-A by the solid line, is plucked, the whole string tends to give on an arc indicated by the dotted line *A*. Actually, however, it will give more at the exact spot where the pluck takes place, producing not only the whole curve represented by the dotted line *A*, but an addi-

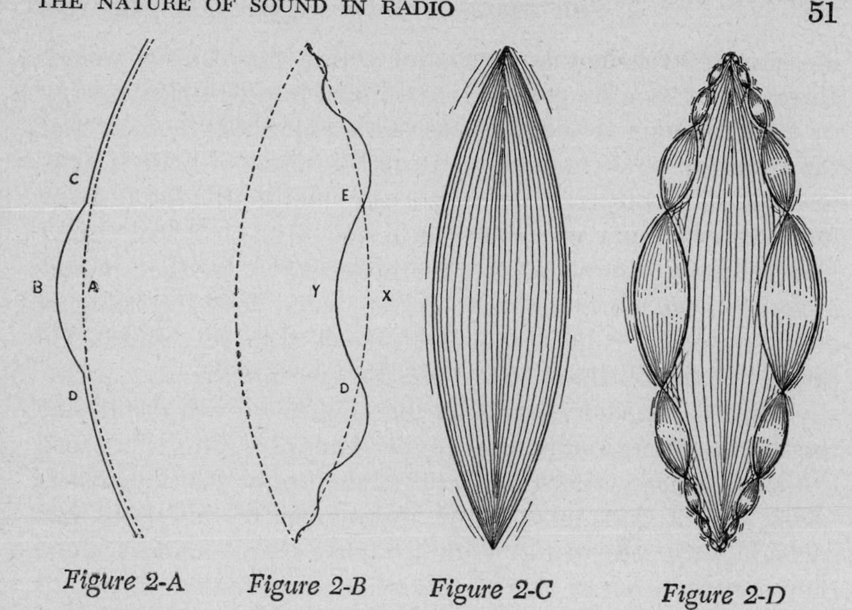

Figure 2-A *Figure 2-B* *Figure 2-C* *Figure 2-D*

tional outward curve in the middle of the string indicated by points *C* to *D*. When the string is released and vibrates in the opposite direction, the curve *C* to *D* sets up a ripple which runs out toward the top and bottom of the string in exactly the same way as a ripple in a child's jumping rope made by simple up-and-down motions of the wrist applied to one end of the rope or to its middle. These ripples are indicated in Figure 2-B. The whole harp string will vibrate in the opposite direction in the Figure 2-A to a position marked by the dotted line *X* in Figure 2-B. The solid line indicates a possible actual pattern of the string labeled *Y*. *D-E* represents a compensating backward motion from the original distance *C-D* in Figure 2-A and this ripple travels out toward the end of the string, the ripples becoming smaller as they reach the end of the string, just as the waves become smaller in a pond where a stone is dropped into the water.

The string is not vibrating as the single pattern represented in Figure 2-C, but rather in a complex pattern superimposed on an over-all pattern as illustrated in Figure 2-D. The result is a complex series of sounds. We will hear, let us say, middle

C as a result of the total vibrations represented by the pattern in Figure 2-C. We will also hear a series of higher-pitched sounds resulting from inner vibrations on the string as sketched in Figure 2-B. Because the string vibrates as a whole body through an arc and also carries several smaller patterns of vibration, we hear two sets of sounds: a fundamental tone which is the pitch to which the string is tuned, and a series of higher-pitched sounds which are called overtones. Strings of different materials, lengths, and diameters may produce the same fundamental tone, but their overtones will vary greatly.

It is the overtones which produce many of the shadings of sound referred to as quality. Certain types of vibrators generate a sound pattern of which the component pitches are known. For example, a violin string sounding a fundamental tone of one will have overtones in a ratio of two, three, four, five, six, and so on, order, and our ear reorganizes this particular tone complex as that of a violin. In this instrument the first overtone will be twice the pitch frequency of the fundamental, the second will be three times the frequency, and so on in the mathematical as well as the musical scale. In similar instruments, however, there may be a quantitative difference. In some instruments, where the overtone pattern goes in a one, two, three, four order, the relative amount of volume of various overtones may differ, and a resulting difference in quality occurs. In addition, some sound sources have overtone patterns containing different components. For example, a clarinet sounds a series of component overtones which run one, three, five, six, seven, eight, and so on. Because of this difference in pattern, there is not only a quantitative difference in the volume of the individual overtones, but also a qualitative difference. This accounts for the difference in quality between two musical instruments sounding exactly the same pitch. Each generates the same fundamental tone, but their patterns of overtones may differ both in components or quality and in quantity of volume.

Any understanding of the quality of sound must take into account this simple principle of the difference in volume and pitch of the overtone patterns. The whole matter of consonance and dissonance can be directly traced also to the complexity of an original sound. If two sounds played simultaneously have overtone patterns with many pitches in common, the combination tends to be pleasing. If the overtone patterns are dissonant, then the combination tends to be unpleasing: the presumption is that there are so many sounds competing for the ear's attention that the result is a jumble and becomes unpleasant. If there are certain sounds in the overtone pattern that tend to repeat themselves between two tones, the result is a simplification of the pattern and therefore it is more pleasing.

The whole subject of fundamentals and overtones can become extremely complex. There is no need for the production director to go into the complex variations, which are of interest only to the research scientist.

There is a second factor which has considerable influence on the quality of sound besides the character of the vibrating body which creates it. This second factor is resonance. Stated in simple terms, the principle is this: quality of sound is governed not only by the characteristics of the vibrator, but also by the nature of the enclosure which surrounds the vibrator. Some sound originations, by their very nature, must be considered in terms of the resonance which is applied to them before they may be heard or analyzed. An example is the human voice. The resonating of the pharyngal, oral, and nasal cavities inevitably influence the quality of the original sound created by the vibrations of the vocal bands.

The influence of a resonator on sound depends on these factors: the rigidity or flexibility of the resonator; the hardness or softness of its surface; its size; and its shape. All these influence the way a resonator will react on sound. It should be understood that a resonator cannot produce sound. It can, however, amplify and control sound. The thin-wooded box on which violin strings are stretched becomes the resonator for the vibrations set up by the strings. If a violin string should be stretched to its normal tautness between two otherwise unconnected points, and then played with a violin bow, the resulting sound would be of low volume and have few of the characteristics of the violin tone that our ear expects. However, when the string is attached to a box of the right size and shape, the vibrations of the string are transmitted to the resonator through the bridge, and the resonating chamber amplifies and controls the sound generated by the vibration of the string.

A piano has a sounding board which is common to all its strings. A flute or a french horn has a long tubelike resonator. The shape of a bell is so designed that the vibrator and the resonator are one. The metal in the bell acts as vibrator and the shape of the metal forms a partial enclosure which gives additional and sympathetic resonance. The human voice has oral, pharyngal, and nasal cavities to act as resonators.

A resonator may be either a partial enclosure to which a vibrator is attached and to the walls of which the vibrator transmits its vibration by direct contact, as in the case of the violin, or it may be a complete enclosure in which the sound takes place. In this last sense a radio studio may become a resonator for all of the sounds generated in it. This may be a desirable or undesirable thing, depending upon the character of the resonance resulting.

Resonance, like other characteristics governing the quality of sound, may be a complex matter. It is enough for the radio production director to realize that resonance controls the quality of sound and that, because the character of the resonator can be controlled or changed, it is possible to control to a very high degree the quality of sound.

Duration

Because sound is a physical phenomenon which occurs within the framework of time, and because the length of the sound's existence can be controlled, duration must be considered as one of the basic characteristics of sound. This fact in itself means little, but when it is realized that the duration of sound can be varied and that varying durations in recurrent patterns may be obtained, one realizes the importance of a simple basic principle. The time factor in sound has significance because sounds of varying length can be built into meaningful patterns. The alternations of sound and silences are fundamental in any sound pattern. All aspects of rhythm and accent depend on this basic principle.

The foregoing paragraphs are far from a complete summary of the physics of sound. They merely attempt to state in the simplest possible terms the basic component characteristics of which sound is made. Objectively speaking, sound can vary in pitch from sixteen cycles per second up to infinity. It can vary in volume or intensity to infinity in either direction. In quality or timbre, it has an infinite variety of minute differences governed by the two basic factors, the character of the vibrator and the character of the resonator. The duration of sound can be varied at will. Having described these basic objective factors of the characteristics of sound, we can now consider it as it is received by the human ear.

The Perception of Sound by the Human Ear

This subject will be discussed from three points of view:

1. The physical characteristics of sound perception: the limitations of perception within the possible spectrum of sound.
2. The operational characteristics of the ear: the habitual stimulus-response reactions which follow certain sound stimuli.
3. The reaction characteristics of the human ear: the inferences, both intellectual and emotional, which the ear makes in response to certain combinations of sound stimuli.

A basic understanding of these reactions is essential to the working artist in the field of sound. Unless he is familiar enough with the physics of sound to control the generation sound to get the desired end result, he is defeated before he starts.

The following facts in outline form cover the physical characteristics of the ear:

1. The ear can perceive differences in pitch and react to sounds that have frequencies ranging from sixteen cycles on the low end to twenty thousand cycles per second on the high end.
2. The ear can perceive volume or intensity of sound which varies from the threshold of perception at the low end to the point of acute pain on the high end.
3. The ear can perceive differences in quality or timbre.
4. The ear can obviously perceive the duration of sound.
5. The ear can, to some degree, perceive the distance separating it from the sound source.
6. The ear can, within limits, perceive the direction from which the sound comes.
7. The ear can perceive limitless combinations of sound at one time.
8. The ear can separate various sound sources and recognize juxtapositions among sources.
9. The ear can, within rough limits, perceive acoustical relationships such as the alteration made on sounds by their surroundings.

Most of these statements regarding the physical perception of sounds by the human ear are self-explanatory. Only a few remarks need to be added. It should be noted that the limits of perception vary considerably with individuals. It is generally agreed, however, that below sixteen cycles per second, pitch drops below the threshold of perception of sound and becomes feeling — a pulsation rather than sound. On the upper end many people do not hear pitches of fifteen thousand vibrations.[1] We judge our distance from a sound largely on the basis of volume plus quality. While our perception of distance

[1] Exceptional cases have been noted where hearing goes as high as twenty-five or even thirty thousand cycles per second. For all practical purposes, however, both these limits are far beyond the normal usefulness necessary. It is interesting to note in the matter of volume that excessive volume can become acute physical pain even while it is still perceptible as sound.

from a sound source is far from accurate, it is reliable within rough limits. The perception of the direction from which a sound comes is possible only because we are equipped with two ears and because sound travels at a comparatively low rate of speed.[2] Sound coming from one side will, therefore, be registered in one ear before the other, and the slight time lapse between registrations allows us to perceive direction within rough limits.

The fact that we can perceive an almost limitless combination of sounds at one time is important to the radio production director, but it is a factor which should not be abused. This knowledge must be used according to the rules of attention, which play an important part in selecting combinations of sound to present to listeners' ears. By juxtaposition of sound is meant the ear's capacity to hear a soft sound at close range and a loud sound at a more distant point and to perceive the two simultaneously. Not only may this simultaneous perception occur, but it may be multiplied into a complex pattern by the perception of differences in pitch, quality, volume, direction, and distance all at one time.

The ear can perceive acoustical relationships. This is another important factor for the radio production director to know. We are all conscious, for example, that a voice talking in the telephone booth will sound different from the same voice in a stone cathedral. The ear is able to perceive these differences caused by resonance and reverberation on the original sound. This knowledge is used constantly in the production of radio programs. If we wish to tell an audience that a character in a play is descending into a rocky cavern, a change in the acoustics by the addition of echo will help to create the illusion.

The Operational Characteristics of the Ear

Not only must we be aware of the conditions of physical perception of sound, but we must also know the manner in which our aural sense disposes of these sound stimuli. A long list of

[2] Eleven hundred and twenty feet per second through air at 20° centigrade.

such operational characteristics might be compiled, but two are of special importance.

1. Many sounds are perceived automatically, and acted on without conscious thought.
2. The ear is selective. The ear attends only to sounds which are meaningful to it at the time.

One may hear a buzzing mosquito and mechanically reach up to brush it away from the face, without once leaving the process of thought already in progress. Even more interesting and important is our ability to hear sounds and draw a prompt conclusion without being conscious of having heard the sound or having drawn the conclusion. We may listen to a salesman's speech and our mind is occupied by his sales talk. But subliminally, we catch certain insincere inflections and conclude that the salesman is not to be trusted. We refuse a convincing factual sales talk, not on an intellectual basis, but by a process of subliminal reasoning, stimulated by subliminally perceived sound patterns. To draw conclusions from this is an uncertain business, yet the fact is that such reactions do take place. Every good public speaker knows the trick of throwing out subliminal cues. More radio announcers and production directors should be aware of its possibilities.

The fact that the ear is selective is a blessing to mankind. If we had to "hear" all the sounds which impinge on our ears every day, the psychiatric wards would be more filled than they are. This would be especially true of city dwellers, on whose ears a multitude of sound stimuli are constantly dinning, with no rest and no interruptions. Nature has protected man by giving him at least partial immunity to sound which he does not need to hear. The ear drum actually vibrates to the sound, but somewhere between there and the brain, the impulse is sidetracked from the conscious to the unconscious level of perception. This process of selection is going on constantly and our entire lives are shaped by the selection. There is, interestingly enough, no index of relationship between volume, pitch, quality, and the perception. One soon learns to ignore loud sounds close at hand if they are meaningless. Thus, the city dweller is kept awake at night in the country by the absence of sound, because that is a strange situation to him. Men working in boiler factories soon cease to hear the din that surrounds them, but can hear and understand much quieter sounds.

This interesting fact has considerable significance to the director of radio programs. To one who is inclined to "load" a production with sound, it is rather startling to discover that the listener does not hear much of the sound the director has prepared, and there is at least a chance that either he will ignore it entirely, in which case time and money have been wasted, or he will be annoyed by its presence, as he neither expected nor needed it. Let us cite an example. Radio production seems to be full of doors opening and closing. If all the energy used to open and close sound-effect doors could be harnessed to a useful purpose, what a contribution it would make to a labor shortage! When you are sitting in the room with another person and that person says to you, "I'm going out to the icebox and get a drink," you listen a moment, make an appropriate answer, or simply grunt, and go back to whatever you were doing. The person goes out of the room. You probably hear neither footsteps nor door opening and closing. At least you do not *attend* to these sounds. Under normal circumstances, then, they are not necessary in the sound-effects routine. It may be argued that simply because these sounds are expected, they should be included even if they are not attended to by the listening audience, because their absence will be noticeable. This position may be tenable under some circumstances; in others it merely results in excess sound. This kind of production detail needs careful thought.

Another common error of beginning production directors is to include in the background of a dramatic scene all the sounds which might occur in real life. In a street scene, for example, the pattern of sounds may be very complex. All that is needed is enough to create an illusion of a scene, and the "mood" appropriate to the moment. This may be done with half the sounds that would actually occur. If the total pattern is used, it may compete with the main center of interest in the scene and distract the audience's attention. Because the ear is selective, and because it bases its selection on momentary meaningfulness, the production director must always conform to these limitations in the management of his program.

The Reaction Characteristics of the Ear

We come now to the most interesting and the least considered set of facts regarding the sense of hearing. For want of an accepted term, these have been called the "reaction characteristics" of the ear. In these characteristics are found some of the most significant factors governing the use of sound to project ideas and emotions. From an artistic point of view, more tenets of radio art are determined by these characteristics than by any others thus far discussed.

In discussing the reaction of the ear to the various phenomena of sound, an attempt will be made to show the application of these reactions in the production and direction of radio programs. It is here that we begin to make practical, down-to-earth use of the seemingly vague and technical facts so far discussed. It should also be noted that the ear seldom reacts individually to a single phenomenon; since we seldom distinguish between pitch and quality and volume, but assess the sound as a whole, some latitude must be allowed in the individual discussion of these factors. They tend to reinforce or offset each other and make untrue some generalized statements.

The Reaction to Pitch

Not only does the listener perceive pitch as a phenomenon of sound, but from pitch alone he draws many conscious and unconscious conclusions about the sound, as well as its source. Low pitches are usually soothing and reassuring. High pitches are generally unpleasant. The facts are, of course, modified by volume and all the other characteristics of sound. A high-pitch, low-volume sound may be pleasing. But if it is both high in pitch and high in volume, it is almost universally displeasing to the ear. Pitch has a factor of diminishing unpleasantness beyond a certain point because the ear is capable of reacting only to a limited frequency range. While the listener cannot dodge increased volume, he eventually ceases to become aware of higher pitches. They tend to attenuate as they pass gradually beyond the threshold of perception. High pitches are usually attributed, in the mind of the listener, to small sources; low pitches, to large sources.

The ear is also arbitrary about the combination of pitches. Just as the painter knows that certain color combinations create an unpleasant, jarring effect, so the painter in sound must be cognizant of the factors of dissonance. Certain combinations of pitch are pleasant, others are definitely unpleasant. What is more, these combinations are more or less exact and can be mathematically determined. Notes *C* and *E* in the musical scale are a pleasing combination. Notes *C* and *D* are not, and we call the result a dissonance. Dissonances have their uses, but they are not necessarily pleasing to the ear. If we complicate this pattern of dissonance enough, we have what are commonly called noises. When one realizes that the ear is sensitive to frequencies ranging from sixteen to twenty thousand and the number of combinations of overtones that are possible, and that what we hear is actually combinations of pitches, one gets some idea of the endless number of pleasant and unpleasant variations which can be achieved. When it is further realized that these combinations can be changed many hundreds of times per minute, the possibilities become astounding. The listener not only reacts to pitch and combinations of pitch, but he also reacts in a fairly universal manner (within a given civilization) to progressions from one combination of pitches to another. In its simplest form this is the basis of all music.

Rising pitches tend to be exciting and have a disturbing, electric effect. Descending pitch progressions have a soothing, reassuring effect. The sliding rise in pitch is a basic factor used in the design of sirens. Part of the fact that a siren is an exciting, disturbing thing results from connotations built around the use of sirens in fire engines, police cars, and so on. Part of it, however, is inherent in the pattern of rising pitch in the sound itself.

It is interesting to note that while there are differences in the degree between different civilizations,[1] the general rule holds true for any people of any language or place. The lower sounds tend to be soothing; the higher sounds to be exciting or disturbing, and these reactions may be counted on from any individual regardless of his background. An individual can be fairly quickly conditioned even to unpleasant sounds. The selective powers of the ear come into play and eliminate from the pattern of consciousness the unpleasant sounds. It might be argued psychologically, however, that the unrest still takes place on a subconscious or subliminal level.

A production director, wishing to build a climax or disturb his audience in some way, will use high pitches. Most production directors, even if they know nothing about the psychology of sound, know that building to a high pitch is one way of getting a climax. It would be much better if they could know why they are doing it, and do it deliberately with a definite end result in mind at the time they plan their program. It would eliminate the necessity for proceeding by instinct, and place decisions on a basis of causal relationship.

The Reaction to Volume

The listeners' reaction to volume parallels that of their reaction to pitch. Sounds of low intensity or low volume tend to be pleasant and soothing. Sounds of higher volume are disconcerting, irritating, and in cases of extreme volume cause actual pain, loss of hearing, or even death. These facts give the production director some pertinent information about the level of volume at which he must work. And yet how many production directors shout soothing information to their audiences! Volume may be used as a reinforcement of pitch or as a reac-

[1] Orientals are much more tolerant of high pitches and dissonances than are Occidentals. Hence conditioning is a factor.

tion against pitch. For example, a very high-pitched sound which might be irritating can be made acceptable if it is handled with low volume. A low-pitched sound which would be soothing and reassuring might be made disturbing by the use of extreme volume. A clap of thunder is a low-pitched sound, but the abnormal volume makes it a terrifying thing. Thus, volume can be used either to counteract pitch or reinforce its natural reaction tendencies. As an application, one might argue that signature music opening a radio program ought to be of fairly high volume to disturb the listener from his normal train of thought and attract it to the program. Quite aside from other factors, volume should be used in this instance as an attention-getter. As an example in the opposite direction, a children's storyteller could hardly use a high-pitched, loud voice and expect to have much soporific effect on his bedtime listening audience. These brief, obvious examples are given only to show how constant are the applications of simple principles in the handling of radio programs.

The Reaction to Timbre or Quality

Here is the most communicative of all the factors of sound in the richness of the information it can bring to a listener. When the production director considers the quality of sound, the possibilities become staggering. The sweet, high *E*-string of a violin and a metal pipe both vibrate, both generate sounds, both have resonance, but what a difference in quality! Compare the sounds of a well-cast bell and that resulting from striking a block of wood such as is used in the xylophone. Compare a harp and a piano, both string instruments, both having a like vibrator and a similar resonator — there is still a difference in quality between the two sounds. The human voice is infinitely more complex than these; its possible variations in quality are myriad. The voices of no two people in the world sound exactly alike. People can imitate each other, and often the quality difference between voices is nothing startling, but there is a difference, and these quality differences are the raw material out of which the production director creates a program.

Obviously, there is a vast number of sound qualities available to a production director. The reason for stressing this point is important. The human ear draws a tremendous number of conclusions from the quality of a sound. We hear a quick, irritable command spoken, and without quite realizing it, we assume that the man who issued the command is a grouch, a prig, or a conceited ass. This assumption comes instantly and without our even knowing why. Directors must know how to control the quality of sound in order to strike these responses in exactly the way they wish. Through the control of quality or timbre in sound, a clever director can make us draw conclusions, can play on our emotions without our being aware of it. That is a part of the art which conceals art.

Student directors will do well to listen to music critically, in an effort to assay the qualities of various instruments. Listen to different noises which surround you every day. The beginning director must trust his own reaction to the pleasantness or unpleasantness of sound and hope that it will have a similar effect on audiences. Try to describe the quality of sound and you will likely fix the effect that it will have on the audience.

The ear assigns big sounds to big objects and small sounds to small objects. It assumes that harmonious sounds come from pleasant objects or people, that dissonant sounds or harsh qualities come from unpleasant things or people. But the ear probably draws more conclusions from the quality of sound than from any other characteristic. For this reason it is one of the most important of the artist's pigments when he is painting in sound. There is the fun of magic in planting ideas, emotions, reactions, in people's minds without their knowing what you are doing or how you are doing it. And that is just what a good production director does all the time. Much of the sheer artistic enjoyment of directing comes in being able to do just that. The secret lies in controlling and being able to use the quality or timbre of sound to telling advantage.

The Reaction to Duration

As we have said, the fact that sound exists in the framework of time is not in itself important. Whether the sound is a long or a short one is not of momentous importance. But when one begins to group into patterns sounds of different time lengths, then the whole matter takes on significance, for it is on the basis of duration and time that rhythms can be created. Rhythm is the strongest, sharpest, most incisive tool with which the production director is blessed.

Rhythm and timing may concern the length of a word, the length of a series of pauses, or the artistic philosophy behind an entire production as it is made manifest in over-all tempo.

Not only can the ear perceive time patterns, but the complexity of patterns which it may receive at one time is almost limitless. Out of a number of varying time patterns which the ear may be receiving, it can always "hear" any one of these at will, or hear and react to the total of all the patterns. This flexibility of perception is constantly used by the skillful production director, who may implant one idea in the minds of his audience with a dominant time pattern and at the same time implant a completely different idea on the subliminal level of perception with an opposing or contrasting time pattern.

It is also known that emotional reactions to patterns of sound in time are fairly universal and similar to all members of the same general civilization. Slow, steady patterns are soothing and reassuring. Fast, staccato, uneven patterns are upsetting and disturbing. Quick, steady patterns have a martial, stimulating effect. Gradually increasing tempos are exciting, stimulating, and tend to make unstable emotional reactions possible. These are not new facts. They have long been known to every musician — to every African medicine man. But they are fascinating facts to the radio production director. When we come to a study of basic rhythm patterns, certain very obvious truths begin to assert themselves. It would be impossible, for example, to build a martial warlike piece of writing on a basic time pattern which was inherently three-four or waltz time. The kinesthetic reaction of the audience simply does not respond in that way. Poets have long known the value of rhythm in writing; and rhythm in radio is merely an aural manifestation of this same pattern of expression. Almost every high-school student has, at some place along his educational route, been exposed to the basic prosodic facts concerning rhythm. The use of the iamb, the trochee, the anapest, and the dactyl to the written expression of ideas has an equal or stronger application in the realm of sound.

It would be impossible for a production director to create the character in a play which he wanted the audience to trust if that character spoke in these rhythms which were essentially erratic, jerky, irregular in pattern. The total combination of patterns would say, "Here is someone upset, unstable, irrational." And no matter what the words that character uttered to establish a smooth, solid, steadfast character, the words would be offset by the inherent rhythm in which they were expressed, and the audience would not accept them at their dictionary value.

In the management of rhythm two fundamental principles must be kept in mind. First, the inherent rhythm in the program must be right for the expression of the inherent idea. Second, the pattern must be varied to avoid boredom. Any pattern ceases to use its effectiveness if it is repeated too often without relief. These two factors in combination will give the production director his basic approach to the application of time and rhythm to a production.

The Reaction to Distance

The ear can determine distance to a certain degree, and this is important to the production director in several ways. By establishing the distance from the microphone of various components of a scene, an entire scene set is accomplished.

Every art form, being basically artificial to begin with, soon develops certain conventions which the audience accepts as part of the medium. In painting, we learn to accept the picture frame and concentrate our attention within the frame. In the theater, we accept the proscenium arch as a part of theater convention. In radio we have developed similar conventions. One of these is that the audience is always "with" the nearest sound source. The audience always wants to place itself with regard to the scene being broadcast, and by this convention, it places itself beside the nearest sound source. Thus, if we hear two people talking quietly in normal tones, we assume we are with them. And if one of them turns and shouts to someone at a distance away, we assume that we, too, are some distance from the person shouted to — the same distance in fact as the person doing the shouting. Just as in good stage play the director ought to be able to control the focus of visual attention of the audience on any given part of the stage at any given time, so should the production director of a radio program be able to control the center of attention of his audience to any component of his program at any given time. His best and most often used tool to accomplish this is the use of distance. Everything else being equal, the ear will attend to the sound closest to it.

By establishing a near sound, distant sounds, and intermediate sounds within a given scene, the production director can fairly accurately tell an audience the size of the scene they are hearing. If in a dramatic scene you hear a door open and a man's footsteps on a hollow wood porch, and then you hear him "Hallooooo," a loud call which comes echoing back after a few seconds, the routine says, more clearly than anything else a production director could do, that the scene is taking place in a large space. It would say mountains, lack of many habitations, solitude, and loneliness. All these are established by a simple acoustical principle back of distance.

Distance and the change of distance are constantly used by the production director to project action within a scene to an audience. This is accomplished by the simple process of changing distances during an actual line of dialogue. The simplest possible application is in what is called the "fade." The character says that he is going into the next room, and as he says it we hear his volume fading off, which says to us that he is moving away from the point at which we are now located. We know accurately and exactly that he is leaving our presence. This is based on the simple matter of increasing the distance between us, the audience, and him, the actor. A warning should be added. Merely moving a silent actor in the studio does not give us an illusion in the change of distance. The movement must be accompanied either by sound or a line so that we can hear an actual change in distance. Fading an actor off is of no avail unless he talks while he fades or unless some accompanying sound effect fades in volume and perspective as he leaves. Incidentally, fading volume at the control panel will not give an effect of increasing distance nearly so well as actually moving the sound source.

As the painter may use converging lines to give a forced perspective effect in a two-dimensional medium, so it is possible to use forced perspective in radio. We can, by technical tricks, make any given distance seem much greater than it actually is.

The Reaction to Multiple Sound Stimuli

In discussing the physical phenomena of the perception of sound by the human ear, it was said that the ear perceives limitless combinations of sound at one time and draws conclusions from a juxtaposition of sounds. What is equally important, this does not within reasonable limits cause any confusion to the listener. A hundred different sounds generated in rapid succession by a symphony orchestra fall quickly into meaningful and easily perceived patterns to the human ear. Such combinations can, and will, be heard singly or as a whole with almost equal ease. Thus, a skillful production director can create simultaneous conflicting ideas in the minds of his audience by giving them two diametrically opposed stimuli at once. Perhaps one is soothing, another is disturbing. By this method a feeling of unrest, of being torn between two ideas, can be projected to an audience.

The ear can not only hear several sounds at once, but it can also judge the sound sources by their relationship. We have touched this point already in discussing distance. Let us cite a simple case from a dramatic broadcast. Suppose the audience hears two men whispering to each other, very close to the microphone. In the distance we hear the intermittent chatter of a machine gun. Occasionally, at a still greater distance we hear the rumble of artillery. Every so often, close to the mike, there is the loud nasty snarl of a ricocheting bullet which interrupts the conversation. The audience, hearing this pattern of sound, will understand what is going on and where they are. They will completely accept a battle scene given to them almost entirely from clues gained from simultaneous perception of various sounds at varying distances and volumes. Such examples could be cited by the hundreds to show how a story or an idea or a reaction can be planted with a listener without his having to do any work and even without his awareness.

The Reaction to Acoustical Relationships

The ear hears, not only sound, but also alterations of the fundamental sound created by the character of the enclosure of the sound. Everything else being equal, the ear will ascribe to a large space sound which has a considerable amount of echo or reverberation accompanying it. It will assign to a small space sound which has little or no reverberation and sounds "dead." These are the principles behind the use of echo chambers and other devices which change the normal reverberation period of the room in which the sound is generated. Sounds have different characteristics when made indoors from those made out-of-doors. No matter what the enclosure, some reverberations are likely to result indoors unless the room is acoustically designed for complete deadness. Out-of-doors, because of the normal lack of restraining space, sound is usually free of any reverberations. In spite of this fact it is not safe for a production director to assume, in closing his scene with acoustical surroundings, that he can make his exterior scenes "deader" than his interior. Although this is really what happens in nature, it is not necessarily a convention which the listener will accept.

Little attempt is made in this country to clothe a scene in the proper acoustical setting. Whether a scene is supposed to occur indoors or outdoors, whether it is played in a cathedral or in a meat market, the average production director places all the scenes in one studio at one microphone with no alterations in the acoustics surrounding the scene. About the only changes are extreme ones, where echo is applied or some kind of artificial dampening is placed around the mike to give an extra dead effect. Between these two extremes little is done.

At the BBC in London, and in certain other foreign stations, considerable attention is paid to acoustical relationships. Studios of varying reverberation times are used within the same show to give an acoustical variation to each scene suitable to what might be expected in real life.

Variation of acoustical relationships can be easily managed by varying the amount of sound absorption in the walls of the studios or surrounding the microphone. The harder the walls the more "bounce" of sound and the longer the reverberation. The more sound absorbent the walls are, and the fewer parallel surfaces there are in a room, the less chance there is for bounce and reverberation. By the use of acoustical screens and other devices, the qualities of any studio can be considerably altered.

The Ear Is Credulous

The ear is one of the easiest senses to deceive. It is perfectly willing in most cases to be deceived. There seems to be a certain sensory pleasure in this deception. Whereas the eye is a hard-bitten realist, the ear is an incurable romanticist, and this difference can be a delight to the radio production director.

There is a folk expression which says, "I'll believe that when I see it." As a matter of fact, it may or may not be true. We do not believe what we see with our own eyes unless what we see happens to check with our previous experience. Suppose this book in your hand were suddenly to rise out of your hand and suspend itself halfway between the floor and the ceiling with no apparent means of support. Even though you saw such a phenomenon, you would not believe it. You would more probably believe that you were having delirium tremens or that someone was playing a trick on you. You would not believe what you saw because it would not check with your past experience. One does not believe that the magician really saws a lady in half, even though the process is carried on before one's very eyes. We accept it only for what it is – an optical illusion. It is this fact which makes the production of fantasy or expressionistic drama on the stage so difficult. Even in the movies, where all the advantages of trick photography are at the director's command, it is extremely difficult to make an audience believe a purely fantastic fact. The eye does not trust its own perception when that perception seems not to check with previous experience. What is more, the eye is unwilling to make concessions to the imagination. It begrudges any variation from the realistic and the factual. This is probably the reason for the slowness of many people to accept surrealist art. A typical reaction to such art is, "I never saw anything like that before," and the mental note is that it does not make sense.

The ear, on the contrary, is extremely credulous. It is quite willing to believe what it hears, and accepts it at face value no matter how incredible it may be. Gossip columnists, who reduce their buzzings to type, may be read with interest, but they are always read with mental reservations and suspended judgments. Word-of-mouth gossip runs riot, and finds acceptance even in the most conservative minds. Why? Because the ear is a credulous sense! We believe what we hear!

If this credulity were not a fact, the furor aroused by the Orson Welles broadcast – now famous in radio history – could never have happened. Had people in New Jersey seen metal monsters creeping across their fields, they would have thought, "What a novel Halloween trick!" or that the Army was choosing a curious time to test new equipment. But because they heard it, they promptly deserted their firesides and took to their haystacks with shotguns. It seems incredible, but when one understands the reaction tendencies of the sense of hearing, it begins to be believable that it actually did happen.

Hollywood producers spend millions of dollars to build authentic sets. They buy battleships, ranches, lease mountains, go to all kinds of extremes to achieve visual reality. And, after all that, the first hint of a painted backdrop brings snorts of derision from a movie audience. In radio, a sound-effects man plays a recording of a foghorn, a woman sighs and says, "Isn't the mist lovely on the water," and the listening audience promptly locates itself on the designated beach and awaits developments. This is possible only because the ear is completely credulous. No one seems to have advanced a sound reason for this deep-seated difference in the acceptance of facts through the different sensory channels. It is strongly demonstrated that it is so, however, and the director of radio programs can count on it. The professional production director, either consciously or unconsciously, uses this fact in every program he directs. If this use can be conscious and deliberate, it can also be vastly more effective.

The Ear Responds Imaginatively to Stimuli

This reaction characteristic is closely allied to the previous one; the ear is not only willing to believe, but to add to a set of stimuli comprehended aurally. There is something childlike in the listener's willingness to "make-believe." The visual sense sits back and says "show me"; the aural sense says, "I see what you mean. I can just hear it." It accepts what is said, and adds details of its own to reinforce the impression. The production director can count on this. Thus, when the audience knows that a character in a play is dead, and they hear his voice coming to them through a filter mike, they are quite willing to accept the fact that he is speaking from the Great Beyond. Efforts to do this on the stage and in the movies have never been completely successful. There is something always a little amusing about Banquo's appearance at Macbeth's feast, even when it is skillfully staged. All the tricks of staging and the diffused spotlights never quite bring the audience to the point of acceptance. How different was the audience reactions to a recent broadcast on the *Day of Reckoning* series over NBC when the Stephen Vincent Benét's script, *The People versus Adolf Hitler,* was broadcast. The prosecuting attorney in this script was Abraham Lincoln, and even though the entire script was highly imaginative, the character of the great President was established in three or four lines and accepted as intended.

An example of the ear's imaginative response to auditory stimuli is the willingness of an audience to shift itself in time and place. A director in a visual medium must go to the trouble and expense of getting authentic costumes, sets, properties, and the other impedimenta of a period play. Radio can do the same job by having the announcer say, "The year is 1590. The place is London." A few essential details following this, a little convincing sound, and the listeners have transformed themselves back to Shakespeare's England with no more trouble than that. They have turned back four hundred years and jumped the Atlantic Ocean as effortlessly as they might turn in their chairs, and just as completely as with the most elaborate visual cues. No other medium offers such flexibility in settings and the management of time.

The Ear Responds Emotionally to Sound Stimuli

It is always dangerous to generalize, but it can be said, with certain reservations, that the eye is intellectual in its response, the ear is emotional. Certainly the avenue to an audience's emotional mood is much more accessible through the ear than through the eye. A scene may be interesting or unusual, but it takes something rather breathtaking to make it emotionally exciting. Sounds, on the other hand, are commonly accepted as emotional stimuli.

Print is the natural outlet for the scholar, the pedant, the academician. But the medium of sound is the peculiar property of the dramatist, whose job it is not only to plant ideas, but to arouse emotions. A sound medium *can* successfully handle purely factual matter. This is proved by the success of radio in the news field. But sound has the additional power of emotional appeal.

These facts are very significant to the director of radio programs. They tell him that he is working in a medium where facts need not be as important to the listener as reaction. Perhaps that is the reason why listeners prefer news commentators to news reporters. The facts seldom stimulate emotional reaction, whereas opinion gives them something to react to emotionally. At any rate, it is important to remember because it colors all approaches to the mind through the sense of hearing.

The Ear Is Highly Sensitive to Tone Patterns

This is true of music, it is true of sound or noise, it is equally true of speech. We have already discussed the ear's reaction to the separate elements composing sound, such as pitch, quality, volume, and duration. When we unite these into tone patterns, whether in sound effects, music, or speech, the possibilities become immediately apparent. The ear is so quick to detect a minor melody in a speech pattern that it can be established in two or three lines. There is as definite a minor melody in certain speech as there is in music, and the listener inevitably draws the same conclusion about both. If a speaker or actor habitually uses a minor speech melody, the audience assumes immediately that he is listening to a defeated person. The audience reacts accordingly.

This principle has endless application for the director. He uses it to achieve characterization in his actors. He uses it in music to establish moods. He uses it in the inflection of the announcer to create good will for the sponsored product. Even the sincerity of an announcer can be detected by the audience on the basis of inflection patterns. Reactions to these tone patterns are well known, but for the sake of completeness, they will be enumerated here. Major combinations are cheerful, bright, happy. Minor harmonies of tone are mournful, depressing, sobering. A rising-pitch pattern tends to be light, exciting. Descending-pitch patterns are more soothing, heavier, more ponderous. Very delicate tones, such as those from a Chinese wind chime, suggest fragile things. More resonant patterns produce a corresponding feeling of strength and power in the listener.

Thus, in sound effects, in music, in voice, and in the combination of voices, these principles can be applied to give an audience the precise emotional reaction to your program that you wish to get from them. A skillful production director will do exactly that.

The Ear Reacts to Time Patterns, Alterations, and Variations

This factor, added to the previous ones, rounds out the case for the power of sound. Regardless of the quality of sound, its pitch, or combinations with other sounds, the very alteration of that sound into time patterns gives the director one of his most powerful holds on his audience.

One of the reasons for its power is the universality of the reaction to it. The steady, throbbing beat of the jungle drum arouses the same reactions in a dock-walloper and a college president, in the rich man and the poor man, in the young man and the old man. There is a complete universal response to rhythm and time patterns which varies only in degree. What is more interesting is the fact that the more elementary the rhythm, the more powerful it is. Power and simplicity seem to be in direct ratio to each other.

This is a tool which no artist working in a static medium can ever appreciate. The painter cannot, nor can the sculptor. The novelist has little sense of its power. But the musician, the dancer, the radio director — because they work with a framework of time — have it for the asking.

Hate can be built with rhythms. So can confidence and suspicion. Of all the devices at the command of the worker in radio, this is probably the most powerful, the most flexible, the most lasting in effect. It can occur in the beat of a drum or in the syllables of a line and be equally effective in both places.

The Ability of Radio to Transmit Sound

Thus far we have talked about the characteristics of sound and the conditions under which the ear perceives sound and reacts to it. In order to round out a complete picture of how sound works in the medium of radio, we must know radio's technical possibilities and limitations in the transmission of sound. We must also take cognizance of the ability of the average radio receiver to receive sound. Both of these factors are important, and they are not necessarily parallel.

We have said that the ear can hear pitches varying from sixteen cycles a second on up to approximately twenty thousand. High-fidelity monitoring equipment in a station may be able to reproduce frequencies from thirty up to fifteen thousand. The station can deliver to the air from thirty to fifteen thousand vibrations, but a sensitive receiver will have difficulty eliminating interference between stations if it receives more than five thousand cycles. The width of the band which may be broadcast and received satisfactorily is conditioned by the fact that stations are crowded together so closely in the broadcast spectrum that thirty to five thousand vibrations is approximately all that can be received without causing interference between stations. In FM (Frequency Modulation) broadcasting, a much wider frequency band can be received because of differences in the tuning device of the receiver, and because the transmission takes place in a part of the spectrum which is not so crowded. In FM broadcasting a signal whose frequency width ranges from thirty to fifteen thousand cycles is possible.

Still one other factor may be considered in finally determining exactly what usable band of pitch frequencies is available to the radio director. A good receiving set, in first-class condition, should be able to receive as wide a band of frequencies as a station can transmit. Actually this is possible. Practically, it is a condition which seldom exists. In the first place, people do not keep radio sets in good condition. In the second, they do not spend as much time and money on their receivers as is necessary to get completely good reception. The result is that, while it is possible to receive the maximum width of frequencies that stations transmit, actually the average, cheap, table-model radio, the midget radio, car radio, and the portable battery set seldom deliver more than sixty to three thousand cycles.

This range of frequencies will include all the fundamental speech frequencies, but leaves out many of the overtones of music. This is the reason why so much music, which may leave the studio with the full richness of all the audible overtones, arrives in the home in a garbled form. The frequency response of the average table-model receiver, which has not had repair or attention for a year or more, delivers little more than half of what is broadcast. This last fact does not necessarily argue that the broadcaster or the production director should lower the standards of his own production. There are certain places, however, where he must take cognizance of these facts in the planning of his program. In as simple a matter, for example, as a cross-fade from one scene into another, this transmission limitation must be noted. If he is working in a control room where the speaker is delivering a full fifteen thousand cycles, he may fade a scene very slowly and be able to hear it all the way down to the bottom of his fade; when he starts a fade-up into the new scene he begins to hear it as soon as a whisper of a sound comes through the fader. As a result, there is a very short period of silence at the extreme bottom of the fade where one scene is ended and the other begins. On a cheap receiving set, however, the receiver may have ceased to function halfway down the fade, while the producer in his control room is still hearing it. The result is that between the two scenes, where the producer was hearing almost continuous sound, the listener was hearing a rather long silence in which nothing was happening. Situations like these force the production director to take a realistic view of how his program sounds to the average radio listener.

The sensible attitude is always to shoot for the best possible production of quality in transmission and to make due allowance for those listeners who must, by reason of their equipment, hear considerably less than is given them.

Radio is also somewhat limited in the amount of volume it can transmit. The transmitter of any station is limited in the volume it can carry on the low end by the volume which is perceptible to the human ear. In other words, the volume must come up to the lowest threshold of hearing. There is also a high volume or intensity beyond which radio cannot function properly. Any radio circuit is so designed that it can translate sound into electrical energy up to a certain volume level with a fairly high degree of accuracy. Where more volume is applied to a microphone than the system can accurately reflect, distortion occurs. The ear no longer gets a true picture of the original sound because of the electrical distortion which takes place between transmission and reception. It is because of this single fact in broadcasting that every control panel in every control room is equipped with a volume indicator. The zero position on the volume indicator is set for the maximum incoming volume which the equipment can accurately translate into electrical energy. Sounds which come in above this fixed zero level are subject to distortion.

Again, the limitations of receivers must be borne in mind. The highly efficient equipment of a broadcasting station can normally handle more volume, distortion free, than can a cheap receiving set. If your own radio receiving set is a powerful one, you will find that it is possible to open the volume control to a point where the loud-speaker begins to rattle and roar and the tones are all distorted. That point at which the distortion begins represents the maximum volume which your particular receiving set can reproduce without noticeable distortion.

The bugaboo of volume has haunted radio production directors since the inception of radio. It made many sound effects impossible for years. The difficulty of transmitting a pistol shot accurately is rooted in the inability of normal amplifying equipment to handle such sudden peaks of volume as are created by the repercussion of the firing of an actual pistol in the studio. Now that many of these problems have been ironed out, there is still the problem of monitoring the total output of a program constantly so that the sum total of all the volume does not go beyond the point which the equipment can reproduce faithfully. It should be understood that this zero level varies from one piece of equipment to another, depending on the design and the type of circuit. These are, however, technical matters and need not concern the production director.

There are many problems, properly the concern of the production director, however, which are influenced by the inability of amplitude modulation broadcasting to handle a wide pattern of volume. One simple case may illustrate this point. Suppose we are broadcasting a symphony orchestra. While the orchestra is playing, the engineer on the program opens his volume control so that the total output of the hundred-odd men playing in the studio comes to a zero level on the volume indicator. A great deal of sound manufactured by many different musicians totals up to a fixed total volume. Then along comes the announcer to announce the next number. The engineer will usually so manipulate his volume control that the one voice is as loud as the total output of the entire orchestra which preceded him. This contrast gives rise to a certain unpleasant sensation in the listener. It certainly gives a production director a sense of frustration, because he must maintain a volume level for the announcer, so that he will be heard. When the announcer is followed by music, the total volume of all the music must not go much beyond that of the single speaker. The result is a loss of power in the music. It should be understood that this is a relative comparison, and either the orchestra or the speaker alone would give the listener a satisfying effect.

Our previous discussion will have clarified the fact that while quality is a characteristic in itself, it is in turn dependent upon volume and pitch. It is therefore obvious that the limitations of quality both as to transmission and reception in radio will be the same as those of pitch and volume. There can be no fuller quality than there are frequencies available to transmit it. While the bracket of frequencies from thirty to five thousand covers all the fundamental tones and some of the overtones of almost any sound that would be broadcast, the higher frequencies might add a richness which in most broadcasts is unavailable. This is not a serious limitation, however.

It is safe to say, then, that commercial amplitude modulation broadcasting as we now know it is a fairly accurate and complete medium for the transmission of sound. There is no denying the fact that present-day frequency modulation broadcasting will allow wider bands of frequencies to be received and a more static-free signal to be transmitted. With the medium now available, however, there is much to be done which has not even yet been explored. We can sum it up by saying that the medium is suitable but not ideal for the transmission of sound.

The Theory of Radio Transmission

No one planning to work in the field of radio should be ignorant of the basic technical principles of his medium. Least of all should a production director ignore these facts.

One must understand three basic phenomena: first, the characteristics of sound; second, the translation of sound into electromotive force; and third, the wireless transmission and reception of this force.

Until the advent of radio broadcasting, sound was man's only medium for broadcasting. It is obvious that sound alone, as a medium, has its limitations. Sound, first of all, travels very slowly (about 1120 feet per second through air, at 20° centigrade). Furthermore, the loudest sound man has devised can be heard only a few miles, which would place an immediate limit on broadcasting in that medium. In the second place, sound is not easily controllable. If one person were broadcasting mere sound, everyone else would have to keep quiet — a difficult assignment. Too, everyone would *have* to hear the broadcast, whether he would or no.

It seems obvious, then, that sound had to be translated into some other form of energy before broadcasting could become feasible. Sound must be transformed into a kind of energy that travels very quickly and in a form which is controllable. Electrical energy is a form which answers both these requirements. It travels at the speed of light (186,000 miles per second), and it can be put on wires and sent wherever desired. No one need be bothered with it who does not choose to be. Furthermore, electrical energy can be sent through the air without wires. Here, then, is a medium made to order. Our only problem is in making the translation. Let us investigate, then, the underlying theories which make broadcasting possible, and take them up in step-by-step order so that we can see the logical progression of happenings as they really occur.

In order to pigeonhole the processes as neatly as possible, let us list the various stages of broadcasting and then explain them in turn. These things occur:

1. Sound is generated. It may be speech, music, noise, or any combination of these.
2. It is acoustically controlled. In studios this is managed by "softening the walls" or by the use of artificial echo, or by other means. This refers to the control of sound waves while they are still in the physical form.
3. Sound energy is translated into electrical energy. The microphone is the instrument that accomplishes this transformation. Henceforth, we are dealing with an electrical force – not a physical one.
4. This electrical energy is amplified. It is very weak in its original form. The vacuum tube accomplishes this amplifying process.
5. It is controlled as to volume and placement. Control is established by the use of conductors, non-conductors, and resistors.
6. It may be distorted. This can be done only by subtraction of frequencies through the use of filters.
7. It is broadcast. This is the function of the radio transmitter.
8. It is received. The home radio set accomplishes this and makes possible the next step.

9. The electrical energy is retranslated into sound energy. This is the function of the loud-speaker. Head-phones serve the same function.

Here is the barest and most simplified outline possible of what takes place in the process of broadcasting. Obviously, books could be and have been written about each one of these steps or even minute parts of each step. Our need here is to understand the principles involved in the whole process, and enough detailed understanding of those steps which the actor, announcer, and producer use in everyday practice to assure maximum efficiency in the handling of their respective jobs.

Establish this list well in mind. Mark this page, if necessary, so that it may be referred to in the discussion that follows. The danger in such a discussion is of getting bogged down in detail and failing to see proper relationships and progression in happenings.

Sound Is Generated

We have already described the nature of this process. For the purposes of our discussion, let us take a simple sound pattern originated by the human voice. Somewhere in a studio, an announcer says, "This is the National Broadcasting Company." The vibration of his vocal bands creates the sound. His tongue, lips, etc., shape the sound into meaningful patterns which we call words, and the resultant push of physical energy (in the form of a molecular disturbance in the air) travels out into the studio.

Acoustical Control

We may think of sound as going direct from the announcer to the microphone. And so it does. But in the process something happens to it. Certain characteristics are added by the space in which the sound is uttered. It sounds one way in an empty stadium, another in a telephone booth. We must control the acoustics of the walls that surround the sound before and while it is reaching the microphone.

Since this set of sounds was generated in a radio studio, acoustical control is achieved automatically. The walls of the studio are sound-treated. This simply means that the walls are made soft enough to absorb most of the molecular bombardment that hits them when sound is generated in the room. If the walls were very hard, this bombardment would hit them, bounce back, hit the opposite wall, and keep repeating this process until the energy was dissipated. Meantime there would be a continual sound all that time. And since sounds seldom occur singly, new ones would be generated which would also continue, and there would be an overlapping of several sounds – all being heard at once. If this overlapping was very bad, a series of words would soon become unintelligible. Using soft-surface walls or sound-absorbent material on the walls damps the reverberation and prevents the overlapping of sounds so that we hear them one at a time. This is the simplest form of acoustical control.

How this is done and how other acoustical changes are achieved will be discussed under the headings "Studios" and "Special Resonance Control."

Translation into Electrical Energy

Once sound is generated under controlled conditions in the studio, it is directed into the microphone. It is here that the change-over from sound energy into electrical energy is effected. That is the purpose of a microphone. The reasons for the necessity of the change have already been established.

There are three different principles on which microphones are made to operate. Only one will be given here. The others will be discussed under the heading of "Microphones."

This principle is: a conductor, vibrating in the field of a magnet, will generate electrical energy of a strength proportional to the force of the vibration and having the same number of cycles as the frequency of the physical vibration.

We must define a few terms before we go further. These definitions are not designed for technical accuracy, but to give a simplified explanation of the phenomena of electrical energy to the non-technical personnel of broadcasting. Here, then, are the basic terms and their meanings:

Electrical energy. A flow of electrons.

Conductor. Any matter which allows the easy flow of electrons along it. Here are some of the best conductors, listed in order of the amount of conductivity: silver, copper, aluminum, nickel, soft iron, and platinum. All these materials are conductors to a fairly high degree.

Nonconductor. This is a self-explanatory term.

Insulator. This is a term for a form of nonconductor used to stop the flow of electrical energy. Glass, porcelain, plastics of various kinds, and rubber are most commonly used, since they are almost complete nonconductors. They are used to stop the flow of electrical energy and are therefore used in "control equipment."

Resistor. This term is applied to materials which have a certain amount of conductivity, but not enough for free passage of an electronic flow.

Ohm. A unit of measurement of the resistance of a substance to the flow of alternating current.

Impedance. A unit of measurement of the apparent resistance of a substance to the flow of alternating current.

Volt. A unit of measurement of electrical energy which refers to the pressure at which it flows. An easy comparison can be made to water flowing through a pipe. The more pressure applied to the water, the faster it flows. The more pressure there is on the electronic flow, the higher the voltage. A normal home-lighting circuit flows at a pressure of 110 volts.

Ampere. A unit of measurement of electrical energy, referring to volume of flow. This may be compared to the flow of water as governed by the size of the pipe. A large pipe, regardless of pressure, will let more water through. A large conductor will let more amperes of electrical energy pass.

Circuit. A term used to indicate an arrangement of conductors which is capable of carrying electrical energy. There must always be two conductors in a circuit — one to carry the energy to the point of application, and one to return it to the source of power.

Direct current. Electrical energy which flows constantly in the same direction. There is a side positively charged, where the flow is from power source to application point; and a side negatively charged, where the flow is from the point of application back to the source of power. These two sides, connected continuously by conductors, form a circuit.

Alternating current. Current whose direction of flow constantly reverses. Thus, the positive and negatively charged sides reverse at stated intervals.

Cycles. The number of times per second that an alternating current changes the direction of its flow.

Decibel. The amount of increase necessary in a given volume for the change to be perceptible to the human ear. This amounts to a twenty-five per cent increase. Zero level is usually considered as the volume level of normal speech. Lower volume sounds are stated in minus decibels; louder sounds as plus decibels.

A study of these terms and an application of the principle stated give us a start in the understanding of the workings of a microphone. It is plain that if we are to translate sound energy into electrical energy, we must do two things: first, create the electrical energy itself, and second, give it exactly the same characteristics as the sound energy which activates it. We must, therefore, have an electrical generator which can be driven by the sound energy with which we start, and the generator must vary the electrical energy output just as the physical energy varies.

We know from our first principle that a conductor, vibrating in the field of a magnet, will create electrical energy. We know that the harder it vibrates, the more voltage it sets up, in terms of volts and amperes. We know further that for each vibration of the conductor we create one cycle of the alternating current pattern. It remains now only to understand how the conductor can be made to vibrate according to the sound energy created in the studio by our announcer saying, "This is the National Broadcasting Company."

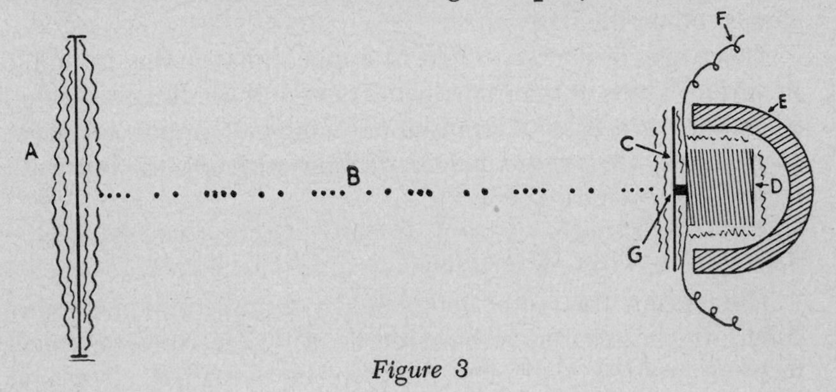

Figure 3

Figure 3 shows how this is done for one kind of microphone. *A* represents the sound source. It may be a piano string or the vibrating vocal bands of the announcer. Whatever the source, it sets up the condensation and rarefaction pattern of molecular movement in the air, creating a molecular bombardment on the microphone as indicated along *B*. In the microphone is placed a thin, stretched steel diaphragm *C* whose function and method of operation is exactly like that of the human ear drum. When the sound-wave pattern strikes the diaphragm, it vibrates. It vibrates the same number of times per second and with the same relative intensity as the originating sound source. We have then, mirrored in the vibration of this diaphragm, the original vibration pattern of the sound source. At *D* is a conductor, in this case a coil of wire, resting between the poles of a magnet *E*. The coil of wire is directly attached to the diaphragm at *G*, so that when the diaphragm vibrates the coil of wire vibrates. This movement creates a constantly fluctuating electrical alternating current. This current goes through a complete alternation or cycle with every full vibration swing of the diaphragm and creates more or less current depending on the length (strength) of the vibration swing. Thus, we have a fluctuating alternating current set up whose frequency (number of cycles) varies with the number of vibrations per second that the diaphragm makes and whose strength varies with the vigor of the vibration. The current thus created is carried off on the wires *F*.

There are, of course, different applications of this principle in various kinds of microphones. These will be discussed later. It is the principle of translation which is important now. Henceforth, we are no longer dealing with sound, but with controllable electrical energy.

Electrical Energy Is Amplified

The current created or generated by the microphone is very small. It is measured in hundredths of a volt. It is too small to be of any use, and must therefore be amplified. It was at this point that radio bogged down for many years until Lee DeForest discovered, and others perfected, the three-element vacuum tube which made it possible to build up the volume of an electrical energy without destroying or distorting the fluctuation pattern. To describe the operation of the vacuum tube would demand more technical explanation than can be justified here. It is enough to know that the tube contains three elements — a grid, a plate, and a filament. When the filament is heated, it causes an electronic flow to the plate. This flow can be changed by the introduction of a second current from the grid and thus caused to increase. In its simplest form, the microphone current is introduced into the grid circuit and this causes a much larger electronic flow from the filament to the plate in the tube, but the pattern or change as represented in the microphone current is maintained, even though the total power is amplified as much as three hundred times.

This is something you can let the engineers worry about. It is enough for the production director to know that this process of great amplification takes place by means of a series of vacuum tubes which may multiply the power of an original microphone current several thousand times, but the pattern of fluctuation remains proportionate. Having been amplified, the energy is strong enough to do useful work, and we must know how it is controlled.

Electrical Energy Is Controlled

We are concerned with two ideas under the heading of control. First, we wish to send this electrical energy where it will be useful to us. Second, we must control its volume. The first control is achieved by means of conductors and nonconductors. Copper wire is the most commonly used conductor and the energy can be sent almost anywhere by the simple process of laying copper wire to that point. Switches are simply a means of breaking the continuity of the conductors and afford a means of turning the current on and off. Insulators are used to keep the current from going to places where it should not.

Control of volume is managed by making use of the principle of resistance. Most commonly used resistors are very fine copper wire, carbon, and german-silver wire. These materials will allow electrical energy to pass, but they offer considerable resistance. If enough resistance is introduced into a circuit, the power required to overcome the resistance is more than that of the current, and it never gets through. All volume controls use this principle. They simply introduce into a circuit a varying amount of resistance. If enough resistance is introduced, the flow of the energy can be stopped completely.

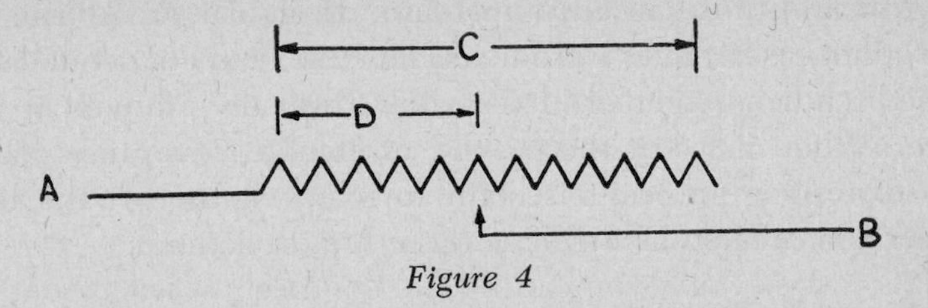

Figure 4

In Figure 4 this is illustrated. *A* represents the incoming current. The full resistance, as indicated by *C*, represents enough resistance to stop the amount of current coming in at

A. If only the amount of resistance is used as represented by *D* and the circuit is brought out at *B*, then only half enough resistance is used to stop the current completely, so at least half of the original power at *A* comes out at *B*. By varying the amount of the resistance used, any given amount of the original power at *A* may be allowed to pass. This variation of resistance is what occurs when you twist the volume control on a radio receiver. As you bring up the volume, you are simply taking out more of the resistance, letting more power come through. This gives constant control over the amount of power at any given point.

Distortion of Electrical Energy

Having translated sound energy into electrical energy, amplified and controlled it, it may be desirable to distort it somewhat. This can be done only by subtraction. We can or should add nothing to the pattern of varying volume and frequencies which is the electrical mirror of sound, but we can subtract from its total. This is done by a process called "filtering." Filters are a combination of inductances and capacities which have the ability to stop the passage of certain frequencies of current. They can be built to stop any particular set of frequencies desired. Thus, a predetermined number of frequencies can be subtracted from the microphone current and a distortion produced. This is how directors achieve the voice "at the other end" of a two-way telephone conversation. It is also the principle of the tone control on a receiving set. When the tone control is set at low or bass, a series of filters take out some of the high frequencies and allow the lower ones to pass at full value. When it is set at low, the reverse process takes place. This distortion process is useful in many forms of dramatic production and will be discussed at length later on.

The Signal Is Broadcast

When the electrical energy pattern has gone through all these procedures, it is ready for transmission through the air. It leaves the studio and travels to the transmitter, which is usually located away from a city to avoid blanketing out other stations and to make possible distant reception.

Two essential steps happen at the transmitter. The first originates there and has nothing to do with anything that has gone before. Huge oscillator tubes generate a radio wave of a fixed length, called a "carrier wave." Each station sends out a wave length of its own. Everyone at some time has heard the announcer of a station say, "This station is broadcasting on a wave length of blank cycles, by authority of the Federal Communications Commission." The Commission assigns to each station a certain wave length; the carrier wave of that station must not vary from it. It is this fixed-length carrier wave which makes it possible for more than one station to broadcast at a time. It makes tuning or selection of stations possible, because it is the length of the carrier wave to which the receiving set is tuned.

Once the oscillator tubes generate the carrier wave, it is forced out on the antenna and ground system of the transmitter under high electrical pressure. The amount of pressure determines the power of the station, the distance the signal travels, and therefore the service area of the station. Forced off the antenna, this signal radiates equally in all directions. Those waves which head down from the antenna hit the ground and are reflected back into the air. Those that radiate up continue into the air from forty to sixty miles until they reach an atmospheric layer known as the Kennelly-Heaviside layer, from which broadcast wave lengths are usually reflected. The upward waves are reflected (in varying degrees depending on atmospheric conditions) back to the earth and continue to bounce back and forth between the earth and the atmospheric layer until they are exhausted. See Figure 5 for an illustration of this. *A* represents the antenna mast, *B* the carrier wave, and *D* the length of this particular wave. *C* represents the voice wave superimposed on the carrier wave.

Now let us examine the second important step which occurs at the transmitter. Coming into the transmitter from the studio in the city is a fluctuating current which is the program or

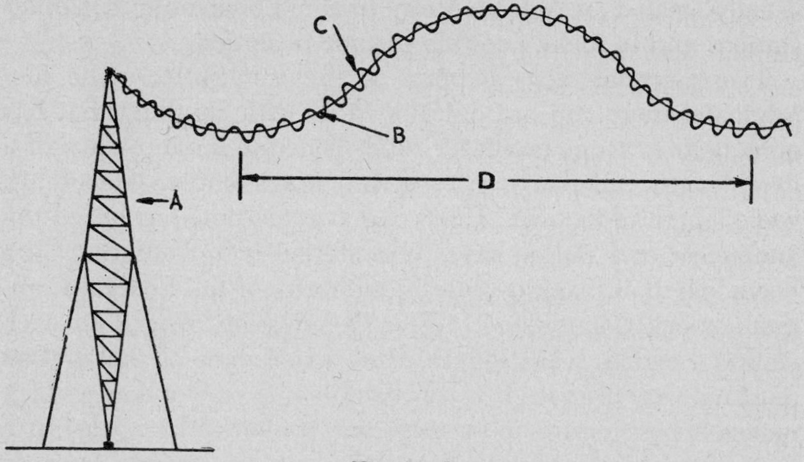

Figure 5

voice current. This current is again amplified and then "placed on the back" of the carrier wave. That is to say, the voice wave is superimposed on the carrier wave as represented by *C* in Figure 5, and thus is radiated or broadcast.

The Program Is Received

All receiving sets must have an antenna of some sort. It may be only a small coil of wire rolled up in a portable case, but it serves the same purpose as an aerial on top of a house. Whatever its form, the aerial intercepts the carrier wave of the station. A tuning device in the receiving set makes it receptive to only one wave length at a time and this can be changed by the tuning apparatus. In the receiver the signal is first amplified because it becomes very weak in the transmitting process. Then the carrier wave is filtered out from the voice wave and discarded. The voice wave which remains is then further amplified and the same fluctuating alternating current actuates the receiving set which was first generated by the microphone.

It Is Retranslated into Sound Energy

The translation of electrical energy back into sound energy is accomplished by the loud-speaker. In order to understand its workings, we must state another principle. Everyone is familiar with the action of a magnet and its property of attracting a metallic body. If a coil of wire is wrapped around a magnet and the coil of wire charged with an electric current, the magnetic (pulling power) attraction is increased in direct ratio to the amount of current in the coil. This is the principle that is used to make a loud-speaker operate. A diaphragm is placed in front of a magnet, which exerts a fixed pull on its center. A coil of wire is then wrapped around the magnet and into this coil of wire is fed the "voice current" with which we have been dealing all along. This current is constantly fluctuating, both as to number of frequencies per second and as to power. It creates a proportionate fluctuating change in the pulling power of the magnet on the diaphragm and thus sets up a varying vibration in the diaphragm. The vibration of the diaphragm is a physical, not an electrical movement, and it transmits itself to the molecules in the surrounding air, just as the original sound source did back in the studio. The vibration pattern of the diaphragm sets up the sounds and words with which we started – "This is the National Broadcasting Company."

In this way we complete the transmission of a set of sounds from a speaker in a distant studio, into the medium of electricity through the air, and back into the home of the listener.

This much and very little more information about the theory of radio broadcasting is helpful to the prospective production worker in the studio or control room. An understanding of the basic principles is the soundest foundation upon which one can build. The details of management may be safely left to the engineers, who are efficient, interested, and proud of their work.

CHAPTER 4

THE BASIC EQUIPMENT OF BROADCASTING

BROADCAST EQUIPMENT will be discussed under five major headings:

1. Microphones
2. Studios
3. Control rooms
4. Control equipment
5. Auxiliary equipment

A production director should know these things about the equipment with which he works:

1. Its principle of operation
2. Its characteristics
3. Its limits of flexibility
4. Its method of operation
5. Its most usual application to radio production directing

This is not nearly so complex as it sounds. There is no need to take a course in electrical engineering to learn these facts. It is perfectly possible to operate a mixing panel from the front without an intimate electrical knowledge of the "how" of the happenings behind the panel. Scores of announcers do just that in small stations all over the country every day. Basic principles are always simple and can be simply stated.

MICROPHONES

This discussion of microphones necessitates the explanation of certain basic terms and principles of their operation. There are two main factors considered in measuring the worth of a microphone. The first is the width of frequencies to which it will respond; that is, how low and how high a pitch will it pick up and reproduce. Some microphones will not respond to sounds lower than seventy-five cycles per second on the low end or above five thousand cycles per second on the high end. Others have a range of from forty on the low end to fifteen thousand on the high end. This width of frequency response is the first factor considered.

The second factor is the accuracy of response throughout the useful range. Some microphones, for example, might respond to a frequency pattern ranging from fifty to ten thousand cycles, but in certain parts of that range, the response might be as much as thirty per cent inaccurate. Other microphones might respond to a range limited from sixty to six thousand cycles, but have an inaccuracy deviation of less than one per cent. When a microphone is tested to determine these two factors, the results can be reduced to chart form which will look like Figure 6. Along the bottom of the chart the ver-

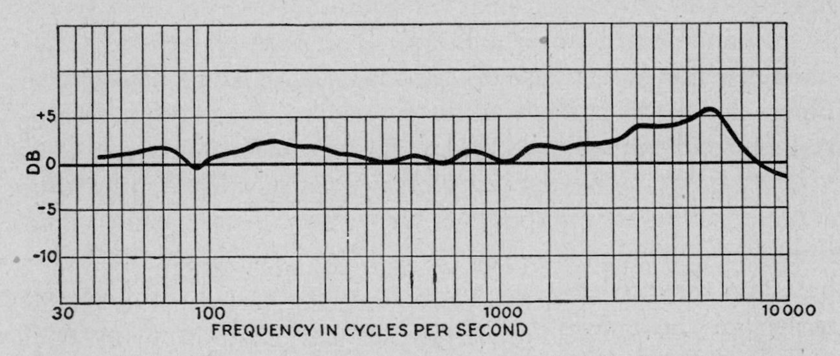

Figure 6. Frequency Response of a Typical 77-B Unidirectional Microphone

tical lines represent the range of frequencies. This chart shows a range of thirty to ten thousand cycles. Along the left-hand side is a decibel scale on which is checked the variation in volume response of a given microphone to various pitches. A good microphone is one whose curve would extend as far across the chart as possible and whose vertical variation is as small as possible. When engineers say a microphone has a very flat frequency response, they mean that it has very little volume variation at different pitches. This is high praise. The flatter the curve, the more accurately the microphone reproduces sound throughout its useful range. The wider and flatter a frequency response curve, the better the microphone.

In addition to those just mentioned, there are certain behavior characteristics of the microphone which govern its usability for broadcast purposes. We need to know if it is subject to "blasting." Will it, in other words, distort under sudden overloads of volume? What are its directional characteristics? What does weather do to it? What will changes in barometric pressure and humidity do to the microphone? The answers to these questions will determine how a microphone is used, for what, and by whom. In the discussion following, these questions will be answered for each kind of microphone in common use.

From a technical point of view there are only three kinds of microphones – velocity, pressure-actuated, and cardioid types. RCA manufactures several models of velocity or ribbon microphones which are extensively used in broadcasting. This microphone derives its name from the fact that a free-moving ribbon, fastened only at the two ends, vibrates in harmony with the velocity of the molecular movement of the air. Of the pressure-actuated type of microphone, there are several kinds. The so-called dynamic mike, the crystal, the salt-shaker, the eight-ball, and several others are pressure-actuated. In this kind the molecular movement in the air bombards a fixed diaphragm and the pressure thus created generates the movement which is translated into electrical energy. The cardioid type of microphone combines the principles of the velocity and the pressure-actuated microphones in such a way that creates what is known as a "cardioid pattern." This microphone uses two ribbons, one free-moving as in the velocity microphone, and the other acoustically baffled so as to react like a pressure-actuated microphone. The result is a microphone which can be made bi-directional, semi-directional, or non-directional.

Since most students of production directing will not have an engineering background, this classification of microphones will mean little. Most non-technical people tend to identify microphones by their outward appearance. For this reason, microphones will be identified by picture and discussed according to their principle of operation, response pattern, directional characteristics, performance characteristics, and common uses.

There are two other kinds of microphones which are of historical interest only, since they have almost entirely been retired from active service in broadcasting. These are the double-button carbon microphone and the condenser microphone. Both were pressure-actuated, but their principles of utilizing the pressure were different from that of the modern microphones. For many years the carbon microphone was the symbol of broadcasting, just as the velocity mike is today. Both of these had many drawbacks, but they did yeoman's duty in the dim dawn of broadcasting.

The crystal microphone is another type not described here, although many crystal mikes are in use today. It was not included with the others because it is seldom used for broadcasting. There seems to be little specific agreement among engineers as to why they have been excluded from the broadcast field, but the consensus seems to be that, although they have a wide range of frequency response, in general the accuracy within that range is not high enough to warrant their use for broadcasting. Crystal mikes work on the pressure-actuated principle. They are akin to the photoelectric cell, which is light sensitive. Certain salt crystals (notably Rochelle Salts) are pressure sensitive, and when a pressure is applied to one face, they develop an electric charge on their opposite face.

Crystal microphones are made by many manufacturers and they come in all kinds, types, and shapes. They are comparatively inexpensive, and as a result are much used in public-address systems, inexpensive recording equipment, and for intercommunication systems. While they are seldom used for broadcasting, they are frequently used in talk-back systems and for other purposes where the quality is not critical. Some manufacturers of crystal microphones claim for them a frequency response just as accurate and wide as other kinds, but they have not been generally accepted by the broadcasting industry.

The Use of Microphones

Production directors are not concerned with the kind of microphones with which a station is equipped, except to be sure that enough different kinds are available to meet their normal needs. The director may safely assume that whatever mikes are available are the best which the station can afford.

What does concern the production director is the kind of directional pattern needed for a specific purpose. While it is dangerous to generalize, certain broad principles may be stated.

1. Dynamic, pressure-actuated microphones are best for out-of-door pickups where wind may be encountered. Their rugged construction also make them best for remote work.
2. The unidirectional or velocity microphone is probably best for musical pickups because of its extreme sensitivity and wide frequency-response range.
3. Non-directional microphones simplify pickup problems in round-table programs and audience-participation programs where many people must be accommodated.
4. Velocity microphones are probably the most useful for dramatic work because their directional pattern allows for fades, and for picking up sound from more than one source with a minimum of cross-talk.
5. Unidirectional microphones are useful when studio audiences are involved.

Studios

There are as many kinds of studios as there are demands on a broadcasting station, ranging from a tiny announcer's booth up to a huge auditorium which may seat as many as two thousand people. Some small stations seem to be able to struggle along with only one or two studios; large network origination points may have twenty or more.

Acoustical engineers have been trying out pet theories for the past fifteen years, and all sorts of trick treatments have been evolved for sound-treating and sound-proofing studios. It is impossible to describe here all these various developments. The student director should try only to understand the basic theories behind some of the treatments and to know the more conventional acoustical arrangements. A talks studio need only be large enough for a small table, a couple of chairs, and a microphone. A large studio is obviously needed to accommodate a fair-sized studio audience, a full symphony orchestra, and a large dramatic cast.

Rooms are treated in two ways to make them into studios. First they are treated to isolate all sound and vibration from without. Second, they are treated to control the length of reverberation time of any sound which originates within the studio. This is a simple statement of acoustical needs. Within these apparently simple limits have been spent years of research by sound engineers. Modern studios are rooms suspended on springs and horsehair within the regular frame of the building itself. Ceiling, floor, and walls have no direct contact with the framework of the building, but are hung from and rest on a series of pads designed to absorb all the shock and vibration to which the framework of the building itself is subjected because of trains, heavy trucks, and traffic. Each studio is also sealed away from any possible seeping-in of outside noises. Few studios are entered directly. Most of them are equipped with sound traps so that a person entering comes first into a little antechamber and closes an outside door before opening a second door to go into the studio proper. These doors are carefully constructed to seal out outside noises. Windows looking into the studio from control rooms, observation rooms, and so forth, are made of from two to four layers of glass with dead air spaces between. Few modern studios have outside windows, but if they have, these are also made of multiple layers of glass. The necessity for sealing up a studio has, incidentally, been a boon to the air-conditioning industry. It is at the same time a large headache because the problem of introducing and circulating fresh air into a studio without creating undesirable air currents which may affect sensitive microphones is no simple task. It is ordinarily accomplished by a complicated system of baffling.

Many early studios were hung with heavy draperies of velour or monk's cloth to absorb some of the sound and prevent the rooms from sounding "boomy." Later, patented wood-pulp materials were used on the walls until it was discovered that termites and other vermin were having a feast. Eventually, rock wool and various asbestos materials came to be used as sound-absorbent materials. The material is placed on the walls and ceilings of the studios in such a carefully calculated way as to bring the reverberation time in the studio within fixed and controllable limits. The microphone is more sensitive than is the ear, and therefore acoustical conditions have to be less live in a studio than they are in the average room. Engineers and acoustical experts disagree on what is the best normal condition for broadcasting, but the normal is probably between five tenths and one and two tenths seconds of reverberation time. Anything above this would be too live or boomy for broadcasting purposes. Anything below this would be probably too dead for ordinary use, taking all the brilliance away from sound.

The most modern studios are so sound-treated that they provide for a variable reverberation pattern in various parts of the studio. The usual arrangement is to build in a live end and a dead end with the center area a compromise neutral between the two. The dead end is heavily blanketed with absorbent material so that it completely absorbs any sound reaching it. The live end will be faced with seasoned wood panels mounted to make them a resonator or sounding board. The two side walls immediately adjoining the live end of the studio may be of similar construction except that they are built in a saw-toothed arrangement, carefully angled to avoid parallel surfaces on either side. Perhaps halfway down the room this saw-toothed arrangement of walls ceases, or it may continue, but in either case sound-absorbent material is applied heavily to make its reverberation characteristics about the same as those of the dead end of the studio. The live end is usually equipped with a heavy drape or curtain on a regular stage traveler so that it may be completely opened or closed at will, thus varying the amount of the live, resonant wall exposed.

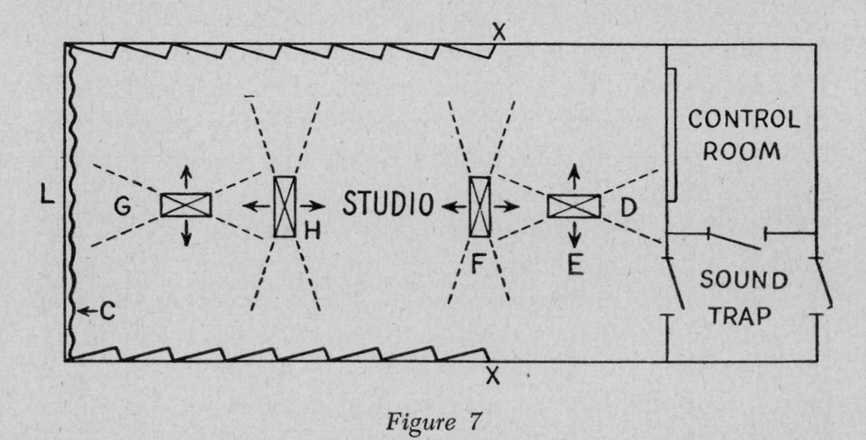

Figure 7

Such an arrangement as this offers the maximum flexibility thus far devised in the control of the acoustics of sound in a studio. Use of such a studio is illustrated in Figure 7. *L* is the live end, *D* the dead end, and *X* on either side shows the point at which sound-absorption panels begin. Placement of a velocity microphone as in *E* would give a minimum of reverberation, since both beams of the mike are headed toward heavily treated walls. A velocity microphone located at *F* and beamed as indicated would allow for considerable reverberation, since the sound directed toward the live end of the studio from *F* would be picked up on the mike and at the same time travel the length of the studio and be picked up again on its way back. A velocity microphone located at *G* and beamed as indicated would offer considerable brilliance, but no direct reverberation, while one located at *H*, with the sound source located on the dead-end side of the mike, would give the same kind of pickup as obtained at *F*, but with a shorter reverberation time. Add to these simple examples the other positions possible in this kind of studio setup, complicate it with the possibility of beaming the microphone horizontally and vertically, and the combinations of quality possible to obtain begin to multiply rapidly. The final variable factor is the draperies at the live end of the studio, which may be opened or closed any desired amount. The whole picture gives some idea of the flexibility of a studio acoustically treated in this manner.

In some studios the acoustical treatment on each wall can be varied. The acoustic panels, instead of being permanently built in, are mounted on hinged panels like window shutters. One side of the panel is heavily sound-treated; the other has a hard surface. By simply swinging the panels around, any needed amount of change can be quickly made. This is an especially useful arrangement where studio audiences are often present. It allows for changing the acoustic treatment in accordance with the number of people in the audience. Each person represents the acoustic equivalent of about 4.6 square feet of sound-absorbent material, gross. Thus, if one program has two hundred people in the audience and another program five hundred, it is clear that there will be a considerable difference in the acoustics of the studio, and some sort of adjustment becomes necessary. The panel method allows for this change with comparative ease.

The increasing popularity of studio audiences is having a decided effect on studio architecture. Many new studios more nearly resemble auditoriums than a conventional studio. They have a stage and stage lighting, with control rooms and sponsors' booths in the positions occupied by the boxes in a theater. It is likely that this tendency will grow, because in many types of broadcasts a studio audience is a highly desirable ingredient of the program.

Studios must, of course, be well lighted and well ventilated. Lighting must be so placed that there is no glare on the control-room window to cut down visibility. They should also be adequately supplied with microphones and electrical outlets. Several microphone plugs located in various parts of the studio make unnecessary long microphone cables stretched over the floor and eliminate chances of people tripping over them. It also makes for neater, more convenient management by the control engineers.

There is one last consideration with regard to studios. They should be well placed with respect to the general architecture of the building to insure a maximum quietness, accessibility, and efficiency. If possible they should be so placed that observation booths, control rooms, and sponsors' booths can have a maximum view into the studios and be easily accessible.

Control Rooms

Ideally, there should be a separate control room looking into each studio. In many stations control rooms are situated between studios so that they can service two and sometimes even three studios. This may conserve space, and it does conserve equipment, but it is a poor arrangement, nevertheless. A studio is more often than not only of use when there is an available control room to service it. If a control room is busy with one studio, it obviously cannot be satisfactorily used as a monitoring room for a rehearsal from a second one. There are any number of stations where this is done every day, but it is far from ideal. The combination of a large studio with an announcer's booth might work very well, since the latter will seldom be used for a program that needs rehearsal. But for larger studios a separate control room for each studio is desirable.

Control rooms need not be large. As a matter of fact, there is considerable virtue in having a small one because, during the production of a radio show, only the production director, the engineer, and possibly an assistant are needed in the control room. People who have no function there cause distractions and a small room tends to discourage extra people crowding in. A room six by eight feet is ample for the average control room. If the studio which the control room serves is a large one, then the control-room floor should be elevated two to four feet above the floor of the studio itself so that the director and the engineer sitting at their operating tables can command

PLATE 1

PLATE 2

THE RCA VELOCITY MICROPHONES, 44-BX AND 74-B TYPES

Principle of operation: Velocity of ribbon type.

Response pattern: Very flat from 30 to 15,000 cycles, for the RCA 44-BX very flat from 70 to 8,000 cycles for the RCA 74-B

Directionalism: Bidirectional as shown in Plates 3 and 4

Characteristics:
A. Very sensitive. It will distort under sudden volume overloads.
B. Attenuates high frequencies when the sound source is closer than 18 inches.
C. Flutters in wind or other moving air currents.

Uses: The RCA 44-BX can be used for almost any purpose, with two important exceptions. It is too sensitive to air currents to allow its use out-of-doors and it is not suitable in situations that can be best handled by a non-directional microphone. Except for these two situations, the 44-BX can do almost any kind of job. Plates 5, 6, 7, and 8 indicate some of the ways in which it can be used. This model velocity and its predecessor are probably the most used microphones in American broadcasting. The RCA 74-B microphone is a new inexpensive model velocity microphone developed to compete in the lower price range. Its principle is the same as the 44-BX. However, it is smaller and less accurate. It is widely used by schools and stations that cannot afford the larger, more sensitive model.

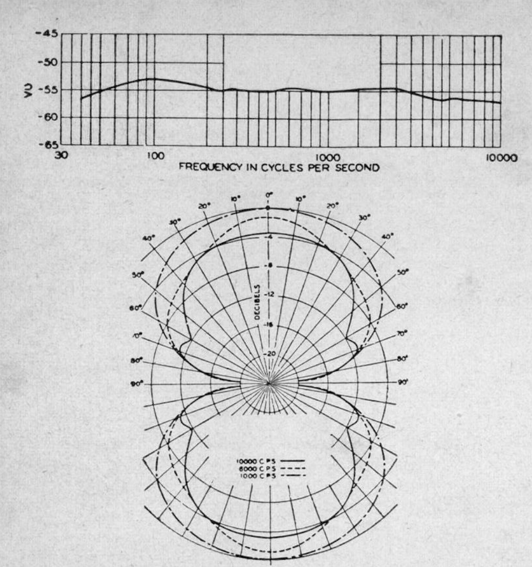

PLATE 3

ABOVE: Frequency Response of a Typical 44-BX Velocity Microphone

BELOW: Directional Characteristic of a Typical 44-BX Velocity Microphone

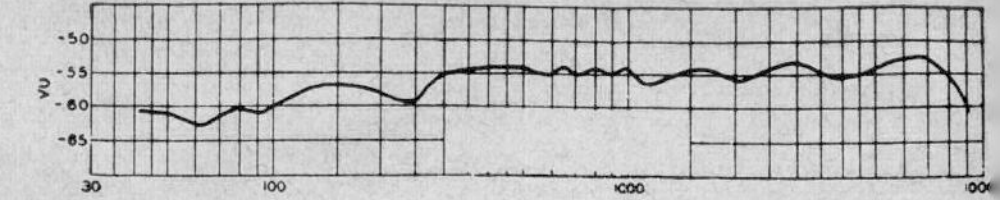

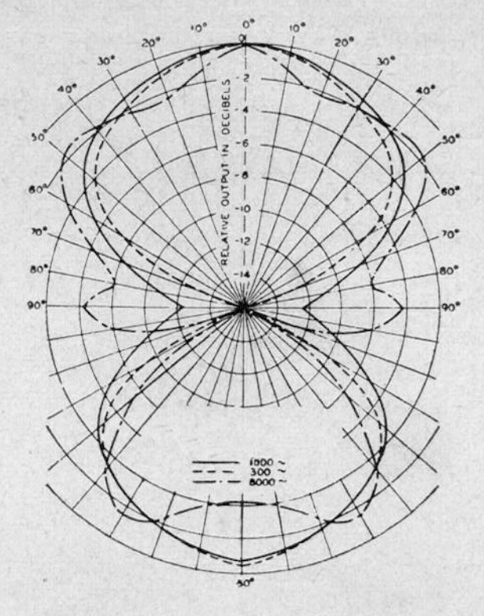

PLATE 4

ABOVE: Frequency Response of a Typi
74-B Velocity Microphone

BELOW: Directional Characteristic of
Typical 74-B Junior Velocity Micropho

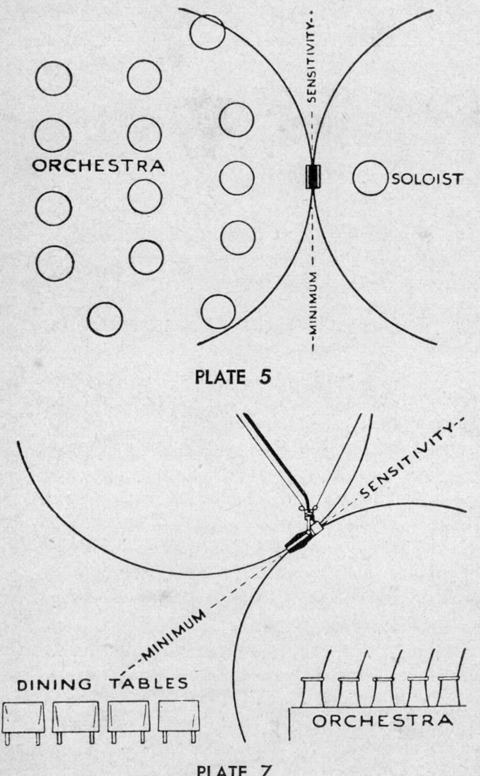

PLATE 7

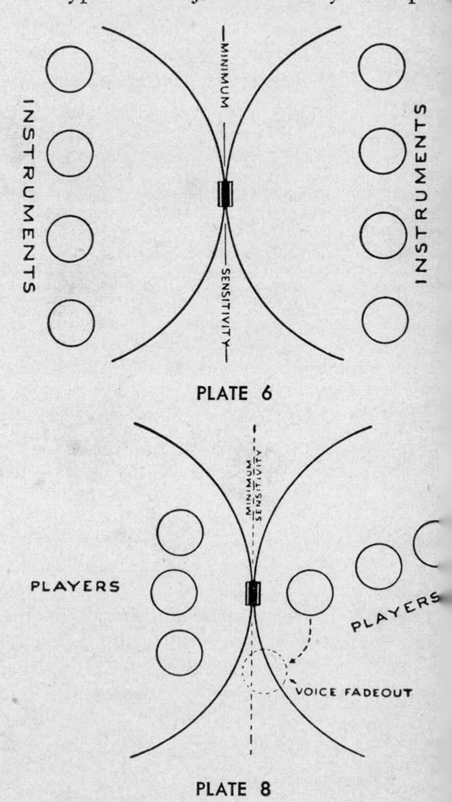

PLATE 8

Studio Set-ups Using the RCA 44-BX Microphone

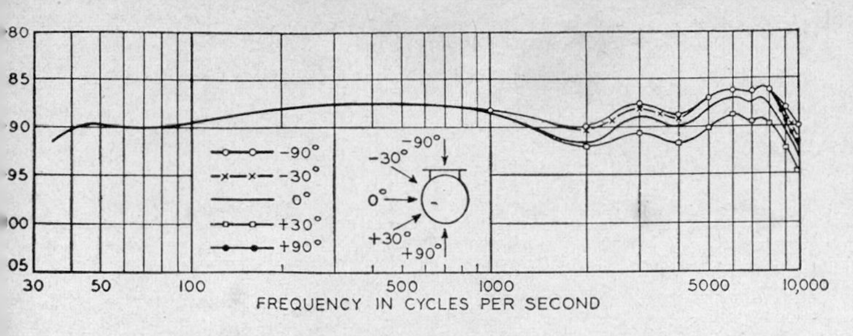

PLATE 9

Frequency Response of the "Eight-Ball" Microphone

PLATE 10

THE WESTERN ELECTRIC "EIGHT-BALL" (630-A) PRESSURE MICROPHONE

Principle of operation: Pressure-actuated type.

Response pattern: Very flat from 40 to 10,000 cycles.

Directionalism: Non-directional.

Characteristics: A. Not sensitive to sudden overloads in volume and not likely to distort.

B. Response pattern fairly constant regardless of the distance of sound source from microphone.

C. Extremely rugged in construction and not subject to weather conditions.

Uses: The "8-Ball," formally designated as the 630-A, excels in two uses. Because of its rugged construction, lack of sensitivity to weather, and because it can be handled without making too much noise, it is often used for special events and sports assignments. It is more satisfactory out-of-doors than a ribbon microphone because it is not so sensitive to wind. Its rugged construction makes it good for remote work. It is also useful in any studio situation where a non-directional microphone is needed. In round-table programs, audience-participation programs, and similar programs where many people need to be around a single microphone, the 8-Ball is useful.

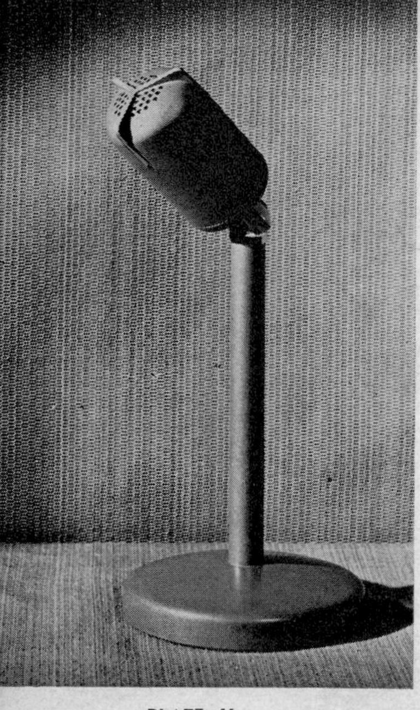

PLATE 11

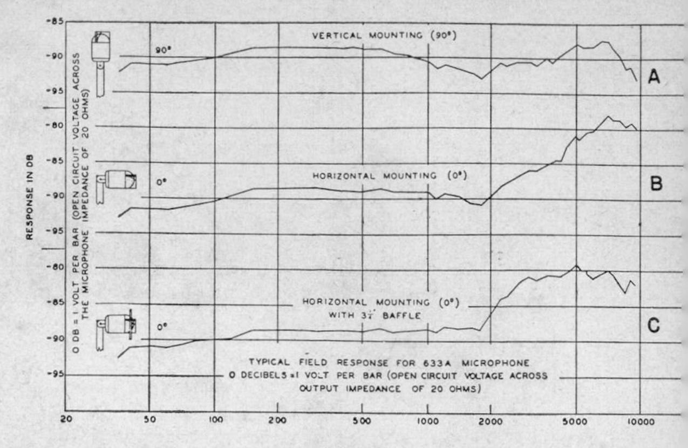

PLATE 12

Frequency Response of the Western Electric "Saltshaker" (623-A) Pressure Microphone

THE WESTERN ELECTRIC "SALTSHAKER" (633-A) PRESSURE MICROPHONE

Principle of operation: Pressure-actuated type.

Response pattern: Fairly flat from 50 to 10,000 cycles.

Directionalism: Either non-directional or semi-directional, depending on whether or not a baffle is used and whether it is mounted horizontally or vertically.

Characteristics: The same as the "8-Ball" microphone or most other members of the moving-coil type of pressure-actuated microphone.

Uses: The uses of the Saltshaker mike, formally designated as the Western Electric 633-A, are much the same as the 630-A. The baffle provided with the 633-A makes it slightly more flexible in terms of its directional qualities. It is also a very inexpensive microphone, comparatively, and therefore is often available where its more expensive counterparts are not. It is slightly less accurate than the 630-A and has a somewhat narrower pattern of accurate response, but it is much used in many stations.

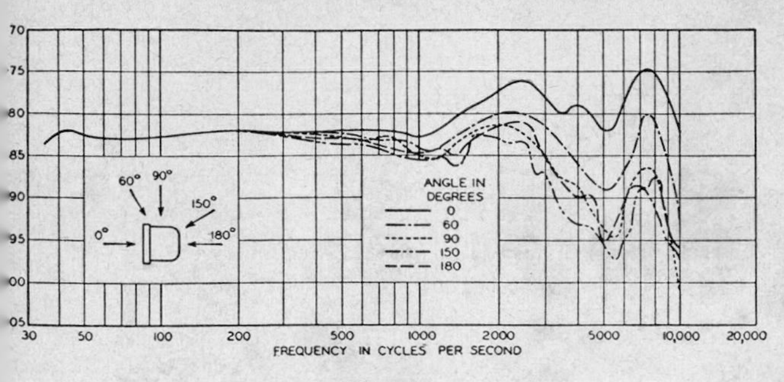

PLATE 13

Frequency Response of the Western Electric Type 618-A Pressure Microphone

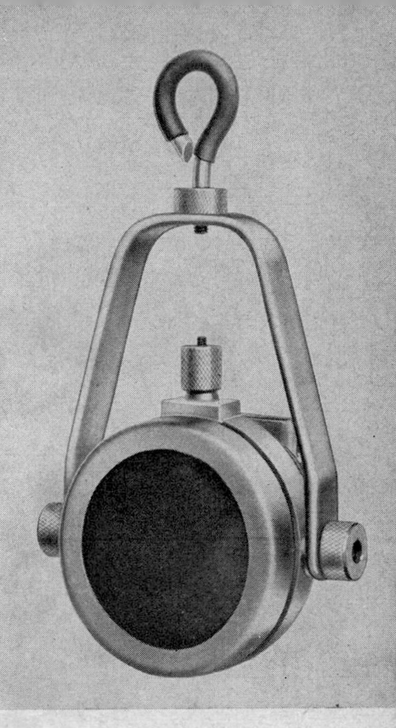

PLATE 14

THE WESTERN ELECTRIC TYPE 618-A PRESSURE MICROPHONE

Principle of operation: Pressure-actuated type.

Response pattern: Fairly flat from 40 to 6,000 cycles.

Directionalism: Semi-directional. While it will respond to sound from all directions, there is some attenuation of high frequencies at 180 degrees.

Characteristics: Introduced in 1931 by Western Electric, this microphone was one of the most widely used microphones in broadcasting for announce work, remotes, and other uses where ruggedness and insensitivity to weather conditions were desirable. It does not blast easily, even from sounds very close to it; it will not pick up wind and makes comparatively little noise when handled. It was, therefore, very good for announce work, especially under adverse conditions.

Uses: The 618-A was widely used as an announcer's microphone and for out-of-doors and remote pickups. Its rather narrow frequency response pattern makes it not as desirable for a music pickup as some other kinds, but for its purposes, it was excellent. It has been largely replaced by improved models of the moving-coil, pressure-actuated types, but there are still many of these microphones in daily service.

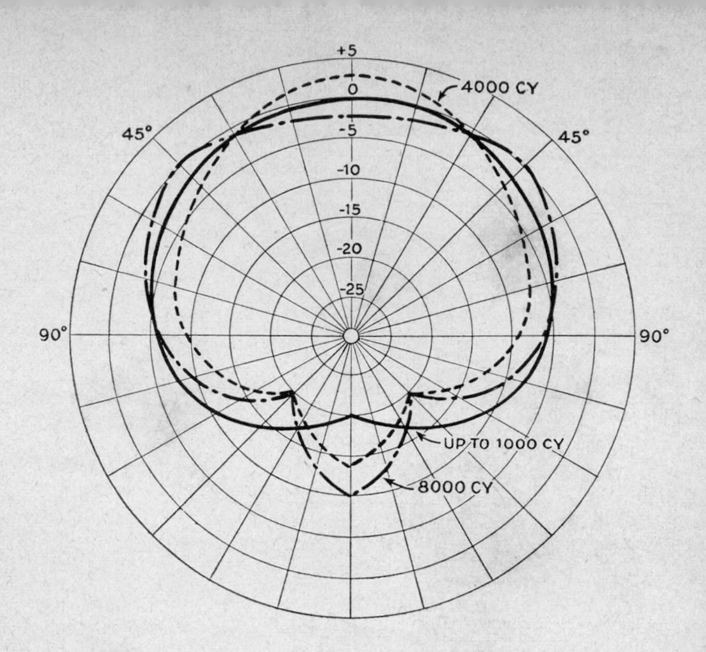

PLATE 16

Directional Response of a Typical 77-B
(Unidirectional Connection)

PLATE 15

THE RCA UNIDIRECTIONAL TYPE 77-B MICROPHONE

Principle of operation: Cardioid type.

Response pattern: Very flat from 50 to 10,000 cycles.

Directionalism: Unidirectional in the cardioid pattern. The actual pattern of directionalism is shown in Plate 16.

Characteristics: This microphone combines all the characteristics of the velocity microphone with the advantage of directionalism. Since it is essentially a velocity microphone, its characteristics are those of the velocity microphone, except for the matter of pickup pattern. It provides all the sensitivity and extremely high quality of the velocity microphone with good control of direction.

Uses: Since its qualities are those of a velocity microphone, it cannot be used out-of-doors or under circumstances where it might receive rough treatment. It is primarily a studio mike, but it has certain specific applications. Being unidirectional, it can be used for audience programs, where a good pickup over a wide angle is desired from the talent and at the same time giving a minimum of pickup of audience noise. It also helps cut down reverberation pickup in a very live place. It is good to use where a microphone has to be placed close to a wall or window, since its pickup of back-slap could be reduced to a minimum. It has application wherever directionalism plus high quality is desired.

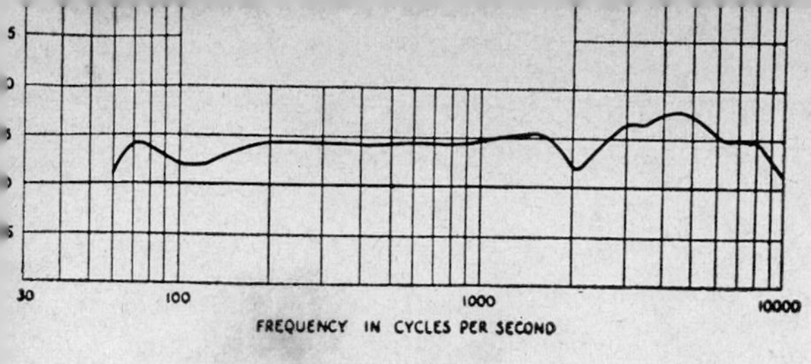

PLATE 17

Frequency Response, MI 4048, Type 88-A Microphone

PLATE 19

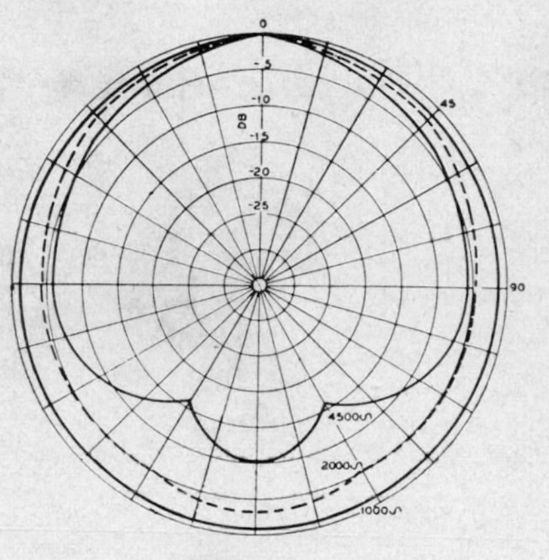

PLATE 18

Directional Characteristics of a Typical 88-A Microphone When Mounted Horizontally

RCA TYPE 88-A PRESSURE MICROPHONE

Principle of operation: Pressure-actuated type.

Response pattern: Very flat from 60 to 10,000 cycles.

Directionalism: Almost completely non-directional. The actual pattern is shown in Plate 18.

Characteristics: It is light in weight, has a high output, and is free from the effects of wind and moisture. It is very useful for remote work, for which it was designed. Because of the high output, it keeps the signal-to-noise ration down and enables its use at very low gain.

Uses: Being one of the latest developments in the field of pressure-actuated microphones, it has been widely adopted for field use. Wherever microphones have to be used out-of-doors or under circumstances where they will receive rough treatment, this microphone is useful. It can also be used in the studio for round-table programs, announce work, and in any other situation where a non-directional microphone is needed.

PLATE 20

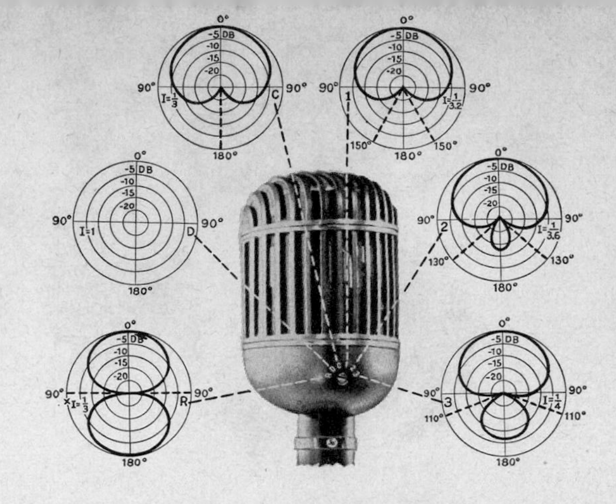

PLATE 21

The Directivity Index (I) equals (Efficiency for Sound of Random Incidence) divided by (Efficiency for Sound of Normal Incidence)

THE WESTERN ELECTRIC CARDIOID 639-A MICROPHONE

Principle of operation: Cardioid type.

Response pattern: Very flat from 40 to 10,000 cycles.

Directionalism: This microphone has three settings, providing three different directional patterns as follows:

1. Unidirectional on the cardioid pattern.
2. Bidirectional on the velocity pattern.
3. Non-directional on the pressure-type pattern.
4. In addition, three other optional cardioid patterns are provided. Any of these six patterns is available through a switching arrangement in the case.

Characteristics: Since this microphone is a combination of an 8-Ball and a velocity-type microphone, it has the characteristics of either when the switch is set in the appropriate position. When it is set in any of the cardioid positions, it has a set of characteristics which are a combination of these. Because of a specially constructed ribbon in the velocity part of the microphone, the manufacturers claim that it is only slightly susceptible to wind noises and may be used out-of-doors.

Uses: Since this microphone combines the other two basic types, it can be used for almost anything, depending on the directional setting employed. There seems to be some doubt about whether for the critical work of broadcasting this microphone is the best choice for out-of-doors work in bad weather. With this exception, however, it is certainly usable under almost any set of circumstances because of its extreme flexibility.

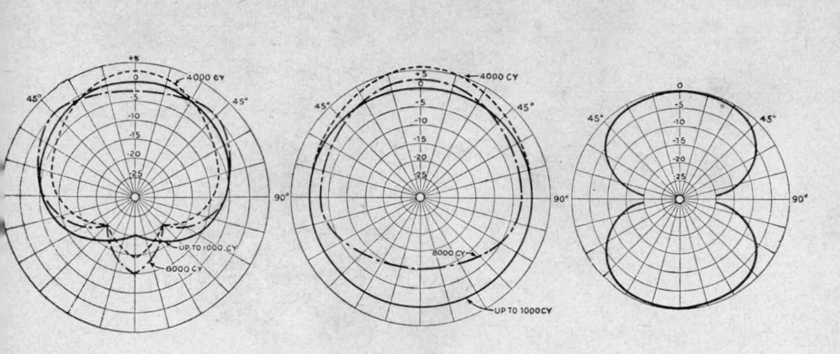

PLATE 22

Optional Directional Patterns of the RCA Type 77-C Microphone

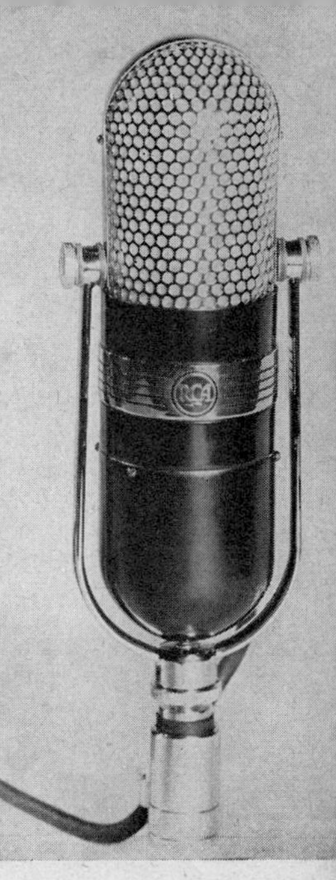

PLATE 23

THE RCA TYPE 77-C MICROPHONE

Principle of operation: Cardioid type.

Response pattern: 50 to 10,000 cycles.

Directionalism: There are three directional patterns available on this microphone. These patterns are:

1. Unidirectional on the cardioid pattern.
2. Bidirectional on the velocity pattern.
3. Non-directional on the pressure-type pattern.

Characteristics: The characteristics, generally, of this microphone are the same as those of the velocity mike. It is very sensitive, highly accurate when used properly. It is not suitable for out-of-doors use, and will attenuate high frequencies slightly when the sound source is too close.

Uses: Except for out-of-doors pickups, the 77-C can be used for anything. Its three directional patterns make it suitable for almost any kind of studio assignment. Its chief virtue is its flexibility. This microphone is a comparatively recent development and is still not in wide use. However, because it offers so much, it may very likely replace many of the broadcast microphones now in service when new equipment is available again.

PLATE 24

LEFT: The RCA 70-C Transcription Turntable

PLATE 25

BELOW: The Western Electric 9-A Reproducer

a full view of the studio even over the heads of those near the window.

The function of the control room is to provide a space that is "sound-isolated" from the studio and still visible from the studio. Both artistically and technically, the control room is a mixing chamber. In this room the production director and his engineer control and mix the various sounds created in the studio and judge the mixing and controlling of these sounds as they come out of the loud-speaker, which is always located in the control room. There is much skill involved in the manipulation of sound in producing a radio show. The only way a producer can judge the effectiveness of the manipulation is to hear it as his listener would hear it from a loud-speaker. Thus, he places himself in a room where he can see his cast, but where he cannot hear them except through the instruments with which he is working. Hearing his program in this way enables him in rehearsals to make whatever changes are necessary to achieve the desired effect.

The control room is sound-treated in much the same way as is the studio. It should be completely sealed against any outside noises. Control rooms are usually sound-treated to give maximum quality for listening. In these surroundings the production director and his engineer work with, mold, change, and reshape the sounds coming out of the studio, both by control equipment in the control room and by changing sound relationships in the studio until the sound pattern is suitable. This brings us to the subject of control equipment.

Control Equipment

Remember that sound is transformed into electrical impulses in the microphones in the studio. These electrical impulses are carried by wires or cables directly into the control room, where they first pass through pre-amplifiers which boost the weak signals to controllable volume. Ordinarily, there is one pre-amplifier for each microphone. Although production directors seldom use more than three or four microphones in any given show, many control rooms are equipped with six or more pre-amplifiers and six control channels so that sound may be picked up from as many as six or more different sources. From the pre-amplifiers the circuits pass to the mixing console. This console contains several volume controls – one for each of the pre-amplifiers and a master control which governs the output of all. It is in this mixing console that much of the art of production takes place. Here the sounds from the various sources are carefully blended and balanced against each other or are faded from one into the other to gain the effects which the director wants.

The mixing panel is a strange combination of a technical gadget and a musical instrument. For talk programs, announcements, round tables, and audience-participation shows, it is merely an electrical device which governs the incoming volume and allows the production director to choose which microphone he wants alive at any given time. In the production of musical or dramatic programs, however, the control console becomes an artistic entity, an instrument of music and dramatic power which a production director can "play" as a skillful artist would play a violin.

For an average studio show a production director will use possibly three microphones, one for his announcer and cast, a second for sound effects if there are any, and a third for music. This means that his mixing console will control three separate sound sources, placing each at its proper level in relation to the others and fading them in or out as the demands of the show dictate. All three of these sound sources will in turn merge into a whole sound pattern which will be governed by the master control. The master control must be handled so that the total amount of sound coming out is of a fairly even volume level. In order to achieve this, the controls are constantly manipulated during a broadcast performance to allow approximately the same amount of sound to pass through at all times. These controls are called "faders" or "gain controls" or "pots," and the process of controlling a program is known as "riding gain." This job is ordinarily handled by the engineer, subject always to the dictates of the production director in all matters except the leveling-off of the output volume. That is of no concern to the director and is purely a technical matter. In the middle of the control console is a single meter whose fluctuating needle shows both the production director and more particularly the engineer the exact amount of total volume which is coming into the control mixer. This meter is scaled in decibels, reading from minus at the left through zero at the center to plus on the right. When no sound is coming into the mixing panel, the needle rests at the extreme left end of the arc on the minus side. As sound begins to pass through the panel, the needle fluctuates to the right. The more volume comes in, the farther to the right the needle goes. It is the engineer's job to see that "peaks," or the loudest points of volume, stay near the zero level on the dial. He is constantly adjusting both the various input channel faders and the master fader or gain to maintain a proper balance of volume between channels, keeping the total output on the meter peaking below zero level on the dial. The meter is called a "volume indicator" and is referred to by technicians and director as the "V.I." The balance between channels becomes important in a complicated musical broadcast where more than one microphone is used to pick up various sections of an orchestra. To do a good job of gain riding on such a program, the engineer needs to know his music as well as his control board.

Mixing consoles or control boards vary widely in appearance and in elaborateness because many of them are custom-built. It is quite common to find control boards with only two channels. Such boards will have two separate gains to control each channel and a master gain for the two. Ordinarily, eight channels are the most which are provided in mixing consoles in this country. In England, where the multiple-studio technique of production is used, the standard dramatic control panel is equipped with twelve channels and a master control.

One should not become confused by the complications of the mixing panel. It has only two functions: (*a*) the mixing of various sounds, (*b*) the control of the total. For practical purposes the mixing panel is used either to fade from one microphone to another, thus changing the source of sound pickup in the studio, or to balance two sounds simultaneously one against the other, as when, for example, someone is talking against a faint background of music.

Too much stress cannot be laid on the power of the mixing panel in dramatic production, and a skillful production director should know his control board as well as the engineer who operates it. He may not be able to wire all the circuits or repair the equipment, but he must be familiar with its operating possibilities.

Amplification

From the mixing panel through the master control the lines carrying the electrical impulses proceed to a panel of instruments usually called the "amplifier rack." The electrical impulses were very feeble at the beginning in the microphone. They have already passed through one set of pre-amplifiers, but since then they have also gone through the mixing panel, and in all the resistance and wiring circuits they have lost some of their power. By this time the signal has been somewhat attenuated and must be amplified several hundred times. In the amplifier rack two things happen. First, the signal is amplified sufficiently to carry to the next point in the system. This is done by a line or booster amplifier. The output of this amplifier supplies a sufficient volume to carry the signal wherever it needs to be sent. The volume, however, is sufficient only for transmission. It is not strong enough for other purposes.

A second function must still be fulfilled in the control room. The output must be "monitored" or listened to. This requires a loud-speaker, which in turn requires another amplifier. So the output of the line amplifier is fed into a monitor amplifier where the signal is built up sufficiently to drive a loud-speaker. The output of the line amplifier also feeds the volume indicator so that it shows the relative strength of the signal being fed out of the control room. A schematic diagram of a typical control-room circuit is shown in Figure 8.

This concludes the circuit in the control room. The output

of the line amplifier in each control room is fed into the master control room where the hour-to-hour and minute-to-minute traffic of the entire station is handled. The master control room in a small station may be the only control room. In that case the output of the line amplifier is sent directly to the transmitter. If the station boasts more than one control room, they will all be connected to a master control room.

No alteration in the program itself is made in master control. It is primarily a traffic-control point through which all programs from the various studios pass on their way to the transmitter. All programs are monitored in master control. An additional volume indicator check is made, the program is still further amplified, and sent on to the transmitter.

A schematic diagram of a master control room might look like Figure 9. Lines from the left indicate incoming program lines, both from studios and possibly from a network. Any one of these may be picked up and fed into a monitor channel. Two or more monitor channels are provided – one for the program actually on the air and at least one other. The reserve channel or channels may be used to monitor succeeding programs, for auditions, or for other services.

Each monitor channel consists of a line amplifier to boost the signal high enough to go along the line to the transmitter, a monitor amplifier to drive a loud-speaker, and a volume indicator and speaker for each system. A well-equipped master control room will also have a spare channel equipped to provide amplification for recording equipment.

The output of the master control room may be sent to several points, as follows:

1. To the transmitter
2. To the network line or lines
3. To recording equipment
4. To an office loud-speaker system
5. Other "remote" points

The signal will always be sent to the transmitter (except in the case of large networks). There is usually also a constant

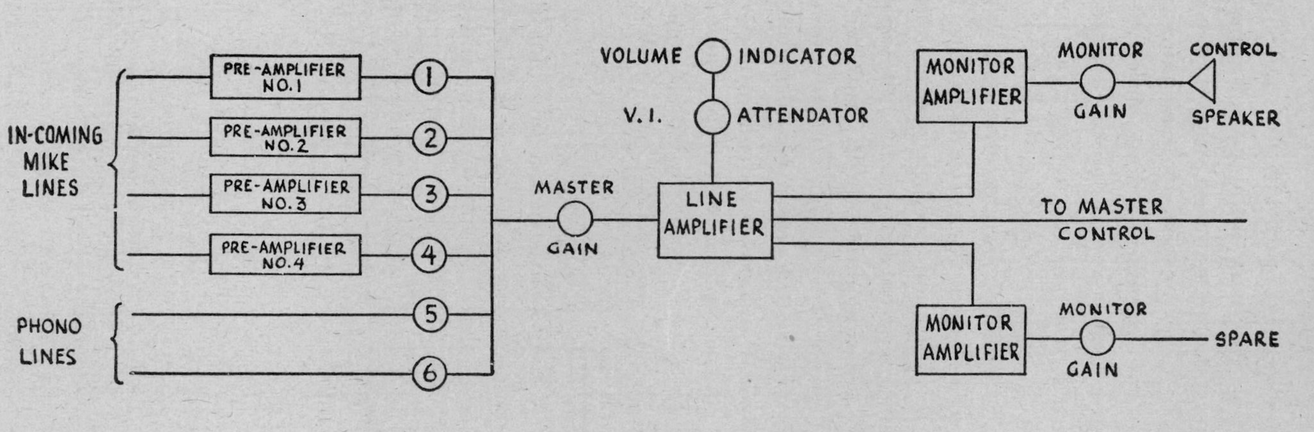
IN-COMING
MIKE
LINES
PHONO
LINES
PRE-AMPLIFIER NO.1
PRE-AMPLIFIER NO.2
PRE-AMPLIFIER NO.3
PRE-AMPLIFIER NO.4
1
2
3
4
5
6
MASTER
GAIN
VOLUME
INDICATOR
V.I.
ATTENDATOR
LINE AMPLIFIER
MONITOR AMPLIFIER
MONITOR
GAIN
CONTROL
SPEAKER
TO MASTER
CONTROL
MONITOR AMPLIFIER
MONITOR
GAIN
SPARE

Figure 8

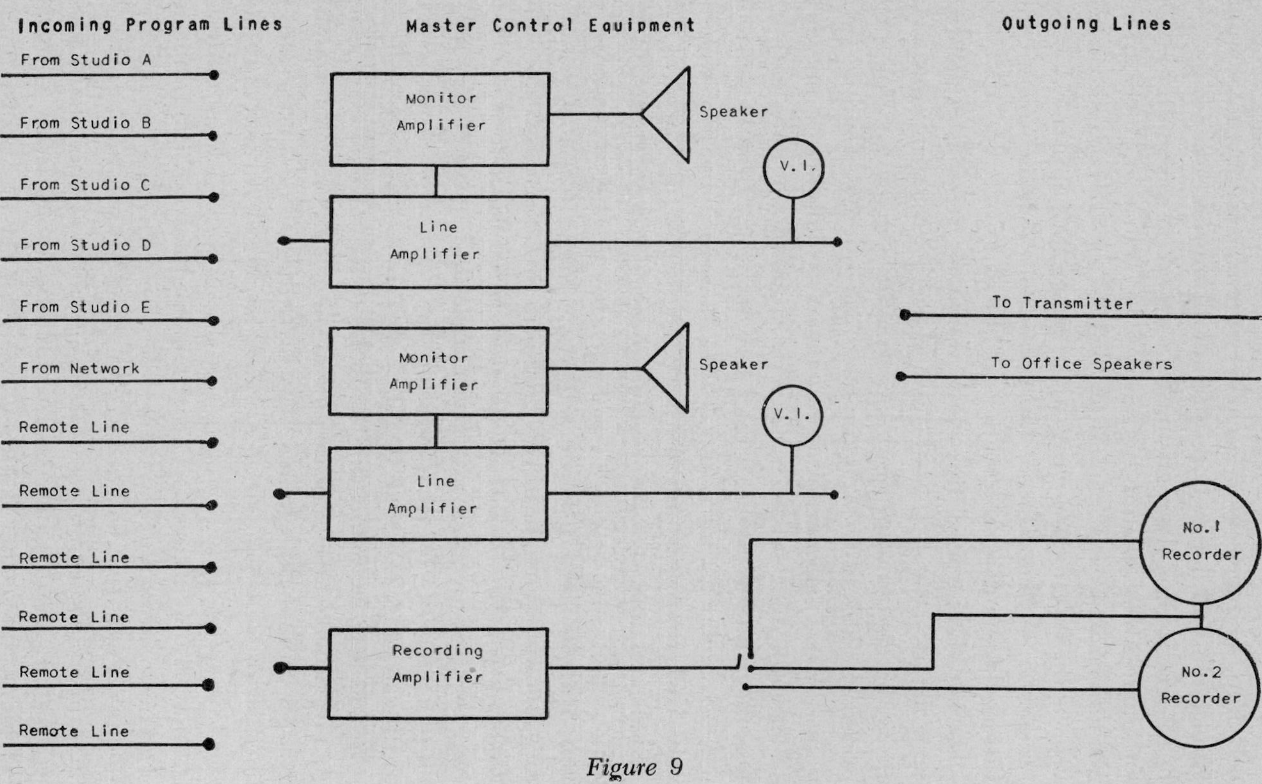
Incoming Program Lines
Master Control Equipment
Outgoing Lines
From Studio A
From Studio B
From Studio C
From Studio D
From Studio E
From Network
Remote Line
Remote Line
Remote Line
Remote Line
Remote Line
Remote Line
Monitor Amplifier
Line Amplifier
Monitor Amplifier
Line Amplifier
Recording Amplifier
Speaker
Speaker
V. I.
V. I.
To Transmitter
To Office Speakers
No. 1 Recorder
No. 2 Recorder

Figure 9

feed into an office loud-speaker system around the station. Other feeds will depend on individual program scheduling. As the program goes through master control, it is monitored for both quality and volume by the master control engineer. This precaution assures a maximum quality of the output at all times and prevents an overload at either the amplifiers or the transmitter so that none of the equipment is blown out in the station, thus putting the station off the air.

Having thus traced the voice signal to the master control room, let us now follow it from there to the transmitter or across the country to other stations where it may go for a re-broadcast. This process is known as "piping" or "feeding" programs. Every station in the country which has a network affiliation of any sort is connected by telephone lines with all the other stations of the same network and with the various network broadcasting points. Thus, a program originating in New York may be simultaneously broadcast in Chicago and Los Angeles and sixty or seventy other points in the country, all of which are connected directly to the original studio in New York by long-distance telephone lines. These telephone lines are an important adjunct to radio broadcasting. Not only do they carry the broadcast program from point to point, but they also provide two-way communications between the originating point of the program and the various stations which are to carry it.

In addition to connecting stations, telephone lines are used by individual stations to connect their studios with remote pickups around the vicinity in which they may be operating. The master control room of a broadcasting station will not only have incoming lines from each of the studios in the building, but may also maintain special telephone lines to various hotels, churches, auditoriums, and the like, from which programs frequently originate. To these origination points the engineers carry microphones and portable amplifier equipment to pick up programs. Such pickups are called "remotes" or "nemos." Telephone lines used in this way are in most respects similar to those used in ordinary interhouse service. They must, however, carry a wider range of frequencies for a longer distance, and in order to insure perfect transmission, most broadcast telephone lines are special installations.

Telephone lines thus used are the property of the telephone company serving the area and are rented or leased by the broadcaster. No station or network owns telephone lines. The lines are serviced and maintained by the telephone company and are leased at fixed monthly or yearly rates. It is interesting to note that the American Telephone and Telegraph Company, which was the original owner of station WEAF in New York City, pioneered the field of telephone transmission of programs and perfected it before they sold WEAF to the then newly formed National Broadcasting Company in 1926. During the last few years networks have paid an annual toll bill that runs into several million dollars for the use of their network of telephone lines.

Transmission

When broadcasting was young, it was a common sight to see the taller downtown buildings spiked with steel masts from which were transmitted the programs of the various stations in the city. As technicians studied the result of their broadcasting, they discovered many phenomena. Some stations discovered many blank spots in their coverage, for example. Others had trouble with fading. As stations became more powerful, they tended to blanket out other stations for listeners close to their transmitters. When transmitters were located in cities, this often meant that many listeners could hear only one station. This problem was solved by moving the powerful transmitters out into the country. It is a common practice now for stations to locate their transmitters from five to twenty-five miles away from their studios. The station master control room is then connected to the transmitter by telephone lines.

The transmitter of a modern broadcasting station is a miracle of self-operation and efficiency. In many such transmitters a single man is on duty, and even a very large station seldom has more than two men on duty at one time. Literally, the transmitter operates itself, and the engineer's duties consist mostly of filling out reports on the various dial readings during the day and acting as a stand-by in case of trouble. Many transmitters maintain complete dual equipment, so connected that if for any reason the operating transmitter is blown off the air, a second transmitter is automatically turned on and continues the broadcast within a few seconds. The chief work of an engineer at a transmitting station occurs when he turns the station on in the morning and when he turns it off at night. In spite of this, his position is a very responsible one because on him falls the necessity of keeping the station on the air if an emergency occurs, and for this reason the best men available are usually put in the transmitter jobs.

One interesting development in transmitters may seem unusual to laymen. Long experimentation has proved that the transmitter carrier wave may to a certain extent be made directional, and broadcasting stations are beginning to use this principle in the construction of their aerial masts. The old two-tower antenna, with the wires stretched between the tops, are now more and more being displaced by single tall towers, the steel framework of which is used as the transmitting area. Sometimes a series of such towers are used when the broadcaster wishes to direct the radio beam in a particular direction.

This directional principle is used by commercial broadcasters who wish to keep from infringing on the territory of another station located in some specified direction away from them. The principle is used to a high degree of efficiency in short-wave broadcasting, where it is more essential to maintain directionalism. Fairly narrow beams of carrier waves may be laid down in almost any desired direction by the careful arrangement of the antenna masts at the transmitter. The British Broadcasting Corporation, which maintains an extensive program of broadcasting to the Empire, has many acres of various antennae at its Droitwich station. Each aerial is pointed toward a definite colony of the Empire and these antennae are used in turn for programs directed to, let us say, Canada, New Zealand, South Africa, Australia, and so on.

AUXILIARY EQUIPMENT

Aside from microphones, studios, and mixing panels, there is another large list of equipment which is now regarded as necessary for even a modest broadcasting station. The inclusion of this equipment under the heading "auxiliary" should not be interpreted to mean that it is any less necessary. It is equipment which is not hooked into the microphone-to-transmitter circuit. In discussing auxiliary equipment some attempt will be made to place the items in the order of their importance and usefulness, although this may not hold for the entire list.

Clocks

Radio is so time conscious and depends for its successful operation so much on accurate time that in this country laymen have come to look upon radio as the final authority in the matter of time. We set our watches by it and govern our comings and goings according to the broadcast time announcements. Well-operated stations pride themselves on the fact that their station breaks come exactly "on the nose," that each program finishes exactly at the end of the fifteen-minute or the one-half-hour period assigned to it.

The importance of time reaches its zenith when a station becomes affiliated with a network. Stations must depend on accurate timing alone to know when they may cut into the network line and expect the beginning of a program. With complete program changes every fifteen minutes throughout the day in some six-hundred network affiliated stations over the United States, split-second timing is a vital part of smooth operation. The number of stations connected to a network changes every time the network program changes. Some stations must drop out for local reasons; others wish to join. The only way they can do this smoothly and without untold confusion is by reliance on a fixed prearranged time- and cue-schedule. For this reason the number one place in importance among auxiliary equipment must be given to the studio clocks. They must be accurate to the second, they must be synchronized with each other, and with Naval Observatory time. Only by complete synchronization can stations check in and out of the network. Every room in the station should be so equipped. Certainly, all the control rooms and studios should be. All reception rooms and waiting rooms, if they do not have standard clocks, should at least have a few available so that talent waiting for programs can know accurately how soon they are to go on. Studio clocks should be generous in size. Those furnished by the Western Union service seem to be satisfactory. They should have a clearly marked face with hour, minute, and sweep-second hand. With such accurate time always available, there is no excuse for a station to be sloppy in its operation.

While we are on the subject of timepieces, it should be noted that an accurate stop watch should be considered part of the standard equipment for every production director. It is possible to time a production during rehearsal by means of the studio clocks, but it is much simpler if the director has a stop watch which he can operate independently. Stop watches should be sturdy, accurate, and should be of the type that allows for cumulative timing. Some studios equip the desks in the control rooms with large-sized stop clocks permanently attached to the table in front of the director's seat. These are useful, but they are a luxury. Most production directors would prefer to have their own timepiece to carry wherever they go.

Turntables

Turntables are a "must" in the equipment list of any station. Without them a good many small stations would find themselves off the air about nine tenths of the time. There are many different kinds of turntables put out by many different manufacturers, but it will be enough here to indicate the divisions among the various main types and the specifications which good turntables should meet. A good turntable unit should have these qualifications:

1. Dual speed. It should be able to play records cut at either 33 1/3 R.P.M.[1] or 78 R.P.M., and have an easily accessible and quietly operating gear shift.

[1] R.P.M. means revolutions per minute.

2. It should be powered with a heavy-duty synchronous motor and provided with a noiseless power switch.
3. Its speed should be constant.
4. It should provide for playing up to sixteen-inch transcriptions.
5. It should be able to reproduce either vertical or lateral recordings.
6. The pickup arm should be free-moving, free of resonance peaks, and long enough to reduce tracking error to a minimum.
7. The pickup arm should be counterbalanced to provide a needle pressure of not more than one ounce.
8. The pickup head used by most stations is a well-built magnetic type reproducer with a permanent jewel needle.
9. The reproducer head should be capable of a frequency response of thirty to seven thousand frequencies.
10. Variable frequency response settings should be provided to allow compensation for differences in type of recording.

Fortunately, most stations, even small ones, are usually equipped with at least one pair of transcription tables that meet these specifications. Plate 24 shows the latest RCA unit (No. 70-C), which is widely used. It is one of the latest and best designed transcription tables available.

Plate 25 shows the newest Western Electric reproducer set (No. 1300-A), which is also found in many stations. These two types of transcription tables or their predecessors manufactured by the same companies are the most widely used equipment in broadcast stations.

Such tables are generally used in pairs so that while one recording is being played the next one can be cued up on the second table. The short announcement habitually used with recorded music programs does not permit time for a change of records on the same table. In a case where an electrical transcription at 33 1/3 R.P.M. follows a regular 78 R.P.M. record, it would take too long to change both records and speed and still provide a smooth-flowing program.

Transcription tables may be located in the studios or in the control room. Regardless of their location, they normally feed directly into the control panel. The direct wire to the control panel makes for the best quality transmission. In addition to the line to control, each turntable or pair of turntables should be equipped with some means for listening to the output of one table while the other one is on the air. This can be done either with headphones or with an independent amplifier and speaker. This allows the operator to listen to a record in the studio or control room, and thus to set the pickup exactly at the beginning of the record to avoid delay when a record is cued in.

Some stations have an announcer's booth which contains a microphone and two turntables to allow the announcer to announce his own programs and change the records and operate the turntables. In some small stations, turntables are sometimes located in the control room and one man has the task of making the announcement, running the turntables, and riding gain on his own program at the same time.

A different kind of turntable with a different set of requirements is used for playing sound-effect records in dramatic productions. A detailed discussion of this type of turntable will be taken up in the chapter on sound effects.

In only a few minor respects does the operation of a transcription turntable differ from the operation of a normal home phonograph, but differences are important.

1. All dry grooves (grooves on which no sound or music is recorded) should be kept off the air.
2. Cueing must be prompt. These two points mean records must be set exactly right.
3. Records must be checked to see whether:
   a. They are vertical or lateral cuts.
   b. Recorded at 33 1/3 or 78 R.P.M.
   c. Whether they play inside out or outside in, the table must be adjusted accordingly.

4. It is a good practice never to handle a pickup arm when the gain is open.
5. Transcription play-back arms must be handled gently. Remember, a good pickup head is only another kind of expensive microphone and should be so treated.

Aside from these differences, a transcription table is just like a phonograph in operation.

Talk-Back System

The convenience of a means for talking back into a studio from the control room cannot be overrated. Unknown a few years ago, such a system is now almost standard equipment. A considerable delay can be caused by rehearsing an elaborate program without the use of such a system. There are no standard talk-backs developed purely for broadcasting. Most of them either have been custom-built by the station engineer, or the station has bought a simple two-way office intercommunication system, of which there are many good ones on the market. These systems, as the names indicate, allow the producer to talk to his cast in the studio to give them instructions during rehearsal periods. They are, of course, never used during an actual broadcast.

The system may be a simple two-station setup between control room and studio, or it may be a more elaborate one which allows the producer in the control room to talk with several different studios or offices. In most systems the microphone and loud-speaker is the same instrument and the change in direction of conversation is effected by turning a two-way switch. Some systems provide only for one-way communication from control room to studio, and the people in the studio talk back over the regular microphone. In this case the talk-back systems are usually connected to the regular broadcast system by relay switch so that the microphones are cut out as soon as the talk-back system is turned on. This arrangement prevents a feed-back between control room and studio.

Most modern installations use the regular channel amplifiers to operate a control-room microphone which may be fed into a studio loud-speaker. Thus, when the talk-back switch is pressed, relays cut the control-room speaker and the studio mikes and connect the control-room mike to a studio speaker. It is common efficiency to have a decent quality of reproduction in the talk-back system, although it need not necessarily meet rigid broadcasting standards.

Remote-Control Equipment

The amount of equipment a station carries in reserve to handle remote-control pickups will depend, of course, on the number of such pickups which a station is normally called upon to handle. Remote-control equipment for a small station usually consists merely of an extra microphone, sometimes a portable mixing panel, and portable amplifiers which are used to boost the signal. These pieces of equipment are taken to the pickup point, such as a night club in a neighboring hotel. The microphone mixer and amplifier are set up and plugged into a telephone line which carries it directly to the station.

Larger stations may have elaborate remote setups. Networks may have, for example, among other things a portable knock-down control room. This is a completely sound-proofed room which can be linked together and set up in short order at some remote point where elaborate production is needed for a show. In such a case, the portable equipment is so elaborate that a complete broadcasting booth can be packed away into cases and transported wherever the need indicates. Much special equipment – such as dynamic microphones with parabolic reflectors, elaborate portable mixing cabinets, and all the other dozens of items which may be needed for producing a program away from the studio – has been built by the larger networks and a separate corps of engineers maintain this equipment and operate it on location.

Some large stations maintain a motor car, bus, or truck which is a small broadcasting station on wheels. This portable station may be driven anywhere and start broadcasting on special short waves in a very few minutes. These roving units actually transmit a program into the air which is received at the station on special receiving sets and then rebroadcast over the station's regular transmitter. Mobile units such as these make it possible for a broadcasting station to cover sports events without arranging in advance for telephone lines. Suppose, for example, a disaster of some sort occurred in New Jersey. Mobile units from the large New York stations could be sent out at once. Engineers could make their equipment ready while the truck or bus was driving out and start broadcasting as soon as the unit arrived at the scene of the disaster. Some stations also maintain truck-mounted recording equipment which can be sent out to make transcriptions. These transcriptions can then be rushed back to the studio, edited, and played over the air as soon as the broadcasting schedule makes it convenient. All such mobile units can, and usually do, use telephone lines whenever possible rather than take chances with atmospheric disturbances by actual short-wave transmission. Usually each truck unit is equipped for short-wave and land-wire transmission and for transcription work.

In general, remote-control equipment differs in no way from studio equipment except that it is more sturdily built and can be fitted into cases to be carried to any point which a program pickup demands. The principle of operation is exactly the same.

Recording Equipment

Because recording equipment is expensive and because well-trained engineers are required to operate it, not many local stations are equipped to make their own transcriptions. Furthermore, some local stations do not find enough use for such equipment to make it worth the investment and the added cost of maintenance. Most of the larger stations, however, are equipped with one or more recording turntables where they may transcribe whatever programs they please.

Radio manufacturers during the past five years have developed recording equipment to be sold at a reasonable price and which is simple to operate. The main stimulus to the recording market seems to be a greater interest in schools and colleges in such equipment. Here it is used for speech and radio training work. The development of new low-priced equipment will enable the local stations increasingly to avail themselves of its use. There are so many uses for good recording equipment that it is rapidly becoming a necessary part of the equipment of a station.

Although there are at least three rather common types of recording, radio has never used but one to any great extent. This is the one called "instantaneous" or "lacquer-disk" recording. Flat disks are covered with a thin coating of cellulose nitrate or some similar material which is very smooth. Into this surface the cutting needle of the recorder cuts a continuous spiraling groove, and in the groove is impressed the pattern of the sound to be recorded. The direction of the vibration may be either lateral or vertical, and both types of recordings are used. Transcriptions are cut at a speed of 33 1/3 revolutions per minute, while standard recordings are cut at 78 R.P.M. By recording at the slower speed, twice as much material can be put on the same amount of space. Thus, on a sixteen-inch record, fifteen minutes of continuous recording can be cut at 33 1/3 R.P.M. These lacquer recordings can be played back immediately and have very high quality for the first few playings. Thereafter the quality drops off, the scratch level comes up, and while not suitable for broadcasting, they may be played many more times for checking purposes. Prewar disks were aluminum, coated with cellulose nitrate. The coating is still available, but aluminum is not, so glass is now being used. The quality is as good, but the shipping breakage is not very encouraging. Various kinds of composition and paper bases have been tried. They are all right for checking purposes, but they are not high enough in quality for broadcasting.

Transcriptions can also be recorded on wax master records, which can be treated in such a way that duplicate pressings can be made from them. The pressings are made of a durable material similar to that of commercial records. They may be played many times before the quality begins to get bad. This is the method used to distribute transcribed programs. Such transcriptions have many uses. It is possible to record an entire radio program in this way, have duplicate pressings made, and furnish one to each station that plans to carry the program. In such instances the agency or sponsor deals directly with the station, buying the most valuable time available that the sponsor can afford. An individual deal is made with each station.

The movie industry, for obvious reasons, has used almost exclusively the process of recording on film. The principle of recording on film is basically the same as recording on disks. The only difference is that the coating is made on film and the cutting needle scratches through it to the transparent film. Play-back is then made possible through the use of the photoelectric cell. A light is thrown on the recording track. Where the needle has cut through the coating, the light can pass through and activate a photoelectric cell on the opposite side of the film. This method of recording offers high fidelity, but the width of frequency range is narrower than lacquer-disk recording. Also it is more expensive. For several reasons, radio broadcasting has never adopted the method of recording on film.

The third method of recording is the magnetic tape. In this method a steel tape is magnetized at various intensities depending on the power of the incoming signal. When the tape is re-run through a play-back machine, the varying amounts of magnetism in the tape are translated into electrical impulses which, in turn, are translated into sound. The tape method has one unique feature. Once a piece of tape is no longer useful, it can be run through another machine and demagnetized. The tape is "wiped clean" and a new program can then be recorded on it.

Recordings have several important uses in broadcasting. One of the most important is for rebroadcast work. In case a station wants to carry a network program and does not have local time available at the time of the network broadcast, the station can make a recording of the program as it comes over the network line and then play the recording locally at the convenience of the program schedule.

A second use of recordings and transcriptions is for the distribution of non-network programs. Many national advertisers prefer to have a program transcribed so that they can bargain individually with stations for the best available time. This has some benefits over putting on a network program which must be taken by all the participating stations at the same time. One of the greatest benefits of such a system is that it is much cheaper.[1]

A very common use for recordings is the making of air checks. Production directors and orchestras often use this method of keeping their organizations on their toes. As the program is broadcast, it is also recorded, and at a later time is played back to the participating group. This allows them to listen to and analyze their performance on the air.

Recordings, to an increasing degree, are also being used for documentary purposes. Recording a program provides a permanent file which would otherwise have died with the last feeble flutter in the ether. Programs which seem likely to be of historical importance are also recorded and filed away for future reference. Those engaged in teaching often find transcriptions an invaluable method of study. Schools, for example, can record from their school receiving set the trans-Atlantic broadcast of a speech by Winston Churchill. This transcription becomes a part of the permanent file of the school. It can be played in history classes, in social-study classes, or wherever it may be useful. Student announcers, actors, and directors will find transcriptions very helpful. It is the most usable teaching tool for the teacher of radio. A radio show can be rehearsed, produced, and recorded, and all the glaring errors, the successful transitions, and the muddled climaxes are permanently recorded in a form which the student can study until he feels he knows where and why he made his mistakes and his successes.

[1] This refers to actual outlay and not to per capita cost of reaching an audience.

The making of recordings is too intricate and technical a process to be described here. Practice is one of the most important elements in the successful making of lacquer recordings, and to those readers who are contemplating the handling of radio equipment, the best advice is to get the equipment and make your own mistakes.

Filters and Equalization

Technicians and engineers have found many ways of distorting sound to help the production director, and often certain kinds of distortion enable him to gain effects he could achieve in no other way. Directors used to simulate the effect of the far end of a telephone conversation by having a cast member talk into or across the mouth of a glass. This was a makeshift arrangement, but it would distort the original voice in the studio to a certain extent and it gave a rough approximation of the effect. Talking through long tubes, megaphones, and even into banks of draperies were used as devices for altering voice quality. Some of these same tricks are still in use. The trouble with them is that there are always variables in the equations and the production director can never be sure of producing the same effect time after time.

Engineers have come to the aid of directors in these matters, and most studios are now equipped with elaborate combinations of filters and equalizers which may be introduced into one or more microphone circuits in such a way that the voice or music quality coming through the circuit can be altered at will. Such filters or equalizers are usually arranged so that any particular band frequencies may be eliminated from the sound pattern as it comes through. For example, a filter arrangement may be used to eliminate frequencies below two hundred and above three hundred and fifty cycles per second, leaving only a narrow band of middle register frequencies. This will create the faraway telephone voice. By eliminating all the low frequencies from a voice pattern or all the high frequencies, other interesting changes can be made, and these can be made to work for the production director who knows how to handle them. Filters can be introduced in such a way, for example, as to let pass only the fundamental tone of music and to eliminate most of the overtones. It can even be arranged so that the fundamental tone itself is filtered out and only the overtone remains or some segments of those overtones. The complexion of a piece of music can be entirely changed and a completely different emotional reaction made to result from such tampering with the normal sound. Details of this kind of manipulation are the job of the engineers, but the production director should be familiar with the possibilities of equalization.[1]

All the auxiliary equipment has its rightful and necessary place in the business of broadcasting. The producer should be familiar with it, know how to operate it, and although he may never be called upon to do so, he should always be prepared to make the proper answer to the engineer who says, "It can't be done." More important, he should know enough to be able to ask the engineer for the things which will help him. Most radio engineers deserve profound respect.

This technical information is necessary to the director if he is to be familiar with the many tricks in his bag. He must know them and have them ready to use in a complicated production. If a production director has a sound knowledge of engineering principles and equipment, his prestige will rise considerably in the engineer's eyes. And the respect of his engineer may be the factor that determines success or failure for a program.

[1] John Mills, in his book called *A Fugue in Cycles and Bels,* treats this and similar subjects at considerable length. It is recommended reading for anyone seriously interested in production directing.

CHAPTER 5

SOUND EFFECTS

EARLY IN THIS BOOK it was stated that the production director was a painter in sound, using a mixing panel for his palette and a loud-speaker for his canvas. In the preceding chapter we talked about some of the production director's equipment — his brushes, palette, and canvas. In this and the two succeeding chapters we will begin to discuss his paints. In general the production director has three sound sources with which to work. These are:

1. Sounds effects
2. Music
3. The spoken word

In this chapter it should be remembered that we are talking about all kinds of production directing and all kinds of programs, not specifically dramatic programs, or music programs, or any special type. Therefore, it should be understood that the term "sound effects" does not necessarily refer only to sound generated by a sound technician for the exclusive purpose of setting the scene for a dramatic show. The term should have a much broader meaning. When the special events department broadcasts the play-by-play report of a baseball game, it is possible to consider the cheers of the crowd and the crack of the bat as sound effects. An on-the-spot interview with a worker in a shipyard may be accompanied by the background staccato of an air hammer banging away at a steel plate. That is a sound effect in so far as its inclusion in the broadcast is deliberate and planned by the production director. One should not, therefore, be too narrow in defining the term "sound effect" for the moment. This is a discussion of those amazing sound sources which the good production director molds as a sculptor does his clay until he creates in his loud-speaker a meaningful pattern of sound for the listener.

The British are far ahead of American broadcasters in codifying and evolving rules concerning various production activities. They have classified sound effects into six divisions according to the purpose they serve. It may not be wise to try to adapt their system to American broadcasting, but their ideas on the subject will give production directors something to think about. They classify sound effects in this way:

1. Realistic confirmatory effects
2. Realistic evocative effects
3. Symbolic evocative effects
4. Conventionalized effects
5. Impressionistic effects
6. Music used as a sound effect

This division and codification is credited to Lance Sieveking.[1]

Since the list is somewhat foreign to people not working at the BBC, it may be well to amplify it enough to make it completely clear. "Realistic confirmatory effects" are those which amplify without adding to the dialogue. The sound of wind howling behind the scenes would be classed as a realistic confirmatory effect if it is placed in the production after or concurrently with its mention in the script.

By "realistic evocative effect" is meant a sound effect which might be a realistic part of the broadcast of a dramatic scene being portrayed, but which is not mentioned in the script itself. For example, if the script simply calls for a scene on a street corner and the production director elected to add a traffic background, this would be listed as a realistic evocative effect, provided no point was made of the traffic in the scene and its only use was to create realism and add mood and atmosphere to the scene. If the traffic were mentioned in the script and was important to the dramatic action of the play in progress, it would be classed as a realistic confirmatory effect.

[1] Lance Sieveking, *The Stuff of Radio* (London: Cassell and Company, Ltd., 1934), pp. 65-66.

"Symbolic evocative effects," Sieveking describes as sound used to explain something of an abstract nature, such as "a record of an abstract rhythm of a churning and insistent nature, definitely not classifiable under the head of music, used to express the confusion in a character's mind." The illustration is Mr. Sieveking's.

By "conventionalized effect" is meant those average sounds which have long been accepted by the radio audience as expressing certain action. It is fairly common practice to use a sound effect of a train as a transition between two dramatic scenes when the audience needs to be told that a character in the play is going from one place to another by train. In this case no attempt is made at realistic production. The sound of the train traveling at high speed is simply used as a device in the same way that the theater director rings down his curtain for ten seconds to indicate the passage of time in the middle of an act. It is one of the conventions of radio.

The "impressionistic effect" is an unrealistic one used to create an attitude in the minds of the listeners. An example of this might be an artificial echo superimposed on a voice or of unrealistic choral chanting to highlight the climax in a nonrealistic play. This application of sound has for its primary purpose a working on the subliminal perception of the audience while some other part of the broadcast is working in the area of liminal perception.

The last item is self-explanatory. Music used as a sound effect is growing in favor among American production directors now in direct proportion to the amount of original cue music being written for broadcast programs. Music is certainly one of the most flexible of all sources of sound effects and it has the additional artistic value of giving an audience the effect of sound without giving them the sound effect. It is perhaps a more artistic way of accomplishing the same results. When music is written to substitute for a sound effect, the whole purpose is to sublimate the realistic sound into an impression, musically conveyed, which, presumably because of the artistic selection going into it, has a heightened effect on the audience.

To many American production directors this whole elaborate codification may seem too complex. A simpler division might be just as effective. For simplification let us use the classification, primary and secondary effects. If we understand primary effects to mean realistic recognizable effects used for realistic purposes, and secondary effects as unrealistic or impressionistic sound used to heighten mood or project emotional powers, we have created enough terminology for our purpose. Again, remember that we are considering as sound effects any sound source that we plan to include in the broadcast which is not music or the spoken word. This will admit many items into many broadcasts under the heading of sound effects which may not have the blessing or execution of the sound effects department as such. In the broadcast of a political convention, the very hubbub and roar in the background of the crowd may be deliberately included to help the listener get the "feel" of the situation. In this case the background roar of the crowd is used as a sound effect. If it is used consciously, it can be better used.

Before proceeding any further, it will be well to establish the reason for sound effects in radio broadcasts. Presumably every time a sound is admitted to the speaker in the monitor control room, it should be admitted with full consciousness of its presence and for a definite purpose. Any sound which does not serve some useful function should be eliminated. After all, the listener has enough competition of sound in his own home. For the production director to furnish competition to his own program in the form of unneeded sound effects is like the design of one of the French bombing planes which was described as having its own built-in head wind. What, then, are the uses of sound?

The Uses of Sound

To Project Action

The microphones scattered around a stadium at a football broadcast are not there to furnish a competitive background of sound for the sports-caster who is broadcasting a play-by-play account of the game. They are there to reinforce his words by the actual sound which is generated as the result of action on the field. It is impossible to broadcast the signals in the huddle and the thump as bodies clash in the line. The next best thing is to pick up the mirroring of that action as it is displayed in the crowd noises made in spontaneous response to the action on the field. In a dramatic show such sound effects as footsteps, doors opening and closing, and the sound of taut cables working in the rigging of a sailing ship are all used to help project the action of a scene being played. This is probably one of the most important uses of sound effects. After all, since radio lacks the visual appeal of the theater, sound effects, even in a real broadcast of a real event, take the place of scenery, property, and lighting in their function of explaining the current actions to a listening audience through the medium of the ear alone.

To Set Scene or Locale

Both in broadcasts of actual events and in dramatic programs the judicious use of accompanying sound is one of the best, the quickest, and the most economical methods of establishing a scene or a locale. In the broadcast of the speech of an important speaker from a dinner gathering, it might be possible, by careful selection of microphone position and other production details, to eliminate almost completely any other background sounds. It might be possible so to arrange the pickup that nothing would be broadcast except the actual words of the speaker and the announcer who introduced him. Even if this could be done, it might be unwise. The rumble of the whispers of the audience, the clatter of silver being put down, and the acoustical bounce of the average hotel ballroom where such functions are held, all combine to make a background of sound effects which says to the listener plainly, "We are now at a banquet, and before long there will be a speaker." It helps the listener to gauge the mood and the locale of the situation better than anything else could do. The same principle, of course, holds in a dramatic scene. Suppose you hear coming out of your loud-speaker the nostalgic bass grunt of a foghorn. Overlaying this sound, which is off in the distance, is the quiet "slap slap" of waves washing up on a sandy beach. There is an occasional cry of a tern or of a seagull coming in over the surf. This pattern of sound allowed to run five seconds would say more than a great many words in describing where we are and under what conditions. The sound itself, with very little reinforcement from dialogue, will set the scene.

To Create Mood or Atmosphere

Have you ever heard the broadcast of the returns from an election headquarters on election night? The reading of the returns tends to be monotonous. But because the broadcasts are usually made from headquarters where the counts are being made, we pick up the background sounds. There is the excitement of constant reports coming in. There is confusion and a sense of something important all made plain and real and obvious in terms of the sound effects which form the backdrop for the announcer who is reading numbers from a page. This whole pattern of background sound tends to establish a mood for us – a mood of expectancy, of being "in at the kill."

It would be easy to establish a mood of peaceful pastoral contentment. A meadowlark singing occasionally in the background, the joyous yip of a dog galloping over a farm field, the swish of wind through the trees and grass, would all help to create a picture of quiet, lazy rural contentment. A mood could be established before a line is spoken – and it could be done completely with sound.

Sound may be used for the achievement of a climax, and it can be extended or intensified by sound. There is a story in broadcasting circles of the first attempt to broadcast, from between the lines, an actual battle in progress. It was supposed to have been a broadcast on the Russo-Finnish front when that prelude to world conflagration was in progress. A remote broadcast from the battlefields before Helsinki were to be climaxed by the actual firing of Finnish guns. Everything went off according to schedule except that the Russians did not know it was a broadcast and started firing back immediately. The broadcasters found themselves in the middle of a first-class artillery duel. This was a climax with a vengeance.

Everyone has heard football broadcasts in which the sports-caster cuts his booth microphone and switches in the pickup of a crowd cheer as the team goes over for a touchdown. After all, all he can do is say that *X*-team scored a touchdown. It remains for the delighted shouts of the crowd to furnish the climax to that particular action, and the smart sports-caster takes advantage of it for exactly that purpose.

There was a play broadcast recently which had for its climax the receipt by a mother of the news of the death of her son in action. Events leading up to this tragic climax were all well planned, and when the letter came the mother read two or three lines – just enough for the audience to know that a letter had been received and what its contents were. Then all that was heard for a full ten seconds thereafter was the slow, methodical crumpling of a piece of paper. So slight a sound as this, so unexciting in its own right, created and extended and intensified the tragic climax.

In any story where action is predominant over dialogue or ideas, it is interesting to note how often the ending is handed over, not to an actor, but to the sound effects department, to create the final and ultimate climax. This job sound is eminently fitted to do.

To Establish Time

The use of sound to establish the time of day or night, or even a period in history, is a conventionalized trick which has wide acceptance among radio listeners and wide use by production directors. How many of the old thrillers can you remember that started out with the ominous striking of twelve o'clock by a grandfather clock? One of the few times that it has been used successfully in a stage production was in the first act of Thornton Wilder's highly imaginative play. *Our Town.* Remember there is a cock crowing off in the distance just as the play begins.

To Establish the Entrance or Exit of a Character

This use of sound can be employed in a real broadcast as well as in the broadcast of a play. The most common example of this application of sound is the matter of footsteps. Footsteps fading away from or into the microphone tell the audience that a character is entering the scene of action or leaving. The tapping of a blind man's cane along the sidewalk or on the floor tells us not only of the approach of a character but something about him. To identify it we should need only to know that a blind man was expected; the tapping of the cane would do the rest.

As a Signature or a Theme for a Program

Probably the classical example of this application of sound is the Chinese gong which opened the *Lights Out* program for years. The more recent use of the cock crowing to introduce *Information Please* is another example of sound used as program signature. Many others could be cited. This kind of signature for a program, incidentally, has not been thoroughly exploited. There is room still for some clever ideas.

To Create an Unrealistic Effect

This use of sound has application only in the radio dramatic show. One of the classic examples was in Charles Urquhart's production of an Author's Playhouse script called *Today – Tomorrow.* In this delightful fantasy Paul Bunyon was demonstrating his terrific powers of playing havoc with Time by yanking Tomorrow right into the middle of Today. This is probably as tough an assignment as a sound effects crew ever received. The delightful fantasy of the solution would be warming to the heart of any production director. Another Author's Playhouse broadcast by the same director, *The Cracken,* told about the capture of a submarine by a prehistoric undersea monster. The sound routine which described the dragging of the submarine into a subterranean cave was a masterpiece of impressionistic treatment. In such application of sound the director and the sound man can let their imaginations run riot, often with excellent results.

For Scene Transitions

Sound can be used as a transition device to separate two scenes under two general conditions. The first is a realistic use in which one sound element of a scene simply sweeps up and over the other elements, drowning them out for a few seconds, and then fades under again as the new scene continues. In this case it indicates continuing action with either a slight time lapse or a change of locale within a larger scene. The use is at least semi-realistic. Second, sound is also used as a transitional device on a purely conventional basis. For example, a scene will end with a man saying, "Hold on – stay where you are. I'll jump in the car and be down in five minutes!" Then we hear, fading in at fairly high volume, the sound of a car running, a screech of brakes, the car door opening and closing, a building door opening and closing; the new scene starts with a line to show that the person in the first scene is the same who opens the new one. In a case like this thc sound is not realistic. It is a conventionalized transition device, to indicate the change in locale, and the manner in which the central character proceeds from one to the other.

Sound can also be used as a transitional device in non-dramatic programs. The bell used in quiz programs to show time out is an example. The cash register in *Information Please* tends to become a transitional sound effect. Even applause, when it is deliberately built into a program, acts as a transitional device between one part of the program and another.

To Create a Montage Effect

A radio montage may be defined as an impressionistic creation of a composite sound picture by quickly superimposing one scene on another. In a montage scene there is no full development of separate scenes, but two or three or four quick lines from a number of scenes are thrown at the audience in quick succession, either merged into each other or separated briefly by climactic sounds or music, so that all the scenes become a unit in themselves. The montage scene can cover a great deal of exposition in a short time, or it can give the effect of many things happening simultaneously and in mounting climactic order. It is a good device if not overused, and sound is effective as the binder that holds the composite parts of the montage scene together.

As an Expositional Device

In the capacity of expositor, sound may be used either impressionistically or realistically. It would be possible to build a complete montage effect out of sound alone which would set forth the action demanded in a certain scene, provided the action called for could be told plainly in sound alone. Suppose, for example, we wanted to tell the audience in a dramatic show that a whole police station is being thrown into a riot of activity, with all the reserves being called out. This might be done by building up a composite sound picture of telephones ringing, of alarm bells clanging, of cars roaring away from the station, of trucks with sirens screaming, and so on. No dialogue would be needed, and the whole exposition could be handled impressionistically in sound alone.

On a realistic basis, sound can do much as a background device to set forth what is going on behind and around the central dialogue in a dramatic show. Suppose the scene takes place on a dock where a large ship is departing. The dialogue may have to do with the actions of two central characters. While this is going on, the background or secondary level of interest of the audience is engaged by a number of sounds, such as the rattling of winches, the puffing and tooting of tugs, the grind of baggage tractors, and so on, all as background activities to a major scene. Examples like this could be enumerated *ad infinitum.* This device must not be overused because there is always a danger of making the background to a scene so interesting that it competes too strongly with the foreground interest. There must always be a harmony of balance to keep the main focus of attention where it should be.

Music as a Sound Effect

When music is used as a sound effect, the execution of the effect falls to the orchestra, the organist, the musical director, or whoever is responsible for creating the music. From an artistic point of view, however, and in the mind of the production director, the cue is a sound effect, not music, even though it may be furnished by the musicians. One of the most common uses of music in this manner is the situation in which the orchestra imitates a train, let us say. That job might just as well be done by the sound of an actual train. From an artistic point of view, however, the use of music to execute a sound effect has the additional advantage of artistic selection which makes the whole thing a little more interesting and allows the production director a little more leeway in the expression of his ideas. Suppose, for example, that in a dramatic show it is necessary to give the impression of a tremendous explosion to show the dropping of a bomb and the consequent blowing-up of a whole block of buildings. Such an effect might be started with a realistic sound-effect explosion, and then picked up by the orchestra and resolved into a music cue highly imitative of the sound but with the additional artistic possibility of sublimating the terrific confusion into an emotional expression of what happens as a result of the sound.

Music used in this way can be a substitute for sound to achieve any of the other purposes mentioned in the foregoing paragraphs. It is not necessarily a special device in itself, but simply a substitute manner of creating sound to fulfill some of the purposes already enumerated.

It is obvious that under certain circumstances a detailed and long sound routine might completely replace dialogue for a section of a program. This could only be true if the sound was completely clear in itself without the lines. Incidentally, this does not often occur. There are so many sounds which are hard to identify that it is dangerous to rely on sound alone for most routines.

When Sound Is Used

One of the major decisions which a production director must make for every program he does is how much sound to use, where and how to use it, and for what reason. A new director should have certain principles to guide him in making the decision. The wisdom which goes into these decisions will determine the artistic ability of the production director.

One principle should be made clear at the outset. No element in a radio program should be included or excluded on the basis of a rigid rule. Every situation is a law unto itself and the decision about how it should be handled must be made on the basis of its inherent problem. It is dangerous to generalize in any art form. A generalization, by its very nature, cannot possibly take into account all the factors in a specific situation. There are, however, certain guiding principles about the handling of sound which can be set down for the beginner to follow until he has assurance in its use. After the "feel" has been developed, he may disregard some of these working principles. But they should be disregarded only when there is a specific good to be gained to offset the danger involved in their violation.

As a general rule, sound should be used only when it accomplishes one of the twelve specific purposes outlined in the preceding paragraphs. No sound should be included just for the sake of adding sound. It should be included only if it has a definite function, and even then it is questionable whether it should be used if that function can be or is already fulfilled in another way. The beginner's tendency will be to load any kind of program with sound. It is better to err on the side of using too little rather than too much. Sound, well applied, should have the same effect and perform the same function as a well-designed stage set in the theater. A setting which is so outstanding or conspicuous as to draw a hand from the audience when the curtain first goes up is a bad stage set. After all, the setting only furnishes the surroundings in which the play itself takes place. It is not an end in itself, and if it calls attention to itself, it will, by the same token, detract from the play. The perfect stage setting will pass almost unnoticed by the audience. That same reaction should be striven for in the handling of sound. No sound routine should be so prominent that it in itself elicits response from the audience. Sound in radio is merely the scenery.

It should also be remembered that sound is usually a background accompaniment to the broadcast, though in some instances and for short times it may occupy the foreground of the listener's attention. Too much sound, or sound used improperly, or sound "out of balance" with the remainder of the program, will prevent the desired effect from being achieved. Sound is the garlic in the salad. It gives it spice, it gives it lift, and a certain fresh fillip, but it should not dominate the program.

In the handling of sound we must remember certain of the basic reaction characteristics of the ear in hearing. These have all been stated and it is now time to apply them. Remember that the ear is selective. It hears only those things which are important to it at the moment. This principle has application in the use of sound for setting the scene and for establishing locale and actions going on in a new scene. At the beginning of that scene the sound is important. It helps to establish the locale, the time of day, and what is going on within the scene. As such we are conscious of the sound, not as sound in itself, but as an important cue to what is going on in the broadcast to which we are just beginning to listen. Under these circumstances sound may have a definite place in the foreground of attention of the listener. As soon, however, as the important expositional function of sound is achieved, then sound ceases to have importance.

It is at this point that something definite should be done about it by the production director. The obvious thing to do is to submerge sound at this point so that it no longer occupies the center of attention. The normal way to accomplish this is by using sounds at reasonably high levels at the opening of the scene and then gradually submerging them until they either are cut out completely or are forced down to such a low level that there is no possibility of their intrusion into the foreground of attention. This must be done subtly or the very change in level will itself be noticeable. When such a device is used, sound should be slowly submerged over a period of a page or a page and a half of the broadcast so that its descent into the background of attention is not noticeable. By handling it in this way, we accomplish the desired effect of having it in the foreground when it is important and relegating it to the background when it no longer has importance. We also eliminate another factor, competition for the attention of our listeners.

Sound used as realistic background for a scene should be handled in the same way. Suppose, for example, we are doing an on-the-spot broadcast in a war plant, where the purpose of the program is to show the speed and efficiency with which war materials are being turned out. We may elect to use a considerable amount of general machinery background to establish the locale and to create a mood of humming activity. To this end we will use some of the background available at fairly high levels in the opening portion of the scenes, but very quickly these will be submerged and held to a low-level background as the interest in the program begins to focus on what is being said rather than the locale in which it is being said. The mechanics of a broadcast should be so set up that control of background is possible. The principle can be applied with equal force to any background sound, realistic or otherwise, in a dramatic program.

The application of sound to a radio program is an artistic job. By its inherent nature, it makes obligatory a selection of sounds to be included. Out of the total sound pattern which might be available and which might be realistically applicable to the scene, those specific sounds must be selected which are typical and which do something important to the establishment of whatever purpose the sound is designed to accomplish. Suppose we are trying to create an airport scene and are using sound to establish locale. Out of all the sounds that might be realistically present in the scene we need only a few. Realistically one might hear a gasoline truck backing up on the ramp, and the banging of a mechanic's hammer inside a hangar. Coming out of the office windows of the flight office might be the tap of typewriters as stenographers make out flight reports. Overhead there might be the drone of a plane circling, awaiting a landing signal. Near-by in the foreground there might be the conversation of two or three pilots, and the rattle of wooden blocks as two mechanics drag them across the ramp. There might be a dozen other sounds which could be present realistically in the scene. It should be obvious that all of them are not necessary. We need to include only that sound which is typical enough to establish the locale. This kind of selection must go on constantly in the application of sound to any kind of broadcast.

The Handling of Sound Cues

In the application of sound to an actual broadcast, one of the questions which the production director must always decide is how it shall be cued. The final decision must be made always in the light of the demands of the specific situation. The following general rules, however, are set down for the guidance of the beginner until such time as he can make his own decision out of an extensive experience. Most of these rules are based on common sense, but they are constantly violated by the beginning director simply because he is not aware of all the factors involved.

If sound is to be co-ordinated with the action of a member of a company, then normally the cue for that sound should be left in the hands of the person responsible for making it. He takes his cue direct from the dialogue of the actor. As an example, suppose the script calls for, and the production director decides to use, the sound of a blow supposedly being struck by a member of the cast. In that case the convincingness of the sound would depend on its timing with the words of the actor who is supposed to have struck the blow. Then the cue would probably not be given by the director, but would be left in the hands of the sound man to time from the lines of the actor himself. Only in this way could the split-second synchronization of line reading and sound be accurately accomplished. Whenever a similar situation exists and whenever it is possible for the sound man to see or hear his cue, then it should be left to him to execute on the actual cue from cast. If there is so much noise in the studio that it would be impossible for the sound man to hear the lines, then obviously some other solution must be found. If this is the case, however, it probably means that there are other surrounding sounds going on simultaneously and the timing becomes less important than if that particular sound were the sole center of attention at the moment.

Where a difficult routine involves several elements of the company at once, the cue should be kept in the hands of the production director. For example, suppose there is a line for a cast member to be followed immediately by a music cue, which in turn is followed by another line from another cast member, then by two sounds in quick succession and a third line from a third member. In such a case so many factors are involved that the execution of the whole matter must be centralized in one man. The logical and only man for this is the production director himself. He would retain all cues to all members of the company so that he could act as the timing reference point for the execution of the complex routine.

Because of the nature of American broadcasting, where the complete program is staged in one studio, it is often impossible for the various members of the company to hear what the other members of the same company are doing. When the orchestra is playing, the sound man is busy, and the cast is reading lines, the total pattern of sound may be such that no one of these is able to hear the others with any accuracy. In cases like this, of course, the cues which control the various parts of the routine must be given by the production director. This is the only way in which they can be successfully handled.

There are two general schools of thought among production directors about the assignment of cues for sound. Some directors feel that they must be absolute conductors of the entire program. They insist on retaining every cue for every action, whether to cast, to sound, or to music, and insist that the members of the company execute each sound or routine on cue from the control room. Another group maintains the diametrically opposite point of view. This group holds that all the cues for a program should be taken by the members of the company. The directors in the first group feel that the over-all handling of the show must remain in their hands. They feel that if they are to conduct a symphony in sound they must have control over it at all times. The main argument brought forward by the second group is that such autocratic procedure tends to take responsibility away from the members of a company and to encourage a mechanical, thoughtless, emotionless kind of performance. As is usually the case with extreme points of view, there are inherent dangers in each. Most production directors who have been through the mill use a combination of the two techniques. They decide whether cues shall be given from control or taken by the members of the company on the basis of the facts involved in each particular routine. Undoubtedly this is the wisest and most correct method of deciding on how sound cues should be handled.

Where sound must be identified before the program progresses, cues should be retained in the control room. Suppose that we wished to set a scene with sound in a small metropolitan bar. We will begin with the sound of a tinkly boogie-woogie piano and overlay that with the rumblings of crowd talk and laughter and the clink of glasses at the bar, and let the pattern establish itself before we begin the dialogue. Obviously here the cues both for the sound pattern and the dialogue should be retained in the control room because the production director can best judge when the sound has been identified and the scene established.

There is one over-all statement which will influence the philosophy of handling all components of the show, including sound. It must be understood by every production director that the show — whatever it may be — does not happen in the studio! *It happens in the control room!* The talent, the sound crew, the musicians, tend to hear only their part of the performance. If they hear the other parts, they certainly do not hear them in their proper volume balance to the whole performance and therefore they get a distorted view of what is happening. It is only after all the component parts of a program have passed through the mixing panel and been balanced, one against the other, that the final proportions of the show are established. This obviously does not happen until the show reaches the control room. For that reason the bulk of the control of a program always must remain with the production director. Where the matter of delicate timing is involved — always a creative thing — and where there are no circumstances to prevent, then the matter of timing may be left with the company, provided those members have proved themselves capable of managing delicate timing. This is especially true of actors. A good production director who has respect for his talent will allow them all possible latitude in the timing of their own lines. After all, there is a different "feel" which an actor creates spontaneously with each performance of a part. Everything else being equal, he should have the right to time that as much as possible.

There is, however, the over-all timing and pacing of the program which few members of any company in the studio can have the insight to understand. This is no condemnation of their talent. It simply means that they are not in a position to hear all the parts of the show in proper proportion. It therefore should be left to the production director to make the final and ultimate establishment of timing, pacing, and the bulk of the cueing in any program. Control should remain in the control room. That is what a production director is there for.

The Director Looks at the Sound Routine

When the production director faces a new program for the first time, he has many decisions to make about handling its sound. One of the first things he probably will do is to look over the script furnished him by the author, and assess the value of the sounds indicated in it. It should be understood that the production director is not obliged to follow exactly the patterns indicated by the writer. If the millennium ever comes when radio writers know as much about production matters as directors, the necessity for having to make a series of decisions about the writer's cues can be eliminated. The director can then assume that the cues are right and proceed to execute and interpret them. That happy day has not yet arrived, however, and the production director knows that his first job is to take the cues indicated by the writer and determine their practicality and usefulness.

The seasoned production director is no longer shocked by what he finds written into the script under the banner of sound cues. He learns to expect directions like these: "Sound of cat walking softly across a thick rug." "The rustle of the *New York Times* slipping off the face of the sleeping man." Similar atrocities can be quoted by the score. The director first must decide whether the sound is necessary or pertinent. His next job is to decide whether or not it can be executed. After all, sound can only fulfill a function which can be described in terms of pitch, volume, quality, duration, and distance. Described in any other terms it is not a function of sound. Writers are, in general, weak in their ideas of what kind of sound should be applied to a program. They tend to be general, vague, and impractical. Very often the author will have a good idea, but its expression would make no sense to the member of the company assigned to execute the sound. In such cases the cue must be rewritten and clarified by the production director so that what he wants will be delivered back to him.

The director must decide the number of men needed to execute the sounds indicated and the amount and kind of equipment necessary, though in some stations the sound effects department assumes this responsibility. For a dramatic program the director may have to plan the studio floor space to accommodate the turntables and bulky sound equipment and leave room for the cast. For a non-dramatic program he will have to consider how many microphone pickups he will need and how they should be located. All this is a part of the production director's job in the preliminary analysis of his program.

The director must decide on his sound routine in the light of the budget available. The sound routine indicated in the program may be too heavy for one man to execute and require two men. If there are budget limitations, he must make corresponding changes. If the program is a non-dramatic one to be done outside of the studio, he must decide how many engineers and how much equipment over and above the regular amount would be necessary to execute the sound routine. This will then have to be checked against the available budget and the decision made as to whether he will ask for a budget increase or cut his sound routine. Budgetary matters are a definite part of his responsibility.

Once the sound has been decided upon, the manner of its execution is not normally left to the production director. If it is something which calls for engineering, he consults the engineering department about its handling. If it is a sound effect that could be created by the sound man, he will normally leave to him the decision as to how it will be created and delivered to the control room. Of course, the production director always retains the right to veto a proposal of any of his company if the results do not please him. How much of this control is retained by the production director and how much is delegated will, in every case, be contingent on the competence of his staff. If, for example, the production director knows that he is being assigned a green sound man, he might retain much more control and more of the decisions than he would if he had an experienced man. This is only common sense. But it should be a generalized understanding that the actual manner of execution of sound, and the decision as to whether it should be manual or recorded or electrical, should be left to the sound effects department. After all, responsibility is a challenging thing and the interest of the company usually rises in direct ratio to the challenge which the production director gives to them. It remains only for him to hold high the standards of performance once the responsibility for the execution of the work has been delegated.

No production director should ever underestimate the genius of the sound effects department. If a sound can be expressed in terms of volume or pitch or quality or distance or duration — that is, if the effect is really in the realm of sound — the sound man can produce it. The length to which a good sound effects man will go and the co-operation he is willing to give are amazing. The fact is a tribute to the creative interest of sound men in general. It is true that they tend to fall into certain routines and repeat certain effects over and over. When this is true, it is because the production director has failed to hold his standards high enough to present a real challenge to the sound effects department. Given the challenge of a hard job, they will nearly always respond to it magnificently.

It is necessary at this point to make a plea for accuracy in sound. Too many production directors are prone to accept the standardized conventionalized sound effect without asking the proper penetrating questions about the rightness of its quality. To too many production directors an automobile is an automobile. There is a vast difference in the quality of sound of various kinds of cars. The recognition of simple differences in basic qualities is often overlooked by the careless director.

In the field of the non-dramatic program there is a similar carelessness in the planning of sound. Unfortunately, the terms "sound" and "sound effects" are so closely identified with the dramatic show as to obscure the real function of sound in radio. It sometimes seems that production directors deliberately go to great trouble to eliminate sound which might otherwise form a highly desirable and useful function in a program. For example, most round-table discussions are conducted in a vacuum. We hear the alternate voices flashing through silence into the microphone and we are asked to visualize a discussion among three or more individuals. This is, on the face of it, an artificial situation. All the normal sounds which might accompany such a program are kept off the air. A cough by one of the members, the dropping of a pencil on a table, the shuffling of notes or the twisting around in the chair by the participants, all these things might lend reality and a third dimension to the broadcast. It is not to be denied that certain meaningless sounds can detract from a program. There is always competition for the listener's attention. But the creation of a round-table program in an utter vacuum does something to eliminate all reality from the situation and to take the element of human feeling out of the broadcast. A little forceful pounding on the table might do something to put a few red corpuscles into the round-table programs that air over our American radio every day. And there is little doubt about the fact that some of them need a few more red corpuscles.

This same argument might be carried into various other kinds of programs. Many of the broadcasts which are being conducted from the Army camps these days have a freshness and a sparkle and a liveness and a zip which is due largely to the fact that many of the previously controllable sound elements in the broadcast are not controllable under camp circumstances. The shuffling of feet in an audience, the whistles and stamps of the enthusiastic soldiers, the general rumble of room noise which is present in broadcast surroundings not especially treated for broadcasting — all these things give a sense of reality and of being present on the scene which is not always heard in a more carefully controlled studio broadcast. It might be argued that these are legitimate sound sources which could be added to any broadcast to give it a feeling of reality and naturalness. This application of the philosophy of sound can be carried straight across the program spectrum and might find applications in many places. Obviously it can be overdone. We must remember basically that meaningless sound tends to be a distraction. But it should also be remembered that certain sounds can be meaningful in a subtle sort of way to give an ultimate reality to a scene.

At any rate, sound is one of our basic ingredients in radio. It should be considered carefully, used judiciously, and made to give its maximum benefit to the program.

CHAPTER 6

MUSIC

THE SECOND PIGMENT with which the production director paints his sound picture is music. Music is one of the most flexible and colorful sound sources at the production director's command. One has only to consider the number of musical instruments available to realize its breadth of tonal qualities and general flexibility. When one adds to the flexibility of instruments the wide variety of kinds of music which can be had for the playing, one begins to see how important and how exciting a thing music can be for the production director.

The history of music in radio since its inception as an artistic medium in 1920 has done much to restore faith in the cultural good taste of the people. Never before has so much good music been available to so many people in any country. It could be argued that the omnipresence of music in radio tends to discourage the personal participation in and execution of music by the general population. This same argument was advanced when the phonograph first became popular. From the point of view of audience appreciation and general knowledge of the great body of good music, no people has ever been so well informed as Americans today. The credit for this must go largely to radio.

Every week the output of the nation's greatest symphonies is available to the listening public at the turn of a dial. American love for music has certainly been exploited by radio, but there is no question either that radio has made a conscientious effort to improve the taste of the public. Already there is a slight but growing preference for good music on the air. Each year the balance between so-called popular music and symphony music swings slightly toward serious music. Popular music itself is getting better as a result of changing public tastes. The orchestration of popular music is richer and fuller and more skillfully done than it was ten or twenty years ago.

It is into this exciting field of music that the production director can step at will. The presence of so many uninspired musical programs on the air is a sad commentary on the skill and insight and understanding of the average program director. With so much richness at hand there seems little excuse for a pedestrian job in the handling of music on the air.

Let us look now for a moment at the functions which music fulfills in radio programs. They have a wide range and they will grow in importance and frequency of use as we learn to master them. This chapter is not intended to discuss musical programs of various kinds. It is our purpose here to consider in an over-all view the place of music in radio and the vast opportunities it offers to the production director.

The Uses of Music

Music as Program Content

Radio's most obvious and frequent use of music is as the basic content of a program. From the smallest local station with its recording library up to the largest network with a staff symphony orchestra, music has a prominent place in day-to-day programming. There are more all-music programs on the air than any other single type. This is probably as it should be, because music is a natural for radio. Music appeals to the ear alone. Visual cues are not necessary for its enjoyment. It can be listened to and enjoyed with varying degrees of attention — it is excellent content for a medium which is often used as a background for other activities. No production director should make the mistake of assuming that his audience is doing nothing but listening to his program. But it is surprising how many directors unconsciously make such an assumption when they plan and execute their programs. Because music can be attended to as a background to other activity, it has an important place in radio programming.

Theme and Signature Music

Even in non-musical programs, music has come to have an important place because it is more often than any other device used as a trade-mark for programs. A certain piece of music is used over and over again to open and close a program in the same way that a manufacturer uses a certain picture or symbol on the package of his product. This use of music is a good and legitimate one.

The requirements of theme music are fairly obvious to state, but very difficult to fulfill. A good piece of theme or signature music must be strongly melodic. It must be fairly simple. It must have a tune which, if it is not easy to hum, is at least easy to recognize. In addition to these factors it must have a style and "feel" which are in harmony with the style of the show itself. If, for instance, it is the signature for a comedy show, the music must be lively, rollicking, and fun to listen to. It should be a short theme, with a beginning and an ending which can be developed and completed in not more than twenty or twenty-five seconds. Total theme patterns including announcements may run as long as a minute. Finally, it must be a piece of music which is adaptable to the instruments available. One piece of music might sound well if played by a sixteen-piece orchestra, but would be completely inadequate on an organ. This factor may be more often decided by budget than by anything else. At any rate, it should be known before a signature is chosen.

The device of trade-marking a program with a piece of music was first thought of by certain band-leaders, who always played a portion of a certain number when they came onto the air for a broadcast. It was later adopted by other kinds of programs and has since come into almost universal use. It is a good device because music, being one of the most flexible of all sound sources, can say a great deal in a very short time. It should not, however, be taken for granted, because most programs use music as a signature, that that is the only way to do it or even the best way. As has already been pointed out in the discussion of sound, there are other ways of creating a signature for a program which may be just as effective. Music will probably remain the most popular one, for a long time, however.

Cue or Bridge Music

With the increasing popularity of dramatic shows, music has developed a very specialized job in this area. More and more, production directors are coming to use it as a transitional device between scenes in a dramatic show. This application of music is a specialized one and has developed as a whole new field in the last few years. No one quite knows how the idea started, but it may very well be that it is a carry-over from the pit orchestra that plays between the acts of a stage performance. Much of the early music used for cues came out of the libraries of the old pit piano players who accompanied the silent films. However it originated, it is an effective means of making a scene transition. In the earlier days of dramatic broadcasting, small excerpts from standard orchestral works were used as short transitional interludes. As radio matured and the artistry of production increased, the idea of writing original music for each play developed. This is an expensive process and demands very talented composers, but it adds tremendously to the effectiveness of a show. The specific how and why of the application of cue music to a dramatic show will be discussed in detail later. It is enough here to state that this is one of the many uses of music in radio production directing.

Music Used as a Sound Effect

This subject has already been touched on in the previous chapter but some elaboration can be made here. Music can be used in this way only when an original score can be obtained and afforded. Writing music to imitate sound requires careful composition and scoring, because of the constant change in the orchestras available. So far as is known, there is no library of scores arranged for imitative music. This kind of work is possible only when there is a composer at hand who can score it for the orchestra available for the show. This fact limits this application of music to radio programming. It is an expensive process and for that reason is not often employed.

Music as the Punctuation in a Program

The use of an orchestra to mark the end of one routine and the beginning of another in comedy and variety programs is so accepted by the listeners that it probably never occurs to them what is happening. A comedy routine not "paid off" in music would seem flat indeed. Comic music introductions are also a standard device on variety programs. Fanfares to herald the entrance of a character, either seriously or in a comedy vein, are constantly heard. The use of music to accentuate and punctuate the division of a program, especially of the comedy or variety type, is probably the most effective means of doing the job.

The same device is used in serious drama. Music is often used to back narration or even a realistic dramatic scene where a slight accentuation of a certain mood or a certain atmosphere can be effectively introduced. Certain production directors who have sufficient budget have gone to the extent of scoring practically an entire play, using music not only for theme and for transitions between scenes, but also as background to actual dialogue. It is played at very low level, but in a proper key to accentuate and underline the important mood and ideas of the program. This process is, again, an expensive one, and is seldom indulged in except by directors who are in the rare and fortunate circumstance of commanding a practically unlimited budget. If the student wishes to study this use of music, he needs only go to any first-class movie and sit with his eyes closed. Hollywood has long used music to back scenes for the specific purpose of mood reinforcement or to point up certain emotional ideas. They have spent a great deal of time and money experimenting with this device and have done some excellent work. To the beginner in radio production who may not have a wide list of recordings to study, the movies represent one of his best training grounds for listening to the use of music in this manner.

Music Can Be Used as a Comedy Device

Not only is music used as a reinforcement of comedy programs for introductions and pointings, but it may become, itself, the comedy in the program. No one could deny this after hearing Bob Burns and his bazooka or Jack Benny and his infamous violin. In these instances and dozens of others which the reader will remember, music is used definitely as a comedy device. The hair-trigger punctuation which Fred Waring gave to his nightly scoreboard of who wins and who loses, using the entire orchestra as punctuation for comedy effect, is an excellent example of the point under discussion. Because this use of music depends on a hairline timing and on an excellent sense not only of musicianship but of comedy, it has not been exploited to its fullest. Very few people are capable of doing the job. But there certainly is a field here which can be developed beyond what we now know. One has only to listen to Prokofieff's *Peter and the Wolf* to realize how far the idea can be carried in terms of semi-serious composition.

The Production Director's Place in the Music Program

No matter what the application of music to a specific program may be, the production director is still, in this field as in other kinds of programs, finally responsible for the program. Nearly all matters of program content and execution are in his hands. There are certain exceptions in the field of music, however, which should not pass unnoticed. The actual programming of a musical show may be the result of the combined efforts of the production director and the musical director. The program may be the sole idea of either with the consent of the other. In any event, agreement must eventually be reached on the matter of programming. By the word "programming" we mean the decision about the routining of the program. What shall open the program? What shall come next? In what order are the component parts of the program to come? How shall they be joined together or kept apart? All these are programming decisions which rest finally with the production director. If he is an intelligent man, however, he will lean heavily on the advice of his musical director in these matters.

There is one place in which the production director in the field of music does not trespass. That is in the matter of interpretation. If a vocalist is singing over the air, the production director will not tell the artist how to present his material. The vocalist is the creative artist in this case and it is up to the director simply to get the artist on the air in the best possible way. The manner of execution is the artist's concern. The production director must see that the vocalist's style is given the fullest support and effectiveness in the way that the program is handled.

Production Director Keeps Hands off the Orchestra

In a program which involves an orchestra and an orchestra conductor, the production director normally does not work with the orchestra. If there are things about interpretation or balance which do not suit him, he should work through the musical director or the conductor. This channeling of authority is necessary to avoid all kinds of confusion in matters of jurisdiction. Again the intelligent production director will take advantage of the skill of the man with whom he has to work and consult him in all such cases. In the rare case of complete disagreement, the production director must take responsibility for the final decisions. When such a deadlock occurs, the best and safest thing to do is to eliminate the controversial part of the program and substitute something else upon which the production director and musical director can agree.

The matter of arranging the music also lies primarily in the hands of the music director. This must be, of course, subject to veto by the production director, but again this is a matter for mutual settlement whenever that is possible. Presumably a musical director has his job because he is competent to do it. The production director takes cognizance of this fact and makes arrangements accordingly. The work of arranging music for a particular combination of instruments, then, is the province of the musical director, subject to the approval of the production director.

On the other hand, the size of the organization with which the musical director will work is a matter for decision by the production director. More often than not the budget will decide this question for the production director. On some occasions the budget may be more than adequate to do the job. The production director may decide, for instance, that even though there is money to hire a full orchestra, the job can be done more effectively by using an organ. In a case like this the decision should lie with the production director. These matters are all so closely tied in with budget, however, that the production director usually makes his final decision in the light of what is available, and that is a matter for the business department of the station.

It is within the province of the production director to ask for specific musical talent. For example, on a certain show he may wish to have a violin section consisting of such and such staff musicians. Normally about all he can do is to "request" these people and see what happens. If trafficking makes it possible, they will normally be assigned to him. This is not, however, always possible, and the production director can only do the best possible with the talent available at the time his program takes the air.

Cue Music Is Producer's Province

In the field of cue music, the production director is the absolute boss. Here music is completely subservient to the ideas embodied in the script and the exact effects which the production director wants are known better by him than by anyone else. The usual procedure is for the production director to talk over with the musical director a desired effect to be gained from the music; once this is established, the musical director will work out the suggested answers which are then heard by the production director and either passed or rejected. This process is repeated until there is a complete agreement between them on each cue. Then the music is rehearsed by the musical director and brought back for final O.K. in the music rehearsal. In this application of music the production director is and must have complete authority even to the manner of execution of the music involved.

In a musical program it lies within the province of the production director to change whole numbers if it becomes necessary to do so. Though he may not have too much to say about the execution of the number beyond making suggestions to the musical director, if for any reason a number is unsatisfactory or does not do the proper job in relation to numbers which precede and succeed it, the whole number can be changed by the production director. This is rightly his authority because his is the final responsibility for the programming of the entire production.

There is sometimes a tendency among production directors who are not as familiar as they should be with music to stand too much in awe of a musical director or of musicians. Certainly it is wise to utilize the background, knowledge, and skill of any member of your production company. One need not, however, stand in awe of a musician simply because he is capable of doing something which you as production director may not be able to do — namely, execute music. The simplest possible approach to music is that it is, after all, only a complicated pattern of sound. Presumably the production director is an expert in the field of sound. This being the case, he has a perfect right to make critical comments on the musicians' work. This is especially true in cases where music is only one of the component parts of an entire show or scene. It does not take musical genius to recognize the rightness or wrongness of a piece of music or an arrangement or instrumentation in any given spot. The young director must remember that music is, after all, sublimated sound. Music, no matter how complex it may seem on the surface, is still only a combination of pitches, of volumes, and of qualities, and these can be altered to get the maximum of effectiveness in any given situation. The director must remember the basic factors he knows about sound

He must remember such simple facts as that rising pitches are exciting, that increasing tempos tend to be exciting, that high pitches and loud volumes are more exciting than low pitches and low volumes. If this simple straightforward approach to music is taken, the production director need not be afraid of music or the musicians.

Music and Station Policy

There are certain over-all considerations in the application of music to programming which must be considered, quite aside from the specific question of the application of music to a given program. Some stations and networks have what they call a repetition rule. The National Broadcasting Company has decreed that no piece of music can be played sooner than two and a half hours after its appearance on the air. This might mean that a piece of music which is absolutely right for a given spot might not be available. This restriction, of course, does not apply to all networks or all stations, but it is a principle which must be reckoned with where it does apply. The reason behind the ruling is perfectly obvious. There must be a certain variety in programming and this variety would be hard to get if a half-dozen production directors, all working individually, suddenly decide to use the same piece of music. The audience would be bored and this would be to the detriment of the programs.

There is another practical condition in regard to music which must be considered by all production directors. In most broadcast stations the whole subject of music is closely related to the unions. Not all stations have agreements with the American Federation of Musicians, but a great many do, and the larger stations and networks are almost a hundred per cent union-organized. This means that the production director must know the rulings and limitations imposed upon him by the contract between the stations or networks and the American Federation of Musicians.

While there are differences in contracts from station to station and from network to network, the basic agreements have certain common factors. In most stations the basic pay of the musicians is fixed by contract. Usually the agreement specifies how many union musicians the station must employ on its regular staff. This number may or may not coincide with the number of staff musicians actually employed by the station. Small stations commonly have only the minimum number required by the union contract. Larger stations may have more than the minimum number.

One of the clauses in standard agreements which has direct relationship to the production director is that regarding working hours. The usual agreement states that a musician may not work more than five hours out of an eight-hour day. That is to say, his total working day must not be more than eight hours and he may not actually work more than five of the elapsed eight hours. The working week is five days out of seven. These rules apply to staff musicians. Where free-lance musicians are employed, there is a regular scale of pay established by the union local, to which the broadcaster must conform. In network operations these details are usually managed by the musical director. In smaller stations the management of hours and of rehearsal time may fall to the production director himself. In any event, they are limitations to which the program, broadcasting, and rehearsal schedules must conform.

Vocalists are not necessarily controlled by the American Federation of Musicians, although they may be. In cases where an artist combines vocal talent with the playing of an instrument, the decision concerning jurisdiction is usually made locally. These borderline cases are always handled by specific agreement between the local union and the station involved.

One of the first things which a production director should do when he moves into a new locality is to familiarize himself with the details of the contract between the Musicians' local and the station or network. He will be held responsible for conforming to these contractual relationships and ignorance of the terms of the contract does not absolve either the station or the production director from infringements. It is, therefore, part of his preparation to become familiar with the local rulings.

Music and Copyrights

There is one other aspect of the control of music which the production director should know. Music is actual property and is so considered by American law. It is subject to copyright and to the protection afforded by copyright laws in the same manner as manuscripts or books or other printed material. There are several organizations which control the copyrights of most music, and the production director should familiarize himself with the station's arrangement with these bodies. Anyone who has followed radio at all will remember the long-drawn-out legal tangle in which the broadcasting industry engaged with the American Society of Composers, Authors, and Publishers. This organization controls a large bulk of the copyright music available in the United States. When the controversy between the broadcast industry and ASCAP started, a new licensing organization was set up by the industry called Broadcast Music, Incorporated. Other licensing agencies which control certain music are the Associated Music Publishers (AMP); and the Society of European Stage, Authors and Composers, Inc. (SESAC).

Payment for the use of broadcast music is usually handled in one of three ways. Most stations pay a blanket fee to one or more of the publishers' agencies in return for which they have the right to use any music on their list with certain exceptions. This fee is paid annually on a basis agreed upon by both parties. Publishers' relations with certain authors and composers make it necessary to charge a special fee per performance for certain pieces of music. These are the selections which are excepted from the blanket contract and which must be paid for at a fixed rate per performance on the air. Recently a third means of payment has been devised: a credit to the musical production in which the number originally appeared. This system has been used to a certain extent by the movie industry. You may have heard an announcer say at the close of a program, "The musical number so-and-so was from the current movie such-and-such released by such-and-such movie company." This announcement is sometimes made in lieu of a cash payment for the use of the music.

When contractual agreements between a publishers' organization and a broadcaster are completed, a list of the restricted music is furnished to the station. Any piece which is controlled by the licensing organization may be considered to be on the blanket list covered by the yearly fees unless it is specifically mentioned on the restricted list. It is understood, of course, that contractual agreements with one licensing organization do not permit a station to use copyrighted material controlled by another licensing organization. If the station has agreements only with BMI, for example, they may not use any ASCAP material at all. There is nothing to prevent stations from making contracts with more than one company.

There is, of course, a large body of music which is called "PD," which means that it is in the public domain. Its copyright or renewal of copyright has run out and it now is common property. It should not be assumed that because a piece is old it is necessarily in the public domain, however. Sometimes the actual piece of music under consideration may be in the public domain, but the specific arrangement available to the station may be a copyrighted one. Arrangements of music can be copyrighted. Clearance must be obtained, not only for the music itself, but for the particular arrangement which is being considered.

There are several companies which specialize in recording libraries for station use. The transcription libraries are usually recorded at 33 1/3 R.P.M. on sixteen-inch disks and are designed to minimize the programming problems in local stations. They are divided into classical, popular, light or semi-classic, vocal, instrumental, and mood music — all the various kinds that would be usable on a small station. One of the advantages of the transcription library service is that all matters of musical clearance are handled at the recording source. It is license free and paid for with the purchase of the transcription service.

These transcription services are sometimes arranged so that a whole fifteen-minute program of music is grouped on one side of a sixteen-inch transcription, even including announcements. The station can play the whole side of the transcription continuously and have a complete musical program including announcement commentary on the music.

Not only can the station buy several different sizes of basic libraries of transcriptions, but a monthly addition service is also available which keeps the library abreast of current music releases. While the building of programs of recorded or transcribed music does not usually require the services of a production director, the director should familiarize himself with the recorded music available in the station because he may be called upon to use it at some time or other. It also offers him an excellent source of various kinds of music which he can study in his off moments and thus fill out his own musical background.

In addition, most stations have very complete libraries of regular commercial records which make up the bulk of the musical fare on the station. These recordings are the same as one would find in a local music store and are played over the air constantly.

As this book is being written, there is a union ruling in effect which allows union musicians to make recordings only for certain companies. This ruling was made by the American Federation of Musicians in an effort to stop the wholesale use of recordings by broadcast stations, in the hope that it would furnish employment for more live talent. Time alone will determine the outcome of this particular struggle, and as yet most stations have not felt the pinch because many of them had large supplies of recordings on hand. However, no new recordings were available to broadcast stations for several months, and only recently have contracts been renewed with some of the recording companies. The current war restrictions on the makings of recordings are also working a hardship on those stations which depend largely on records for their music. The shortage of materials would make it difficult to release new recordings even if the union restrictions were not in force.

Whether the source of music is a piano, a magnificent pipe organ, a full symphony orchestra, or only a commercial recording, all are music. They are all available to the production director. They are a part of the stuff out of which he creates an artistic entity which ends in the loud-speaker as a broadcast program. Grouped together, they form one of the three basic sources of sound which the production director may use in the creation of his program. As such they are a part of the basic warp and woof of radio and should be handled with all the thought and insight and respect of which the production director is capable.

CHAPTER 7

TALENT

THE most important pigment in the sound-painter's box of colors is talent. Sound is important. Music is endlessly flexible. But the final power and the ultimate in diversity is reached in the human voice. For our purposes in this chapter, the term "talent" will be used for all the people who appear on radio programs, regardless of their particular *métier*. It should be understood to include announcers, actors, singers, comedians, politicians, ministers, school teachers, and so on. It will embrace that whole vast parade of individuals who daily stream through hundreds of studios and give voice to the thousands of programs which radio sponsors every twenty-four hours.

The handling of talent is the most complex problem with which the production director is faced. His mixing panel cannot talk back to him, even though his engineer occasionally does. His sound is a mechanical fact contrived from a mechanical source for the most part. His music, although it is produced by individuals, is a result of long centuries of refinement so that it has its own rules and laws. But in talent one faces a complex problem indeed. A producer must always remember that he is dealing primarily with sound and he must look upon talent as producers of sound. His judgment of their work must be always based on the effectiveness of the sound they create. It may be words, it may be music, it may be meaningless symbols, but it must be carefully contrived to achieve a specific effect.

If the problem were as simple as this, it would be easy. But sound, as it emanates from talent, is a purveyor of ideas. And ideas are purveyed by human personalities. It is at this point that a production director meets the ultimate in complexity.

This discussion of talent is a generalized one applying equally to all kinds of programs. It will endeavor to set forth the basic principles which should guide the selection of individuals to appear on the air. It is obvious that there is a wide difference between a capable or even an inspired actor working in the field of drama and, let us say, an expert in home economics who does a daily broadcast on good housekeeping. Each kind of talent deserves a detailed discussion of its own, but there are certain principles which should be applied to all, and which should serve as a standard for every person who aspires to work in radio.

This chapter will deal with talent under four headings. First, there will be a discussion of the *selection* of talent. Second, the *development* of talent will be discussed. Third, one must consider the *use* to which talent is put. Finally, the matter of *relationship* between the production director and his talent must be established.

The Selection of Talent

Sources of Radio Talent

At a radio station, sometime during the long broadcast day between the pre-sunrise sign-on and the exhausted sign-off gasp of the announcer at night, there will appear almost every kind of individual under the sun. They come in all shapes and sizes, with talents ranging from a questionable yearning after opera to a decided ability for hog-calling. The butcher, the baker, the candlestick-maker all want their day at the microphone. Radio does an amazing job of giving these people a chance to appear.

The allied arts furnish one of the most profitable sources of talent. Radio has borrowed from the stage, from the concert hall, from the platform, from newspapers, and from magazines. It has borrowed from any source that might furnish talent either in the sense of performance or in the sense of knowledge or experience in a given field. Much of this borrowed talent came into radio and found a natural home there. Other individuals failed completely in their efforts to adapt themselves to a new medium. Much of our present radio talent came to radio without any experience at all in meeting the public.

People in this category came and were successful because of their basic and deep-rooted knowledge of a specific field of activity about which they could speak with authority.

One of the greatest lessons in show business is to be learned from the observation of this transplanting process. It is interesting to note that the success or failure of talent in the new medium cuts across all styles and kinds of performance. There have been politicians who were expert in the rough-and-tumble haranguing of an audience face to face, who were completely inadequate in the medium of radio and unable to master the techniques required. What holds true for political speakers, unfortunately, has also been true of some outstanding stage talent. Many of the great names in the theater became interested in this fascinating new medium with such a vast audience and wished to become a part of it. Some of them had the innate good judgment to recognize that this was a new medium with artistic laws of its own, and they approached it in the attitude of students who had a lesson to learn. Stage stars who approached radio this way and had the good fortune to find good teachers have made excellent contributions to the art of radio drama. It is unfortunate that there is almost an equal number of talented theater folk who have been completely unable to make the transition. It is not always *ipso facto* evidence of their own unwillingness to learn. Some of them failed to find a teacher. There are some directors in radio who, faced with a big-name guest star from the theater, fail utterly to fulfill their obligation as teacher to a student in a new medium. The unfortunate result is that the stage personality under such circumstances fails to do good work.

There are, inexcusably, stage stars who hold radio in complete contempt. On those rare occasions when the fee is too tempting to turn down, they step into the studio, unwilling to admit that the techniques of which they are masters are not adequate to the situation. These people fail miserably in radio and they fail through their own ignorance and shortsightedness in their approach to their work.

This inability or unwillingness to make concessions to a new medium is not confined to actors alone. There are a great many ministers in this country who have felt that radio was the answer to their prayers. Here was the way to reach a large and sympathetic audience with their religious message. They then proceed to follow the same outworn, outmoded approaches which were bad even in their own pulpits, but which, in the new medium, block them completely from a listening audience. This experience could be duplicated in almost any other field of endeavor in which radio has a part. Some of the people borrowed from other fields came to radio and were willing to learn. Still others came, willing to learn and were able to find no adequate teachers. And there was a last, unfortunate group who came with contempt and no willingness to learn. These facts make it evident that artists borrowed from parallel media, even though they have a preliminary background, are not an unmixed blessing to the talent pool of radio. Some of them create more problems than they solve. Not only was that true in the early days of radio; unfortunately it is still true. It can be said to the everlasting credit of a great many production directors that it is less true now than it was ten years ago.

The best advice that anyone can give to a production director who has to work with talent drawn from a parallel field is to urge him to proceed on the assumption that his talent is ignorant of the ways of radio but willing to learn. Any director, no matter how humble, has the right and the obligation to tell any talent whatsoever what he wants done. The measure of a man in any one field is not necessarily his measure in another. It is the duty of the production director to tell such artists what they should do. Regardless of how famous the artist may be in another medium, the director owes it to himself and to his performers to do a job in pedagogy.

The second pool of talent on which radio can draw is the group of those well-trained and competent technicians who, for one reason or another, are not satisfied with, or completely successful in, parallel media. There are, in America today, a great many singers who have aspired to the concert or operatic stage, but who lack the potential for success in those fields.

These same people, turning to radio, find a medium in which their talents are acceptable. There are many parlor voices heard on the air every day which are completely successful on radio, but which would have been failures on the concert or operatic stage. What is true of vocalists is equally true of the other kinds of talent which radio uses.

A third source of talent for radio is the large pool of people which radio has itself discovered and developed. One need only sit in the production office of any large network for two or three days and listen to the constant stream of applications for auditions to realize how many people aspire to a career in radio. Many of them have no training, no background, no reason at all for their aspirations. A few come with a thorough grounding and an excellent background which give them an excellent chance for success. The gleaning from this group is small indeed. Any production director who finds one good performer out of five hundred auditions feels that his batting average is reasonably good. This high degree of selectivity does not mean that the talent field in radio is overcrowded. Exactly the opposite is true. There is always less talent available than there is demand. The fact that so many people have to be auditioned to find one usable person is no commentary on the competition within the industry. It is merely a commentary on the inability of most people to meet the requirements of radio.

The wide ratio between people auditioned and people accepted is not quite as strange a phenomenon as might appear at first glance. One is forever hearing a comment worded something like this: "My friends tell me that my voice is just the kind that ought to be on the radio." Many of the people who are rejected have no other recommendation than that for their audition. Most people would not think of going into the Corn Exchange Bank in New York and saying to the vice-president: "My friends tell me that I have just the kind of personality that ought to make me a success in the banking business. Will you therefore give me a responsible position?" They take it for granted that in the banking business one starts at the bottom and works up. Not so in radio. A chance remark from a friend is enough to send a housewife skittering off to the nearest network studio for an audition. Is it any wonder that production directors have to listen to so many auditions before they find one able person?

In spite of the long odds against the talent-seekers, radio has discovered and developed a great deal of first-rate talent. Even against odds of five hundred to one, they have plowed through a tremendous mass of listening, and culled from it a good many people with a high degree of skill in the business of appealing to the American public. This fact is testimony to the perseverance, the patience, and the faith of the men in radio who are willing to look through so many haystacks for so few needles.

All the major networks and most large stations conduct auditions regularly. There are very few important radio stations in the United States where one cannot get an audition by the simple process of asking for it. Because of the large volume of traffic handled, it is not always possible to get an immediate audition. But if one is willing to wait, eventually he will get the call which says he will be heard on such-and-such a date at such-and-such a time. These auditions consume a good many hours of the time of important staff members each week. Contrary to popular opinion, the auditions are listened to with keen interest. It is true that production directors are quick to spot what they think may be talent and equally quick to spot lack of talent. The fact that they may look bored with an audition may only be the result of having very quickly made up their minds that no talent is there. They still have to listen to a good deal of the prepared material which the talent brings in. It may be very disheartening to the auditioning talent to see the apparent lack of interest in an audition board. But it is a refreshing sight to see the enthusiasm and eagerness with which that same board of auditioners listen to someone they think may have a spark of real ability. If there is even a faint hint of promise, the average audition board will go to great lengths to give it a chance to develop and grow. After all, there are fewer good people available for radio than there are good jobs. It is the industry's recognition of this fact which keeps going the exhausting and exhaustive search for talent which is a constant routine in most radio stations.

The reward for the unending search comes with the finding and development of those who turn out to be successful in the medium. Radio has done a good job of developing its own people — people who were not talent until they found their stride in radio. It is interesting to note that there is a whole group of these people now who have reversed the original talent flow by branching out from it to the screen and theater. One needs only to mention such names as Bob Hope, Bing Crosby, Dinah Shore, and a host of others to show what radio has discovered and developed and in turn given to other media.

So much for a generalized discussion of the selection of talent. Let us get down now to specific cases of how the actual process takes place. To begin with, stations and networks are constantly auditioning people. Those who pass a successful preliminary audition are called back for a special audition. The people who are successful in the special audition are then entered in the talent file kept by every well-run station. The file will include actors, commentators, announcers, singers, instrumentalists, and a host of others who have something to give to the public.

It is, therefore, natural that a production director faced with a talent problem will first turn to the station or network file to see what is available. Usually in every organization there is one person responsible for keeping the records and for interviewing auditionees. That person will have at his or her fingertips an amazing collection of data which can be helpful to the production director.

In large cities there is also a registry of talent to which the production director may turn. These registries are clearinghouses for talent, the go-between for talent and the people who need talent. For example, there are half a dozen such talent registries in the city of New York. Any radio actor who is in the market for work will probably be registered with one of them.

If the production director's talent problem cannot be solved by his own station's file, he may logically turn next to the registry. These registries have complete information on each person registered with them, and it is always available to the director in search of a specific kind of talent.

Another source of talent is the agent. There are quite a few agents in the larger radio centers who make a business of finding, developing, and placing talent. Some of them are exploiters. Others do a real job and may spend several thousand dollars developing an actor or a singer. These agents usually concentrate on vocalists and teams by acts rather than on individual actors.

Still another source of new blood may be the talent scout. Some agencies and networks employ such men for the specific purpose of following up leads on talent possibilities. While the amount of talent uncovered in this way is small, it still must be taken into consideration.

There is one other source to which the production director may turn – the AFRA office. AFRA stands for American Federation of Radio Artists; it is the union to which most radio talent belongs. It covers the field of acting and announcing and certain classes of vocalists. It forms one of the most important union contacts in the talent field. It is the radio equivalent of Actors Equity for theater people and the Screen Actors Guild for movie people. It is affiliated with the American Federation of Labor. Wherever AFRA has a local, a guild-shop contract is in effect between it and the broadcasters. Of course there are hundreds of local broadcasting stations which do not have a local in that community. In such cases, however, the talent requirements of the station are extremely simplified and the need for such organization is not existent.

So far as the production director is concerned, he has a direct obligation both to his station and to the union to be familiar with all the local rules in effect, so that he can conduct his work accordingly. His work must fall within the confines of the contracts made between the local and the station or network. It would be impossible in a brief discussion of this sort to outline all the rules which AFRA has set up to govern its members. The rules are not even uniform between different locals. It is enough to say that the production director, when he first goes in to a new station job, should immediately ask for a handbook of AFRA local rules and regulations. These he must not only understand but in many cases memorize because they will affect his day-to-day relations with his talent. He must know, for example, how to keep track of the time on his cast. He must know when he can double characters and when he cannot. He must know the penalties involved for calling rehearsals which he does not meet, and all the other myriad factors which control his relationship with talent. These need not be regarded as inhibitions on the production director. They are simply rules of conduct by which he must abide. They are complete enough to codify all normal procedures. In case of doubt on any given point the new director will always do well to call the station's legal staff for a decision. This kind of checking, before the fact, often obviates the necessity of much explaining after the fact.

As a footnote to this discussion on AFRA it might be well to mention that engineers also have their union and the production director must be familiar with the terms of this contract also. This is less likely to affect the production director because such contracts usually govern only working hours and the handling of equipment. In any well-organized station these matters are handled by the engineering department and the traffic department, and the production director need not be concerned in detail about them. He will gain respect from his engineers, however, if he is familiar with the terms of their contract and abides by them. It is this kind of understanding which avoids all sorts of unpleasantness and personnel problems.

Casting

Having discussed the sources of talent and the rules governing the use of talent, we come now to a matter of great importance – the principles governing the selection of talent. It is one thing to find a source of talent; it is quite another thing, having found the source, to decide among several candidates for a given position. To guide him in matters like these, the production director must have a sure sense of values and a long background of experience in doing the job. Even so, the best showmen admit they make enough mistakes. Even with a definite set of principles to guide him, the experienced production director will often make mistakes in judgment. Another difficulty in this matter of describing principles of judgment is that they must inevitably be intangible. Talent is not something which can be subjected to blueprint. Because it deals with human beings and matters of personality, it cannot be reduced to a mathematical formula. At best we can only make certain generalizations which can be translated into specific and defensible action.

For any given talent problem the first consideration must be the "rightness for the job." Presumably the production director has carefully analyzed his talent needs. He knows the kind of person he needs to do a particular job. It may involve certain personality traits. It may involve specific skill backgrounds. It may involve a great many tangible and intangible factors, but they all add up to a general set of specifications which must be fulfilled. So the first test of any talent is how he meets those specifications — his general rightness for the job.

Let us take a specific problem. Suppose we are looking for an announcer for a children's adventure program. Certain requirements become apparent at once. We must have a voice with a certain amount of fun and excitement in it. We must have a voice which is able to speak to children in their own language on their own level without appearing to talk down to them. We must have a fairly virile voice. We should have a voice which expresses an interest in and an understanding of children and what they like. It is perfectly obvious that a man who may be admirably trained to handle the Metropolitan Opera broadcasts need not be the right person for this kind of job. And yet he may be exactly the right person. Milton Cross has done both jobs for years. The first consideration, then, is rightness for the job.

The number two consideration will probably be freshness of approach. Radio seems to be a business that encourages clichés. It encourages imitation. It too often seems to offer a premium for anyone who can do the job exactly the way somebody else does it. Actually this is not true. There are so few people who can develop an individual style or a new approach to any job in radio that when such a person does come along he is soon followed by a large body of imitators. Directors seeking a new approach and being unable to find it are prone to take imitators of other people who have been successful in finding something new. This may in itself be a mistake, but it is frequently a second-best which a production director may have to accept.

What is meant by freshness of approach? It means simply the discovery of a new way to do an old job. One of the most common problems in commercial radio is to find a good commercial announcer – a voice that is able to sell. Certain styles of handling commercial copy have developed and there is a tendency for announcers to fall into a common mold. At one time almost every announcer of network commercials made his delivery formal, stylized, with a stilted diction which practically screamed the fact that he was reading from copy. Then came a man who insisted on ad-libbing commercials. What an heretical idea! But he had something. He had a freshness of approach, a sincerity and earnestness which the announcer reading from copy could never quite achieve. He was immediately successful and had consequently a large body of imitators. The production director, then, should always be on the lookout for a fresh approach to the job.

The next clue one must look for in the selection of talent is what we shall call, for want of a better term, a trade-mark. If a person can be so individual or specialized in his work that his performance is always recognizable, he can be a great asset. When production directors get together for shop talk, one always hears a great deal of praise for the flexible actor or announcer. There is admiration for the man who can do a number of jobs and who can do equally good work on all of them. From a long-time point of view, however, it seems wiser to encourage individuality or individual style in talent.

Audiences like to be able to spot people, to recognize them immediately. They may even prefer this individuality to rightness for the job. They may forgive someone's inadequacy for a specific occasion if he brings to it the stamp of his own personality. This may be only another expression of an age of specialization. It seems more likely, however, that it is an inherent, if unspoken, desire in an audience. No one can debate the fact that many great actors have worked on this principle. They make little or no effort to submerge their personalities in a rôle. They do make efforts to find a play which matches their own style and their own personality. But in every play in which they appear they appear as themselves. It can be technically argued that this is not acting. From a practical point of view, however, that talent seems to be the best box office which has an individuality strong enough to flavor everything an actor does.

Individuality of style may be something that is natural or it may be something which is consciously cultivated for the specific purpose of trade-marking the actor. In either case the end result is the same. It gives the great American public a handle, a password for that particular person. It is one of the short cuts to building up an individual to important proportions. The homely, down-Indiana speech of Elmer Davis and the quick, hybrid diction of H. V. Kaltenborn are quite different, but in each case there is a distinguishing trade-mark, a constant factor which colors everything they do. This trademark is in itself a desirable and useful thing. It is something to be looked for in the selection of talent.

High on the list of consideration in the selection of talent is the ability to take direction. Remember that our basic premise is that radio is a symphony in sound in which the production director is the conductor. As conductor he must at all times maintain a tight and complete control over his production.

This is not possible with talent that has no innate ability to take direction. The ability to take direction is not a mechanical thing. It is that, but it is much more than that. Naturally, any production director wants to work with talent who can do the little mechanical jobs in the exact way in which he asks. He wants an actor who will fade in a line if he has been instructed to fade it in, without having to be reminded at each rehearsal. But taking direction means much more than the ability to remember mechanical details.

The ability to take direction means, in the final analysis, an open-mindedness to suggestion, a willingness to be dominated by the director. It implies an intellect keen enough to perceive what a director is driving at and a technique skillful enough to translate the desire into proper responses. It must also mean that the talent is flexible enough to be able to do what the production director wants done. Very often an actor can understand what the director wants, but finds himself unable to comply with the request because of his lack of flexibility. Some announcers need only one suggestion to give them an idea. At the next reading they come back with exactly what the director wants. Others require a long and detailed explanation before they are able to deliver what is wanted. Still other announcers are so inflexible that, though they can understand what is wanted, they are unable to deliver. Some are so mentally inflexible that they cannot give in to the demands of the director, while some are so completely insensitive that they cannot even understand what the director wants. Any director, before he has worked with talent very long, will meet the whole gamut of talent skill. He will soon develop a deep affection for the announcer or speaker or actor who can comprehend what he wants immediately and deliver it back on the next reading.

Naturally, any production director will look for co-operative talent. It is always a desirable quality in any personnel equation. It is particularly important in radio, where an entire production is never the work of one man, but the result of cooperative work of a group of individuals co-ordinated under the management of the director. The production director will be wise to choose talent with a high degree of co-operative spirit. Because of the time pressure in radio there is little room for temperament. There is still less room for professional jealousy. The actor or announcer who insists on "standing on his rights" will probably soon find that he has no rights upon which to stand. He is simply not called for work.

There must be a high degree of sensitivity in talent. Regardless of the kind of talent under consideration or regardless of the job to be done, sensitivity to the needs of a situation, to the emotional texture of a scene, to the suggestions of the director, are all requisite. Ability to take direction is important, but it also implies that the talent is supplying something to the equation. How much any individual person on the microphone end of the broadcast brings to that program is governed largely by his sensitivity to the particular situation. Whether it be an actor attacking a part or an announcer on a special-events show, there should in each case be that "feel for the occasion" which marks good talent. The production director will be wise to keep this in mind when he is selecting his personnel.

Every production director is aware of the value of a "spark plug" in a company. There are some rare individuals who, quite aside from their talent, have the quality of inspiring interest and aliveness in their fellow workers. By heckling, by cajoling, by sheer animal spirits, some people are able to invest a quality of excitement and desire to do a good job in other people. Such people have a great deal to offer the production director. Often the difference between a good program and a bad one is the morale of the company. A person who can spark-plug a group of people, who can incite in them an inner excitement to do a good job, is a valuable addition to any company. Production directors will often cast someone who might be a second choice for the particular job just because of this ability to create interest in other people.

Few production directors will put up with the professional grumbler. A man's talent must be outstanding to keep him in work if he is such a person. Healthy criticism is one thing.

Habitual discontent is something else again, and it is this latter trait which the production director should be on the lookout for and sidestep whenever possible in the choice of talent. One such person can do more to destroy the morale of a company than a good person can do to build it up.

There is one final factor in the selection of talent which any intelligent production director constantly takes into consideration. That factor is experience. There are plenty of cases where a production director has cast an actor in a rôle, knowing that he is using his second choice. He may feel justified in the decision because the second choice is an experienced actor. His first choice may have been an unknown quantity. As such he is a question mark, and there are always more question marks than a production director can deal with anyway. He is loath to add one of his own volition.

Often the factor of experience is counted on by the production director to offset the other deficiencies that an auditionee may show. Where time is of importance – and there is never enough of it – the production director will do everything he can to insure himself of an experienced company. This is a factor which is, of course, not peculiar to radio. Every person dealing with personnel takes it into consideration.

But experience is often the direct opposite of freshness of approach. A director often has to make a decision between a person with a new idea which is untested and an old hand at the game with less originality. His final decision in such cases should be made on the basis of the specific problems involved in the casting. The final rightness of any person for any job may be, and often is, enough to offset a lack of experience. It is in matters like these that the production director exhibits himself as an artist. His decision in such cases may mark the difference between his success as a director and his failure.

So much for the selection of talent. We have outlined the sources from which talent may be drawn, we have talked about the working conditions which govern the talent, and we have tried to set up certain principles for the selection of talent. We come now to the next important problem which involves the human equation.

THE DEVELOPMENT OF TALENT

Development of talent on a local station is usually an unsupervised process. The person learns by the process of trial and error without much help or criticism from the station or anybody in it. As stations increase in size and consequently in size of staff, there is more time available for the important job of developing talent. In the networks, where the development of talent reaches its ultimate importance, a considerable amount of time and thought and money goes into the process. It is not a thing which can happen overnight. It is a long-time process. In doing it the network gambles a considerable amount of time and money on its judgment. It is forced to invest a substantial amount of capital in an individual with nothing but the judgment of its production directors as evidence that there will ever be any return on the investment.

The development of talent may be an informal process which means little more than assigning talent to progressively more difficult programs under capable direction. An auditionee who shows promise as an actress may be assigned to a series of bit parts under various directors. No special attention will be paid to her, but she will have an opportunity to learn by working with various directors and by having the benefit of observation and experience. If she learns by this, she will be assigned to more demanding parts until she has matured into a full-fledged, capable actress.

Sometimes the process is a deliberate, planned campaign to take an individual and make him a "name" on the air. This often occurs with announcers. Some staff announcer may develop a special interest in a certain kind of work. A station happens to need an outstanding person in that particular area. After looking over the candidates for the position, the staff announcer is chosen. There will follow a long series of publicity stunts, assignments which will be calculated to put him in the public eye, and jobs which will force him into a development of his field of specialization. Thus, by a process of special assignments of jobs, by judicious publicity, and by actual instruction from capable staff members, a person may be built from an anonymous member of the announcing staff into an important name on the air.

There have been instances when vocalists have undergone a whole process of supervised training and come out as full-fledged talent. For example, a girl singer may show some promise in a routine audition. She may be called in and given some help by one of the musical production directors of the staff. After this another audition will be arranged in which the staff orchestra will furnish the music for another test recording. If this shows promise, the entire staff may be placed on an all-out audition basis. The continuity department will be asked to furnish a special script for her. The music department will make special arrangements of a series of numbers that suit her particular style. An orchestra will be used for the arrangements. An announcer will be assigned to the program. The whole program will be rehearsed just as though it were a production going on the air. When it has reached the highest point of perfection attainable by that particular vocalist, an audition record will be made.

This record will be studied by the program planning board or a board of production directors or another group of critics on the staff, and suggestions made to the vocalist. This process may be repeated several times and the decision finally reached that she is ready for the air. She may be then given a small spot on another program or an occasional spot of her own, and allowed to develop by experience. When she has undergone as much of this process as seems possible, the organization then offers her program or her talents to a sponsor. This kind of build-up process is not at all unusual. Capable talent does not just happen. It is usually the result of long, carefully planned instruction and development, directed by a farseeing program department.

There are several unfortunate aspects to this whole business of developing talent. One of the quite human but nevertheless regrettable aspects of the problem is that some highly skilled, extremely patient production director who remains anonymous may be the one who develops the twenty-five-dollar a week stenographer into a three-hundred-dollar a week actress. More often than not the actress never realizes what has been done for her and proceeds on the assumption that she knows all the answers after a few months' training. The fact that she has been taught everything she knows by the director is seldom given the credit that it deserves. Directors may cease to work on talent development unless they are given encouragement and recognition.

Another setback to the development of talent was the FCC ruling which denied to broadcasters the operation of talent agencies. While there might be legitimate reason for the Commission's ruling in this instance, it does work certain hardships on the people interested in developing talent. It is natural that no organization is going to spend much time and money developing talent only to have it taken away by a competitor. Since broadcasters can no longer control their talent through agencies they have to depend entirely upon the good will of their talent to repay them for the time and money spent on their development. Naturally this has inhibited greatly the program of building up of new talent by the networks.

Unfortunately, there are whole areas in broadcasting where nothing is being done about the development of new people. The field of comedy is one of the most glaring examples of lack of foresight on the part of the networks. It takes a good many years to create a polished, accomplished comedian. This is no simple process which can be completed in a six months' trial-and-error period of instruction. The number of top-flight comedians available to American radio today could almost be numbered on the fingers of two hands.

The time may come when broadcasters will set up some kind of organized process for developing new talent. This process is already getting its start in certain well-founded radio departments in the universities. They can, however, do little more than find the original talent and start it on its way. The long process of developing talent to the point where it is ready for network appearance must be the responsibility of the industry itself. One of these days the need for such a program may become so acute that the industry as a whole or certain parts of it may do something constructive about it. It is certain that at the rate at which radio is using up talent something will soon have to be done to meet the situation.

The Use of Talent

Let us assume for the moment that there is plenty of talent available. Let us also assume that we can afford the talent that we need for our purposes. There still remains the responsibility of the production director for the intelligent use of the talent. It is quite possible to have all the talent in the world and still so misuse it that poor showmanship results. It is obvious, therefore, that a good director must know at least the basic principles of how talent should and can be used.

The first principle in the use of any talent is that it be given a proper vehicle for its display. If there is a vocalist or a comedian or an educator or a newscaster who has a specific ability, then the first important principle is to give it a proper kind of vehicle. Sometimes several false starts are made before a proper formula is reached. While some of this work has to be done by trial and error, thoughtful analysis and careful planning will do much to obviate the necessity for too many false starts. It should not be assumed that because a person has talent he may be put in any kind of program. A very able individual may show up poorly on a program unsuited to him, and do a brilliant job on another which happens to lie within his particular *métier*.

The matter of audience types at various times of the day must also be considered. There are certain comedians who seem to be naturals for morning programs who have failed utterly to amuse or entertain an evening audience. Announcers who may do a good job on a swing-shift show might be unacceptable to morning audiences constituted largely of women. Talent must be distributed so that it can, in terms of time, be available to the proper audience.

A warning should be made here against the star-studded program. A program loaded with outstanding personalities usually fails to live up either to its advance publicity or its expectations. The mix is too rich for the average taste. There is too much chance for a clash of temperaments. There is always the possibility of a conflict over the spotlight. Such shows usually depend on the stars and not enough either on script or direction to make them successful. A show too rich in talent, like a dinner too rich in sweets, can get highly indigestible very quickly. Ordinarily a program that has only one star spot in it turns out to be a better program. The entire program can be tailored to display the talents of the star. The expense is less astronomical. There is little chance for a clash of temperaments and no quarrel over who gets the spotlight. All these things tend to create a unity which is often lacking in the so-called star-studded program.

Another item which the production director must remember is the proper use of time. There are two aspects to this. First, a cast which is not working must still be paid if it is an official rehearsal period. This means that there is money going out for which the sponsor gets no commensurate return. Second, a cast that is not kept busy is not kept interested. The better a director keeps his company busy, the more likely he is to get an interesting and interested performance from them. Nothing is more congealing to talent than to be called to rehearsal and then sit long minutes and sometimes hours without doing a thing. It quite rightly seems to the actor to be an utter waste of his time, even though he is being paid for it. Any actor who is worth his salt resents that kind of inefficiency. Rehearsal calls should be so planned that the people who work scenes together can rehearse together. Very often rehearsals can be so planned that people who have little to do can be allotted a minimum amount of rehearsal time. Quite often there may be only one or two people in a program who need a considerable amount of rehearsal. By calling the rest of the cast for the basic minimum time which AFRA allows, enough money can be saved to compensate for overtime spent on important members of the company. This is intelligent use both of time and talent and is usually practiced by every good production director.

Another consideration in the use of talent is the achievement of a proper balance. If a program is predicated on the use of a central figure, then all the other talent should be chosen to combine with, contrast, or highlight the qualities of the central figure. It would lead to confusion to cast two men on a round-table program whose voices were similar, whose ideas were similar, and whose backgrounds were so parallel that no striking difference of opinion might emerge. The audience could not tell them apart by their voices. Their ideas would not clash enough to make a round-table program interesting, and the lack of intellectual challenge will mean a dull broadcast. The same matter of balance can be applied to dramatic casting. The art of contrasting voices and personalities is an interesting problem. It is a phase of directing which is too often ignored.

Finally, in considering the use of talent, one must remember that talent is, fundamentally, sound. It is a reflection, in sound, of the pattern of a personality. Within certain limits the pattern can be controlled by the production director, but in certain respects it is beyond the control even of the actor himself. The production director must protect himself by proper casting and by careful selection of the right people to achieve all the end results he wants on a given program.

One last warning should be given to beginning production directors. Talent is talent whether it is an unknown, unheralded announcer or a comedian famous from coast to coast. When a production director is placed in charge of a program, his superiors expect him to be in charge of that program regardless of the talent on the show, the caliber of the people involved, or the importance of the program. A production director has only one duty: he must furnish a good show. In order to do that he must, regardless of who his talent happens to be, exercise his authority in the execution of his duties. If his talent is good, they will recognize that authority. If it is not good, it does not matter. Good talent is good only in proportion to the intelligence of the use to which it is put. The production director will do well to study the principles of the use of talent and conform to them.

The Relationship Between Production Director and Talent

We come now to a very important topic and one upon which there is no agreement of opinion. There are as many ways of handling relationships between director and talent as there are directors and talent. No hard-and-fast rules can be laid down. Some directors can carry off an intimacy with their casts which would wreck another director. The whole problem of personality differences must be taken into account in discussing the proper relationship between a production director and his talent.

The beginning of any such relationship must be founded in mutual respect. The production director should lay the foundation in his choice of talent. If he has a voice in the choosing of the talent for the program, presumably he chooses somebody for whose work he has respect. It is up to him then to conduct himself so that the talent will have respect for him. This can be accomplished only if his conduct inspires respect.

The one sure way to gain respect from a company is to outguess them, outdecide them, and outwit them. If you can top every member of your company in every department without making a great point of it, you will automatically gain the respect of your group. If you know enough about the problems of your engineer not to ask foolish results of him, you will have his respect. If, in addition, you show some genuine understanding of his job and his problems, you will have no difficulty in getting his loyalty. What is true of him will be true of other members of your company. If you have done thorough preparation, if you know specifically what you want, if your ideas are definite and well founded, you are in a position to make executive decisions. If those decisions are wise, your cast is quick to sense it and quick to respond with a confidence and a loyalty that makes for top-flight programs. But if your work is sloppy, if you make decisions after you get into rehearsal and then have to reverse them – in short, if you do slipshod production, you cannot hope to have the complete respect of your company. Naturally, when they give themselves into the hands of a director, they want to feel that they are in the hands of a capable person who has given some time and thought to the job. Once they are convinced that a director has done that, they are quite willing to go along with him.

A production director must be a firm disciplinarian. Firm discipline does not mean harshness. It does not even mean that he has to be stern in his reactions. It simply means that he has certain rules by which he operates and certain standards of result that he expects from every member of his company. He accepts the best they can do as his rightful due and acts accordingly. If he gets less than that from his company, he has a right to demand it of them. If these demands are properly made, they will be at least respected.

It is human nature to take all the leeway one is allowed. When a company working under a production director discovers that they can do what they please and get away with it, that director has lost a major battle. He may lose his whole artistic war for just such basic reasons as this. Equitable discipline breeds respect as well as efficiency. The firm sense of control of a company is essential to the proper carrying out of the complex pattern of activity of a radio program. Laxness in one department will breed laxness in another. The more complex the program, the more reason there is for the director to be firm in his insistence upon his control of the program. Firmness of discipline cannot be achieved by a director who lacks understanding. Senseless discipline which does nothing but soothe the ego of a director is equally out of place. Good discipline is so tacitly understood between director and company that the subject never comes up.

The next point is a debatable one, but the majority of directors will probably agree that social relationships with talent should be avoided whenever possible. Some directors may have the rare ability to preside as an amiable host over the luncheon table one minute and to become a strict disciplinarian over the same people ten minutes later. If the personality of the director permits him to bridge that gap, no harm would probably come from casual social relationships with his talent. However, intimate and extended social contacts with talent tend to break down the barrier which divides an administrator from other employees. It is the rare director whose judgment can go completely unclouded by intimate social acquaintance with talent. Friendship and other contacts may get in the way of his artistic judgment. Undesirable pressures may be brought to bear. All these things are possibilities which the wise production director avoids if possible.

The foregoing should not be taken to mean that a director should remain aloof from his company. He dare not be unaware of them as individuals because the whole problem of personality is so intimately bound up in most talent problems that ignorance of their personalities would be dangerous. Much of a director's judgment of talent must be predicated on a fairly comprehensive knowledge of the temperament and the capability of his talent.

A director should know his talent so well that he understands the quirks of their minds and their habits of thought. Only by this kind of knowledge can he make the wisest use of his available talent. It is perfectly possible to know a personality reasonably well without engaging in too much social contact with that person. A good director will make it his job to be acquainted with his talent and to understand them, but at the same time maintain a certain detachment and "psychic distance" which will protect him in making unbiased decisions.

Finally, and in some ways most important of all, a production director should observe his own rules. If he insists that a cast be in the studio and ready to rehearse at six o'clock, then he himself must be ready at six o'clock. He dare not demand things from his company which he himself is unwilling to give also. Talent is slow to accept a double standard of rules. If the director lays down certain principles for the conduct of rehearsals, his cast will expect him to observe them likewise.

It is extremely difficult to get and hold the loyalty and respect of a group of people if you are not willing to play the game according to the rules which you yourself created. If you expect your talent to be thoroughly prepared before they come to a rehearsal, you yourself must be equally well or better prepared. If you expect them to be punctual, you must be punctual. If you expect them to meet high standards of performance, you must yourself be able to conform to those standards. All this is a part of the pattern of leadership and it is only common sense to recognize its wisdom.

In relationships with fellow human beings (which includes talent), the Golden Rule is a fairly safe and workable principle of operation. There is a saying that the man who is satisfied with nothing but the best manages to get it a surprising amount of the time. This certainly is true with directors. After all, the final measure of the stature of a director is his ability to draw from his company the performances and standards of work which he is willing to set for himself.

Our discussion of talent might be summed up this way: Basically, when we are dealing with talent we are still handling the rudimentary colors with which we will paint our sound picture. After all, talent, in its final essence, furnishes us with sound. But, where our sound effects might be reproduced from a recording, the sound effects of speech are reproduced by individuals who have minds of their own, wills of their own, and artistic philosophies of their own. The extent to which a director can take advantage of the contributions of his talent and at the same time retain firm control of his entire production will determine his artistic success. If he can somehow take into consideration all the human factors in the equation and still maintain enough aesthetic distance from the personalities of his company to see them objectively as patterns of sound or voices coming out of the loud-speaker, the better he will be equipped to do his job.

Thus far in this section of the book we have described the tools with which the production director works. We have looked at his equipment and at the various sources of sound which will be the components of his finished product. Having obtained some idea of what materials the director uses and something of the manner in which he uses them, we come next to the matter of the procedure by which all the daily miracles of radio are accomplished.

3

GENERAL PROCEDURES

CHAPTER 8

GENERAL PRODUCTION PROCEDURE

THE PROCEDURE in production varies considerably. Different practices are approved in different stations, and even though there might be a common denominator, it would, of necessity, vary with the size of the station, the kind of program, and the budget available. All these are variable factors which must be considered when one sets out to describe production procedure.

An attempt has been made here to set forth a basic procedure which is used, with some variation, in most stations and networks. The pattern is flexible enough to admit almost any kind of program type, although various of the steps in the procedure might be short-circuited in programs which do not involve some of the elements listed here. This outline should be regarded as a basic, all-inclusive procedure. Variations from this procedure must certainly be made in many individual instances, but in each case the variations should be made with a purpose. In general the outline given here is sound for almost any kind of program the production director may be called upon to do.

The Program Is Chosen

It may be chosen by a program planning board. It may be turned in by an advertising agency. It may be an idea dreamed up in the continuity department. Or it may have come directly from the office of the president of the company. Depending on the kind of program and the details of its origin, the production director who is ultimately assigned to do the program may or may not have had any voice in its choosing. In network operations, which are fairly highly specialized, it is somewhat unlikely that the director will have much to do with choosing the program. This may be a matter for the program director or the program planning board. Once the decision has been made to go ahead with the program, then the next logical step is taken.

A Production Director Is Assigned

In most network operations there is a production manager working under the program department. Once a program has been passed for broadcasting, it is turned over to the production manager, who in turn assigns it to a member of his staff to put on the air. Every effort should be, and is, made to assign to a program a director whose particular interest and talent make him useful for that program. This is an ideal to be striven for, but something that is not always achieved in actual practice. Even in fairly large networks, the staff of production directors is usually comparatively small. In such cases sometimes the sheer press of traffic makes it impossible to assign the production director to a program who might do the best job on it. But no matter through what machinery it is done, the second step is the choice of and assignment of a production director to see that the program gets on the air.

The Production Director Studies the Script

Many directors like to read a script through completely before they make any decisions as to how it is to be handled. They read it in an attempt to get a fresh first impression like that which the listener will get when he hears the program. During this first reading the production director makes himself as nearly as possible into the kind of person he visualizes as being the audience for the program. He tries to guess what the audience will like and what it will not like. He tries to estimate the human interest or comic or tragic value in the story. Impressions formed on this first reading may prompt decisions which will govern the entire production. Certainly after the first reading, the production director will begin to have fairly definite ideas about how he wants to handle the program. He will check on its acceptability to the public. He will scrutinize the dramatic structure or the program structure of the script and try to make whatever comments he thinks necessary for the rewriting of the script into acceptable air form. At some time while he is doing the first reading, he will make a preliminary timing in an effort to estimate whether the show needs to be added to or cut. This timing can only be approximate, but it is enough to give the director some idea of how he is going to have to handle time.

On subsequent readings the director will make a very detailed analysis of the script to see what rewriting may have to be done. He will attempt to spot all the technical flaws which must be covered before the script goes into production. These are some of the specific things for which he will watch:

1. Is the opening clear, short, interest-provoking? Is the over-all structure right?
2. Does the program have a good fast start and proceed from minor climaxes to a major climax?
3. Is there proper identification of all the personnel of the program?
4. Have any matters of company policy been missed in the check-over by the continuity department?
5. Is the climax at the close of the program handled deftly and effectively?
6. Are there any unproducible features in the script?
7. Are the sound and music well handled?

On the basis of the decisions made after the preliminary readings, the writer of the script may be called in for a conference and suggestions made for rewriting. Following this conference, a revision of the script is made along the suggested lines and returned to the production director for approval.

All this is predicated on the assumption that there *is* a script. In some kinds of programs, of course, this is not true. In a music program, for example, there is nothing in the beginning except certain talent and a general program idea. The "script" in this case is the music — and this the director will probably choose. In certain round-table programs there is no script. Again a special procedure is called for. What has been said here about the editing process holds true only if a script is the push-off point of the program. Programs which spring from other diving boards will be discussed later.

The Director Makes a Production Analysis

It is at this point that the capability of the production director first displays itself. The caliber of any program on the air is probably determined by the skill and thoroughness of the production analysis. This is where the artistry of the director is displayed. It is the production director's "homework." He will go through the script or program idea again and again until every last decision has been made in his own mind. Once the production analysis is finished, the director should have little further need for making decisions. The rightness or wrongness of his decisions in this session will be the gauge of his power as an artist. Not only will he formulate his basic concept about how the program should be directed, but he will also decide on a hundred details which will then become matters for executive orders and interpretation. The creative process, such as it is in directing, takes place when the director makes his production analysis.

It should be understood here that the term "production analysis" is this author's. It is not a term which is in general use. As a matter of fact, probably very few professional directors sit down and analyze their problems to arrive at decisions regarding any given program. Experience has taught them that certain things need to be done. But even without calling it a production analysis, most directors nevertheless go through something of the process which will be outlined here.

As the first step in his production analysis, the director will establish clearly in his own mind the aim or the end result which he hopes to achieve. To begin by setting a goal to be reached is good tactics. Everything else will be colored by that decision, so it must be made first. To whom is the program directed? What reaction is wanted from that audience? What is the purpose of giving this program to that particular audience?

The decision about the purpose of the program should not

be treated lightly. It is often the case that the establishment of the aim of the program is made by the sponsor or the program department and handed as a readymade goal to the director. If it is not done this way, then the director must make his own decision. This point is more complex than it sounds, because of the multiplicity of reasons for which programs are broadcast. For example, consider a round-table program. Such a program might have as its purpose the indoctrination of the public with certain ideas. It might aim to create intellectual controversy, with resultant consideration of certain issues. It might be designed for the purpose of stirring the minds of the audience about a specific problem. It might be devoted to the primary object of bringing to the radio audience the thoughts and reactions of certain authorities on the question under discussion. Regardless of what the aim may be, it must be clearly established in the mind of the production director, because every subsequent decision he makes will be against this background.

The next thing that the production director must do is to make a decision about the type of production. If it is a dramatic program, he should know whether the play is a comedy, a farce, a melodrama, or a tragedy. If a musical program, he must decide whether he wants a classical program, an all popular program, or some variation between those two. This pigeonholing of the program into certain pre-set purposes has certain drawbacks, but it has the virtue of forcing the production director to a clear decision about the type of program he is going to do.

The next decision is about the basic approach to the problem. The director must establish in his own mind an approach to the show. By production approach we mean the whole general philosophy by which he will attack the program. Having studied the author's intent, he must then see how closely it can be followed. He must decide, if it is a play, whether he is going to treat it realistically, or satirically, or romantically, or with some combination of these. Everything will be keyed to the decisions made on this point.

He must study in detail the structure of the program. Regardless of the kind of show, a careful study of structure should be made. Obviously, the structure of a dramatic program is probably the most complex, but a study of structure should not apply only to dramatic programs. There are sub-climaxes and climaxes in any musical performance, for example. Regardless of the type of program or the purpose for which it is being broadcast, an analysis of its structure is essential. It forms one of the cornerstones of the final job.

The preliminary guiding decisions having been made, the question of talent must be taken up, if this has not already been provided for. Most musical programs use the same basic talent all the time. Hence, the talent, in such a case, would be one of the things the director is given along with the assignment to do the program. However, if talent is needed, careful study must be made of the talent required by the program. Many production directors go to the extent of putting down in outline form the requirements for each person in the broadcast. It is at this point that the director should decide about the talent he will call for auditions. For certain assignments on the program that seem fairly simple, he may call only one person. If there are difficult rôles in the show and he is not sure of his talent, he may call several people for one job or one part. Whatever has to be done to outline the talent requirements of the script at this point, he does.

His study of the talent problem will also give him some notion of schedule. He will make a decision as to how long it will take him to cast the program. In some cases it might be a matter of minutes. In others it might mean searching for a solid week to find exactly the right person for the job.

A Staff Is Assigned to the Program

In some stations the production director may have a choice of staff. In others he may have to take the staff assigned to him. If the production analysis reveals that it is a very difficult program requiring special skill in certain areas, the director will often make a special plea for certain staff members on the ground that they may be more experienced in that particular kind of program. Most stations and networks try to allow the director as much freedom as possible. However, from a practical point of view, it is only under ideal conditions that a director can always select his staff, because of complications with the regular work schedule of any production group. If the production director cannot choose his staff, then he indicates the size and kind of staff he needs to various department heads who, in turn, will assign to him whatever help is called for. Suppose, for example, that an organ is to be used for theme and cue music on a dramatic program. The station staff may boast three organists. If it is possible, the music department will assign to the production director the organist whose background would make him best fitted for the job.

However the assignment of staff may be handled, the director in his production analysis lists the number and kind of people he will need for later requisitioning. Planning well in advance often permits him to get his requests in early enough to secure specific people whom he may want on a given program.

He will decide on his studio needs as a result of the production analysis. The kind or type of program or the number of people in it may necessitate a large studio, or the problem may be so simple and the staff so small that almost any studio would do. As a result of his analysis the production director will indicate in his notes the size of the studio he needs, for the guidance of the person in charge of studio assignments.

Another step is for the director to sketch out, either in his own mind or in a rough diagram on paper, the studio layout which will work best on the program involved. It may be a simple program with one announcer and an engineer. In that case there is no need to worry over a studio setup. On the other hand, some programs are very complex, requiring a number of different pickups from various points in the studio. Then the arrangement of the studio must be so made that each sound source can be picked up independently, with a minimum of cross-talk between microphones. In a complex variety program with music, the matter of studio layout becomes extremely important. The program may call for an orchestra, an elaborate group of sound effects, and a fairly large cast working on two or three different microphones. Carefully thought-out location of equipment is essential. If special effects are used in the program, a detailed and accurate studio layout is all the more helpful. Production directors who have been in the business a long time seldom bother to write such things down. Long years of training have accustomed them to carry many details in their heads.

Problems like the accommodation of a large cast in a small studio necessitate very careful planning. All component parts of the show should be within easy vision line of the control room. The assignment of people to certain places in the studio, the placement of the microphones, and a great many other details must be considered when a studio layout for a program is being prepared.

Along with the studio layouts, the director during his production analysis will make at least a preliminary decision on the mike setups and placement. In his analysis of the show he must solve the pickup problems with a minimum number of microphones. An inexperienced director may have to make a paper solution of his problem and reserve final decision until he can try out his ideas in the studio. A more seasoned director, familiar with acoustics of the studios in which he works, can forecast with reasonable accuracy the results he will be likely to get with any given microphone arrangement.

Some stations keep check charts of various microphone setups from one job to another. These charts are often very helpful to a production director. They can give him an idea of how similar problems have been handled in other productions. The director can get the chart out of the file, study it, and profit by it in forming his own ideas of microphone placement. Matters of studio acoustics, of convenience in handling traffic, of visibility from the control room, all make the microphone setup a troublesome problem. But they are considerations which must be taken into account and provision made for them.

The production director should list any special effects which the program calls for or which he wishes to add to the show. The special effects will usually be the sound department's job, though they may have to go to the musical director or the engineer. At any rate, any special effects are listed and either mental or written notes made about them at this time.

The director must then make some kind of estimate of the amount of rehearsal time necessary for the program. On the basis of this estimate the traffic department or the program director will later assign the proper kind of studio and the amount of time that he needs. Some programs may require practically no rehearsal at all. Others may need a lot of rehearsal time. This, of course, depends upon the complexity of the program and the number of people involved. It will be different for each kind of program.

The production director next studies and makes the final decision on the handling of the sound. There are, of course, many kinds of programs in which sound is not used. In that case obviously this part of the production procedure would be omitted. In looking over the script, the director may accept all the writer's suggestions about sound, he may add some of his own ideas, or he might throw out all the sound indicated in the script and write in his own sound pattern. This would represent an extreme case, but it has been known to happen. How much sound the director will use and how he will use it will depend on the kind of script he has and his production approach to it. At any rate, during the production analysis the entire pattern of sound is worked out on paper and planned for later rehearsal and execution.

If music is involved in the program, the same process must be followed. It may be a musical program, in which case this process becomes the number-one step in the entire production procedure. Music is chosen, and only *after* that is done can the director proceed. Everything thereafter is tailored to the music. If it is a dramatic program, the production director will look at each spot where the writer has indicated music in the script. He will first decide whether or not he will use music

If he decides to use it as the script indicates, then he must decide what kind to use. These decisions will be colored by his budget and the talent available. He may add other music cues which the author did not indicate. He may cut certain music cues and substitute sound or some other transitional or background treatment. Out of this study will come notes copious enough so that when the director sits down with the music director, he will have specific recommendations to make of exactly the kind of music he wants, how long he wants it, and the specific feel of the music cues in each place in the script. This detailed preparation makes it possible for him to speak to the musical director with definiteness and authority.

The detail with which a production director will plan, and the decisions about music, will depend on several factors which vary in each situation. In general, the more capable his music director the more the production director can leave in his hands. If a capable musical director is available, the production man might do little more than indicate the approximate kind of the music he wants and the general feel of it, leaving the actual execution to the musical director, subject always to his approval. If he feels that the staff assigned to him is not completely competent, he may do a very detailed analysis of each music cue and hand to the music director a complete description of each bit of music, even including suggestions for instrumentation and references to musical passages that might net the proper cues. Whether it is only a cursory job to guide the music director or a complete analysis, the decisions must be made at the time when the production director can study his script in peace and quiet.

The next and final step in the production analysis is the making of provisional cuts. It is difficult to estimate very closely the playing time of a script by simply reading it. Even when the cast does it in reading rehearsal later on, only an approximate timing can be achieved. If the director is able to get his script to within a minute of his final timing at this point he is doing well. It should be noted here that if any allowance is made, it should be on the side of generosity. It is easier to cut a long script than it is to stretch a short one. In actual production, the reverse is true. Any production director would rather be ten or fifteen seconds ahead than to be behind that much on the air. Picking up time is a difficult process and one that may easily show up in the production on the air. But a program can be stretched twenty or thirty seconds over a half-hour period without much apparent damage to the final results, provided it is done skillfully, and if the stretch is made over the whole program. However, at this stage of the game it is much better to have a little extra script or music with which to work. Stretching a script thirty seconds is not difficult. Stretching it two or three minutes means adding material and this is a difficult job for the production director to do. It is rightly in the province of the continuity department. Therefore, the production director should be sure when he edits the script in the first place that he has enough material.

The director should, if he is a good workman, have certain possible cuts all ready and marked out in his script. These should be made while he is doing his production analysis, when he can give considered attention to the best places in which to make cuts. If it is possible to do so, the production director should make provisional cuts of varying length. If he can find a thirty-seconds cut all in one place, and add to that two or three of fifteen seconds and two or three of ten seconds and a couple of five seconds, he is in a position to "make change" when it comes to bringing the program to time in the final rehearsal stage. If he is, for instance, forty-five seconds over, he can then bring his program to time by making only two cuts. He can cut his spot of thirty seconds and one of his spots of fifteen seconds and without any further to-do, the program is on time.

Too many production directors ignore this little mechanical detail of preparation, which is unimportant in the final rehearsal stages if you are ready for it and may be a matter of paramount importance if you are not ready for it. Many production directors spend the last fifteen minutes before a broadcast tearing their hair while trying to find spots to bring a program down to time. They are, in the meantime, giving their company the jitters, they are taking chances on last-minute changes which cannot be rehearsed, and they are taking the highly paid time of talent to do a job which they could have done much better in the quiet of their offices.

By the time the production director has completed his analysis, he should have all the answers he needs to put his program on the air. He is familiar with the structure of the entire program with which he is working. He knows who his staff is going to be and is prepared to talk to each of them. He knows how much physical equipment and space he needs and for how long. He knows the exact disposition of all his elements of sound within the space which he has requisitioned. He is prepared to talk to the sound department and to the music department and to make specific requests of them. And he is prepared to bring his program within the time allotted. All this is done in an unhurried, thorough manner well ahead of the hustle and rush of actual rehearsals.

The Script Is Duplicated

By this time all the changes in the script which can be foreseen at the moment are made. The director has requested a rewrite from the author and he has made his own notes and changes in the rewritten version that he thinks will stand when the program goes on the air. Having arrived at this point he is now ready to have the script duplicated. The production director's only responsibility here is to decide on the number of copies he will need and to see that a master copy of the script gets to the duplicating department. This is done by mimeographing, multigraphing, hectographing, or, in some cases, merely by making carbon copies on the typewriter. However it is done, enough copies of the script must be provided for the director's company plus the number of copies required for filing purposes. It is always better to allow for a few extra scripts than to be too miserly in the estimate. Even professional talent has been known to lose script. Requests may come in from responsible people for copies of broadcast which the station or network wishes to oblige.

It is an interesting fact that after twenty-two years of radio broadcasting, the industry has developed no standardized format for the typing of a script. This is true in spite of the fact that much of the talent on radio is free-lance, working in all the studios in a given city. This would argue for some kind of uniformity among stations and networks.

Certain provisions should always be made in the duplicating of scripts. The title of the program and the number of the page should appear on each page of the script. It is helpful if each line of the script is numbered. This is the quickest, most accurate means by which the production director can refer to a specific spot in the script. All sound effects, music cues, and stage directions should be clearly separated from the lines which are to be spoken by the members of the cast or company. The common practice is to put into lowercase everything that is to be said over the air, reserving CAPS for instructions, for sound and music cues, and for the names of the characters who are to speak. Talent learns to make the eyes skip over the capitalized lines and not read them on the air. Perhaps the student of this volume may be able to do a little missionary work in the matter of establishing a common format for the reproduction of scripts. A common system of typography might be beneficial to the entire industry. Certainly there is no reason for not taking advantage of the small mechanical details of composition which will facilitate rehearsal and obviate mistakes on the air.

The Staff Is Chosen

At this point in the procedure a staff is assigned to the program. As was indicated earlier, the manner of assignment varies from one broadcasting organization to another, depending upon the way in which a staff operates. Though in most organizations an effort at least is made to give the production director the people he wants to work with, it is usually the job of the heads of the other departments to make the final decision as to what staff members will be assigned to what programs. Practical matters of union hours and schedules must be taken into consideration as well as normal traffic problems. In rare cases the program director or production manager might take exception to the production director's judgment of the amount of staff needed. This will happen rarely, however, and is not a serious problem.

Space and Equipment Is Scheduled

At the National Broadcasting Company, a special clerk is responsible for the assignment of studio space. The man assigned to sound effects on a program will clear with his chief and see that proper equipment needed for the show is free at the time of rehearsal and broadcast. He is also responsible for seeing that that equipment is in the studios and in operating condition in plenty of time to start the rehearsal when it is called. The engineering department sees to it that proper microphones and all the other engineering equipment is in the studios, installed and ready to be used at the time the rehearsal is called. This whole process of scheduling is more a matter of traffic than anything else and is often handled in a routine manner by certain departments in the organization.

Staff Conferences

The next step in the production procedure is a series of conferences between the production director and his various department heads. In the series of conferences with the sound technician, the engineer, the musical director, or whichever of them are involved in the program, the director will outline his approach to the program as he has determined it in his production analysis. Detailed discussions of the points which affect each department will create good understanding between the director and those who must work with him. There is no standard procedure for the handling of the conferences. Sometimes a general conference is called in which all the department heads working on a show meet for a common discussion. Sometimes individual discussions are held between the production director and the individual department heads involved. Sometimes a two-minute chat while waiting for an elevator will suffice. The handling of that matter is for the individual to decide. In some cases it is more economical to get a whole group together and talk the program over. In others it is merely a useless waste of time. The decision on this should normally rest with the director in charge of the program.

The Script Markup

At about this stage of the game, the production director will sit down and mark up a master production script. This process simply puts into symbols and notes on his script all the plans for executing what he has worked out in detail in his production analysis. There is no standard system for marking up scripts. Many production directors work so much in detail that by the time they have their plan complete they have memorized it, and they use almost no markup at all. Others make copious notes and numerous signals to themselves on their script. This is a matter for individual tastes. It is only necessary that the director have all his decisions at his fingertips. If he can crowd it all into his memory, fine. If he cannot, then his script should be so marked that he knows exactly what he had planned to do with each line and each sound and each music cue in the program. If the production schedule is not too heavy, a director may very well memorize his entire production. If, as is so often the case, he may be working on several shows simultaneously, this may be impossible.

To avoid confusion and misunderstanding, certain things should be definitely marked. For example, all the places in the script where the director wants cues taken from control should be indicated. He may want to indicate cross-fades or montage treatments or any of the other special techniques he plans to use. He may even want to mark up in marginal notes climactic speeches and indicate rhythm and tempo of individual scenes and of over-all tempo. Practice differs widely here. The only requirement is that he have his entire plan where he can get at it.

Where students of production directing are working on a script and it becomes desirable to change student-directors in mid-rehearsal, it is wise to have some kind of a common mark-up system so that everyone understands the marks of everyone else. This is a purely pedagogical necessity and is not, of course, obligatory in professional production directing.

Auditions Are Set Up

The next step in the production procedure is to arrange for auditions for casting talent. The production director may have to get on the phone and call his own prospective cast. If he is working in a large station or a network office there is probably a casting clerk whose job it is to contact talent. In such a case he indicates either the people or the type of people he wants and says when auditions will be held. Most production directors soon become familiar with the available talent, and for almost every part they are called upon to cast, they have certain specific suggestions. They would like to hear Actor X and Actor Y and Actor Q, and they might also tell the person in charge of calling that if he has any additional ideas to include them in the call.

A studio must be scheduled for casting auditions and an engineer must be present. A definite time is set when the program will be cast. The more foresighted a production director can be about getting his cast call well ahead of time, the better off he is. There are two reasons for this. The good talent is always in demand, and if a director wants to assure himself of a top-flight cast, he must put out his call far enough ahead so that he can have a chance to get some of the people he wants. Also, if the casting is done fairly early, it gives the publicity department a chance to publicize the program. Casting done at the last minute has little publicity value.

It is wise to announce the rehearsal schedule when people are called for casting. In this way, if they already have previous engagements that will conflict, they can be saved the time and energy of auditioning for your show.

Casting

Both in making cast calls and in the actual process of auditioning for casting, the principles of selection discussed earlier in this chapter should be kept in mind. These are the basic principles that will govern the production director in the choice of people for any given program.

A production director will do well to get his scripts to his auditionees one day before they come to the studio for tryouts. This is an ideal which is not always possible because of the press of time, but it does give cast members a chance to study for the rôle for which they are being considered and allow them to do a better job on first audition. It will also give the production director a better idea of who is likely to be a flash-in-the-pan actor and who is likely to grow with the part.

Casting is not a process which should be rushed. On the other hand, there is much useless waste of time in casting when the production director is not properly prepared for the job. The director should be able to make a precise fifty-word statement of exactly what the program is all about. He must be able to sum up for the entire list of auditionees the heart of the broadcast and what he as director wants to do with it. He should then outline succinctly and concisely the need for each person in the company. If it is a dramatic play, he should have his characters pegged and specific descriptions of them ready. It takes time to ad-lib a description of a character. A careful, methodical director will often write out or have typed concise descriptions of various characters in the play being cast. These might even be sent out with the script if it goes out ahead of time. They give the actor or other talent a specific and concrete set of specifications of what the director wants. A director should also have at hand a list of spots in the script which he wants to use as tryout material. If this is all typed in advance of casting, the director will save himself a lot of lost motion and casting time.

There are some basic principles which should govern all casting regardless of what kind of program is being set up. The first rule is to cast on mike, always. Since the program is ultimately to be aired over a microphone and through amplifiers and loud-speakers, it is under those conditions that the cast should be chosen. Second, the production director must observe the rule of contrast. He dare not cast two excellent actors, both capable of doing good work, if their voices are too similar. If the item of contrast is ignored, it will only confuse the listener, regardless of the excellence of the individual jobs of the two people.

The actors cast or the talent chosen should all be in the same key. Except for comedy purposes it would be bad business to cast a heavy, oldtime, Shakespearean type of actor with a modern, flip, glib comedy actor. All the people called presumably will be pretty much in the same key. That is to say, they will all be people who can play together and make the audience accept them as people who would probably be together in a common scene.

The production director must constantly guard against the flash-in-the-pan performer. This is the kind of person who does a brilliant job on audition, but never progresses an inch beyond his first audition, having within himself no capability of growth. On the other hand, some people who do not make an outstanding showing on audition may be the kind who will grow until their final results bear little resemblance to the quality with which they started. It improves and richens and deepens as the rehearsals progress. Everything else being equal, this is the kind of person the production director looks for.

Not only contrast but variety must be sought in the selection of people to go into a program. There should be enough different kinds of talent to provide an interesting pattern of sound. This matter of over-all variety is important, because the ear likes a change of sound quality in the same way and for the same reason that the eye likes a change of sight quality. That is the reason that movies seldom hold one camera angle more than thirty or forty seconds. The constantly changing visual approach lends interest and excitement to the story being told. The parallel situation is true in radio where a constant change in voices not only helps to distinguish characters, but gives the whole sound pattern an interesting variety which is pleasing to the ears of an audience.

It should not be necessary to warn the production director that courtesy is due auditionees. Unfortunately, this basic tenet of decent behavior is not always observed. Production directors who are not the capable, understanding people they should be may make the mistake of assuming that because they have the power of hiring they are also obliged to be rude to auditioning talent. The director should always remember that he has to work with the company. The more he is liked and respected, the more and better work he can get from his company. One does not gain respect by being rude to people.

Talent should not be held any longer than necessary in an audition. It is bad management for a director to hear an actor who obviously will not do and then keep him sitting around the studio for another hour while presumably making up his mind and hearing other people. He will do the actor a service by telling him he is not what is wanted at once rather than letting him sit around and wait in doubt. Many free-lance actors have several engagements a day and the director will do well to be considerate of them in this respect.

In the casting process it is quite permissible to do a little directing just to see if you can help an actor approach what you want. After all, one of the things that the director wants to know, if he does not already know, is how the actor can take direction. Hence it is worth doing a little directing while casting is going on, just to determine how a new person can take direction. It must never amount to rehearsing the show. Talent must and should be paid for that.

Certain mechanical details must also be taken care of at the time the casting is done. Once the director has selected the cast, several things must be made clear. Rehearsal schedules must be announced. A repetition of the rehearsal schedule should be made at the end of the casting call to be sure that all members of the company can make all rehearsals. All other matters of importance to the company, such as how they shall dress for the broadcast and what time they have available between rehearsals, should be completely announced.

The Final Selection of Music

Sometime in the production procedure the director will sit down with the musical director or his organist, or whoever is furnishing the music for the program, and listen to the music which has been chosen. The production director may ask for certain changes, may turn down, or may accept the work, and he may do this with each cue. For one cue he may say that it is exactly what he wants. In another cue he may wish the addition or subtraction of a few bars. A third cue he may vote out completely. This process is kept up until there is agreement between the production director and the musical director about all the music involved in the program.

The Sound Is Finally Selected

The same process outlined for music is repeated for the sound effects. If the sound is comparatively unimportant and fairly standard, such a prerehearsal check of sound may not be necessary. After all, most of the standard sound effects are repeated by the sound effects department dozens of times a day. They can be done on cue without rehearsal. Effects of this kind can be taken for granted by the production director.

If there is some unusual sound, or sound which may be particularly difficult in cueing, the production director may choose to hear it and pass on it. If there are sound routines about which he is in doubt, they should be listened to and straightened out. Sometimes it is difficult to make a final decision on a sound routing until it is actually heard in conjunction with the lines. In this case it is always wise to have a provisional substitute plan ready so that time will not be lost in the critical last minutes before dress rehearsal.

A careful production director will check everything that has anything, even remotely, to do with his broadcast. If it is to be watched by a studio audience and tickets are issued, the careful director may check on the number of tickets given out, to be sure that he has a good house, but not more than the studio will accommodate. In a large network, where the page staff or guide service is used to handling studio audiences, the production director can usually take efficient handling of audiences for granted. In a less elaborate setup, such details, which are of no importance to the production *per se*, may need to be checked by the production director himself. Certainly if there is any item that can influence the production in any way, the question should be raised and solved by him as early in the process as possible.

The Program Is Rehearsed

Naturally, rehearsal routines vary considerably with the type of program to be produced. Some programs, by their very nature, cannot be rehearsed. Some may have to be rehearsed meticulously over a period of days. Between these two extremes the general average of procedure can be outlined here. It should be understood that this is only a hypothetical rehearsal schedule; it might be condensed into fifteen minutes or expanded into fifteen days, depending on the demands of the script or program.

The first step in the rehearsal process is for the talent to get acquainted with the material. In a dramatic program this may mean a table reading of the script. In a musical program it may mean for the musicians to play through the music for the first time. In a round-table program it is probably a preliminary discussion of the topic by the participants in an effort to clarify their ideas. For any program it is the process of getting the talent and the material together for the first time. How this is done, and exactly what is done, will depend on the type of material and the type of talent.

Also in this first rehearsal period a rough timing should be made so that the production director will know, in general, whether he will have to cut or expand the material to fill the allotted period.

The next important step is the microphone rehearsal. At this point the production director and his talent part company. The director retires to the control room where he can hear the rehearsal over the mikes and the talent, of course, stays in the

On the Air

Having completed this much of the production procedure, the program is now ready to take the air. A thoughtful production director will never rehearse directly up to air time. It is always wise to give a cast a little time to get their breath and rearrange their scripts and get out of the studio before broadcasting time. Therefore, the final dress rehearsal should be scheduled so that a period of five to fifteen minutes is available before air time. Besides giving the cast time to freshen up and get ready to do a good job on the air, this grace period gives the production director a chance to check over the last-minute details which so often arise. During this time he can talk to members of his company about final corrections. He can check with his engineer on exact signals for getting the show on and taking it off. He can check with his sound man on any details that he wants changed or adjusted. He can check over the timing on his script. All these things can be handled if the director allows himself a little grace period prior to the broadcast.

It is wise to have the entire company in the studio at least two minutes ahead of air time. A cast member may be very responsible and be in his exact place at the right microphone when the program goes on the air. But if he is not in the studio thirty seconds before air time and comes wandering in exactly on the nose, it does something to upset the equilibrium of a director. It is a healthy practice to give the company a stand-by warning at one minute and again at thirty seconds. Amateurs watching professional production directing should not be taken in by the ease and offhandedness with which these things are done. There is little surface excitement and no feverish dashing back and forth in the last minutes before broadcasts in a well-run program. It is all done casually and easily.

The production director should take his show on the nose. That means that he should be ready to start his program at the exact time that he is supposed to start it. He must wait until he has the go-ahead from his engineer before he can proceed. Even if this means delaying the start of the broadcast several seconds, it must be done. There is no use starting a program until that studio is connected into the master control room or the transmitter or wherever the program is being sent. In network operations this almost invariably happens right on the nose.

During the broadcast the control room should be kept absolutely quiet. The production director must concentrate. He has a list of myriad details to which he must attend and he must constantly be listening to the program. Every sound in the control room which is not a part of the program should be eliminated. Many directors will not allow anyone in their control room except their engineer. Others are a little more lenient, but in nearly every case they insist upon absolute quiet from any guest or spectator. Certainly the practice of having extra people in the control room should not be encouraged. Even when they are absolutely quiet and motionless, they may inhibit a production director or distract him unwittingly. Too much happens too fast in radio for this kind of distraction to be allowed. Any production director is well within his rights to ask anybody to leave his control room that he does not want there.

During the airing of the program the production director makes a constant check on time. The secret of easy timing of a radio program consists in correcting errors before they get too large. It is unwise to allow a program ever to get more than ten or fifteen seconds off. Ten seconds can be picked up easily. Thirty seconds may be insurmountable. The problem of time, of course, varies widely with various kinds of programs. In some every element of the program is rehearsed and timed down to the last few seconds. On others nothing but the roughest sort of timing is available before the program airs, and it is up to the ingenuity and skill of the production director to see that the program comes off at the appointed minute and second.

Time adjustments should be applied where they are the least

noticeable. They need not necessarily be adjusted when they are first noticed. For example, suppose you are producing a dramatic program and you suddenly discover that your leading man has slowed up his pace and you are fifteen seconds behind. The scene which is playing may be such a delicate one that you are afraid to tamper with it by asking your cast to speed up. In that case you need only to hold them steady on that pace and prevent further loss of time until that scene is finished. While the program is on, you can look ahead and find a place in the script where you think the pace can be picked up to good advantage. When that place occurs, the speed-up signal will put the show back on time.

Care should also be exercised in the handling of time with various members of the cast. A production director may soon discover in a rehearsal that some of his cast members can speed up or slow down very easily; others are so fixed in their time pattern that any attempt to change their timing will destroy their handling of the lines. Therefore, the director must ask those members of his company who can do it most easily to make his time adjustments for him. The making of time adjustments during a program should be handled as a matter of routine. No director, no matter how much he is suffering inside, should make it apparent to his company that he is worried about time. That is his job and his responsibility and not that of his company. If he displays a great deal of concern over it in the control room, it will tend to disconcert his company and they may do a ragged job. No matter how tough the time problem becomes, it should not become apparent to the cast in the studio. They may be asked to speed up or slow down or make adjustments, but these adjustments should be asked for calmly and in a matter-of-fact manner. If the company once senses that the timing of a program is all off and that the director is worried about it, they will let it have a bad effect on their work.

The matter of keeping a program on time is one of the greatest concerns of the beginning production director. After a director has five hundred shows to his credit, he will learn that time is a thing which can be played with. It can be molded and condensed or stretched in such a way that the audience is seldom aware of it and in such a way that the program always ends on time. Time becomes something which can be handled easily and unobtrusively. Nevertheless, it must be handled!

Every production director should so conduct himself in the control room during a broadcast that he inspires confidence in his company in the studio. No matter how badly he is attacked by the green jitters, the company must never see it. If something goes wrong during a broadcast, a director must not rage and make frantic motions or tear his hair. This will not fix the mistake and it will do little to inspire confidence in the company member who made the mistake. Few people make mistakes deliberately on the air. They are trying to do their best. The director must recognize this and give them confidence and encouragement during a performance rather than express criticism and rage in pantomime through the control-room window. No matter how badly a program is going on the air, confidence and encouragement are what the director must create. Only in that way can his company do the best job of which it is capable.

During all the checking of time and the watching of balances and the throwing of cues which go on during a broadcast, the production director must reserve a part of his mind to listen objectively to the sound coming out of his monitor speaker and evaluate it as disinterestedly as possible. He must always keep in mind his audience. As C. L. Menser, vice-president in charge of programs for NBC, says, he must put himself in the position of the "little lady in Oskaloosa, Iowa, who is listening to the program." In the midst of all the hurly-burly he must still listen objectively, and say to himself, "Does this make sense? Do I understand what is going on? If I could turn this off, would I keep on listening to it?" The maintenance of this kind of objectivity in the rush and tension of a broadcast is difficult, but the success of a director is often measured by his ability to do just that.

Cueing

Something should be said here about cueing. The production director can do much to eliminate errors and keep a show running smoothly by the way he handles the cues which he gives to his company. A few basic rules will help immeasurably in making cueing satisfactory. First, a cue should be definite and not tentative. Do not make two or three false starts before you actually give the cue. To do so upsets the timing of the members of your company. Never give a cue without first making eye contact with the person for whom it is intended. If the director has his nose in the script, he may cue accurately and concisely, but he may throw a cue at the precise second when the actor looks away momentarily. Second, make the cue direct. Point right at the person who is to get the cue. In case the studio is so arranged that two or three people are working one behind the other and there may be some question about who gets what cue, arrange special signals so that each member of the company will be sure of the cue which is coming to him or her. Third, execute cues in the way the response is wanted. If a line is to be grabbed, give the actor a quick, concise-cue gesture. If it is to be taken easily and slowly, give the cue in the same way. If you want volume suddenly faded up, give the volume increase cue vigorously, and if the fade-out is to be slow and gradual, make the fade signal the same way. A company will unconsciously follow the director's manner of cueing in their handling of the lines.

Finally, during a broadcast the director should watch the studio, the control room, the company – not the script! Some directors prefer to work without a script and memorize every cue. Most directors work with a script, but they dare not keep their eyes glued to it during the entire broadcast. The script is there only as a reminder of what is to be done – not as a detail sheet to be followed slavishly. The director should know his script so well that a casual glance at the page will tell him what is coming up. Thereafter he watches his company, his engineer, his announcer, his sound man, his music director. Those are the elements upon which he must keep watch and with whom he must establish *rapport.*

A great deal has been made in fan magazines and articles on radio of the system of hand signals by which the production director communicates with the various members of his company. This system of hand signals has been regarded as a kind of secret-service code for the radio industry. As a matter of fact, it is nothing of the sort. It is a utilitarian means of silent communication between the control room and the studio to relay such simple information as may be necessary for the adjustment of an element of a radio program. Every office seems to have its own peculiar system of cues and hand signals, and many of them are not universally accepted. There are a few, however, which have not only been universally accepted by radio, but which have come to be widely used in a slang sense outside of radio, and have, in fact, become an addition to the language itself. It should be understood that hand signals can be improvised as they are needed, provided only that the production director remembers to tell the cast what they mean before he uses them. Every time a peculiar situation arises, it may necessitate the creation of some kind of signal for a specific purpose only. This can be done as needed. The following signals are fairly standard and will be understood by anyone in the business.

Stand by. This is a preparatory signal which can be used to precede other cues. Its common use, however, is to warn the company of the first cue which will put the program on the air. The cue consists of simply raising the arm above the head vertically.

Cue. The cue is simply the go-ahead signal to execute whatever should be done at the particular time. A cue may be given to any member of the company for any purpose. The member of the company will know what to do because of the context of the script itself, and he simply waits for an order to do it from the production director. A cue consists of pointing at the person who is to execute it. It should be done from the stand-by position. When the arm is upraised in the stand-by position, it is merely lowered to horizontal, the finger pointing to the person involved. That is all there is to it.

Speed up. If the production director wishes the company or any member of it to pick up the tempo, he indicates it by rotating an index finger clockwise. If he needs a considerable amount of time picked up, he will rotate it rapidly. If he needs just a little time picked up, he will rotate his finger slowly. The manner of execution indicates the degree of the need.

Slow down. The signal to slow down the tempo or to stretch the time is indicated by a gesture which looks as though the production director were stretching a rubber band between his two hands. Again, the manner of execution will not only indicate what needs to be done, but how much time needs to be stretched.

On the nose. This term has been absorbed into the language as slang and is familiar to almost everyone. When the production director touches his index finger to the tip of his nose, he means that the program is running on time.

Move closer to the microphone. This direction can be given to the company by placing the hand in front of the face, palm inward. This tells whoever is performing in the studio to move closer to the microphone.

Move back from the microphone. This direction is given by placing the hand in front of the face, palm outward, and tells whoever is performing to back away from the microphone.

More volume or louder. The indication for more volume is given by extending the arm with the palm upward and raising the hand either slowly or quickly to indicate how much more volume is needed. This cue may be used to sound, music, or cast as the case may be.

Less volume or more softly. This direction is indicated by extending the arm with the palm down and dropping the hand gently or quickly, depending on the manner in which the direction is to be executed.

Okay, or everything is all right. This is the signal which every performer hopes to get from his production director in the control room. It is a circle made with the thumb and index finger extended toward the studio. This is another gesture which has been popularly absorbed outside of radio and nearly everyone is familiar with it. The okay can be used in a hundred different ways during the broadcast. It will answer an unspoken or gestured question from the floor. It will terminate any kind of adjustment made by other cues. For example, if the production director signals an actor to move into the microphone, and the actor starts doing so, as soon as he has reached a satisfactory level, the production director will give him the okay signal. The signal is frequently used to indicate to the company on the studio floor that everything is going well and it is also used as a signal of encouragement.

Cut. The cut signal simply means that the production director wants something or somebody to stop. It is indicated by drawing the index finger slowly across the throat. It can be used to terminate anything from a complete broadcast to any part of it, depending on the circumstances under which it is given. To avoid mistakes, it is sometimes preceded by the cue signal. For instance, the production director points to the sound man and gives the cut signal, which means he wants a particular sound stopped. If some members of the cast are doing a crowd effect behind the dialogue, he may point to them all and give the cut signal to stop the crowd effect.

Conclude with the chorus. This is the cue given to musicians or a music director to indicate that the production director wishes the number concluded at the end of the chorus. This direction is indicated by raising the arm with the fist clenched. This cue is also used in some places to signal the network announcer to give the network cue, which is usually the announcement of the name of the network. This use of the cue is not universal, however.

Play the theme. This direction is given to the musical director by making a rough "T" with the thumb and index finger. Some production directors use the index fingers of both hands to make a "T" for indicating this signal. It tells the musical conductor to start playing the music.

Use the first ending and repeat the chorus. This direction is also used only to the musical director or musicians and tells them that the music needs to be stretched to the extent of repeating a whole chorus. The cue is made by holding up one index finger to the musical director.

Use the second ending and conclude. This is another musical direction which is self-explanatory. It is made to the musical director. It is indicated by simply holding up two fingers with the rest of the hand clenched.

Used along with the specific signals, and equally as effective, are the facial expressions and pantomime which the production director will unconsciously use in conjunction with his cues. A smile and an encouraging nod in conjunction with an easy speed-up signal will tell the talent that only a little speed-up is needed. A vigorous nodding of the head and a frown accompanying a vigorous speed-up signal may indicate that the situation is serious and that the talent must race as fast as possible. The production director will find himself using all sorts of pantomime to get his ideas over. If the direction is a complicated one, he may even resort to writing it out on a piece of paper and holding it up to the control-room glass for someone to read and relay to the proper member. For all normal purposes, however, the standard cues will suffice and they are familiar to everyone who does professional radio work.

Paper Work

There is a certain amount of paper work for which the production director is responsible in almost every station or network. There is always the matter of station policy to be checked. This, in networks, is usually checked by the continuity acceptance department. They are human, however, and do miss things. There is also the curious circumstance of copy which sounds differently and may have different connotations when read aloud than when it is read in print. In all matters like this, the production director is the final court of appeal. He must also time all commercials, he must sign the music sheet, he must sign the master copies of the script, and file a complete corrected version of the program as broadcast. He must file a talent report indicating who worked on the program. If there were any errors in the program or any times off the air or any other irregularities, a written report on these must be made. In some networks the exact timing on each musical number or occurrence of music on the program must be recorded. Whatever paper work is required by the station and the network must be done by the production director and actual air checks made on all the items while the program is on the air.

Managing the Show

The production director must remain flexible during the program. This is particularly true in the case of comedy and audience-participation programs. It is also true to a limited extent in dramatic programs. Sometimes on the air things happen unexpectedly which may be good. A comedian may start ad-libbing from the script and develop a brilliant series of gags spontaneously. The seasoned production director will listen to these spontaneous outbursts, evaluate them, and then do something about them. Either he will allow them to go on and make proper adjustments in his program or he will try to get the company back on the script. In audience-participation shows completely unexpected things sometimes happen, and the director must be able to handle them and to take advantage of the good parts of spontaneous accidents on the air. Sometimes actors hit an inspired performance which may result in a somewhat radical change in the timing of certain scenes. If the timing is good and seems to fit with what has gone before, a good production director who is experienced in his work may accept it, even though it is different from the rehearsal, and then make proper adjustments later on for time so that the program does not lose by the variation. No matter what happens, the production director must be flexible enough in his ideas to accept what is good and fix very quickly what is bad.

At all times the good production director will keep a firm,

if unobtrusive, grip on his program. This need not mean bullying a company into complete subjection. Rather it should give them a satisfying sense of working under a director who knows his business. A director who insists on tight control over his company can exercise the control in such a way as to give a company confidence and sureness or to irritate them. It is firm management which gives the company assurance which should be striven for.

It is always a good practice to keep five or ten seconds leeway in time available. If the program is ten seconds under, it can be easily stretched to end on the nose. If it is ten seconds over, adjustment is more difficult. Most production directors prefer to have a little time leeway to play with. If the show is just a little bit under, it removes the feeling of pressure which can be very distracting to a director.

Finally and above all, the program should end on the nose. In the case of a network program the time is usually known. The usual sign-off time is thirty seconds before the hour ends; in some cases the chimes or network signature comes in twenty seconds before the next program. Whatever the predetermined time is, it should be met accurately. If there is any variation it should be on the under side. A show should never run over time.

After the Broadcast

The production director's first duty is to his company. It is good policy and good public relations to thank your company for a good job. If you do not feel that they have done a good job, you may not want to be hypocritical enough to give them a pat on the back, but do not make the mistake of going into a critique session immediately after a broadcast. In most cases, if the company has made a sincere effort you owe them thanks for the job. Every production director should strive on every show to get from his company the "plussage" which makes for an outstanding program. If he gets it, he owes the company thanks for it. If they have done a good job they will appreciate the thanks. If they have not, this is no time for severe criticism. Incidentally, do not forget the bit part players, the people with minor jobs on the broadcast, the sound crew, and the engineer. They are all a part of the company and deserve consideration.

Do not try to hold critical sessions in the immediate post-broadcast period. The company is not ready for it. They are too excited and keyed up from the program to sit down calmly and analyze it. They have not had time to build up objectivity and aesthetic distance from their job. In most cases the criticisms will be individual and not group criticisms, and they should be delivered privately. It is both desirable and healthful to schedule a play-back on a program whenever this is possible. If the program is recorded, the cast may be told when a play-back will be available or a poll may be taken as to the time when the company can all get together to hear it. Professional actors do not do enough of this kind of thing. The best ones, however, are always eager to get a critical check on their work. And nothing is so critical or so objective as a recording of a broadcast.

Immediately following the broadcast the director should make a final check of the script to see that there is a corrected copy as broadcast, that it is signed, and that the music sheet is also signed. This is a part of the paper work. If there is additional paper work, see that it and all reports are filed promptly. In case something has gone wrong with the broadcast, an immediate report of the mishap should be made. If the broadcast occurs during the day, an immediate call to the production or program office is indicated. If something goes wrong with an evening broadcast when the offices are closed, the report should be on the production or program desk by nine o'clock the next morning. This allows the responsible person in charge to know what has gone on within his organization and to meet comment and criticism from the outside with full knowledge of the facts. In large network organizations sometimes program directors or production managers are called to account for something which has happened on a program about which they know nothing. Prompt reports from production directors give them all the ammunition they need to answer any questions which may arise. It is protection for the production director and also for his superior.

4

APPLICATION OF PROCEDURE

CHAPTER 9

THE PRODUCTION OF TALKS PROGRAMS

THUS FAR, this book has been concerned with the general principles which apply to all kinds of production directing, and with laying down the broad outlines within which all the activity of production must occur. It is now necessary to see how those broad principles are applied to specific production problems and specific program types.

One more understanding must, however, be reached with the reader. Production directing is a term which usually has network connotations. Local-station men shudder at the word. They will insist — some of them — that there is no such thing as production in a local station. It is true that there is no "production" in the network sense of hiring a cast of eight or ten actors, an orchestra of twenty-five pieces, a high-priced script writer, and a network production director to produce a program. Nevertheless, there is a considerable amount of "production" done in a local station every day. In essence there is production work going on every time a program originates at the station. In this section of the book an effort will be made to cover all kinds of production situations, local as well as network. The same job which a production director on a network may be assigned to do might fall to the announcer at a local station, but it will still be considered production.

One of the simplest programs to produce and one which occurs frequently on all kinds of stations is the talks program. Since it is one of the easiest, it is a logical place for the first production attempt to be made.

How, then, does one produce a talks program? That question cannot be answered except in the light of a second question: What kind of talks program? Specific procedure can be suggested only in specific situations. Each kind of talks program involves certain problems and they must be dealt with accordingly. In order to classify the various kinds of talks programs for purposes of discussion, the following outline may be helpful:

1. Straight talk
   a. A staff member speaks
      One of the announcers does a news program; the woman announcer does a "Household Hints" program; the farm director talks about crops. In each case the speaker is a professional radio person.
   b. An outsider comes to the studio to speak
      The director of the Community Chest makes an appeal for funds; the president of the Literary Club does a book review; a minister does a sermon on the air. In each case the speaker is not a professional radio person, but comes to the studios to speak.
   c. A series of talks.
   d. A remote pickup of an outside speaker.
2. The interview
   a. A visiting celebrity is brought to the studio for an interview.
   b. The radio goes to the interviewee
      Before the war every station had a "Man-on-the-Street" program. Radio goes into plants now to interview workers and for many other kinds of on-the-spot interviewing.
   c. Feature programs may be built on the interview form.
      A case in point is "Hobby Lobby."
   d. Educational or instructional programs can be built on the interview format. Any subject from "How to bake a cake" to "Fire prevention" may be exposited in the interview form.
3. Round-table programs
   a. Continued programs built on a definite format.
   b. Single programs growing out of special subject matter or situations.
4. The Forum or Town Hall type of program
5. Audience-participation programs
   Some such programs involve music. These will be treated

in the chapter on variety programs. Here only all-talk programs will be discussed, such as:

a. Quiz programs
b. Spelling bees
c. Stunt programs

One of the most difficult problems in producing talks programs is to overcome the hazard of their simplicity. In comparison with a complicated dramatic program, they seem so simple and easy to do that there is danger of not doing what needs to be done. There is temptation for the production director to think, "Oh, talk, huh? Well – all I'll have to do is hold a watch on it." Even though talks programs are simple to produce, there is more to the job than timing them. There is real danger in the production director becoming so absorbed in *how* he is doing his work that he may neglect to look closely enough at *what* he is doing. Production techniques can become more interesting to him than the content. This is always dangerous.

In a talks program, content is the most important item and it is with content that the production director must chiefly concern himself. This calls for some interest in and knowledge of the subject at hand – an excellent illustration, by the way, of the necessity mentioned earlier in this book for a production director to have a broad cultural background. Obviously, no director can be an expert in many fields of subject matter. He may be called upon to produce a talk for National Education Week in the morning and a discussion on Pan-American problems in the afternoon. But if he has a general background and is used to wrapping his mind around complicated problems, it will help him greatly in quickly acquainting himself with the subject at hand. It will also help him to become interested in it. After all, if a production director has reasonable intelligence, and interest, it is easy to put himself in the position of the listener and evaluate the speaker's efforts. He can then be in a position to advise the speaker about his content. And content is the most important item in a talks program.

In discussing all kinds of production problems, the reader

should check back to the outline of basic production procedure in Chapter 8 of this book. The production of all kinds of programs will be made in terms of this outline, with specific application to program material being drawn directly from this basic procedure.

Producing the Straight Talk

A Member of the Station Staff Speaks

This kind of assignment is simple, indeed. Stations usually do not assign production men to such programs, even if the stations are large enough to have a production staff, except in the case of network operation. In network operation it is standard practice to have a production director cover everything – even the simplest kind of operation. In this kind of program there is little for a director to do. When one is assigned, it is usually as insurance against mishap rather than from any actual need.

When a member of the regular staff speaks, it is usually one of the announcers doing a news program or the women's program director doing a talk to women or some similar program. In any case the person speaking is an experienced broadcaster and presumably is thoroughly conversant with the content of the program. In a news program, the copy has been prepared by experts. In a talk to women, probably the person doing the broadcasting is an expert on the subject and, more likely than not, wrote the copy herself. The speaker will also be familiar with the stringent time schedule of radio and skilled in finishing a program on time. If, in addition, it is a regularly scheduled program, most of the ordering of facilities and personnel will be taken care of in the normal station routine so that even these chores may not fall to the production director.

The reading and editing of the script is done, not by the production director, but by the staff member who is to read it. The production analysis also is done by the reader. Since this is a solo performance, none of the technical matters present special problems. The study of the script for interpretation is largely a matter for the performer. If it is a new program or a single program, facilities will have to be ordered and staff and space scheduled. If it is a regular program, all this is done as routine with no attention needed by the production director.

The "staff" in this case will consist of the engineer, and he will have nothing more exciting to do than to set up a microphone and turn a few switches on and off. Script markup is not necessary because there is nothing to mark up. There is no casting to do, no sound to provide, and the only music needed is for a stand-by if the situation seems to warrant it.[1]

Rehearsal usually consists of reading the copy through once for final timing, with the production director holding a stop watch. The director will mark down the elapsed time every minute, half minute, or fifteen seconds, depending on how critical the timing needs to be. This gives him a standard against which to check while the program is on the air, since the markings are made right on the script. If the program is long or short, the speaker will make the proper time adjustment. No cue rehearsal is involved, because there is only one element in the program, and cues, except for the beginning and end and time signals, are seldom used. Those mentioned are automatic and need no rehearsal.

What, then, does the production director do in a case like this? First of all, he keeps track of timing the program on the air. He does this by comparing the air times with the rehearsal times and adjusting them. If the speaker is ahead of his rehearsal schedule, the director will give him the signal to slow down. If he is behind schedule, he will signal him to speed up. When he is back on schedule, the director will give him the "on-the-nose" signal.

The only other way in which the production director can help is to act as a guinea-pig audience during the dress rehearsal reading and offer whatever constructive criticism he can. Because

[1] A stand-by program is one provided to fill the time, either in case a program finishes ahead of schedule or in case it is unable to air. Good programming usually indicates stand-by programs where talks are involved or whenever any remote program is scheduled. In the case of networks, it is usually a pianist or organist. In station operation, it may simply be a transcription that is ready to be used.

there is so little to do, directors often do not do this. This is an important part, however, of the production director's work and one of the few ways in which he can be really useful in this kind of program. He can make suggestions that may clarify the copy. He can suggest changes in line reading to make the broadcast more interesting or understandable. He can check pace and rate and make suggestions. He can look for mispronunciations. He may even make suggestions for changes in routining, by which is meant the order in which items are broadcast. For example, a home economics expert might have several recipes on the program. Clarity, rising interest, or some other factor might give the director reason to believe that an alteration in the sequence of these items might improve the program. After all, he can be objective. He can, on the read-through, put himself in the position of the audience much better than the speaker can. In ways like these the director can be of real help in a talks program, even though the speaker is an authority on his subject and a professional broadcaster.

In the actual broadcast, the director is responsible for timing; he must do whatever routine paper work there is connected with the assignment; and he must stand by for emergencies. In the last case only does he get a real workout. Otherwise, this is probably the simplest of all assignments in production.

An Outsider Speaks from the Studio

When the speaker is someone who is not an habitual broadcaster and not a member of the station or network, the task of producing even a simple talk begins to grow in complexity. It is still a comparatively simple kind of production, but an element of uncertainty has been added. If the speaker has been well chosen by the program department, the production director may still safely assume that he is something of an authority in his subject. He cannot assume either that he is a good speaker or an experienced performer on radio. These two factors put more responsibility on the director and give him additional tasks.

Once the production director is assigned under these circumstances, he may be faced with considerable work on the script. In a network organization, the department sponsoring the speaker would probably see to the script. Either that department (such as public service or special events) or the continuity department might help the speaker with his manuscript. In a station with a less elaborate organization, whoever was assigned to the program would probably be called upon at least to pass judgment on the manuscript. He might even have to write it.

In case of a network, the continuity department will see that the speech does not violate any matters of policy. In less imposing organizations, the director may have to be responsible for this. Early in the process, once a first draft of the manuscript is ready, the director may make a preliminary timing with the speaker to get an idea of whether the manuscript will have to be cut or expanded. Finally an acceptable speech is ready in script form.

The production director must see that suitable continuity is written for the open and close. It may be provided by the continuity department or he may have to do it himself, depending on the size of the station.

The production analysis on this kind of talks program is very simple. Certainly the determination of the aim or purpose of the program is necessary, but this will be evident if the speaker has been helped with his manuscript. If not, it should be read and studied before rehearsal. The main structure of the speech should be familiar to the director. Talent is no problem. Staff is simple. Only an engineer is needed, and an announcer. In most stations the production director is also the announcer.

A word might be said here about studios for talks programs. Some elaborate stations layouts provide for a talks studio that is designed to look as much like a library in a private home as possible. The theory is that if a speaker is inclined to be confused by all the gadgetry of radio, the homelike surroundings will reassure him. That reasoning probably had more validity in the early days of broadcasting than it does now, when almost everyone who has anything significant to say to the public has made frequent radio appearances. Nevertheless, such a studio is nice and if one is available, talks should be scheduled into it.

The microphone setup will be no problem for the production director, but for a student there are some pointers that are as helpful as they are obvious. Microphones are sensitive creatures. They resent being kicked or blown into. They react unfavorably to sudden explosive sounds such as might emanate from a platform orator. They do not respond sympathetically to being handled. All these things an inexperienced speaker may do to a microphone, either through ignorance or absent-mindedly while nursing his mike fright. It is wise to address the speaker to his microphone in such a way as to minimize the possibilities of any of these things happening. A pressure-actuated microphone is recommended for speakers who are inexperienced, because it is less likely to blast if there is a sudden change in volume or if the speaker gets too close. It is a little less sensitive to being touched and is semi-directional, which means that there is less likelihood of picking up extraneous sound in the studio during a broadcast. The best arrangement is to suspend the microphone from above, either from a cable from the ceiling or from a goose-necked microphone stand, whichever is available. This reduces the likelihood that the speaker will handle a microphone stand which might rest on a table, tap a pencil on the table, or even brush papers against the stand, all of which will cause noise. It is well to seat the speaker at a padded-top table. Most inexperienced speakers feel more intimate, at ease, and relaxed sitting down at a table than standing. Something about standing up suggests orating and talking to large crowds of people. Since this is undesirable in radio, where person-to-person contact is what is wanted, it is well to encourage any practice which will make the speaker feel that way. If the speaker is seated in an armchair that is pulled up closely to a table, he is hemmed in by the furniture to the point where he cannot vary his microphone position too much. He is somewhat held on beam by the chair and table.

At least a half-hour of rehearsal is recommended for a fifteen-minute talk. This allows time for a read-through and suggestions before going on the air. If the rehearsal time is too long, a speaker will have a chance to get worried and jittery.

It is well to provide a stand-by program to fill, in case time gets out of hand. Speakers frequently increase their pace on the air and come out as much as two or three minutes ahead of the rehearsed timing. This is too much time to fill with ad libs, and the only protection against this exigency is a stand-by for the remaining time.

Having made all these decisions (which, in the case of a trained production director are not decisions at all, but the execution of routine), the director now sets to work. He orders the script duplicated, with copies for the publicity office, files, announcer, engineer, director, speaker, and any extra ones which may be desirable. Having done this and scheduled a studio, announcer, and engineer, there is nothing more to do until the rehearsal preceding the program.

Depending on the individual speaker, it is sometimes wise to check by telephone early on the day of the broadcast, to be sure everything is in order. Speakers have been known to forget or misunderstand broadcast times. A telephone call is good insurance.

The rehearsal is an important period in the talks program. Certain mechanical details must be attended to. The speaker must be balanced on the microphone. The speech should be read through. During this rehearsal the production director checks and notes time in his script every minute or thirty seconds, with a time notation every fifteen seconds during the last couple of minutes.

Next, the manner of timing the program will be discussed. Perhaps the speaker has considerable presence of mind and seems to be master of the situation. In this case the director might explain the speed-up and slow-down signals to help in jockeying the program to end on time. This is not recommended unless the speaker seems to be very calm and collected. Another device is to provide alternate last pages of different lengths and make provision for reading the appropriate page to adjust the time. Perhaps it will be best to give the speaker a two-minute, a one-minute, and a half-minute signal, and then explain the cut signal so that the director can give him an idea of the time toward the end. An even better arrangement is to provide a long and a short closing announcement for the announcer, so that any necessary adjustment in time can be made by the experienced announcer rather than the non-professional speaker. Which of these timing systems is used will depend on the experience of the speaker and the degree of nervousness he exhibits. It is a good general practice to worry the speaker about time as little as possible.

Once the speaker has gone through his copy, certain other suggestions may be made which will be helpful. If there are difficult sentences that look like potential flubs, they should be rewritten. If the speaker is pounding too hard, he can be shown how to ease up. If he reads in a monotone, underlining certain emphasis points in the copy may help him. Perhaps he is reading too fast or too slowly. All these things are subject to suggestion by the director. Most speakers will appreciate them if they are tactfully put. Finally, be sure the speaker's and the production script are in order.

After these things are done – and it is well to have them done at least five minutes before going on the air – the director's main job is to set the speaker at ease and to relax him as much as possible. Tension and mike fright are two of the worst enemies of good radio speaking. Talk to the speaker about the weather, football – anything under the sun that is safe and neutral and commonplace. Hunt for a topic that the speaker will talk about and get him started on it. As long as he is talking interestedly, his attention is distracted from the thing that may give him the jitters. The director must keep track of the time, but no point should be made of it. The speaker should be back at his table at least a minute ahead of schedule so that he can settle down without a sense of being rushed. The whole center of attention should be on the speaker and what he is talking about rather than on a lot of hurried last-minute instructions which will only confuse him and make him tense.

If it is possible, the production director's best place in a talks broadcast is with the speaker. Sometimes in network operation this is not possible because the director must be available in the control room in case of emergencies. Certainly, from the speaker's point of view, the director can do his best work right at the table with the speaker. It will give the speaker confidence, to begin with. It also gives him an audience. If the director looks interested, the speaker will tend to speak to him more and more, and this gives a real sense of audience contact that is good. Also in case of timing difficulties or script mix-up, or any of the other things that might go wrong, the production director is right there to scribble a note or arrange a page, or point to the manuscript. In local stations, where all such production work is done by the announcer anyway, being in the studio is automatic.

Going on the air should be preceded by a half-minute warning. If the speaker has a cough in him, now is the time to get it out. During the actual broadcast, the director must note any variations from the script, if any. They might turn out to be important, especially if the subject is a controversial one. The timing on the show must be watched — unobtrusively — and adjustments made if that is the way time is to be handled. As much time as possible should be spent watching the speaker and reacting to what he is saying. This kind of implied encouragement is very helpful. As the program progresses, the time problem will unfold itself, and whatever needs to be done can be decided more or less at leisure. If the director is worried about the timing of the program, he must not let the speaker see it. That is the director's problem. Whatever plan is followed, the speech should be ended as calmly as possible, but ended on time.

The announcer and the production director are the station's or the network's best public relations experts. They are the "fronts" for radio. This should be remembered all through a talks program preparation and broadcast, but particularly in the post-broadcast period. Be gracious after the program. The director is in the position of host and should act accordingly. It is well to remember that, although this may be only another show to the director, it is likely to be an event to the speaker – one which he will remember and talk about for a long time. He may have, in the case of networks, traveled several hundred miles to make it. A good director must somehow sense this importance of such an occasion to the speaker and participate in it. The speaker should be thanked for coming and for doing the job. There is always a let-down period following a show and the wise director can help ease it for the speaker by being nice to him. The director's schedule may be very full, but whenever possible, time should be allowed for a little post-broadcast period to spend with the speaker. It is only sound public relations. It will, if properly handled, create one more and possibly several more loyal listeners, and listeners form radio's box office.

A great many talks originate outside the studios. In such cases very special problems are often created which do not occur at all in studio broadcasts. This whole subject will be discussed in the chapter on producing special events programs. While not all speeches broadcast outside the studios are special events programs, most of them are, and this is the department which is usually assigned to handle them.

Producing a Series of Talks Programs

Laying out and planning a series of talks around a central idea is properly program planning and not program production. In a network the production director will seldom, if ever, be called upon to do such a job. In smaller broadcasting organizations, however, this is a task which often falls to one of the staff men. Again it should be acknowledged that local stations seldom have men on the staff who are labeled producers or production directors. Local staffs are not organized that way. But the announcers, the program director, or some one else does a considerable amount of production work, nevertheless. The following suggestions may help to guide the student faced with building a series of talks for the first time.

The first consideration is a central theme or topic around which the series is to be built. Such a program will have one of three purposes: entertainment; the creation of informed opinion or at least speculation on topics of current importance; or instruction. Whatever the purpose, a topic chosen for a series of talks should rate high in human interest, usefulness, and originality. People are not always keenly interested in the things which concern them most. For example, a discussion program on taxation certainly hits everyone, but this topic would hardly create a sparkling program that would seriously compete with Bob Hope. Therefore, stress should be laid on good showmanship and human interest in the building of talks programs.

A second consideration in building such a series is the talent. Who can speak effectively on such programs? What kind of talent is best? A speaker should be a recognized authority in his field. If a station were building a program to study wild life, the first measure of a speaker would be his knowledge of wild life. A speaker should have a good voice: at least, it should be one that is easy to listen to. He should have a certain presence and sureness in his speaking which will make people believe he knows what he is talking about. He should be an experienced speaker. Speaking, like any other skill, improves with practice. A speaker who has had that practice is usually a better speaker. Some people, however, who seem unable to do effective speaking on a stage or platform often pan out very well in the intimate medium of radio, so it is not safe to generalize. Speakers are usually better if they have the ability to speak extemporaneously. Even when they are reading prepared script, such speakers generally do a better job. Some of the spontaneity of their extemporaneous speech carries over into their prepared and read speeches. Finally, the speaker should have as much personal "color" as possible. The public seems to like individuals – people who are not just like every other person, people with a personal stamp of their own on their speech, thoughts, and actions.

If speakers can be found who fulfill these qualifications, and if the topics are chosen with care and consideration of the tenets of good showmanship, talks programs, either singly or in a series, can have real merit.

Producing the Interview Program

The interview is another kind of program based on talk. As such it is a legitimate part of this discussion. There is one circumstance which is nearly always common to all radio interviews. The interviewer is a member of the broadcasting staff. The interviewee may be anyone, but there is nearly always at least one professional radio person on the program. This fact makes the production of interview programs comparatively simple from a purely technical point of view. The burden of the work does not lie with the production director, but with the interviewer. The interviewer is usually an announcer on the staff, although he may be working in radio in some other capacity. Directors of women's programs, directors of public service programs, farm directors, religious directors, members of the sports or special events staffs, all use the interview technique at some time or other.

In a network organization the production director has little to do for the interview program. It is planned by whatever department sponsors it and the bulk of the work on it (which is primarily concerned with content) is done by the interviewer. About all that remains for the production director to do is, first, to act as audience critic of the program and make suggestions; second, to get proper microphone balances and take care of technical details; and third, to start and stop the program at the right time. None of these things is a matter of great difficulty.

Outside of network organizations, the staff member conducting the interview is usually the same person who is responsible for building the show and producing it. For students who will find themselves in this position, this discussion may be helpful.

Like any other general kind of program, interviews break down into certain well-known types, and there are certain parts of the production procedure that are different for each type of interview. The common types might be listed as follows:

1. The celebrity interview
2. The man-on-the-street and on-the-spot interviews
3. Interview for instructional purposes
4. Serial interviews built around a feature program idea

Each of these could be further broken down into still more specific types, but the problems involved from a production point of view would not change greatly.

All interview programs may be either ad-libbed or read from script; the situation and the interviewee will determine which method is used. Even the wartime restrictions on ad-libbed programs do not usually affect the interview because the broadcaster tends to control the situation. After all, the interviewer asks the questions and this is a positive means of controlling the content of the program. If a prospective interviewee is radical enough in his views to make it necessary to confine him to a script, he is probably not a desirable interviowee in the first place. Whether or not an interview is read or ad-libbed will depend on the importance of the subject, the glibness of the interviewee, and the purpose of the program. During wartime nearly all military personnel appearing on the air, especially if they are talking about the war itself, are required to work from a manuscript which has been read in advance by the proper authorities. Subjects of a highly technical nature, when handled in interview form, are often read from script because of the difficulty in correctly expressing an idea spontaneously. If the subject is very important or very complex, the interview which is completely written out may prove to be the safest and best.

When the interviewee is not a very articulate person, a complete script is desirable. Of course, a highly inarticulate person has no place on an interview program, but occasionally such a person must be used because of his position or office. If this is so, by all means use a script to conduct the interview. Sometimes an interviewee is too articulate. A person who talks easily, but finds difficulty in sticking to the subject, may often be better when held to the subject by words on paper.

In all other cases an ad-libbed interview is preferred, provided that the director does not assume "ad libbed" to mean unprepared. As a rule, more preparation is necessary for an ad-libbed interview than for one which is written out, but because it *can* be done with less preparation, it often is. This is a grave mistake. It is true that time can be filled up very easily with an ad-libbed program for which there has been practically no preparation. To do a good ad-libbed program without preparation is next to impossible.

Producing the Celebrity Interview

Assuming that the production of the interview program is to be done by the interviewer (which is the case in all but network operation), here is a suggested production procedure: There is no script to study and analyze. Rather, a script has to be created. The script may be only penciled notes or it may be a fully written script, but it must be prepared. The director's first job is to find out as much as possible about the visiting fireman. Why is he a celebrity? What facts about his life or his work are likely to interest the audience? What are his personal habits? What kind of personality is he? What are his idiosyncrasies? These are all important questions and must be answered – not necessarily on the air to the audience, but for the benefit of the interviewer. Some of this information can be had by cursory research. Some of it is obtainable only after a preliminary meeting with the celebrity in person.

Audiences are interested in two main kinds of information about celebrities. First, they want to know how and why their lives are different from those of the audience. Second, they want to know how they are the same. The double-barreled interest of differences and common denominators can always be counted on. We are interested to know how a great actress got that way and how it feels to be that way, and we are equally interested if she is suffering from a toothache, even as you and I. This information will help in building the content of the broadcast.

Too often an interview becomes a formless thing from lack of planning. The most interesting facts are divulged first and the whole show runs steadily downhill in interest. The rules of good showmanship hold for the interview as well as for any other kind of program. The interest should mount instead of slope off, and the program should have a climax. This can only be obtained by saving some of the best information until the end and building toward it.

Having outlined the main body of the content, the director must then provide an open and a close for the program. From this point on, the procedure is pretty much routine. A small studio should be scheduled, and appropriate microphones, chairs, tables. Half an hour of rehearsal is not too much time for a fifteen-minute program, even after the bulk of the work is done.

Most of the other mechanics of production are either automatic or unnecessary. Scripts are usually unnecessary beyond the original carbons. The staff will consist of an ongineer. Conferences and study of the script are unnecessary. Casting, sound effects, music, are all out of the picture. One thing, however, should not be forgotten in the celebrity interview. The press and publicity department of the station should be consulted and helped in every way possible. The celebrity will nearly always be good for valuable space in the local press. All this brings us down to the business of rehearsal.

The first item in the rehearsal schedule is a conference over the questions to see that they are all acceptable to the guest. Others might be unearthed. If the celebrity is not at ease, it is the first job of the director to loosen him up, so to speak. He must be made to feel at ease. Celebrities may be accustomed to the routine. They may even be bored with it or resent it, but do it for professional reasons. If this is the case, the director has the problem of awakening a genuine interest on the part of the guest. Voice levels must be checked and set.

Finally, a rough allotment of time to be devoted to the various questions must be decided upon and a set of signals arranged between the interviewer and guest so that the program can end on schedule.

The broadcast itself is simply the execution of the carefully worked-out plan. The interviewer must be sure that all statements are clear and understandable to the audience. If the guest makes a statement that is obscure, the interviewer must be alert to ask leading questions which will clear the matter up. He must also avoid taboo topics by the same process. The interviewer is the voice of the audience, drawing out the facts that will interest the listener.

The broadcast must be managed by the interviewer in such a way that all the topics are covered and the planned amount of time spent on each one. Care must be taken to provide enough time at the end to avoid a hurried close. The close is something that can be planned and written in advance and does much to smooth out any raggedness sometimes apparent in an ad-libbed program. Back-timing of the close is the secret of a smooth ending.

Producing on-the-Spot Interviews

Two important differences between on-the-spot interviews and the celebrity interview cause some difference in procedure. In the first place, being out of the studio imposes remote conditions on the director. In the second, he may have no notion whom he is going to interview until the moment it happens. These two facts alter the production procedure somewhat.

Most popular of the on-the-spot formulae for interviews is the man-on-the-street program. There is scarcely a station in the country that has not had such a program at one time or another. Why? What is the reason behind such a program? There are two answers. This form of interview is useful as a sampling poll of public opinion and people are nearly always interested in other people's opinions on current topics. There is therefore considerable interest in a program which stops the first five people who happen along the street and asks them a question which is looming large at the moment. The other justification of the program is pure entertainment. It is a mild form of making fun of people or playing jokes on them.

Whether the intention is serious or funny, there is a formula for questions on this kind of program. The first questions usually asked each participant are personal ones which identify the interviewee for the audience and get the subject used to talking into the microphone. Easy to answer questions such as "What is your name?" and "Where do you live?" accustom the interviewee to the situation and prepare him either for a gag or to give answer to a serious question, depending on the kind of program that is planned. Whether or not such programs are interesting depends entirely on the skill with which questions are formulated and on the quick wit of the interviewer in handling the situations which arise. Even though the script consists only of the open and close and a few questions, it is still one of the most critical factors in the broadcast. The questions must elicit funny answers if a comedy program is planned, or, if it is serious, the questions must be ones in which there is genuine and widespread interest. Many small stations used to feel that all that was needed for a man-on-the-street broadcast was a man, a street, a microphone, and an announcer. Nothing can be more dismal than such a situation unless it sets out specifically to accomplish a definite end.

The complete production analysis is useful on this kind of program. What is the aim of the show? What type of program is it to be? Serious? Comic? Informative? On the basis of answers to these questions a production approach is outlined. Is the best procedure to be coldly analytical, scientific in sampling (to the extent that each person is asked the same question in the same way), formal in manner of presentation; or can the aim best be accomplished by being easy, informal, friendly? This question will have to be decided in the light of the purpose of the show.

What kind of people should be sought for interview? Will

the choice be completely random? Will it be divided by sex, by age, or in some other manner? This decision will have great influence on the kind of program which results.

The staff for such a program will probably consist of three people. In most cases an engineer with remote equipment will be needed, although many stations solve the program by dropping a mike line out of the studio window. An announcer to do the interviewing will be needed. Another person should be on hand to round up interviewees and have them ready at the microphone so that there will be no time lost on the air. This third person can also help the announcer handle traffic, take care of troublesome onlookers, and in general assist in the smooth operation of the broadcast.

Some kind of pressure-actuated microphone is indicated because only these are comparatively free from noises caused by wind. Most often the announcer will carry the microphone right in his hand, thus controlling the beam and assuring a good pickup both from himself and his interviewees. This makes a very mobile and flexible unit. If desirable, the announcer can move more or less freely from place to place, talking as he goes. All he needs is a sufficiently long microphone cable and someone to help him to manage it. Necessary telephone lines and facilities must be ordered to pipe the program back to the studios.

The rest of the production procedure is not applicable here. There can be, by the nature of the broadcast, no rehearsal. There is no script, no music, no cast to balance. It all happens only when the program actually takes the air. Timing is very simple on such a program. The announcer or the assistant has his stop watch synchronized with the station clocks. It goes until time is up, minus whatever is necessary for the standard closing.

One danger of this kind of program has not been mentioned. There is always the possibility that some hoodlum will start using profanity into your microphone or do something else equally childish in the spirit of what he thinks is good clean fun. There must be a constant vigilance against obscene material on such a program. It does not often happen, but just enough instances of such things have accumulated in the past to make it necessary that the person on the job shall always be wary of it.

Of course, there are all kinds of on-the-spot interview programs besides the man-on-the-street formula. Microphones are being taken into factories, the stock exchange, baseball parks — all kinds of places and for all sorts of reasons. The same general production problems, however, exist in all instances and the variations usually indicate their own self-explanatory variants.

Producing the Instructional Interview

So far as technique and physical procedure are concerned, the informational program which is cast into interview form offers no problems not already discussed. From the point of view of content and format, however, there are a few important variations to note.

Whether the program is done from script or ad-libbed from a carefully prepared outline, there are certain requirements which it must meet. In this kind of program both the interviewer and interviewee are working together toward a common end. In many cases both may be part of the station staff. A certain body of information is simply cast into question and answer form to make it more palatable to the listener. Sometimes the interviewee is an authority in the subject matter under discussion and the interviewer is a member of the station staff. The first requirement is that the information intended for the audience reaches them in an intelligible way. Uncommon terms must be defined. Complex procedures must be simply explained. If instructions too complex to remember (such as recipes) are included, provision for time to write them down must be made. All these factors must be taken into consideration.

The usual procedure in such a program is for the announcer or interviewer to play the rôle of a questioning audience. It is up to him to ask questions, either planned or spontaneously, to clear up the subject matter being presented.

The Interview Series

Like the talks series, the interview series is more of a problem in program planning than in production. Production problems will be settled by one of the appropriate methods already outlined. Occasionally, however, a production director or one of the members of a local station staff will get an order to build such a series of programs.

A case in point might be a program called *He Does an Odd Job*. The whole point of the program might be to bring into the studio each week a man engaged in an unusual occupation. He would then be interviewed with the idea of telling the audience about his work.

The first requisite of such a program series is to find an "angle," an unusual or interesting idea around which to center the series. The idea may be a very casual one indeed, such as *Luncheon at the Waldorf*, where very little, indeed, lends continuity to consecutive programs. The locale and the interviewer are about all each program has in common with the rest. Still, it is an angle and one that serves the purpose.

One factor in this kind of program is new from previously discussed forms. The interviewer becomes one of the personalities on the show – perhaps even its star – and the interviewees are merely passing guests.

In conclusion, there are certain facts which can be summarized about the production of interview programs.

1. Be sure the interviewee is properly introduced to the audience.
2. Humanize him as early in the broadcast as possible.
3. If the interviewee is frightened of the radio situation, use easy questions in the beginning that he can answer without thinking.
4. Gradually shift the spotlight from interviewer to interviewee by asking questions which require extended answers.
5. Keep it moving and keep it on schedule.

6. Keep it easy, human, and three-cornered between interviewer, interviewee, and audience.
7. Avoid a hurried close by keeping track of time.
8. Leave your guests with a good regard for you and the station.
9. Do not let guests be too technical without calling for proper explanations.
10. Keep always in mind those basic human interests which make talk interesting and people interested.
11. Never, never do an interview program without proper preparation.

Producing the Round-Table Program

The production of round-table programs, like the production of most other kinds of talks programs, is difficult to discuss because it is hard to know where to draw the line between production and program-building. The mechanics of getting the program on the air are, strictly speaking, production. What goes on the air and who says it are problems of program-building. In a network these two aspects are handled by two different departments. In station operation there is no such cleavage and the problem is much simpler to discuss, since a clean-cut division need not be made between the two subjects. It should be understood that program-building is the important part of arranging a good round-table program. The mechanics of producing it, once it is built, are simple, indeed, and neither difficult nor important. This discussion, however, will confine itself to production, since there is already in print at least one excellent discussion on the subject of building round-table programs which should be required reading of every prospective production director.[1] In passing, it should be pointed out that some of the best round-table programs on the air are produced neither by stations nor networks, but by college and university personnel who assume complete responsibility for their programs, even to furnishing a production director. In cases

[1] Judith Waller, *Radio: The Fifth Estate*, Boston: Houghton Mifflin Company. (*In preparation*)

like these the production director is also the program-builder, and one person, doing the whole job, has created some of the best round tables on the air. The University of Chicago Round Table and the Northwestern University Reviewing Stand, to mention only two, are handled in this manner.

Round-table programs, like any other kind of talks program, may either be read from script or ad-libbed from a carefully worked-over outline. War restrictions seriously limited the use of ad-libbed round tables on many stations, but a few still exist. The ad-libbed method is infinitely to be desired.

Whether the program is to be done from script or from outline, the production director, upon receipt of the script, starts his production work. His first decision is one of policy. Is the subject suitable for discussion on radio, and are the topics outlined within the bounds of station or network policy? Does the script or outline seem to provide for real discussion and prohibit single long speeches by any participant? Do the different participants present divergent points of view? Are all the possible points of view represented by the participants? Is the outline orderly and logical? Are the participants properly introduced and identified in the opening? All these things must be considered by the director under the heading of the script.

The director then proceeds to his production analysis. Since his work is largely mechanical, there is a tendency among production directors (who have not had a part in building the program) to come to such a production poorly prepared. Even though someone else has worked out all the business of content and participants, the director is still responsible for delivering them intelligently to his audience. He should, therefore, be cognizant of the aims of the program. He should know the general style in which the program is handled, or, if none has been set, create one. Will it be informal and chatty, terse and concise, argumentative, combative — or what? The style depends on the aim of the program and the audience at which it is leveled.

The director is obligated to study the structure of the program. In the first place, is there a structure? If not, it is up to him to create one. The participants and the builders of the program bring the director nothing but facts and people; he is still responsible for welding those elements into some kind of organized pattern. The program should have a planned opening, introduction to material, to personnel, development of material, and summary and conclusion. The director should have these parts of the structure mastered so that he can help intelligently with the broadcast.

One of the criticisms most often leveled at round-table programs is that they never get anywhere. Their conclusions are not clear. Of course, the purpose may not include the reaching of any conclusions. Such programs, however, are often muddled because the audience cannot dredge out an outline from the mass of seemingly heterogeneous conversation. A director can help in this respect by insisting that outline and transition points are clear.

The production director should know something about his participants and their points of view. What he has time to find about them is often very sketchy, but even a little information will often help in making a point or clearing an issue.

The staff for such a program is simple. A stand-by program or musician is usually arranged for in case of trouble. An engineer is, of course, necessary, and an announcer. Unless the moderator is a constant in a series, the talent on the program will usually appoint one of their number to act in this capacity. If this has not been done, the production director should make such an arrangement. Someone must be responsible for moving the program along from one topic to the next.

A small talks studio is most suitable and, ideally, all members of the round table should be working on the same microphone. Some kind of pressure-actuated microphone is indicated.

The remainder of the production procedure can be passed over up to the time of the rehearsal. Rehearsal time for such a program should never be less than double the air time and should possibly be more. During the rehearsal the production director should watch for these things:

1. Balance the voices so that they are approximately the same level.
2. Make routine warnings about not handling the microphone or stand, or rattling paper.
3. Take an over-all timing of the rehearsal, with breakdowns to show how much time was spent on each topic.
4. Check closely for statements that might run contrary to station policy.
5. Make sure that members address each other frequently by name to help the audience connect a name with a voice.
6. If any one participant tries to make a speech, break it up.
7. Watch out for undefined technical terms which the audience might not understand and translate them into common terms.
8. Encourage participants to translate abstract facts and figures into specific terms.
9. Keep all the participants in the discussion, and in a good humor.
10. See that time is allowed for some kind of definite summary at the close.

Certain other matters of mechanics need to be decided upon. If the program is a continuing one with certain members frequently appearing on the panel, many of these matters of mechanics become a standardized part of the program arrangement. If this is not the case, the production director will have to arrange them. How, for example, will members of the round table indicate to each other that they wish to speak? The common method is for the member who wishes to speak simply to raise a hand or finger to indicate that he has something to say. This avoids too much interruption or too many occasions in which more than one participant is talking at once. The moderator should have some sort of hand signal to indicate that it is necessary to move along to the next point in the outline.

Some directors of round-table programs feel that a complete

rehearsal is undesirable. It tends to take the edge off the spontaneity of the program. The Northwestern University Reviewing Stand sometimes, in lieu of a rehearsal, makes a recording of the program several days ahead of the broadcast. Participants are then allowed to hear the recording and see what was good and what was weak. This recording, made several days ahead of the broadcast, does not impair the spontaneity of the program so much and still gives the participants the benefit of a very objective check on their program. In the event that no rehearsal is scheduled, a warm-up period in which the participants talk back and forth for a few minutes ahead of the program serves to bring the men to concert pitch. This pitting of the men against each other before the broadcast makes for a fast start.

When the program takes the air, the production director has a new set of responsibilities. The introductions must be quick and concise and the group should get into an important point as early as possible. During the progress of the program, the director must keep a sharp watch for these specific things:

1. Any single participant must be prevented from monopolizing the discussion.
2. Dull spots in the program must be picked up.
3. Technical terminology must be explained.
4. If personal animosity arises, it must be smoothed over.
5. If any participant wanders from the subject, he must be tactfully but firmly returned to it.
6. Transitions must be made clear and obvious.
7. The program must be kept on its time schedule.
8. Unbroadcastable material must be avoided — by the moderator breaking in if possible. In extreme cases the program might have to be taken off the air.
9. A proper summary must be made.
10. The program must be stopped in time to make a smooth close.

In the post-broadcast period, the production director also has certain duties. He must remember that he is host for the station or network or sponsor. Even though he has other duties, he should stay with the participants long enough to thank them, take care of any questions, and give them a suitable send-off. This is just sensible, courteous public relations.

Producing the Town-Hall Program

In general, the production of town-hall type programs is the same as the handling of a round table, with two important exceptions. The first is the combination of prepared speech and ad-libbed rebuttal with questions from the floor. The second is the presence of a studio audience which brings into the problem a new element.

The usual town-hall program is routined something like this: three speakers, representing opposing views on the subject at hand, make three set speeches expressing their views; each speaker makes an impromptu rebuttal; and finally, the meeting is thrown open to the audience, members of which may address questions to any one of the speakers.

This kind of program requires a moderator to act as chairman, to introduce speakers, and to manage the questions following the formal portion of the program. This person is usually the feature personality on the program and appears each week. The guests, of course, change with the topics. In addition, an announcer and engineer are needed and enough reliable help to manage the selection of the questions from the audience. How many people are needed for this job depends on the manner in which the questioners from the audience are picked up.

The problem is aggravated during wartime because of the necessity of guarding against planted questions or the use of the program as a means of communication between enemy agents. All ad-libbed programs during wartime must have the strictest of supervision. Only those programs where the content is firmly in the hands of the broadcaster or of people in whom the broadcaster has the utmost confidence are allowed to continue ad-libbing. The current practice in some town-meeting programs is for the questioner to write out his question on a card which is passed to an usher. The usher reads the question, assures himself that it is innocent and legitimate, and only then signals to the moderator to recognize that particular questioner. Some other programs announce the topics and speakers on preceding programs and ask listeners to submit questions by mail. This allows them complete control of the content of the program.

There are several ways in which questions from the audience may be picked up. An engineer on the stage may use a microphone with a parabolic reflector which can be beamed or aimed at the questioner from the stage as he is recognized by the moderator. This is a simple and fairly efficient method. Sometimes ushers have portable microphones on long cables which are carried up and down the aisles to the questioners.

In the town-hall kind of program, so much depends on the content — which is in the hands of the moderator — that the production director becomes a relatively minor cog in the machine. At the most, he can help the moderator in keeping track of the content because he is somewhat more detached from the program in his control room than is the moderator out on the studio floor or the auditorium stage. For the rest, he is there to see that nothing contrary to policy reaches the air and that the talk has an excellent technical pickup and reproduction. He can supervise the engineers who make the actual pickup of speaker or questioner and see that it is all understandable to the listener. Beyond these things, his work is subordinate and unimportant in comparison with the moderator, who is really the key man on such a program.

Producing the Audience-Participation Program

Audience-participation programs are often a kind of variety show involving music, guest stars, and specialty acts. These will be discussed under the heading of variety programs, and this discussion will concern itself only with programs made up only of talk. Quiz programs, spelling bees, and various kind of stunt programs fall into this classification.

The Quiz Program

Writing a script for a quiz program is an interesting and tricky business, because only one part of the script can be written, yet it must be so constructed that whatever the script elicits in terms of answers must be safe to broadcast, fun to hear, and fit into what has gone before and what comes afterward. In the quiz program the production director is often in on the planning of the program from the beginning. Since so much of it will be ad-libbed, his advice and knowledge are invaluable in the building of the script.

The production analysis of a quiz program is not a very complicated one, since nearly all of them tend to be alike. In a dramatic program every individual show has its own problems. In a quiz program the problems are the same for almost every show. Therefore, once the formula is solved, it can be used on show after show. The purpose is almost invariably entertainment, though occasionally it might have educational or instructional overtones. The style will be informal, chatty, gay, easy. The attitude toward the program must be informal, with every effort to make it seem effortless and spontaneous. The structure, since the program is largely ad-libbed, will be loose and easy, but in spite of this it must follow out the basic tenets of good showmanship and contain conflict, rising interest, a climax, and a dénouement. The informality of such a program should not deceive the production director into thinking that there is no structure. Its very informality makes it more necessary than ever to strive for some sense of climax. The tempo must be fast without giving the audience a feeling that the contestants are being unfairly rushed.

Talent becomes an item of major importance in the quiz program and unlike most other talks programs, the talent problem usually falls to the production director rather than to the people responsible for building the program. The talent problem is twofold. The first and biggest problem is the master of ceremonies or quiz master. Upon the choice of this key person the entire success of the program may rest. The other talent problem is that of securing contestants who will fit the program.

Since the quiz master is so important, this subject deserves special attention. When a production director picks a master of ceremonies, he is looking for a combination of attributes that is difficult to find. Such a person should be reasonably literate to begin with — a trait that is not always present among "show-biz" people. He must not be merely glib. He must be highly articulate. He must not only be able to keep words coming, but he must choose words and ideas which have pertinence, humor, and good taste. He must be alert and able to take advantage of every break in any situation. He must be capable of instantaneous decision and have enough innate good taste to make the right decision in a large percentage of cases. He must have a keen sense of humor and some ability as a gag artist. He must have an infectious kind of good humor and an ability to spark-plug others into having a good time. In short, he is the one-in-ten-thousand persons who can make a successful master of ceremonies.

The problem of finding good contestants is less difficult, but its occurrence is frequent — every time the program airs. Every well-designed quiz program should have some definite set of guiding principles about the selection of contestants. In most such programs the contestants are drawn from the audience. This means that first there must be an audience. How is this managed? It is not so simple as merely announcing that a quiz program is to be put on and that people are invited. Once a program is established, the audience may come, but in the beginning, at least, an audience must be provided. This can be done by issuing special invitations to groups or organizations. It is usually facilitated by offering prizes. On some quiz programs the audience problem has been solved by inviting special groups each week and choosing contestants from these groups to pit against each other. Teams might, for example, be selected from two schools in a city and the studio audience might be composed largely of students from the two schools. With this kind of audience an interesting rivalry is already inherent in the broadcast before it starts. Less, then, has to be furnished by the program. The ideal contestant on a quiz program is one who is as near as possible to the average level of intelligence of the listening audience. The charm and audience interest in a quiz program is vicarious participation. Every listener is unconsciously pitting himself against the contestant on the program. The listener also likes the conflict of a contest and the clash between two rival forces, but basically his interest is in his own reaction to questions. A contest presupposes two fairly evenly matched teams. If the listener can win easily or never win in his unspoken conflict with the contestant in the studio, he loses interest. If the two elements are fairly evenly matched, the interest is greatest.

The production staff for a quiz show will contain an engineer, announcer, master of ceremonies (who might be the announcer), an assistant to manage the contestants, and a scorekeeper. The station's staff of guides will, of course, be called upon to handle the studio audience. The largest studio available will usually be scheduled for such a program. Possibly a small platform will be placed on which the contestants will sit.

Cardioid microphones are commonly the answer to the pickup problem in an audience show. Their directional pattern allows the director to select his sound sources with the maximum of efficiency and to eliminate a great deal of undesirable sound. If one contestant at a time comes to the microphone, a velocity mike which can be used by both master of ceremonies and contestant may be best. If more than one contestant needs to be at the microphone, it may be best to give the master of ceremonies a separate mike and have a microphone for the contestants. Giving the contestants a separate microphone has one virtue: it can be adjusted to the volume of each person. People who are not trained radio speakers may vary widely in their levels and it is easier for the engineer to level these variations off if he has a separate microphone to use for the contestants.

One last item remains in the production analysis. There

must be provision for ending the program on time. Some "rubber" must be provided in the show to be stretched, or squeezed into the time limits. Experience will soon indicate how many contestants and how many questions can be managed on a half-hour program. If there is no music, talk must be provided which can be included or left out to bring the program to time. A clever quiz master can generally fill the time with ad-libbed remarks with little difficulty, but it is well to make provisions to come to time if he cannot. Contests are usually handled in rounds. A complete round of questions might take three minutes. Suppose there are only two minutes left to fill? Then what? There are many devices for filling this time. For example, the two high-scoring contestants may compete for one short round to fill the time. If the time is under thirty seconds, it can often be filled by applause from the studio audience. However it is to be managed, the plan should be decided on at the time the production analysis is made.

In this kind of program sound effects and music are seldom important. The program cannot be, by its very nature, rehearsed. So there remains only the ordering of scripts, personnel, studio space, and equipment.

Staff conferences will probably be held to make clear to all members how the program is to run and what they are to do in emergencies. Publicity and press should not be forgotten on an audience program. Prizes should be obtained and ready. Dress for the occasion should be indicated. If properties are needed, they should be procured. The proper number of tables and chairs and their placement should be indicated and ordered. The answers to all questions should be double-checked and the authorities known.

It is common practice to admit audiences to the studio fifteen to thirty minutes ahead of the broadcast. They must be given time to get in, be seated, dispose of wraps, get the coughs out of their systems, and be prepared for the broadcast.

In the five or ten minutes preceding the broadcast, the audience is "warmed up." This is handled in all sorts of ways, but a common procedure is outlined here. The announcer on the program comes out and introduces himself. He welcomes the audience on behalf of the station or network and the sponsor if any. He may even tell a couple of stories to get the audience in a good humor. He then introduces the members of the staff, ending with the master of ceremonies who is always the star of the program. The latter then outlines the method of the broadcast and the contestants are chosen and brought up front to the platform. If any special conduct is expected of the audience, they are told about it and asked to co-operate. This whole warm-up period is designed to create fun and interest on the part of the studio audience and in the contestants so that it will be contagious for the listening audience when the program takes the air.

On the air, the production director has comparatively little to do. He is responsible for getting a good pickup of all the voices. He must see that no unbroadcastable material goes out over the air, which is something of a job since many of the elements of the program are unknown and unrehearsed. Even a known quantity like the master of ceremonies may, under the stimulation of a given situation, suddenly come up with a joke or a gag that must not go on the air. These things do not happen often, but they do occasionally, and they are the concern of the production director. For the rest, he keeps track of time and acts as sideline coach for the master of ceremonies, in whose hands the show really rests. He may send out notes from control, suggesting that the pace be picked up, or that such and such a contestant be soft-pedaled or whatever suggestions he thinks may help the program. He is, of course, responsible for getting it off the air smoothly and on time.

One warning should be made regarding the post-broadcast period. A careful record of answers must be kept. Names and addresses of winners must be obtained and kept on file. Once in a while something happens to cause a dispute over either what was said or whether or not a correct answer was given or who won the prizes. The only protection against such trouble is complete and accurate records.

The same courtesy should be accorded the audience as is

PLATE 26

ABOVE: The Carroll Sisters and Russell Wilk

PLATE 27

BELOW: Louise Massey and "The Westerners"

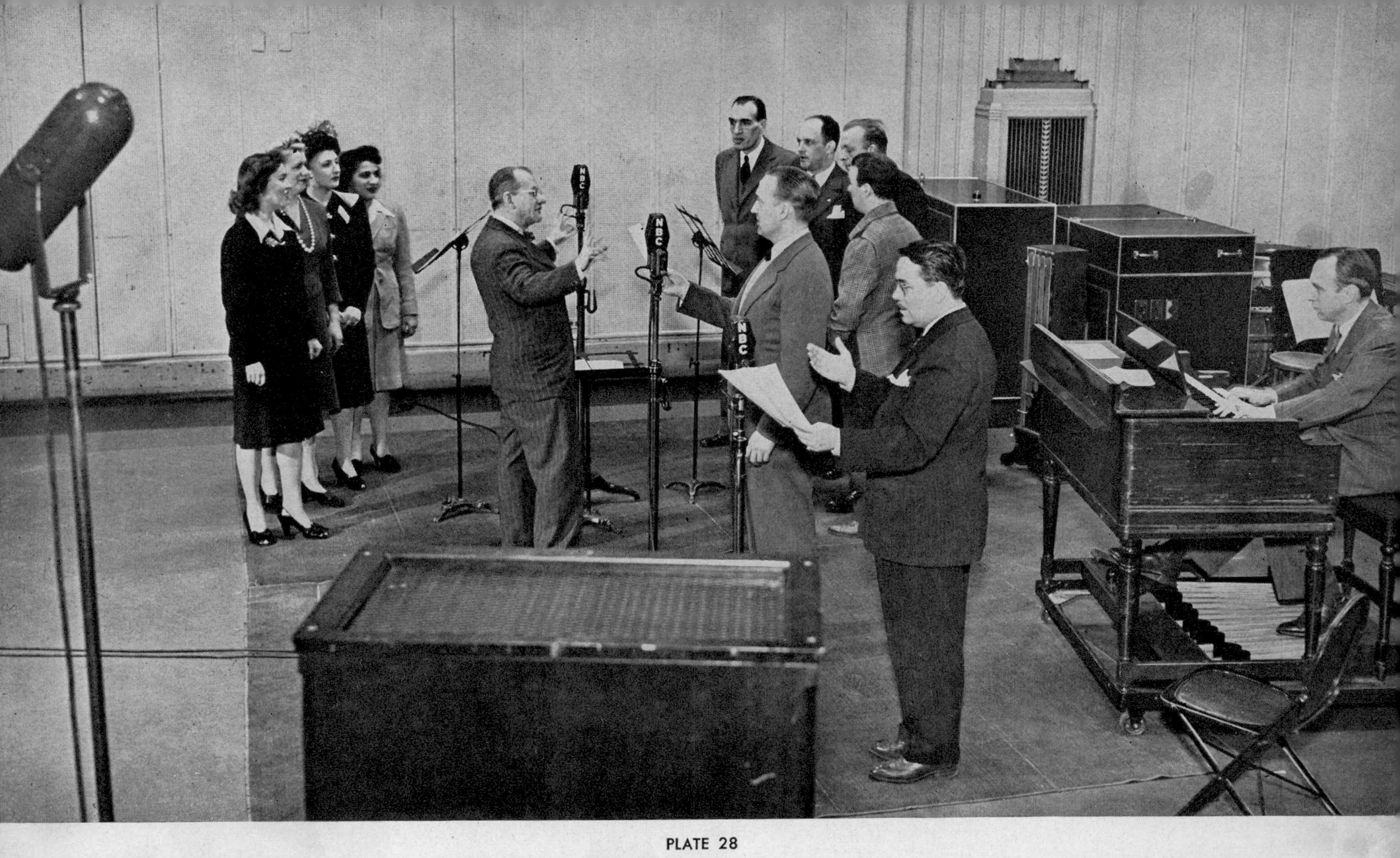

PLATE 28

Arrangement for Choral Group in "Hymns of All Churches"

PLATE 29

NBC Symphony Orchestra Conducted by Toscanini in Studio 8-H, Radio City, New York

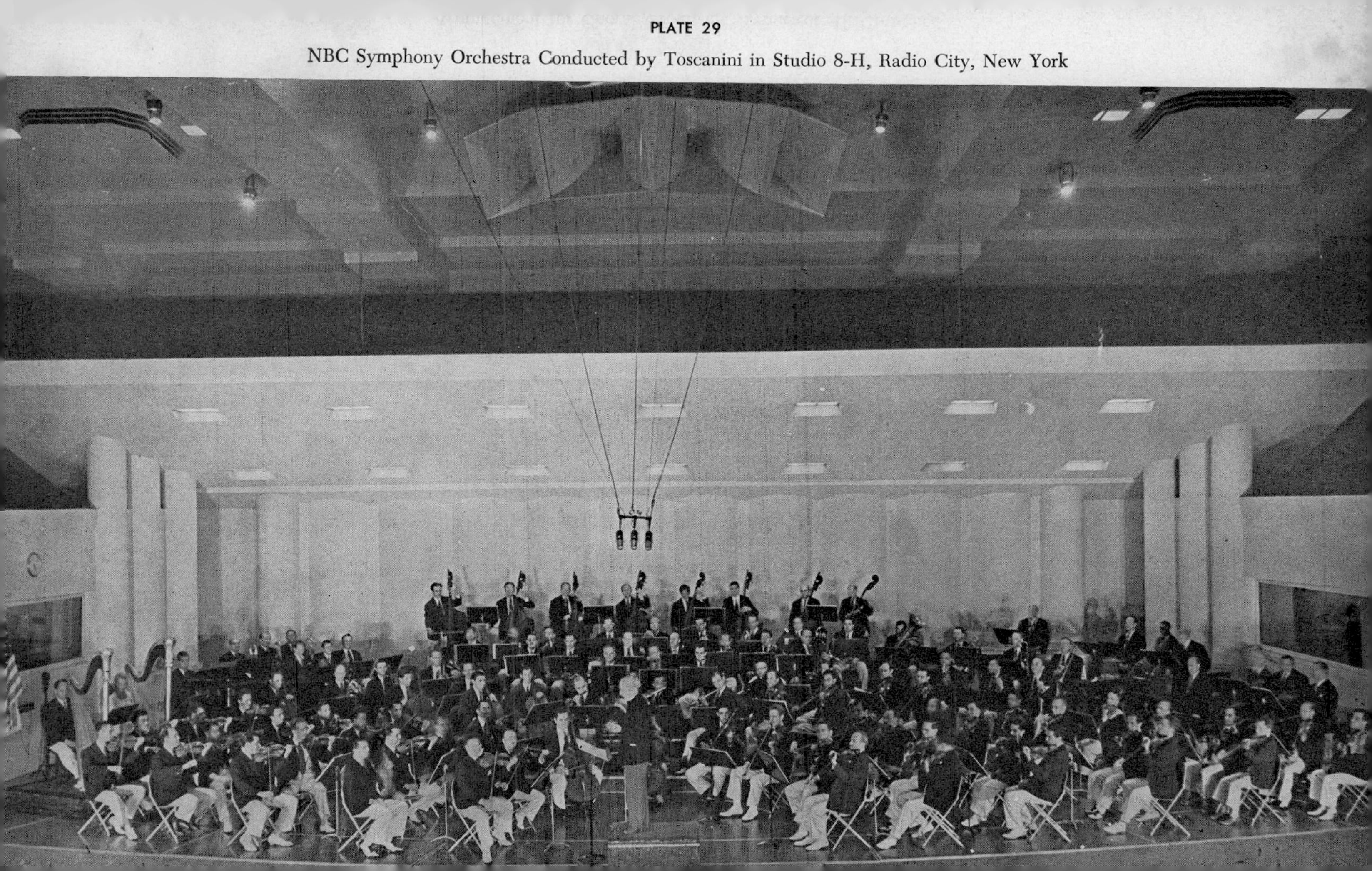

PLATE 30

"March of Time" Broadcast

given to a guest speaker at the close of the broadcast. The station is host. Good will and respect can be easily created by being nice to the audience. This is usually handled by the announcer or the master of ceremonies, but whoever does it, it should not be overlooked. Five hundred guests in the studio probably mean five hundred listeners next week. And listeners are what keep radio stations on the air.

Spelling Bees and Stunt Programs

Essentially the same problems appear in spelling bees and various other kind of stunt programs involving a studio audience that are encountered in the quiz program. In the case of the spelling bee, the number of contestants may be larger, which will influence the microphone pickup and a few other technical problems. Some matters must be determined in advance and understood by all contestants, such as the rules governing the contest and the dictionary to be accepted as authority. Since each broadcast, however, is tailored to the special requirements inherent in the program format, it is difficult to be specific about solutions to production problems.

Stunt programs provide all sorts of challenges to a production director because of the variety of pickups which he may have to make. There is absolutely no format for a stunt program. It seems that the more original and the crazier the stunts, the more fun they are to the audience. A director may be called upon to provide a pickup of anything from an apple-bobbing contest to a transcontinental telephone call. So well is the work usually done in this area that the ordinary listener takes it for granted. The student of production directing can learn much by listening to a program like *Truth or Consequences* and then working out a production analysis for it. This will give him some idea of how much work and planning goes into the production of these programs. Because they are varied, because the problems are always new, such programs are interesting to produce and fun to work with.

CHAPTER 10

MUSICAL PROGRAMS

NETWORK PROGRAM DEPARTMENTS have been wise in their decision to separate production staffs in order to provide specialists in the two major fields of drama and music. The production of musical programs is radically different from any kind of non-musical production. While there are certain elements in common, and while the basic procedure is similar at least, there are many marked differences. The main difference, which accounts for all the others, is this: all other programs stem from the written or spoken word; musical programs stem from a musical score or musical instruments. This simple fact alters considerably the procedure in producing a musical program.

Before things get too complicated, it might be well to outline simply and briefly the major tasks of a musical director in producing a music program. His problems are:

1. To pick the right talent
2. To pick the right music
3. To get a "frame" or "angle" or program idea to clothe the program
4. To make a proper "routine" of the program
5. To achieve a balanced pickup of the program
6. To control the time on the program

These seem to be simple and obvious tasks. They are obvious, but they are far from simple. A good musical director is a man with a rare combination of talents. There are very few top-flight men of this sort in American radio.

The origination point of a musical point is different from that of any other kind of program. Most other programs originate in a planning board or the continuity department or in some other department of a station or network. They arrive at the production department only when the plans for them have progressed well toward the jelling point. Music programs, on the other hand, may (and very often do) originate in the production department. The reason for this is simple. Music programs, as often as not, originate with talent. A vocalist comes along who has something different and distinctive about her work. A production director hears her on audition, recognizes the possibilities. A special audition is set up and a recording made. Other members of the station staff hear it, agree with the production director, and plan a program around this new find. Thus the program has its inception in a vocal audition.

Let us look at another example of a program which is already on the air. Suppose that we have a ten-piece orchestra, a popular vocalist, and a man who does semi-classical vocals. This combination does a regular daily program over the station or network. When it comes time to plan the next day's program, where is the beginning point? On the production director's desk. The first step in building such a program is the choice of the music. This is the job of the production director, in consultation with the musical director or orchestra conductor. Between them they sort out the music with which they are deluged every day by song pluggers and choose the selections to be used. Assuming that the talent is known, then the music becomes the beginning point in building the program. This is the province of the production director.

Compare this procedure with a round-table program, where the production director may know nothing about the program until he is handed the script and introduced to the participants an hour before the program goes on the air. The music director is in on the planning of the program from scratch.

It is true that occasionally a program will start with a vague idea handed down from a program director or a planning board. It might be decided that the station is weak in classical music and that another instrumental classical music program should be added to the daily schedule. But this is about as far as the plan progresses until a musical production director is called in. He will be consulted as to what talent is available, and when this is decided, he will choose the music that will appear on the program.

It is thus apparent that the musical production director is more than an executor of someone else's ideas. He is often in the position of program planner as well as producer. This is necessary because of the very nature of music programs. Early in the planning of such a program someone must be called in who can not only read words on paper, but who can also read *notes* on paper and know what they will sound like when translated into the concerted effort of a group of musicians.

Talent, then, is the beginning point of all musical programs. In radio drama the script is the beginning point. Actors are hired for single programs on the basis of their suitability to perform in a given script. In music, the reverse is true. Music is chosen which is suitable for a certain artist or group of artists. This is true for two reasons. Music bears a great deal of repetition: drama does not. There is always a scarcity of dramatic scripts, since they must be forever new; there is always an abundance of good music, since the total published output is always usable and reusable.

Because musical talent occupies this enviable position, all facets of the program stem from this point. Everything that happens in a musical program is predicated on the use of certain talent. Choice of music, orchestrations and arrangements, script — everything comes after this important decision is made. It should be understood, of course, that the music *is* the script of a music program.

Because the musical production director is usually the ranking musical expert in the network, it is he — in conjunction with the musical conductors and directors — who pass on talent, choose the music and decide on the format of the musical program. Our task, then, is to set forth some of the principles that guide a good musical production director in the execution of his duties.

Choosing Musical Talent

The task of choosing good musical talent is difficult because there is no formula. Good musical talent is not a thing to be measured by scientific test. It is a matter of opinion — and it is trite to say that opinions are individual matters. The best that a musical production director can hope for is a high percentage of right guesses. He will inevitably miss sometimes.

The problem of choosing talent is further complicated by the fact that decisions sometimes hinge on non-musical factors. Two vocalists may have equal training and technical skill and experience. One can "sell a song" and the other cannot. The *x*-factor of personality, which has little to do with music, becomes the deciding point in this instance. Showmanship, appearance, personality, must be considered along with musicianship.

The musical director must also contend with a wide variety of talents. He must pass judgment on everything from an oboe player to the virtuoso of the musical saw. In his day he talks to pianists, organists, torch singers, hill-billy guitarists, arrangers, composers, song pluggers, piano tuners, tympanists, and zither pluckers. He must deal with the whole field of musical literature from the Gregorian Chant to boogie-woogie. Obviously, no artist, no musicologist, no musical production director can be an expert in all these specialized fields. He usually develops a kind of judgment which is part experience, part deep-seated knowledge of music, part hunch, and part sheer metaphysics. This is bolstered with a knowledge born of making many mistakes. Out of it comes a kind of sixth sense which tells a good musical production director when he is hearing something good from new talent that the public will accept.

In spite of all the mysterious hocus-pocus which goes into the choosing of musical talent, there are certain practical measuring sticks which can be applied. The first of these is technical skill. Does the artist have great manual or vocal skill? Is he adept at reading music? Accuracy, precision, flow — in playing or singing — are highly desirable.

Sound musical training is desirable. There are many "natural" musicians, just as there are many people who play glibly by ear, but they are seldom able to meet the exacting standards of radio. Such people usually have stringent limitations on their repertoire and all their work tends to sound alike. So, regardless of native ability, good training, and plenty of it, is highly desirable.

A musician must have a "good ear." This means accuracy of pitch, of course, but it means more than that. It means the ability to hear and dissect music. It means the ability to segregate a theme from a complicated pattern of music. It means a strong melodic sense and all the intangible connotations built around that phrase.

Versatility is a virtue under certain circumstances. A staff musician who can play four instruments well is obviously more useful than the musician who can play only one. He is usable under more circumstances and in more combinations. Some musicians can play only classical music or only popular music. Such people limit their own usefulness by their lack of versatility.

An artist should be widely acquainted with the literature in his own field of music and well acquainted with all music. To be specific, a hill-billy violinist who has collected many folk songs from many parts of the country, and has really made a study of them, is a more valuable asset than one whose repertoire is bounded by "Red River Valley" on the north and "Home on the Range" on the south. Perhaps it is too much to expect, but if that same violinist is not a total stranger to "The Marriage of Figaro" he would be even more useful to have around.

Perhaps most important of all, in the measurement of musical talent, is the determination of an artist's "feel" for music, whatever that may mean. That is an intangible that looms so large it can easily become more important than all the others. Music is an emotional thing. Perhaps the "feel" for music simply means that the artist is capable of responding to the emotion inherent in the music which the composer originally wove into the score. It may find expression in the figures which a musician weaves around a central theme. It may be evident only in the delicate timing of a simple melody, simply played. Perhaps it is only the emotion which a musician feels as he reads the notes, which somehow finds expression in the delicate touch of fingers on strings or lips on a reed. Whatever it is, and however intangible it is in origin, it is easy to recognize. Even an untrained layman who knows nothing about music can hear two pianists and pick out the one who has a "feel" for music. That certain "plussage" which lifts music out of the mechanical realm of notes and time and pitch and volume and makes of it a living vivid thing – that "feel" is obvious when it is heard. The reader has undoubtedly sat in many so-called intimate night clubs where a succession of entertainers were contributing to the constant din. And then an artist came along – perhaps just another piano player among several other piano players – and the din stopped. By some strange alchemy of attention, everyone had stopped talking and were listening. That pianist, because he had a "feel" for music, added something compelling to his playing – something that stopped the buzz of table conversation and made people listen.

Recently an audition was held at NBC for a pianist. The auditionee was supposed to be a fine master of the classics and the board listened for some time to crashing crescendos and rippling glissandos as the pianist moved through Beethoven, Haydn, Mozart, and Debussy. One of the listening board spoke up.

"Play 'Stormy Weather,'" he said.

"I don't know it, and I haven't the music here," the pianist replied.

"Try it," the man insisted.

"But I don't play that kind of music." The pianist was almost plaintive.

"Try it anyway," the board member insisted.

The man sat a moment at the piano and then started playing – very tentatively. At first, there was only the simple melody. Then, as he began to get the "feel" of it, he began to expand the melody, adding his own figures, ad-libbing as he went. The figures he added were all classical. They were not the flourishes which a "pop" pianist would have used, but they were right. They supported the mood of the music and no listener could fail to see that this man knew what that music meant.

When he had finished, the board member explained that, in his opinion, that was the test of a musician. If a specialist in the classics could deal intelligently and sympathetically with a piece of popular music, he must have something.

When a production director, on an audition, hears these qualities making themselves evident, he knows that here is talent he may find useful. Here is someone worth adding to the staff. Not all musicians can have all of these recommendations, but they are likely to be chosen in direct proportion to the number of these virtues that they have.

So far the discussion has been generalized for all musical talent. When it comes to choosing individual performers, there are certain additional considerations which must be taken into account. One does not often find readymade star performers. A production director sees potential solo performers. He is therefore not only estimating present accomplishment but future possibilities. One of the first things he looks for is a willingness and an ability to grow. The musician who *feels* that he has arrived *has* arrived – as far as he will ever go. The true artist, in his own mind, never arrives. Only with that attitude is progress possible. So the production director, in his search for a star, looks first for someone who is willing to learn and eager to grow.

Experience is a sound foundation on which to build. Hence, the more previous experience an artist has had, the less will have to be acquired later, because there is no substitute for appearing before many audiences and on many programs. The more experience an artist has had, and the more varied those experiences have been, the better are the chances of building a star.

Personality is one of the most important factors in a potential solo performer. It is impossible for an audience to accept completely an artist's work unless it also completely accepts the artist. The two are inseparable in the minds of the audience. This is not a conscious association, but it nevertheless deeply influences the audience. It can be argued that personality is less of a factor on radio than on the stage or concert platform, and this is true. Still, something of the person does come through on radio, and if the artist is able, not only to perform, but to charm an audience as well, his chances of success are greater.

Finally, the production director looks for uniqueness or style. Style is that peculiar characteristic quality with which a performer colors his work. Nearly every great musical artist has one. Sometimes it happens by accident; sometimes it is the result of painstaking development. However it comes about, it must be acquired before a musician can hope to become a star solo performer. In a world which is too full of too many things, distinguishing marks are necessary. With so many musicians competing for public attention and favor, the newcomer must have a style which somehow makes him stand out. The public likes to be able to identify their favorites and a distinguishing style helps them do so. Often a production director may recognize potentialities in a performer which mark him as star material. He may then take a hand in developing a style for the performer.

Along with this list of positive virtues, there are some negative qualities against which the production director must constantly be on guard. Most of these can be overcome with skillful handling, but some of them may prevent an artist from ever becoming important.

Chief among these negative qualities is temperament. This is usually an expression of egomania and as such accomplishes little except making the artist a difficult person with whom to work. There is a rare kind of temperament which is good — the temperament of perfection. Once in a while one encounters an artist in whose make-up there is no compromise with perfection. Such a person may be difficult to work with because he refuses to accept anything short of his own best and that of people associated with him. If this perfectionism is mistaken for temperament, it is the production director's mistake.

Another trait which the production director will do well to avoid is a stylist whose style dates itself too sharply. It is a temptation sometimes to accept a stylist just because they are fairly sure to catch the public's fancy, without stopping to consider how long that style may hold interest. Any style which definitely dates itself is dangerous. Any style, furthermore, which is extreme will probably be short-lived in popularity. An extreme style is apt to find wide and quick acceptance, but it seldom lasts for very long because it *is* extreme. The easy-going, informal, yet easily identified style of Bing Crosby has kept him popular for years. Since the process of building up a star is long and expensive, a production director must protect himself against picking a star who turns out to be a comet.

Problems in Selecting Music

The next big problem of the production director in this field is the choosing of music. Here, again, the director finds himself faced with choices for which there are no mathematically correct answers. Only opinions can be expressed, and the production director must be sure that the public supports his opinions a good safe majority of the time. As in the case of talent, however, there are a few sound guiding principles which the production director must keep in mind.

The first consideration in choosing music is whether or not it is suitable for the talent available. It is obvious to say that a song should not be chosen which is entirely beyond the range of the vocalist available for the program. Neither should a symphony be selected which called for massed string effects unless the strings are available to play the piece. One would hardly choose a Bach fugue for a seven-man swing combination. These are all obvious examples, but it is possible to make this mistake in choosing music when it is not so obvious. Perhaps a vocalist has a pleasing quality when he sings quietly, but becomes harsh and strident when he opens up. If a director chooses a piece of music which has to be sung loudly for correct interpretation and value, he must compromise on the performance. Either he sacrifices the needed volume to the detriment of the music, or the pleasing quality to the detriment of the singer. Mistakes in judgment like this can, and do, happen frequently.

Directors should not be guilty of assuming too many limitations. Because a girl's whole experience may have been in singing with a dance band, he may not safely assume that semiclassical music is beyond her. A director can only know that after he has tried it. Therefore, in choosing music for any kind of talent, it is wise to experiment until the limits of that artist's capacity has been determined. It is dangerous to "type" a musician without some experimentation. Having determined what the limits are, however, the choice of music must be governed accordingly.

The popularity of a piece of music is the next thing to consider. Popularity is a fluid, quicksilver kind of thing, and contrary to first impression, it applies to the classics as well as to popular music, so called. It comes and goes very rapidly and at the most unpredictable times. Only while a piece of music is riding the crest of popularity can the production director be fairly sure of his choice. When a song is just being introduced, he has little except his personal judgment to go on. It may or may not catch on. And certainly it is difficult to know when a piece has passed its day of popularity. There is nothing deader than yesterday's popular song. Classical music, of course, moves in much slower cycles. However, the pattern of popularity is a moving one. The production director must be aware of that movement and make proper allowance for it in his choice of music in any given circumstance. One should not understand that popularity is the only factor in governing choice of music. If this were true, no one would dare introduce new music. Popularity is only one factor in the problem.

If a piece of music is new, the production director must make his best guess as to the potentialities of the song. After all, the playing of a piece of music on the air might involve the making of a special arrangement for a large orchestra – a process which involves considerable expense – and he must not waste money on songs which will not have some chance of catching on. Musical production directors are being constantly bombarded by song pluggers who will do anything to get one of their tunes on the air. Pressure of this sort must be resisted when the judgment of the director does not tally with the enthusiasm of the plugger. On the other hand, the director must be on the lookout constantly for new songs, because, especially in the field of popular music, popularity is short and listeners demand new tunes all the time.

Normally, the production director is obligated to achieve a certain homogeneity in the music selected for a given program. Usually a better effect is made on the audience if the music on a program is all the same general type. Under ordinary circumstances it is not good planning to mix Beethoven and boogie-woogie into the same program. Sometimes a production director, in an effort to please all sorts of listeners, succeeds only in losing them all. More and more listeners are doing selective listening. They listen to certain music programs because they get the kind of music they like. If they do not get it, or if they get only an occasional number, they will choose some other program where there is more consistency. There are, of course, some exceptions to this rule which will be stated later. It should not be understood that all the music on any given program should be exactly alike. But it should be, normally, of the same general type.

The next consideration is variety and change of pace. This may sound like a contradiction of the preceding rule, but it is not. Variety and change of pace can be achieved within the same general type of music. A program of dance music, for example, might contain a melodic ballad, a dreamy waltz, a fast fox trot, and a hot swing number – all in the same program. There is homogeneity because it is all dance music, and still there is variety within this basic type. Even in a single number, variety should be achieved through arrangement.

There must be maintained a certain amount of variety among adjacent programs. Most networks maintain some kind of a clearance center so that all musical programs appearing on the network are checked at this point. NBC has a rule that the same number may not be played on the network a second time until two and a half hours have elapsed. Thus, if the production directors of two programs being broadcast within that time limit ask for the same number, the one who asks last is refused the clearance of the number. This is sometimes an inconvenience in programming, but it saves the listener a great deal of unintentional repetition. This same kind of check also prevents too much day-to-day repetition. If too many programs want to use a number within a given time, some limit is placed on its use to prevent a reaction against it.

Another factor governing the production director's choice of music is the audience for whom the program is designed. There are many kinds of music and great numbers of people who like each kind. The production director presumably knows the kind of listening audience he has or wants, and this will, in turn, color his decisions. The age group at which the program is leveled is one consideration. The time of day is another. Young people like lively, popular music and are apt to be very well informed about the latest music and orchestras. Older people like the older favorites and semi-classical music. It would be bad programming to play lullaby music on a breakfast program. It would be equally bad to try to hold an after-school high-school audience with a program of hymns. All these factors have to do with the audience and in turn with the choice of music.

The purpose of the program will also affect the director's choice. If the purpose is to help the listener relax after a busy day, this marks some limits on the list of numbers available. Wayne King became famous for this quiet, soothing kind of program. On the other hand, if the program is designed to beat time for jitterbugs, the music will be chosen accordingly

Many other examples could be cited, but these are sufficient to emphasize the fact that the program will influence the director's choice of music.

Special occasions, holidays, seasonal programs, will give the director ideas for choice of music and also may limit his choice of music. A program of Christmas carols that might be highly appropriate late in December would seem rather out of place in May. On the other hand, a production director, faced with the problem of building a program for Armistice Day, would have many obvious suggestions ready at hand. It is always wise to keep an eye on the special events calendar for aid and ideas in selecting music.

Choice of music is inevitably governed by its availability. All broadcasters have some sort of working agreement with some music publishers or their representatives. To radio, the American Society of Composers, Authors and Publishers, and their arch rivals, Broadcast Music, Incorporated, are the most important. There are, however, several other licensing agencies which own considerable bodies of music rights. All broadcasting stations maintain some kind of clearance machinery with which program builders and production directors can check to see whether the rights are available on specific music. NBC maintains an elaborate department of music clearance in New York and all music used on the network, regardless of point of origination, must be approved by Music Rights in New York before it can be broadcast. Some similar system is maintained by all networks and stations. Only in this way can they protect themselves from claims of infringements. It is seldom that a network production director finds a piece of music unavailable. Contracts are usually so extensive that almost any piece of music which is really necessary may be had by some kind of arrangement. What the problem of music clearance could mean was brought home painfully to production directors during the Network-ASCAP disagreement. For the duration of that disagreement, no ASCAP-controlled music could be broadcast and ASCAP controlled a large percentage of the then popular and semi-classical music in existence. It was out of this predicament that Broadcast Music, Incorporated, was born.

Another consideration is the kind of "stock" available. "Stock" refers to the standard arrangement sent out by the publishers of the music. When a publisher issues a new piece of music, he ordinarily pays an arranger to make arrangements for piano, vocals, and for a standard dance orchestra. A production director might very much want to use a tune, but eventually turn it down because of a bad stock arrangement. Perhaps the stock arrangement is all right, but not suitable for the combination of instruments he has on the program in question. Of course, if a director is working where arrangers are available and special arrangements can be written for the talent on the program, the problem is greatly simplified.

The final, and in many ways the most important, consideration of all is the director's evaluation of the intrinsic worth of music. Certain music can be tagged as obviously cheap and shoddy while other music has at least some merit. Within these rough limits it is not difficult to separate the wheat from the chaff. Musical production directors owe it to their listeners to give them as little cheap music as possible. There is plenty of good music — enough to make it unnecessary to broadcast shoddy music. In passing, it is interesting to note a decided rise in the musical tastes of American listeners which can be almost entirely ascribed to radio. Thousands of examples of the use of cheap music on the air can be cited, but for the most part there has been an honest effort to make good music available to the listener.

Finding a Program Idea

Having decided on the talent and chosen the music, the next problem the production director faces in starting a new program on the air is the format or program idea. The true musician may ask why it is necessary to have an idea for a program. Why is it not enough to play music? If one is to judge by the output of many stations, there is plenty of support for this point of view. Hundreds of programs are broadcast every day whose only central idea seems to be the announcer. The resulting program is often a hodge-podge. A good musical program should have a central idea around which the program is built. There are at least three reasons why this is true.

First, as we have already pointed out, listeners like to know what to expect in a program so they can tune in the kind of thing they like. If a program has no central idea, there is likely to be no continuity to the program; consequently listeners, not knowing what to expect, will not tune it in regularly. A central idea is a rallying point around which a listening audience can be built. Second, a central idea helps to trade-mark a program. With seventeen thousand-odd programs broadcast every day on American radio, there is terrific competition for the listener's attention. Unless a program has some distinguishing mark there is nothing unique that the listener can remember. This has nothing to do with the kind or quality of the music which appears on the program. It simply furnishes a convenient handle for the program. Finally, a program built around some idea which will connect the various musical numbers together and give some continuity to the entire program is a more satisfying artistic unity than a heterogeneous collection of numbers. It satisfies an unacknowledged desire on the part of the listener for unity, for organization of material, for the creation of a meaningful pattern.

"Your Hit Parade" is an excellent example of a musical program built around an idea. In essence it is a program of the latest popular music. But the construction of the program around the simple idea of finding the ten most popular tunes each week gives the whole program an importance and a meaning that it could never have achieved without the central idea. Just playing the music would not have given the program the following it has. The Toscanini broadcasts have come to have a special meaning to listeners. Everyone knows that these programs bring the listener the best in symphony music. The idea is as simple as that. But it is enough.

"The Chamber Music Society of Lower Basin Street" is one of the outstanding examples of cleverness in the building of a musical program. This program – basically just a popular music program – transcended the normal trite pattern of such programs and became a literate, gay, clever piece of satire as well as a good popular music program. The Fred Waring program has done another outstanding job in building a musical program around an idea. It lifts the program out of the mob and gives it a twist which is easy to remember, pleasant to hear. "Hymns of All Churches" is another case in point.

Sometimes a day-to-day idea can be superimposed on an over-all program idea to good advantage. "The Contented Hour" for example, which has its own over-all format, can and often does devote a whole program to a special occasion such as Thanksgiving or Easter or some special holiday. Not only is the general program idea present, but within that idea some special occasion is observed. Such a central idea which provides a tight core around which a program may be developed and which, at the same time, offers sufficient latitude for taking advantage of special occasions is a good program format indeed.

This is a good place to make a plea for decent continuity on musical programs. There is comparatively little that can be written for a musical program. This is as it should be. But there is a tendency to laziness on the part of continuity departments – as there is in all humans – so that even the little continuity required is often dull, uninspired, and repetitious. It descends to the pattern of "The next number will be . . ." The fact that there is very little continuity is all the more reason why it should be good. The continuity is part of the attractive packaging of the program and should not be neglected.

The Structure of Music Programs

To the uninitiated it might never occur that there could be such a thing as structure in a music program. Everyone is vaguely aware that there is such a thing in drama, beginning with inciting action and proceeding to climax and dénouement. A well-built musical program should have a structure just as well planned. The plan need not be obvious to the audience, but the audience will get the effect. In a program of symphonic music there is comparatively little latitude for building a structure because one number may take practically all the broadcast period. However, where a program runs a full hour, and three or four numbers are included, some sense of structure can be achieved even in that kind of program.

The best structural formula seems to be as follows: Open quickly with something that will seize interest; allow the audience a little rest after the opening high point; build another high point with dramatic material; put in something light to give the audience a rest, a change of pace; finish with the most spectacular number on the program for a climax. Theme music at the close, or continuity by the announcer, or both, may be used as dénouement. Even in symphony programs where the numbers are long and most of the music is serious, there is some opportunity to build this kind of pattern into a program. In programs using less pretentious music, routining of this kind is much simpler.

Aside from symphonies, most music numbers play anywhere from two to five minutes, with the average being somewhere around three. This allows five to eight numbers in a half-hour program, and two to five numbers in a fifteen-minute program, although it would be rare to use two five-minute numbers on a fifteen-minute program. A musical production director will choose his material with structure in mind and may very probably pick specific numbers because they might make good opening, middle, or climactic numbers. He will balance vocal numbers against orchestra numbers, heavy ones against light ones, fast against slow, comic against serious, until he achieves a pattern which he thinks will be interesting to the audience.

He must choose an opening number which will catch and hold the audience's interest. He might select a rather fast, highly colorful tune for the purpose, using his full orchestra if he has one. This might be followed by a slow ballad, using a vocalist to give it variety, and this by a comedy number where either a vocalist or the orchestra or both have a good time with the audience. Then a slower number might be put in to get ready for a climax by contrast. Finally, the most showy, most brilliant and dramatic number of the program would be put in to achieve the high point. This is, of course, only a suggested routine. There are many other ways of handling the same problem. The point is that the problem should be recognized and handled.

Variety and change of pace are the important points to remember, with the emphasis coming on the first and last spots in the program. The first spot is the attention getter, the last is the program climax. The more different elements a production director has to work with, the easier is his routining problem. If the program is an orchestra show with a man and a woman vocalist and a vocal team (a fairly standard arrangement) there are all sorts of combinations available. If the program talent consists only of a pianist, the problem is more difficult, but there are still ways of building a structure into the program. In other words, the program is built instead of being thrown together.

Theme music helps in constructing a music program. It lays the foundation of the structure in the opening and puts the flagpole on the top of the close. It gives a program a sense of completeness by coming back to the starting point. It makes the full turn and is therefore aesthetically satisfying. Many programs use *segues* or connectives between numbers to give the program continuity and to maintain an impression of pace and movement. As soon as a number finishes, some small segment of the orchestra, the harp and piano for example, will quietly play background music for the announcer while he introduces the next number, and then the background music will immediately resolve itself into the new number. In this way music makes a connecting tissue between the numbers on the program. Why this is so satisfying to listen to is hard to say, but it certainly is. For one thing, it gives the program flow and continuity. It breaks the idea of stop and start, it helps the audience to make a good transition from one piece to another, and it furnishes contrast to the numbers themselves. It is not a good idea to precede the climactic number of the program with such a *segue.* In that case a full stop is good. It tells the audience, "Here comes something special. This is something set apart from the rest of the program." This use of connective music is not obligatory. It is simply a useful device in making a final pattern for the structure of a music program.

Basic Types of Music Programs

Thus far the discussion has been generalized. When it comes to a matter of specific procedure, however, it is no longer possible to generalize. One must talk in terms of specific materials and a given situation. Since there are so many kinds of music programs, it may be well to get the most common types in mind before plunging into the problem of how to produce them. Talent, time, instrumentation, music, are all variables in a music program, and each of these variables or any one of them may cause enough difference in the program to make a radical difference in the entire production procedure.

Here is a list of program types which are the most common. Readers will probably know of programs which do not fit into any of these categories, but if so, such programs will be simply a different combination of some of the basic types listed here:

1. Recorded or transcribed programs. These may be anything from a full hour of symphony music on records to a five-minute specialty program. Such broadcasts are the backbone of much local station programming.
2. Piano program.
3. Two piano program.
4. Electric organ.
5. Pipe organ.
6. Piano and patter program (where the pianist also sings).
7. Vocal soloists of all kinds.
8. Small vocal groups. Trios, quartets, etc., usually have some kind of simple accompaniment, such as piano or guitar. They should, of course, have a full orchestra.
9. Small combination instrumental and vocal groups, such as "The Ink Spots," "The Westerners," or any hill-billy

group where the entire group plays and sings, going from one to the other.

10. Novelty groups – anything from harmonica choirs to jug bands.
11. Small instrumental groups:
    a. Salon music groups.
    b. Chamber music.
    c. String ensembles.
12. Concert orchestra, playing popular, classical, or semi-classical music.
13. Full symphony orchestra.
14. Choral or choir music.
15. Band music (usually military).
16. Dance orchestras:
    a. Sweet bands.
    b. Hot bands.
    c. Novelty groups.
17. Combined units, of which the most usual is, possibly, concert orchestra with choir or choral group, although many other combinations occur.

It should be realized that this division refers primarily to the kind and combination of instruments and voices. For each one of the groups there could be a wide variety of music types, which means additional production and programming possibilities within each of these divisions.

The Production Routine

The first step in the production of a musical program is the setting of the idea of the program. If the production director is assigned to a program that is already in existence, this will be set and he need only become familiar with it. If not, he must create the program idea in consultation with the proper staff members. He will know whether the program is to be serious or light and in general how he will have to approach his work. If the program aim is to furnish quiet, soothing, reminiscent music for late in the evening, all his thinking and decisions must inevitably be colored by that basic intent. If the purpose is to create a flash feature program in the middle of high-priced evening time, the procedure will take another tack and decisions will certainly be different. Whatever is done must be done against the basic decision.

The production director is now ready to start building the program on paper. First, the numbers are chosen. Usually about twice as many numbers as will be used are put down to begin with, so that in case some of the numbers do not clear, or if the time is wrong on them, there will be additional numbers cleared that can be substituted. This procedure safeguards the director against unforeseen circumstances.

Having chosen the numbers, with all the factors in mind which have been previously discussed, the next job is to assign them to the available talent. If there is only one artist on the program, it is simple. When an elaborate musical program is being planned, however, this job may be complex, although the choice of music originally has been strongly colored by who is available to do the numbers.

Having chosen the numbers, the appropriate stock is selected for the talent to be used. This will be done with the help of the music librarian. On well-known numbers, stock arrangements will be available for almost every imaginable kind of talent – everything from concert orchestra to a full choir. If there is money and talent available, the production director may elect to have special arrangements made for the program. Sometimes arrangers will use a piece of stock as a working base and write new arrangements, and if this is the case, the production director, musical director, and arranger confer on how the job is to be done.

Finally, a routine is made. This can be only tentative until actual timings are known, but at least it gives the director a working plan on which to proceed until he has all the data he needs. A routine is simply a list of what happens, and in what order, on a program. It shows which numbers the director plans to use and the order which he thinks will be most suitable. This routine will be arranged according to the principles of program structure previously discussed. These arrangements may be made by the production director, but more likely they will be made by him in conference with the musical director if there is one on the show, or with the talent if it is a small organization. When all these decisions are made, the routine is sent to continuity and a script is ordered. In the meantime, the production director goes ahead with his plans.

If a guest artist is regularly featured on the program, the guest is chosen and consulted about the music.

The next step is to arrange a staff for the broadcast. If the program is a regular one, it is likely that the same staff will serve on each program. If it is a new show and a staff has to be chosen, there are certain requirements which the production director must consider. He will want an engineer who knows something about music and one who has had some experience on music programs. A really good studio engineer can be of great help to a musical production director. He can anticipate the director's needs in monitoring and he can also assist in making the original studio setup. This is a delicate business, and one in which the production director will appreciate all the help which a good engineer can give him. The director will also need an announcer who has a style that is right for the program. In spite of the fact that announcers sometimes sound as though they were all cut from the same piece of cloth, there is a considerable difference in the styles, voices, and understanding which they bring to a piece of copy. An announcer who sounds formal and dignified would hardly be a natural choice for an informal program of dance music where the rest of the program is easy, chatty, folksy in style. There are two other recommendations which an announcer should have, ideally, to make him suited to any given music program. One is a knowledge of the kind of music on the program and the other is a love for it. In spite of everything, if an announcer really likes something and knows enough about it to have reason for his likes, that feeling comes through to an audience. They can sense his respect for the material. This adds a certain "plussage" to his announcing which often is a valuable asset to the program. Musical directors are so few, even on a large network staff, that the production director will seldom have a choice about conductors, although naturally he will want the best man available.

The production director's next concern is a studio. Whereas in many kinds of programs the only real concern is size, in a music program the matter of acoustics and dynamics becomes important. Studios seem to develop personalities much in the same manner as the old Model T Ford. In spite of uniformity of design and great care in construction, studios differ rather widely in their acoustical properties, and the musical production director soon becomes aware of the peculiar properties of each one. If the musical program is a small one, he may have a choice of several studios and he will naturally try to get the one that will give him the most musical brilliance. If the program involves a large group, his choice may be seriously narrowed, since most stations do not have a great many studios large enough to house a large-sized musical group. In the case of a pipe-organ program, however, the director would have no choice at all. He would, of necessity, use the studio in which the organ was installed. The main consideration is the acoustic quality of the studio, and the director wants as much brilliance as possible without boominess. He will soon learn which of the studios can give him this acoustic quality.

This brings us to a point in the production analysis which in other kinds of programs may be largely a utilitarian matter, or a matter of convenience, but which in music programs is of the utmost artistic importance. That is the matter of studio setup and microphone placement.

Studio Setups for Musical Programs

Since every music program presents its own special problems in pickup, it is impossible to generalize on this subject. Only in specific cases can recommendations be made. Even then, no hard-and-fast rules can be laid down because the ear must be the final judge of any setup. For every problem in musical setups, the following must be considered:

1. The placement of the instruments or artists with relation to each other and within the studio.
2. The number of microphones to be used.
3. The placement of the microphones.
4. The angling of the microphones.
5. The height of the microphones.
6. The kind of microphones.
7. The kind and amount of distortion to be used.

The engineering department of the National Broadcasting Company is categorically committed to the principle that the best musical pickup can be made only on one microphone. The feeling is that if a musical group is properly balanced within the studio and within the unit, the best possible pickup can be achieved by one microphone. In spite of this commitment, few musical programs of any complexity are broadcast from a single mike. Some elaborate musical programs which NBC does are picked up on as many as six different microphones. Obviously, there is a difference between principle and practice. It is true, of course, that when the entire orchestra is playing, the pickup is usually made on a single microphone, but as soon as solos come along, or even when a single section of an orchestra is featured, that section regularly has its own special microphone. Engineers, however, and many production directors alike seem to stand pat on the principle.

Another principle on which NBC engineers are very firm is the matter of distortion. Certain engineers and musical production directors have felt that brilliance can be added to an orchestra by the addition of just a little echo to the broadcast. This is done, not by hardening the studio walls, as one might suspect, but rather by adding echo artificially with an echo chamber. This can be controlled at the mixing panel so that as much or as little echo as desired can be added merely by turning a knob. The NBC engineering staff is unanimous in its condemnation of this procedure, although it is used on several large commercial shows and is used by other networks.

It is generally agreed that a ribbon or velocity microphone

is the best type to use for a musical pickup if it is at all practicable. This is first choice. In cases where directional control is necessary, the unidirectional microphone is recommended. The velocity microphone is the number one choice because it is the most sensitive and has the widest range of frequency response. A musical program demands a wider frequency response than any other kind. Figure 10 shows exactly what the comparative frequency range of various instruments is. The unidirectional or cardioid microphone, since it uses the velocity principle of operation, offers the widest frequency response available in a directional microphone. Where cross-pickup is undesirable, this microphone is recommended.

Studio setups cannot be discussed without including the subject of balance, since the whole purpose of a setup is to achieve a proper balance. Let us define setup as the arrangement of instruments and microphones within the studio. In balancing, we rearrange the setup and shift the elements around until each instrument comes in at a proper volume in relation to all the other instruments for all the music to be played. If more than one microphone is used, there may be several different balances used within a single number as one microphone is cut out and another added in, according to the arrangements being played. All setups are made for the purpose of achieving, in rehearsal, an ideal balance between the various elements of the program.

A Setup for Pianos

There are several ways *not* to set up a studio for a piano pickup which the beginner should avoid. The microphone should never be placed under the lid of the piano as has sometimes been done. A setup should never be used where the lid of the piano is down. This will kill all the brilliance of the pickup and cut down on the definition. The microphone should never be placed on the bass side of the keyboard, because the lower notes tend to have more volume, and if the microphone is on that side of the piano, there is not a perfect balance between the bass and treble parts of the music.

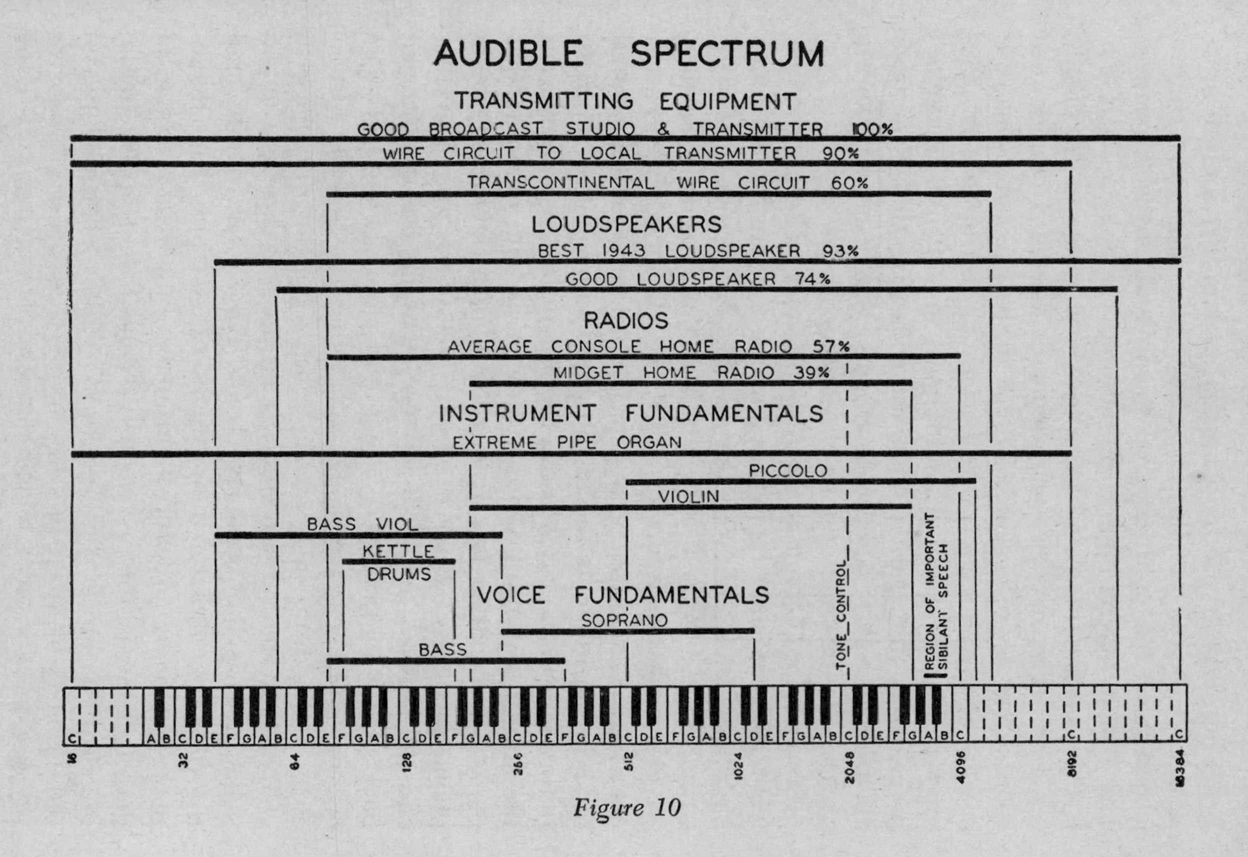
AUDIBLE SPECTRUM
TRANSMITTING EQUIPMENT
GOOD BROADCAST STUDIO & TRANSMITTER 100%
WIRE CIRCUIT TO LOCAL TRANSMITTER 90%
TRANSCONTINENTAL WIRE CIRCUIT 60%
LOUDSPEAKERS
BEST 1943 LOUDSPEAKER 93%
GOOD LOUDSPEAKER 74%
RADIOS
AVERAGE CONSOLE HOME RADIO 57%
MIDGET HOME RADIO 39%
INSTRUMENT FUNDAMENTALS
EXTREME PIPE ORGAN
PICCOLO
VIOLIN
BASS VIOL
KETTLE DRUMS
VOICE FUNDAMENTALS
SOPRANO
BASS
TONE CONTROL
REGION OF IMPORTANT SIBILANT SPEECH
16
32
64
128
256
512
1024
2048
4096
8192
16384

Figure 10

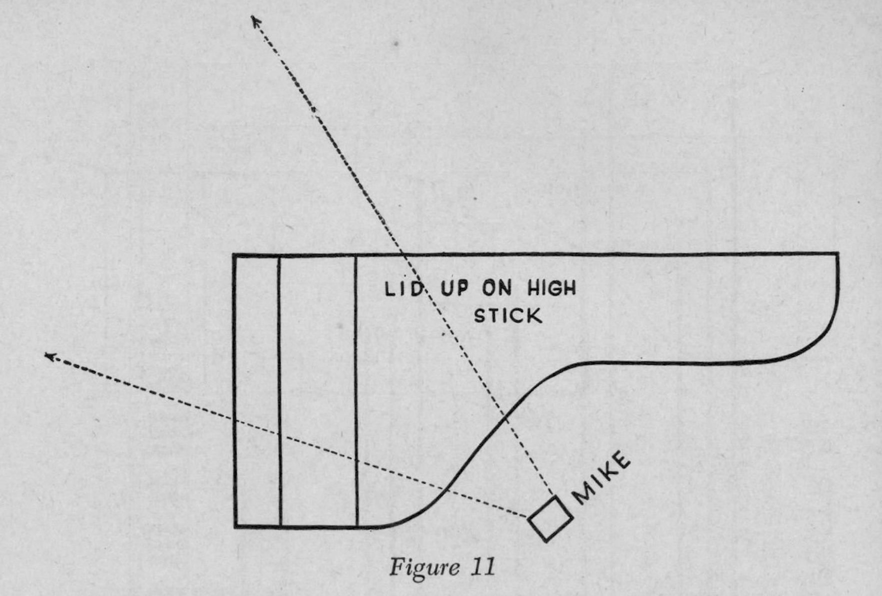

Figure 11

Properly, a microphone for a piano pickup should be located as shown in Figure 11. Notice that the microphone is placed in the curve of the piano on the treble side, tilted down toward the strings and beamed diagonally across the piano. If the piano is to be played in intimate or popular style, the microphone should be about five or six feet high. If concert or classical music is to be played, the microphone can be moved back slightly and raised to a height of eight or nine feet. The relative position is the same except that it is a little farther away and a little higher. This allows for the difference in volume between the two styles of music.

For a two-piano pickup the best arrangement is to dovetail the pianos as illustrated in Figure 12 and place the microphone between them at a height of about five feet and beamed diagonally across the two pianos as indicated. The lids should, of course, be up on the high stick. A fairly good pickup can also be made if the pianos are arranged with their keyboards parallel and a mike hung at the foot of the pianos between them. In this arrangement the lids must be removed.

Where the pianist sings also, as in the case of some song-

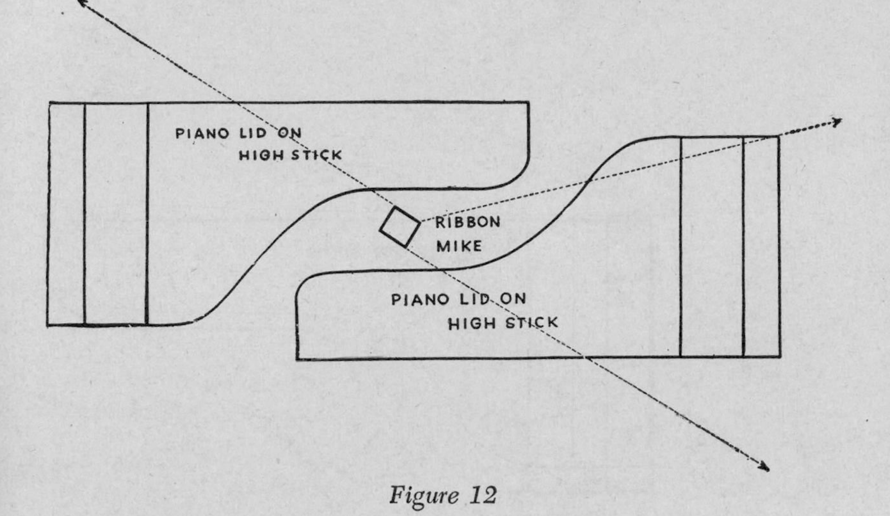

Figure 12

patter programs, a boom-mounted mike may be used, so angled that the dead edge of the mike is beamed toward the sounding board of the piano. This allows for a balance between voice and piano.

Little can be said about setups for pipe organs, since no two organs are alike and since so much depends on the installation and the acoustics of the studio in which the organ is located. If an electric organ is to be used, a ribbon mike is set up in the beam of the organ speaker. Considerable difference of opinion exists about the distance a microphone should be from the speaker. Some engineers think it should be very close to the speaker. Others insist that there should be at least twenty feet between microphone and speaker.

Setups for Small Ensembles

A string trio consisting of piano, violin, and 'cello make a nice combination for certain kinds of music. Figure 13 illustrates a satisfactory setup for getting this combination on one microphone. In all these illustrations, approximations will not do. Often moving an instrument six inches one way or another will destroy the balance. So both angles and distances must be reasonably exact.

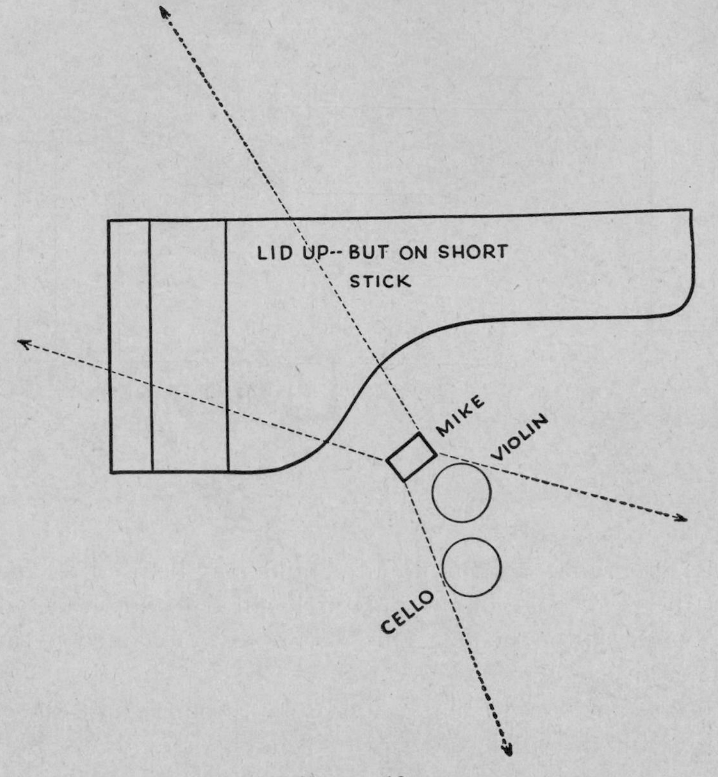

Figure 13

If a piano and violin are to play together in duet fashion, then the setup illustrated in Figure 13 will serve very well, minus the 'cello. If the piano is to be only an accompaniment for the violin, then each instrument should have a separate microphone, so placed as to minimize cross-pickup.

A string quartet setup for two violins, a viola, and 'cello is illustrated in Figure 14. This is the first time a split setup for similar instruments using both sides of the microphone has been shown. This principle can be used for any kind of setup, even a full concert orchestra, although such a large combination seldom uses the split setup. Another good setup for a string quartet is to arrange the artists in more or less standard

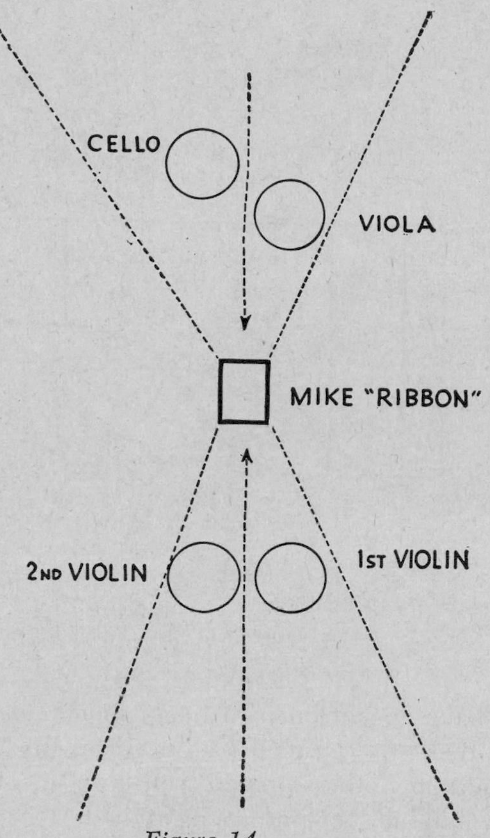

Figure 14

concert setup and then hang a microphone over the group beamed down on them from above.

A larger string ensemble setup is illustrated in Figure 15. In this illustration a special microphone is used for the celeste. If the celeste were not in the combination, then one microphone would be used for the rest of the group. This arrangement would be an excellent starting point in balancing an orchestra.

Small Vocal and Specialty Groups

Radio has encouraged all kinds of small vocal and instrumental combinations to offer their wares to the public. Some

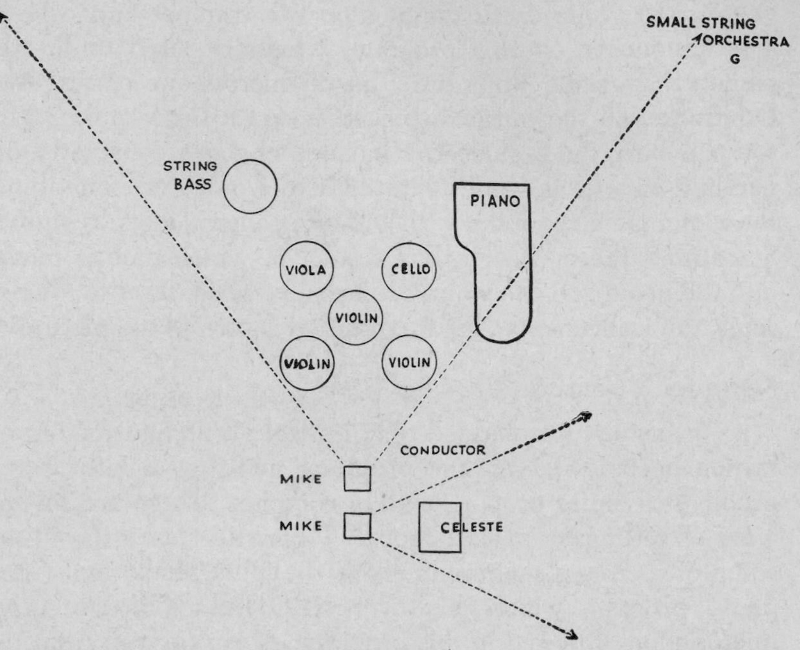

Figure 15

of these have caught on in a most phenomenal fashion. The Mills Brothers, the Boswell Sisters, "The Ink Spots," the Dinnings, and many others are all well known. There are several so-called hill-billy combinations which have wide regional fame, and almost every station has at least one such combination that is broadcast regularly. Since these vary so much and since there are often half a dozen combinations within each such small organization, it is not easy to generalize. Shown in Plate 26 are the Carroll Sisters and Russell Wilk, their arranger and accompanist. It is an interesting setup, since this combination uses both piano and celeste to accompany the trio, who all use the same microphone and all work from the same side of the ribbon mike.

Plate 27 shows "The Westerners" and Kurt and Louise Massey, a popular group on the air. This combination uses a singing combination of three voices, two soloists, and a basic instrumental group composed of a string bass, accordion, guitar, and violin, with doubles on the trumpet and celeste. The announcer on this program, which is heard under the name of "Reveille Roundup," has a microphone of his own. Otherwise, all the music is picked up on a single mike. This setup is very fluid, since the balance changes constantly depending on who is being featured at the moment. Sometimes the violin is on the mike with the other instruments as shown. Sometimes the accordion has a solo, in which case it moves into the beam and the violin drops back. When Louise Massey sings, the instruments take the position shown in the picture.

Setup for a Concert Orchestra

As instruments are added to a musical group and the organization becomes larger, the problems multiply and the setup problem becomes proportionately complex. There are several ways of setting up such a group. Figure 16 shows the disposition of men and microphones for the "Roy Shield and Company" program which airs over NBC from Chicago. Five microphones are used in this program, as can be seen from the illustration. For all full orchestra pickups a single 44-B microphone is used at a height of about nine feet, tilted slightly downward. A second microphone is used directly above the string section and beamed vertically down on top of the string section. This microphone is placed at a height of about seven feet and directly over and in the center of the string section. A velocity microphone is also used here with the one live side beamed down toward the string section and the other toward the ceiling of the studio. A third microphone is used back of the brass section for special pickups of either muted brasses or woodwinds when the instrumentation or arrangement calls for such. This microphone is placed between the brass section and the woodwinds so that musicians from either choir can have easy access to it. It also is a velocity mike beamed at right angles to the general setup line of the orchestra. The fourth microphone is a 77-B unidirectional microphone which is placed near the conductor's podium for Rheinhold Schmidt and Jean McKenna, soloists on the program. The fifth micro-

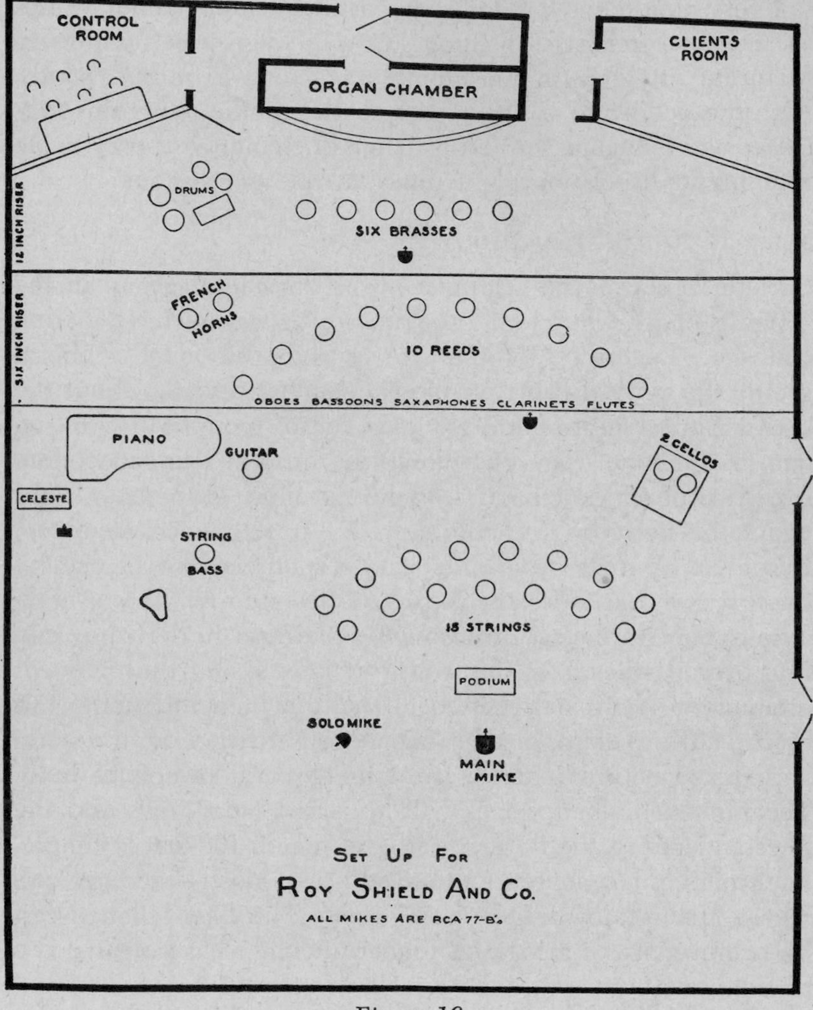

Figure 16

phone is the regular announce mike up by the "delite" box at the control-room window.

What may not be completely apparent in the sketch is the very thin arrangement of the musicians. Doctor Shield spreads his orchestra out much more than conductors of most other such programs. The entire floor space of NBC's largest Chicago studio, Studio A, is taken up with the setup for this program.

Every conductor has his own particular ideas about setups for concert orchestra pickups. They all agree in their main features, but there is considerable variation in minor details. Also the acoustics of the studio in which the program originates will influence the setup. The same conductor may make a different disposition of his men in different studios.

Setup for Choral Groups

Plate 28 shows the arrangement of the choral group in the "Hymns of All Churches" program which airs over NBC from Chicago. Regardless of the size or composition of a choral group, the general principle of arrangement remains about the same. For straight choral work the entire group will work on one microphone. The chorus will be arranged in succeeding segments of concentric circles with not more than six or eight people in each row. Suppose there are twelve voices involved. If it is an all-male group, first and second tenors will occupy the first row, baritones and basses the second row. It is usually wise to elevate the second row on a platform so that they can sing over the heads of the front-row people and thus prevent attenuation from that section. Usually a high microphone is used for this pickup, placed seven or eight feet from the floor. If a mixed chorus is used, the same general principles hold. The highest-pitched voices will be in the front rows and the lowest voices in the back rows. The reason for this is simple. High pitches attenuate more quickly than lower, and women's voices are usually lighter than men's. The best balance can be achieved by putting the higher-pitched voices nearer the microphone.

Setups for Military Bands

Figure 17 shows one possible arrangement of instruments for a band pickup. Most bands are fairly large organizations with much heavier preponderance of brass and percussion than is usual in any other type of music. Because this is true, the setup changes somewhat to make allowance for this variation.

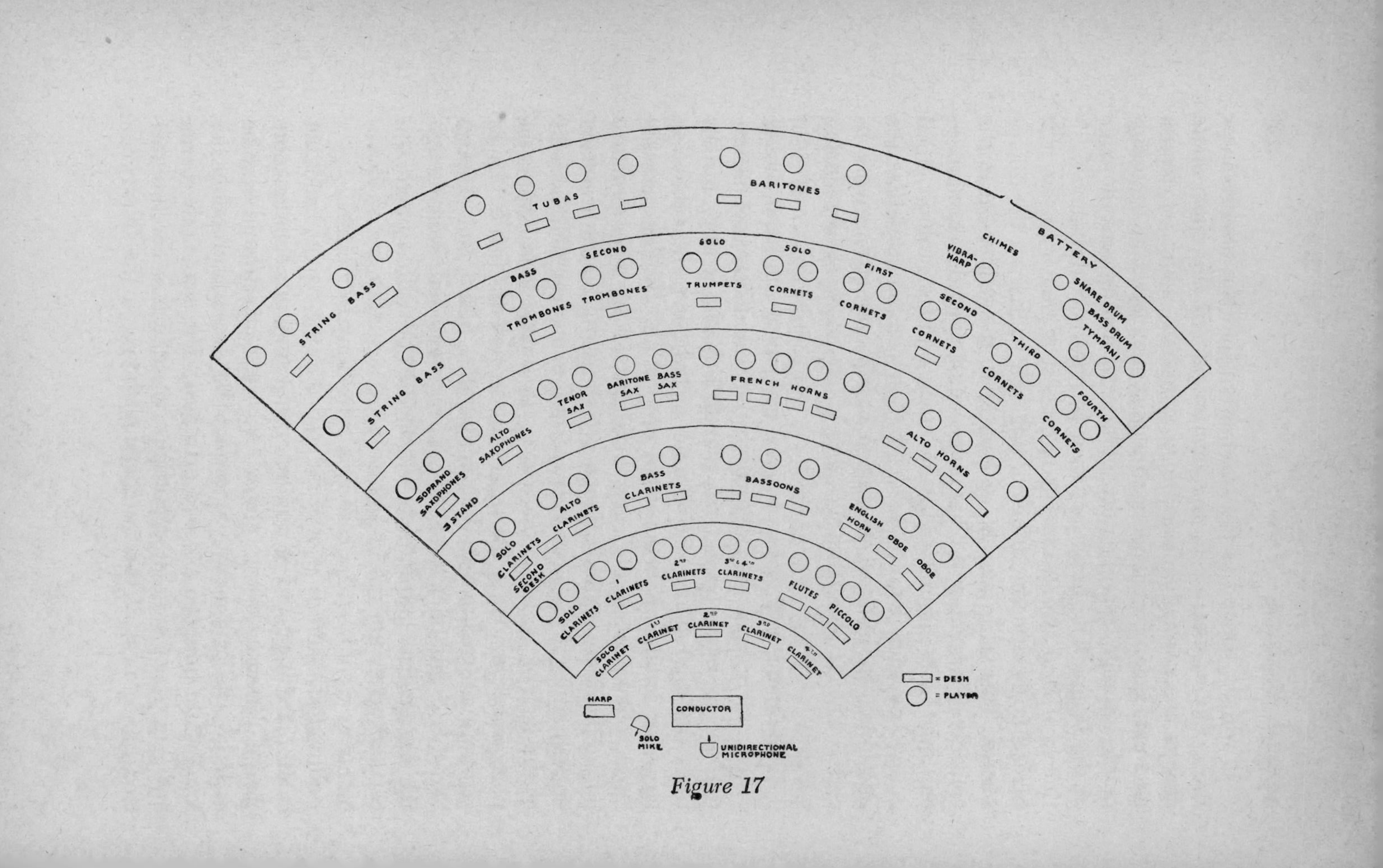
STRING BASS
TUBAS
BARITONES
BATTERY
CHIMES
VIBRA-HARP
SNARE DRUM
BASS DRUM
TYMPANI
STRING BASS
BASS TROMBONES
SECOND TROMBONES
SOLO TRUMPETS
SOLO CORNETS
FIRST CORNETS
SECOND CORNETS
THIRD CORNETS
FOURTH CORNETS
SOPRANO SAXOPHONES
3 STAND
ALTO SAXOPHONES
TENOR SAX
BARITONE SAX
BASS SAX
FRENCH HORNS
ALTO HORNS
SOLO CLARINETS
SECOND DESK
ALTO CLARINETS
BASS CLARINETS
BASSOONS
ENGLISH HORN
OBOE
OBOE
SOLO CLARINETS
1 CLARINETS
2ND CLARINETS
3RD & 4TH CLARINETS
FLUTES
PICCOLO
SOLO CLARINET
1ST CLARINET
2ND CLARINET
3RD CLARINET
4TH CLARINET
= DESK
= PLAYER
HARP
CONDUCTOR
SOLO MIKE
UNIDIRECTIONAL MICROPHONE

Figure 17

It will be noticed in the band setup that the reeds occupy the positions nearest to the microphone in the spot where strings are normally placed in a symphony setup. Tympani and percussion instruments still must be placed at a considerable distance from the microphone and well toward the edge of the beam. The brass section is in relatively the same position in a band as in a symphony orchestra; that is to say, it is placed fairly directly on beam, but well back from the microphone. This setup may be of interest to the reader because a considerable number of band units occasionally do some broadcasting. In communities where union rulings prohibit it, of course, no such work goes on, but in communities that are non-union, high-school or college bands very often give concerts. This is also true of military bands, especially during wartime.

If the number of pieces in each section of the band should differ widely from the proportions illustrated here, compensation can be made by moving that section closer to or farther from the microphone, depending on whether the section is larger or smaller than the usual proportion. By this means a band which is not perfectly balanced in its own structure might be brought into balance. High-school bands are often not made up of the proper proportion of instruments because of the lack of available musicians. In such a case compensation must be made for the size of the section of the band by its position with relation to the microphone. Again, for a pickup like this, a ribbon microphone is recommended even though the degree of definition may not need to be quite so high and certainly does not go through so wide a quality arc of instruments as would be the case in a symphony orchestra.

Obviously there is a lot of difference in the size of bands. A small marching band of a military unit may not contain more than eighteen or twenty pieces. A large concert band may be as large as a symphony orchestra. The average probably lies somewhere between the two extremes. The size of the band, however, is not of great importance, since, if it is a well-organized band, most of the instruments shown in the illustration will be present. The variation in size will only mean a variation in the size of the various instrument sections. One band may have two cornets while another has ten, but the cornet section is the unit to be considered in balancing the band for broadcast purposes.

Setups for Dance Bands

There is probably as much variation in the composition of a dance orchestra as in any other kind of musical unit. It may range anywhere from the very small unit of perhaps five men up to an orchestra which is for all practical purposes of full concert size. Not only is there a difference in the composition of a dance band, but a considerable amount of doubling goes on. Every member of the reed section of a dance band may play two or three different instruments, and the color of the whole orchestra will change depending upon which instruments the various band members are playing in any given portion of a piece of music. Finally, dance bands are strongly stylized. Some bands play almost exclusively hot music, in which case the emphasis will be on volume, noise, and pace. Other bands play almost exclusively sweet music, which means that more emphasis will be placed on melody line and less on rhythm. There will probably be more strings in such an organization and fewer reeds and brasses. Even the general kind of music played will be consistent with the style of the orchestra itself. Therefore, there are many variables in this whole field of dance bands.

There are, however, certain basic concepts which are common to all such organizations. Most dance orchestras are organized into three groups, the brasses, the reeds, and the rhythm section. The brasses will be composed of trumpets and trombones; the reed section will often include all kinds of saxophones from tenor to bass, and in addition will feature clarinets, piccolos, and flutes, and possibly oboes and bassoons; the rhythm section will consist of piano, guitar, bass viol, and drums.

Very often two microphones are used for such a pickup. On

one side of the bandstand will be two rows of instruments with the reeds in front and the brasses behind, both in the beam of a single microphone. At one side or the other of this group will be the rhythm section, which will also have its own microphone, to allow for making a proper balance between brass and rhythm.

If one or two violins are included in the group, they will normally be placed with the rhythm section, because that will give them a spot in front of the rhythm mike where they can be picked up and amplified. Strings playing against brasses do not have much chance unless they can be brought into balance. If the dance band is a large one and there is a regular string section along with the reeds and brasses, then another kind of setup is called for. This will normally follow the general pattern of the concert orchestra setup, with strings in the first bank, reeds in the second bank, and brass and percussion in the third. Other instruments like the guitar and piano will be placed out at the edge of the beam on the second and third tiers. An interesting symphonic jazz arrangement with orchestra can be made by using a split setup on two sides of a ribbon microphone. In this kind of setup, one side of the microphone will have violins, violas, 'cellos, string bass, and piano. There will be a harp on the dead edge of the microphone and on the other side will be saxophones, other heavier reeds, brasses, and percussions. By placing the microphone somewhat closer to the string section than to the saxophones a reasonably good balance can be obtained on this bidirectional basis. This setup is very flexible so far as pickup is concerned, but there is a danger that the conductor may not be in the best acoustical spot to hear and balance his orchestra. If he is, he has the difficult problem of trying to conduct in two directions at once, as his band will be spread out on his left and right. If he moves his podium back to where he can see both sides of the orchestra, he is moving out of the direct line of sound and is not in a good position to balance his orchestra.

Setups for Combination Units

By combination units are meant units in which orchestral music, vocal music, and choir are combined into a single musical unit. An excellent example of this kind of musical program is "The Contented Hour" which has been on the air for a great many years. This program is under the musical direction of Percy Faith.

This program talent has a concert orchestra of thirty pieces, a mixed chorus of twelve male voices and four female voices, and a bass and soprano soloist. The program usually consists of a semi-symphonic treatment of popular or semi-classical music. Anything from Irving Berlin to Gilbert and Sullivan, from "Old Black Joe" to "Ave Maria" is fair game on this program. It is characterized by a brisk staccato handling of arrangements with strong emphasis on melodic line. The program originates from NBC's Studio A in Chicago every Monday night. The setup is illustrated in Figure 18. Nine microphones are used. Number one represents the over-all master orchestra microphone which is used to pick up the total orchestra when it is playing. Number two, a velocity microphone beamed vertically over the string section of the orchestra to augment it during special string passages. Number three is also a ribbon microphone beamed at right angles to the general line of the orchestra and is used for reeds and brasses and muted brass solos. Number four is a special microphone beamed on the vibra harp for certain pickups featuring that instrument. Microphone number five is a 77-B raised to a height of about five feet and is used to pick up the full mixed chorus of sixteen voices. For some vocal arrangements the choral group is split, with the twelve men working on one microphone and the four women on another. In this case the pickups are made on two 77-B microphones indicated as numbers six and seven. These microphones are at normal head height and are mixed against each other and against the orchestral accompaniment when it is used. Number eight is another 77-B used for the soloist on the program and for the

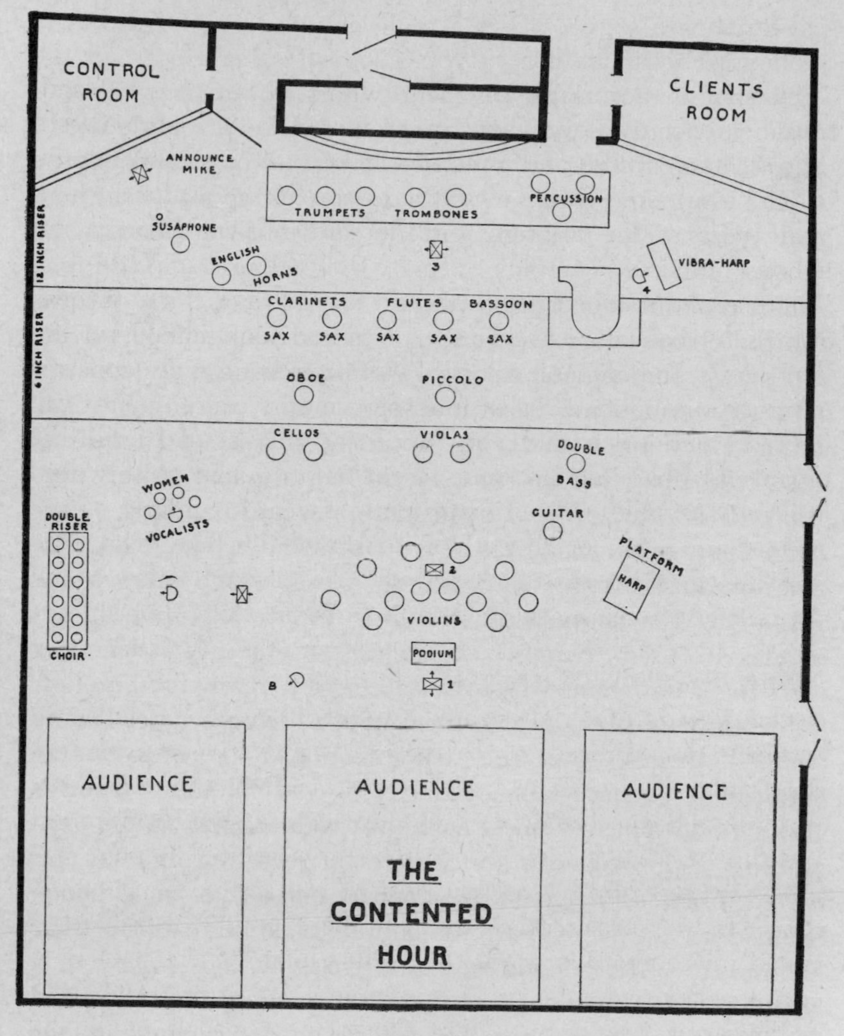

Figure 18

announcer. Number nine is the NBC announcer's microphone at which the program is opened and closed and where network and station identification is made. It should be understood, of course, that never are all these microphones in operation at the same time. Four is probably the largest number that might be used at any given time. If, for example, a musical number is set up where a male chorus carries one part, a women's chorus another, a vocal soloist is featured, and the orchestra is accompanying the whole thing, microphones number one, six, seven, and eight would be in play. Microphones two, three, and four are used only for emphasizing short passages in an orchestration or to pick up a solo bit here and there as the arrangement demands. Even though the whole thing looks complex, actually the pickup is fairly simple. The use of directional microphones for the chorus and soloists allows for balancing them against the accompaniment of the orchestra. Sometimes even a 77-B microphone is used in the number one position. This has some merits, since "The Contented Hour" has a studio audience and the use of a unidirectional microphone helps some to cut out audience noise where it is not desirable. Since this program is heard regularly on the air, as are many of the others mentioned in this book, the student can listen to them and see the kind of balance and over-all effectiveness these setups make possible.

Setups for Symphony Orchestra Pickups

Considering that the organization of a symphony orchestra is fairly standardized, there are surprising variations in the disposition of musicians and orchestra choirs for broadcast purposes. Each conductor seems to have a slightly different idea about what makes the best possible arrangement of the musicians for an orchestral pickup. One practice is fairly common. In the broadcast of a symphony orchestra usually a single microphone is used. Few symphonies have long concerto passages where a single instrument is featured and especially few of them occur where the instrument is a low-volume one. More often, various passages are taken by whole choirs of the orchestra rather than by individual players. Because of this and because the arrangements are more orthodox and do less solo work, it is comparatively easier to achieve a good pickup of a full symphony orchestra on a single microphone. The microphone is commonly placed twenty or thirty feet in front of the director's podium, slightly off center to keep any artificial build-up of harmonics, and at a height of about fifteen to twenty feet, depending on the acoustics of the shell or stage or studio in which the orchestra is sitting. Plate 29 shows the NBC symphony studio, and with Arturo Toscanini conducting, as it is set up in Studio 8-H in Radio City, New York. This group is generally acknowledged to be one of the finest symphony orchestras on the air and a great deal of time and technical research has gone into the placement of musicians and general acoustical and microphone treatment to give the program the maximum effectiveness. Although three microphones show in the picture, only one is actually used, the others being emergency microphones which can be cut in if anything should go wrong with the one which is on the air.

Figure 19 shows in diagrammatic form the disposition of the instruments in the NBC symphony orchestra setup. In the first and second violin, and in the viola and 'cello sections, two musicians play from a single stand so that each circle in those sections represents two players. There are one hundred and fifteen musicians in this organization. Plate 29 and Figure 19 show two different setups of this same organization.

Several other variations on the symphony program setup are

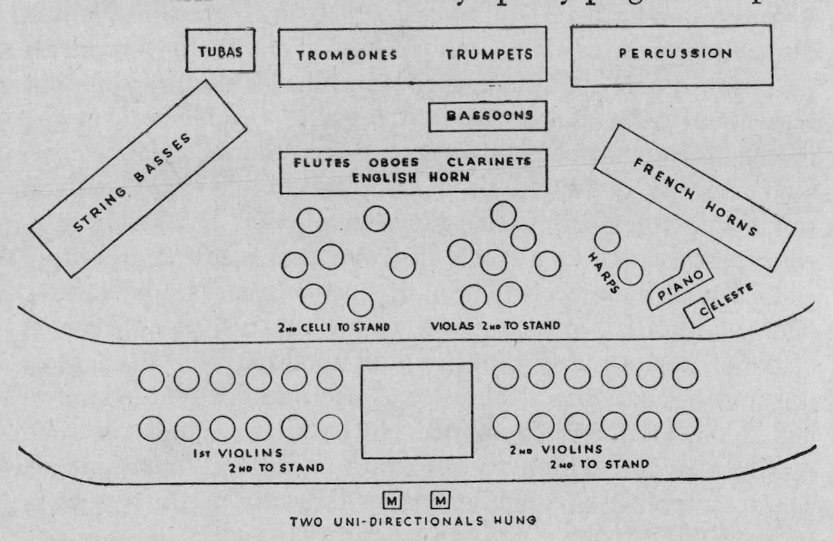

Figure 19

possible. Some conductors, for example, prefer to have percussion on the right, string basses in the center, and brasses on the left. Other conductors reverse this process. The exact placement of the various sections of the orchestra are admittedly a matter of taste and will vary somewhat with the acoustics of the studio involved. In general, however, there are certain underlying principles which need to be observed. Strings will normally be given the preference over all other instruments; that is to say, they will be more directly on the beam and closer to the microphone than any other instruments, with violins closest, second violins next, violas next, and 'cellos next. The woodwinds come in the next position. Piccolos, flutes, clarinets, oboes, and bassoons are usually very near the center of the beam and right behind the strings. Next come the horns, and farthest away are the basses, trumpets, trombones, and percussions. Pianos and harps are always placed well out to the edge of the microphone beam and fairly far away, usually on the edge of the group. This disposition of the orchestral choirs is based almost entirely on two factors, the volume of the instrument and its general pitch register. High frequencies tend to attenuate quicker than low frequencies; therefore, the first violin will carry less well than a 'cello and a string bass will carry even more. Trumpets and trombones are among the loudest instruments in the orchestra and are placed well back from the microphone. Tympani, percussion, and basses all are fairly high in volume and low in pitch and can also be well back from the microphone. Having established these general principles, and made proper allowances for the difference in players and studio acoustics, the production director who has to balance a symphony orchestra will then proceed to shift his people in these dimensions until the balance is achieved. It should be remembered that to lessen volume an instrument can either be moved back from the microphone or around to the edge of the beam. To increase volume it can be moved more directly on beam and closer to the microphone. With these simple facts in mind the process of balancing the group is largely one of trial and error.

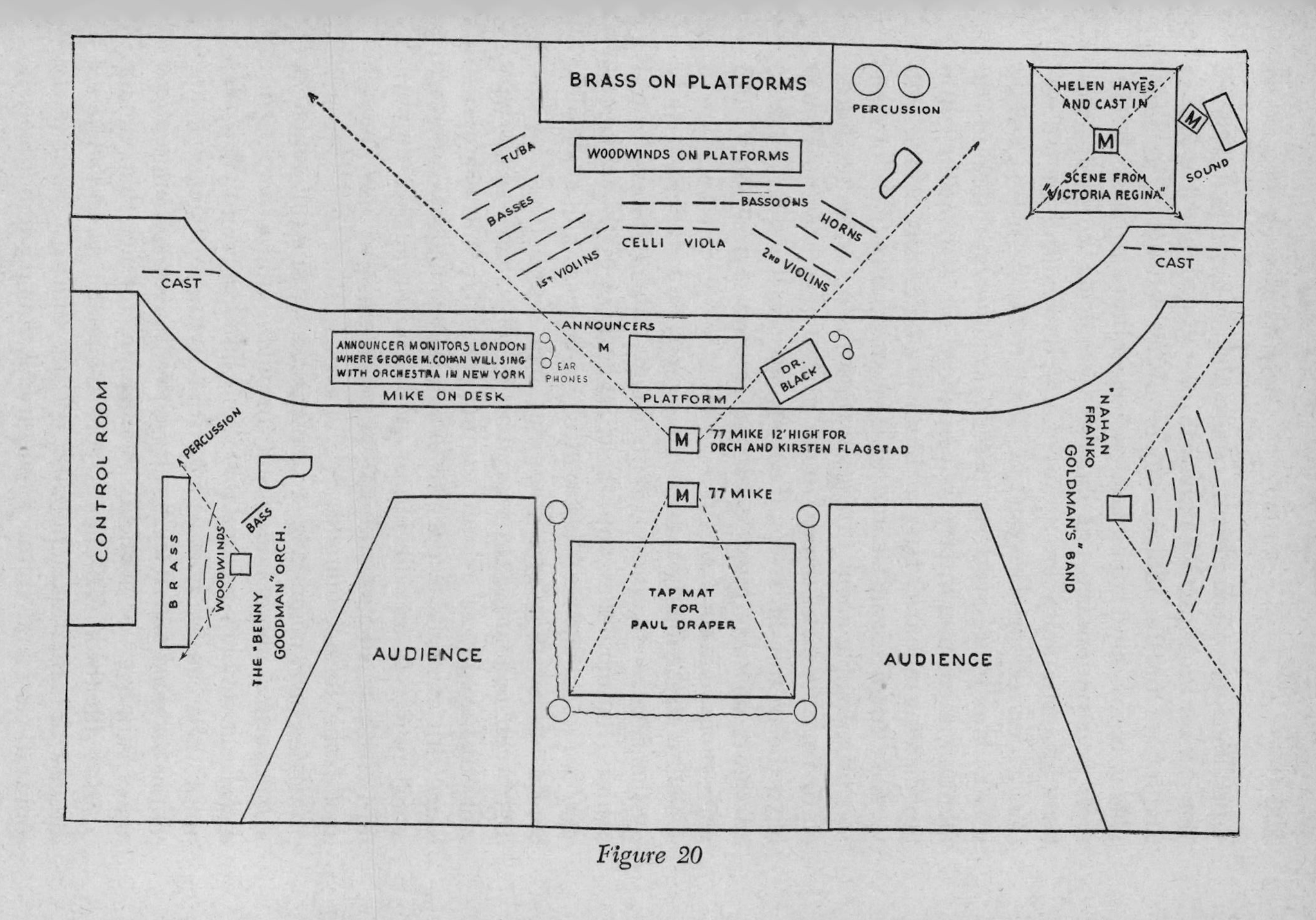
BRASS ON PLATFORMS
PERCUSSION
HELEN HAYES, AND CAST IN
M
"SCENE FROM "VICTORIA REGINA"
M
SOUND
TUBA
WOODWINDS ON PLATFORMS
BASSES
BASSOONS
HORNS
CELLI
VIOLA
1ST VIOLINS
2ND VIOLINS
CAST
CAST
ANNOUNCERS
ANNOUNCER MONITORS LONDON WHERE GEORGE M. COHAN WILL SING WITH ORCHESTRA IN NEW YORK
M
EAR PHONES
MIKE ON DESK
PLATFORM
DR. BLACK
"NAHAN FRANKO GOLDMAN'S" BAND
CONTROL ROOM
PERCUSSION
M
77 MIKE 12' HIGH FOR ORCH AND KIRSTEN FLAGSTAD
M
77 MIKE
BRASS
WOODWINDS
BASS
THE "BENNY GOODMAN" ORCH.
AUDIENCE
TAP MAT FOR PAUL DRAPER
AUDIENCE

Figure 20

Just by way of completely confusing the reader, Figure 20 illustrates a broadcast which came out of Studio 8-H in NBC's Radio City on the "Magic Key of RCA" broadcast in 1938. This is supposed to have been one of the most complex broadcasts ever undertaken. As can be seen from the illustration, three separate music groups were involved: a full concert orchestra under the direction of Doctor Frank Black, Edwin Franko Goldman's band, and Benny Goodman's orchestra. In addition, there was Kirsten Flagstad, soloist, Paul Draper in a tap dancing number, Helen Hayes in a dramatic scene from *Victoria Regina,* and George M. Cohan singing from London to the accompaniment of Doctor Frank Black's orchestra in New York. Add to these factors a studio audience and you have the picture of a very complex broadcast indeed. Figure 20 shows how the huge stage and Studio 8-H in New York was set up to accommodate it.

Setups are strongly influenced by not only the number of musicians, the diversity of instruments, and the presence of soloists, but more than any other single thing by the orchestration or arrangement of the music itself. Most so-called classical music was written for the concert hall. Any special effects, solo work, or unusual arrangement of music had to be adaptable to listening in a large auditorium. If a vocalist was to sing with an orchestra, for instance, she had to have enough vocal power to top the entire orchestra during her number. If a violinist had a solo, he had to be able to play loud enough to top the accompaniment.

Modern composers and arrangers have taken advantage of the fact that microphones and amplifiers allow them to use comparatively low-volume tones and build them up artificially until they can be featured in solo spots. All the so-called crooners, male and female, are a product of the microphone age. Without the artificial increase in volume that can be made with the mike, their voices would be useless. On the other hand, there is a peculiar quality that can be achieved only at very low volumes which has found an enthusiastic audience among lovers of popular music. Along with low-volume vocal effects, modern composers and arrangers like the effects to be gained from muted brasses and strings. These effects are sometimes much too low in volume to be set against the full orchestra without artificial amplification. With the possibility of balancing a soft, low sound against much higher volume sounds which is possible in radio, all kinds of new effects can be used. Arrangers are fond of using these combinations. When such arrangements occur in a score, the production director must take them into consideration in planning his setup.

Rehearsal Procedures

After the problem of setups has been decided, at least on paper, the production director considers any special effects which the program may contain, or which he may wish to add. Echo is a case in point. Some directors feel that a certain brilliance is added to musical programs with a small amount of echo. This amounts to creating a distortion effect, and NBC musical production men are opposed to it as a matter of principle. There are, however, several well-known and widely heard musical programs on the air that use this effect, and it must be admitted that the whole thing is a matter of artistic opinion. Certain passages in the score may give the production director ideas for special effects, not originally contemplated. If these come up, they are discussed with the musical director and a decision made as to whether or not they will be used, and, if they are to be used, how they will affect other elements in the program.

The next step is to estimate the rehearsal time needed for the program. It is difficult to generalize about the rehearsal time necessary for musical programs because there are so many variables to be considered. New arrangements take longer to rehearse than stock arrangements. It takes longer to rehearse forty men than it does five. It takes much longer to work out a fast-moving precision routine than a simple standard treatment of any piece of music. The more diverse elements that go into the program, the more time it takes. For example, it is much simpler to set a number with a concert orchestra than to set one – perhaps the same – number when it includes a violin solo, a baritone solo, and a special chorus by a choir. The addition of other units necessitates additional rehearsal.

Here are some typical musical programs with their rehearsal schedules. "Reveille Roundup," starring Louise Massey and "The Westerners," uses a total rehearsal time of two hours. About twenty minutes are spent in working on each number. "Roy Shield and Company," an elaborate program with a concert orchestra and two guests soloists, uses five and a half hours to rehearse for a fifty-minute program. A small popular group from the orchestra, known as "The Savants," does one number on each program, and this group usually rehearses that number for about forty minutes. A little more than an hour is spent in a dress rehearsal and the balance of the time is spent rehearsing and polishing individual numbers. This is a complicated program, since it uses nearly all original arrangements and some original music.

"The Contented Hour," sponsored by the Carnation Company, and one of the better-known musical programs on the air, rehearses seven hours and twenty minutes on one portion or another of the program, which uses a concert orchestra, soloists, and a mixed choir. The normal disposition of rehearsal time on this program is as follows: On the Friday preceding the Monday broadcast the chorus is rehearsed for two hours. This is a note rehearsal and is not put on the microphone. On the day of the broadcast the chorus rehearses on mike for an hour, from 12:00 to 1:00 P.M. From 1:30 to 3:30 the orchestra rehearses its numbers. During the last hour of this time the chorus is also present to rehearse the numbers involving both chorus and orchestra. From 4:00 to 4:15 the orchestra rehearses with the soloists, Josephine Antoine and Rheinhold Schmidt. From 4:15 to 5:15 the entire group – orchestra, chorus, and soloists – put the finishing touches on all their numbers and a dress rehearsal is scheduled for 5:15. The time from 5:15 to 6:20 is used for spotting any rough places in the program and for making cuts which will bring the program to time. The program takes the air at 9:00 P.M. C.W.T.

Having planned for rehearsal time which seems adequate, the production director's next concern is to study the score. He may even go so far as to work out a complete microphone routine for picking up every number. He needs to know the score for the whole program very well, because this is the basis of his work. The score is to the musical production director what the story script is to the dramatic director. A study of the score will tell him exactly what his job is going to be in balancing and he can plan solutions ahead of time.

One of the things the director looks for is a place to cut. At this point in the proceedings, he has no notion exactly how long the score will take to play. If it is a standard work, he can find out what it usually runs, although every conductor will have his own timing on a piece of music. Especially in longer classical numbers, this will vary considerably. He must, therefore, be ready to make suggestions for bringing the program to time.

The production director now orders the scripts. In conference with the writer from the continuity department, he will plan what is to be said about each number and the general flavor of the script for the whole program. The continuity must, of course, match the quality of the music. Serious music calls for serious continuity and vice versa. Suitability and cleverness and originality are the keynotes here. A brilliant show, musically, can be bogged down into a mediocre affair by poor continuity. It cannot be overlooked that an announcer has the spotlight on a musical program some of the time, inevitably, and he must be of the same caliber as the music on the program.

There is a lot of music library work to be done at about this time. A folder must be made up for each musician of all the music which he will play. For instance, the oboe player must have all the right oboe music for every piece in the routine in which the full orchestra participates and for special numbers in which he appears. This example has to be multiplied by the number of people involved in the program, each folder being different. Furthermore, the order of music in the folders should be the same as that on the routine plan. While this is a job that has no great complexity, still it takes time, and if not properly done can waste a great deal of a valuable rehearsal.

The production director must next schedule his staff. This can be considered to mean himself, the engineer, and the announcer. If it is interpreted to mean the musicians, too, as it might in the case where a staff orchestra is to be used, the scheduling of staff is a complex problem. Most union contracts provide that musicians work a five-day week, an eight-hour day, of which they can actually play only five hours. Since staff musicians often work on different programs in different combinations, it is sometimes difficult to juggle matters so that the right combination of men is available for the right programs at the desired rehearsal time. The problem is so complex, in fact, that once a week's programming has been set, it is very difficult to find anyone willing to upset it. While the problem of assigning staff musicians is not properly in the sphere of the production director's activities, he must be concerned with it, since these men form the talent of his program. Naturally, he wants to get the best people for his program and he wants to get them for as long a rehearsal period as is possible.

The next step in the process is the scheduling of space and equipment. In a large and well-organized network this may amount to little more than asking the studio clerk for an assignment. Everything else will follow as a matter of routine. The maintenance or setup department will see that the proper number of chairs and music stands are in place at the proper time. The engineering department will inquire about microphone requirements and have them on hand and ready. All the other odds and ends will be taken care of in a like manner.

In a station not so organized, the musical production director may have to take care of many of these matters himself. Even in a large organization, special requirements may have to be arranged for. If, as a case in point, a director doing a choir program decides that he needs several risers or platforms for his choir, he will probably have to order them specially, since this is not a routine matter which the department concerned would know about. If a certain studio must be used and it is necessary to have a Hammond Organ, it might have to be specially scheduled. If a program requires the use of a pipe organ, arrangements would have to be made to use the studio in which the organ is located, or, if that is unsatisfactory for any reason, then the organ studio would have to be piped in to the studio used for the program and an extra engineer and two-way telephone connections for cues provided. These should be arranged for by the production director. In doing music programs, all sorts of special needs arise and must be dealt with as they come along.

The director now sets about the task of marking up his script and score for production. In most musical programs this will mean only the making of a few notes on the score about what microphones are to be used at a particular point, or where changes in microphone combinations will occur, based on the arrangements and the music. This markup, if any, will usually be made in conference with the conductor.

With this much preparation the production director is now ready for rehearsals. Rehearsals of a musical program tend to divide themselves into three general stages, although there is considerable variation in practice, dictated by the kind of group and the kind of music involved. Whether or not the rehearsal is formally organized to divide into these classifications, the general process must be fairly standard. First, the musicians must learn the music. Next, the music is put on the microphone and the unit is balanced and timed. Finally, all of the elements of the program are put together in their proper order in a dress rehearsal.

During the first meeting of the talent, whether it be only a pianist and his music, or a full symphony orchestra, certain things have to be done. The music has to be checked. If it is a large group, there may be many folders, and some of them may be wrong. With the music all in order, it is run through casually to see what it is all about. If it is original manuscript, as it may very well be on radio, then the wrong notes will have to be cleaned out and the parts checked for workability. If it is original music, this may be its first playing and the conductor may decide that the music needs a little doctoring. This may mean only changing a few notes, or it might mean slight rearrangement of orchestration or the shifting of certain melodies or harmonies from one section of the group to another. Whatever needs to be done is done to make the music workable at this time. Having cleaned up the score, it now must be learned. With the excellent staff musicians available in most stations and networks, this is usually only a matter of going once or twice through the music to become familiar with it. This is followed by a process which is much more lengthy and patience-trying. The interpretation of the music must be tried out and determined. If the musicians are under a conductor, he should have decided on this interpretation in advance, using the rehearsal only for the purpose of making his group understand and give him back what he wants. In the case of smaller combinations, such as a girls' trio, it may result in a good deal of trial-and-error work. This, however, is one of the most important parts of the rehearsal, since music depends so largely on its interpretation for individuality.

A meticulous conductor may go over and over an eight-bar passage eight or ten times until he gets from his ensemble exactly the interpretation he wants. This takes work, since he is dealing with human beings who are, after all, fallible and who may have their own ideas about how a piece of music should be done. Not that a good musician will dispute interpretation with his conductor. He may simply miss what is wanted because he is unconsciously conceiving it another way. Anyone who has ever visited a church choir rehearsal knows what the problem is. The only difference is that a higher degree of perfection is required of the radio conductor and his demands are answered because he is working with thoroughly trained, highly skilled musicians.

Having learned the music and understood the interpretation of a piece, it must be rehearsed until the performance is smooth and flawless. It must be remembered that this entire process must be repeated for every number on the program. Some may be perfected quickly and passed by. Others may require a great deal of work. Whatever needs to be done must be done, however, and, what is more, done within the allotted rehearsal period. All this work is done by the talent and supervised by the conductor, if there is one. The production director will listen, and perhaps make comments or offer advice, but as yet his real work has not begun. His only tasks at the moment are to learn the music as thoroughly as possible and to get accurate timings on all the numbers at the last run-through of each. This matter of timing is important, since no conductor will pace even a standard work at quite the same tempo as any other conductor, and in a long piece of music the difference may even be measured in minutes. Certainly there will be seconds of difference between conductors and talent and so each piece has to be timed as it is performed by a particular group. The production director will then have the announcer read his copy and time each segment of it. If the announcer is not available, he may read it himself and get a fairly accurate idea of how long it will run.

With this much information, the director is ready to check the workability of his routine. He may have something on paper that looks like this:

	Minutes–Seconds
Theme	:20
Announcer	:25
Stardust	2:34
Announcer	:16
My Hero – vocal	3:25
Announcer	:20
I'll See You Again – Orchestra, Trio	3:30
Announcer	:15
Louisiana Hayride – Small Combination	2:20
Announcer	:10
Theme	:30
Announcer	:15

A little simple arithmetic will tell him that his program will run 14:20, or fourteen minutes and twenty seconds. Normal time necessary to fill a fifteen-minute program is 14:40. He is, accordingly, twenty seconds short of filling his allotted time with the present routine. It is so close, however, that it presents no problems. Five seconds can easily be lost in time between cues. An extra eight bars can be played on the closing theme and the twenty seconds is amply cared for. It remains only for the production director to warn the musical conductor that he will take a long theme at the close instead of the standard one and the program is on time. Several other solutions might present themselves. Perhaps an eight-bar repeat on the close of any one of the numbers would be effective. If so, this might take up the time. If the production director knows his group well enough, and if the music would stand it, he might plan on a very slightly slower tempo over the whole program and his routine would be on time.

Suppose for the sake of an example that the added time had been 1:28 over. This is too much time to adjust in any of the ordinary ways. Something more radical would have to be done to the routining to make it work. Two things would suggest themselves at once to the director. The first would be to cut one chorus out of one of the longer numbers. If this could be done without throwing the whole arrangement out of balance or without cutting any of the prominent talent out of an only appearance, this might be a workable plan. This might take, let us say, 1:05 out of the time, leaving the program still 23 seconds long. Again, 5 seconds might be stolen from the opening theme by fading it under the opening announcement and 15 taken from the closing theme in the same manner, and there would be only 3 seconds to account for, which could easily be made up in increased tempo of the whole show and in giving quicker cues between numbers. If, for any reason, it is impractical to cut out any part of any of the numbers scheduled, the only solution would be to substitute another number which timed more nearly to requirements. It will be remembered that in choosing music for the program originally, the production director cleared extra numbers for just such an occasion as this. These numbers are usually some that have previously been done by this group so that there are known timings, and they have been rehearsed and set before. A quick once-over to refresh the musicians' memory, and the substitute number can be moved into the program.

The introduction of a new number might necessitate rerouting the program. It might throw two similar numbers together which would make the program seem monotonous. It is a simple matter to switch the order of the numbers and the new routining is now on time and properly varied.

All sorts of problems in making out a final routine will present themselves, but if a production director has extra music of varying lengths cleared, something can always be done about rearranging the routine to fit the time allotted.

Balancing the Program

The next part of the rehearsal is put on mike. Here is where the musical production director begins his hard part of the rehearsal period. He must listen to the talent and bring it into balance; that is to say, he must listen to all component parts of the program and juggle them until they are all heard in a proper volume relationship. With small groups this is a comparatively simple affair. As the number of musicians or musical units increases, the job becomes amazingly more complex.

It should be remembered that a setup has already been made. This setup represents the production director's prerehearsal guess as to how the balance can be best achieved. He arrives at this setup through previous experience with the same or similar elements in a program proceeding in good scientific manner from the known to the unknown. Using the setup planned in advance, the production director now refines this rough plan until he hears each part of the program in a satisfactory manner. Even on a program with which he has had previous experience, a production director can hope to do no more than achieve an approximate balance with his original setup. The reason for this is that there are so many variables in the situation over which he has no control.

In balancing an orchestra, for example, the director must consider all these factors in achieving a suitable setup and balance:

1. The Orchestra
   a. Size of the orchestra
   b. Type of orchestra (concert, dance, novelty, or symphonic)
   c. Types of arrangements or repertoire
   d. Quality of arrangements or repertoire
   e. Personnel
2. The Studio
   a. Size of studio
   b. Acoustical properties of the studio
   c. Temperature and humidity
3. Microphones
   a. Type of microphones available
   b. Number of microphones available.

This outline of the factors which the production director must consider was formulated by George Voutsas, now with the armed forces, but formerly a member of the music production staff of the National Broadcasting Company. About balancing the orchestra, Mr. Voutsas had this to say: [1]

> Now is the time to work out the finer details and to eliminate the glaring flaws. Perhaps a trumpet player with a particularly brilliant tone is cutting through the entire orchestra like a knife. He must be moved more off beam or farther away to perfect the ensemble. Maybe the woodwind section is weak. To correct this the microphone may have to be tilted down a little more in order to pick up the section properly. Maybe the mike is a foot too close to the string section, thus favoring it to the exclusion of the woodwinds. Perhaps the tympani is too loud. Maybe he is too far back near the corner of the studio and the walls acting as a reflector send the tones rolling out

[1] In a lecture delivered before the production classes of the Northwestern University Summer Radio Institute, July 15, 1942.

over the studio. Perhaps the percussionist is feeling particularly healthy and is beating his instruments with unnecessary vigor. Perhaps the balance sounds poor because the orchestra is neglecting to observe fine shadings and important dynamics marked into their parts. The director of the orchestra may be asking his group to force their playing because his podium may be set in a dead spot making it impossible for him to hear and direct his orchestra properly. Moving the podium two or three feet might remedy the situation.

Sometimes a production director will exactly duplicate a previous setup only to find it all wrong. There is the same director, the same musicians, located in the same way in the same studio, but they do not sound the same. It may be because a certain selection has been over-arranged or under-arranged. Again it could be because of a week of rain and a high degree of humidity in the studio. These faults and problems can be discovered and corrected only after the setup has been arranged and the production director is locked in the control room listening over the speaker.

About the number of microphones needed for an orchestral pickup, Voutsas says:

The single microphone pickup is to be particularly favored because it is the most natural, reducing to an absolute minimum unwanted reverberation, technical hazards and because it leaves the orchestra shading and blending in the hands of the musical director where it belongs.

On the other hand, radio has created versatile super-orchestras and musical arrangers; consequently the demands on repertoire and style are so great that in order to present the music properly to the listener, additional microphones have to be used in order to reinforce sections or to facilitate the pickup of certain instruments or combination of instruments in order to bring to the listener the effects and tonal colors demanded by those arrangements. These added microphones are brought into use from time to time as required and are seldom, if ever, all utilized at once for fear of a maximum amount of reverberation caused by identical sound waves striking various microphones at various intervals. Needless to say, such a condition robs the balance of clarity and definition. All fine music arrangers take this into consideration when they arrange for certain orchestras and programs, therefore one might safely say that they arrange for the microphone as well, using it as a medium for the various effects. I have in mind such orchestras as those of André Kostelanetz, Roy Shield, Meredith Wilson, Dave Rose, Morton Gould, and Percy Faith.

Whatever the cause of an orchestra being out of balance, the only means of bringing it into balance are:

1. Moving the players and instruments
2. Adding or taking out microphones
3. Re-arranging microphones
4. Changing height or distance of microphones
5. Changing the method of playing the music

In other words, the whole problem of balance is solved by getting just the right amount of each choir of the orchestra into the proper microphone to mix with every other choir to achieve the perfect blend of volume which brings each in at its proper level for all parts of a program. This juggling process the production director does during the first microphone rehearsal. The illustrations here have referred to an orchestra. The same kind of process will apply to any musical group, because the problem is essentially the same regardless of the kind of group or kind of music.

The production director is now ready for his dress rehearsal. During the dress rehearsal, which should be an uninterrupted run-through of the entire program, the production director is after specific data. First, he wants to get an over-all idea of the feel of the entire program. So far he has heard it only in isolated segments, and these usually interrupted. He will recheck all balances during the dress rehearsal to be sure his solutions of all problems are satisfactory. The announcer will be put in and any places where the announcer works over music will be checked to be sure that the two go smoothly together. Both the musical conductor and the production director listen for errors in interpretation, wrong notes, and so on, in the music, and notes are made for subsequent correction.

Finally, a segmental and over-all timing is established, so that the director knows exactly how long each number runs and each announcement. He may, if he is doubtful about time, even make internal timings within a number so that certain passages which could be cut have a known timing.

If the dress rehearsal was ragged, the director may end with a page or two of notes to be handed out. Some of these may be to the engineer, some for members of the orchestra – which will usually be delivered via the conductor – some for the conductor himself. Others will be notes about balances, to remind the director himself of faulty spots. And so it goes. Some of these notes accumulated during the rehearsal may require a quick spotting to smooth out any correction that is made. Others will require only a word of warning. Whatever must be done to correct each of the notations made by the director during the dress rehearsal should be done immediately after it is finished.

The production director now makes a final check on his routine. If his timing was close enough to assure him that he can make his air timing, there is nothing further to do. If, however, it is still too far off (which it should not be if the director has done his work well), then some change must be made in the routine, either by internal cuts in a number or by substitution to bring the program to time. Normally, no good director would substitute numbers this late in the proceedings. Usually some minor time adjustment would be sufficient. Whatever adjustment is made must be checked with the entire ensemble to be sure that everyone is cognizant of what is being done. One piano part out of place could wreck a whole number.

Once on the air, the production director's hardest work is done. The greatest load of responsibility now lies with the talent and the conductor who is directly responsible for the execution of the program. The program must, of course, start on the nose as soon as the director gets an all-clear from the engineer. The director is also responsible for seeing that the right microphones are open at the right time to duplicate the effects achieved on the final balance in dress rehearsal. If the engineer is a top-flight man, this will be a needless precaution, since he will have the routine memorized anyway. Few engineers, however, know their music this well, and the help of the production director is usually needed to call and check the various changing balances as they come up during the progress of the program.

The director will, of course, handle all necessary cues to announcer and talent. He may indicate balances which he wants changed either to the engineer, the conductor, or the talent, depending on the situation. If two different spots are being picked up on two different mikes, then he checks the engineer for balance. If orchestra is drowning a soloist, the director might ask the soloist for more volume and indicate to the conductor to hold the orchestra down. Whatever balance change has to be made, the director indicates. These should be slight if the dress rehearsal has been well handled.

The director must keep the program on time. If it is beginning to lag, he may indicate a slight increase in tempo to the conductor and ask the announcer to speed it up. This will not mean an alteration of interpretation. It will only be restoring the program to its rehearsed pace. Finally, of course, it must be ended on time. Here is a point that is worthy of some discussion. In a musical program it is very easy to employ the lazy man's method of using theme music to fill any odd time left over in a program and simply play theme until time to sign off. This always leaves a ragged end on the program and most directors will agree it is poor production. But the path of least resistance often leads in that direction; it is so easy to let theme fill and fade it at the appropriate time. A program ends, however, with so much more of a flourish if the theme music comes up to its own climax and the program ends exactly on the nose. There is a thrill in such an ending which comes only with perfect precision work, and every director owes it to himself to earn that little extra thrill.

Over-All Considerations

There are a few general considerations which the musical production director must always keep in mind. He should be a musician. But he must be more than a musician, and he must consider factors other than musical factors in the building of a musical program. He must remember that he is not only a musician, but a showman as well, and given the choice between building a perfect bit of music and a perfect show, he will always choose the latter. After all, music of a perfect nature is appreciated only by a few trained musicians, but a good show is something that appeals to everyone, and it is for everyone that radio operates.

The musical production director must also remember that there is more to a musical program than music. True, that is the most important component, but it is not the only one. A program of good music could be defeated by bad handling of other aspects of the program. Hopelessly dull continuity, a monotonous, dead announcer, poor engineering — any of these things could defeat a musical program even if the music were good. The production director, in his concern with the music, must not overlook the importance of these other items which can add to the luster of his show or tarnish it badly.

The production director must keep an eye on the pace of his whole program. The talent and the conductor will, for the most part, be concerned with the rightness of individual numbers. Furthermore, they are embroiled in the execution of the program. The production director has the opportunity and the responsibility for keeping the bird's-eye view of the whole program, and pacing is one of the most important considerations. It might be important enough to warrant changing the attack on an entire number. But whatever is necessary, the program must have an over-all pace and dash that makes it interesting and listenable.

The production director should never make the mistake of assuming that an audience wants "corn" if in his mind corn means inferior music, shoddily done. No production director can afford to set himself up as an arbiter of musical taste. Educators have come to the startling conclusion, after years of research, that individuals differ! We do not all like the same things. Some people like symphony. Others like wild swing music. Others like hill-billy music. Still others like hymns. None of this is *good* music or *bad* music. Each is a "kind" of music. And it can be good or bad, depending on how well it is done. While production directors may tend to specialize on certain types of music, they should not praise one type and damn all others. What they can and must do is to insist on getting the best possible music within any one type. No production director should take the attitude that, because he is working on a program of hill-billy music, there is no need to work. He dare not assume that it is all bad music, anyway, and that it does not make any difference. No matter what the type, he should always try to get the best talent there is available and do the best job that he can do. That kind of an attitude would soon eliminate the word "corn" from the radio vocabulary.

In the few brief years of its existence, radio has done more to educate American taste for music than any other force which has ever been at work in the country. Radio has done a job that it may well be proud of. But the job is only now begun. There are still worlds of wonderful music with which the public is not familiar, and which need popularizing. This is a task which radio is eminently fitted to attempt and to which the radio production director must contribute with every musical program he puts on the air.

CHAPTER 11

PRODUCING THE NEWS AND SPECIAL EVENTS PROGRAM

MOST NETWORKS have in their organization a department called "News and Special Events." Local stations may simply refer to it as the news department. Whatever its name, and whatever its place in the station's organization, there is some department which is responsible for the handling of news programs on the air.

Let us look for a moment at the news and special events department of a network. Such a department has for its purpose three major functions. First, it supervises the gathering of all news copy. The network has three major sources of news information. Most networks have a series of domestic correspondents who operate in the same way as reporters for large newspapers. They will be scattered around the country in strategic locations in large cities. Washington, of course, is well covered by radio correspondents. Most networks also have a rather large staff of foreign correspondents – men who travel about the world wherever news is breaking, to give the network direct, from-the-spot reports. The network will also probably buy the reports of one or more of the regular wire services which furnish news to newspapers and radio stations, such as the Associated Press, the United Press, International News Service, Universal Service, and Trans-Radio. The special events and news department of a large network will probably subscribe to two or three, or perhaps all, of these services. The chief of the department will dispose his staff of correspondents in exactly the same way as the editor of a large newspaper or news-gathering organization. Both his domestic and foreign correspondents may be moved around as the pattern of news shifts to various points in the world. Most of the world's capitals are covered as a matter of routine and many correspondents are reserved for special assignments. In these times nearly all the traveling correspondents of a network are concerned with gathering news and are consequently spotted in the various war theaters to the best possible advantage. From these sources — the network's domestic and foreign correspondents and from the press services — the editors of the news departments gather thousands of words of news every day. These editors are responsible for covering the big news breaks of the world.

The second function of the department is to digest and edit the reports. Editing should be understood to consist of two separate tasks. First is the process of selection. Out of the total mass of material, which may run into hundreds of stories and thousands of words each day, that which seems most interesting and significant is selected for broadcasting. Obviously all the stories which come in cannot be used in the limited time available on the air. Once the news is selected, then it must be either written or rewritten into proper form for broadcasting. More will be said about this under the heading of news-writing style.

Having selected the news, the second part of the editing process is to build news broadcasts. This will consist of assembling copy, rewriting wherever it is necessary, and timing it for reading on the air.

The third general function of the news and special events department, as its title indicates, is to cover all so-called special events which occur within its area. A special event may be roughly defined as a one-time occurrence. If a new subway is to be dedicated or a highway opened or if a governor is to speak at a local convention — all these things would be considered special events, to be handled by the news and special events department. Most sporting events which are covered by radio are also handled by this department. Although most sports are seasonal, it must be remembered that there are usually several sports in season simultaneously, so this part of the work creates considerable activity in any news and special events department.

The staff of a news and special events department usually consists of a chief, who is responsible for the administration and operation of the whole department; a staff of correspondents, who are disposed to the best possible advantage over the field of coverage; a staff of news rewrite men, who edit and rewrite all the incoming news; and a staff of analysts, who may help in the preparation of news in special areas and who also do broadcasting. The news and special events department of a national network may be a fairly complex organization, since several such departments will function within the same network. NBC has news and special events departments in New York, Washington, Chicago, and Hollywood. In addition, of course, offices are maintained now in London and correspondents are scattered all over the globe. The co-ordination of all these offices and the routing of news to them is a very complicated business.

What is the relation of the news and special events department to the over-all organization of the network? The answer to this question is different for every network, but in general this department may be considered as a part of the program department of an organization because it is primarily concerned with the development and broadcasting of programs of a special type. In some networks it is completely autonomous, reporting directly to the organizational head of the network. This is the case in NBC. In other cases the department is considered as a unit within the program department and reports to the vice-president in charge of programs. In this latter instance it is on a level with the production department, the music department, the continuity department, and all other departments which are concerned with the preparation and broadcasting of programs. Regardless of where it fits into the general organization of a network, most news and special events departments tend to be fairly autonomous. This is a highly specialized kind of work and has a minimum of contact with other branches of the program department. Close contact is maintained with the announcing staff because the regular announcing staff usually reads the news programs, except for broadcasts made by special news analysts. Since the copy for such programs is prepared by the news writers in the department there is little contact with the continuity department — certainly much less than any other type of program. There may be some contact with the production department where special events broadcasts are concerned. Most news and special events departments do not have a staff of production men who do only this kind of work. When a production director is needed for a special events broadcast, he is usually assigned out of the regular production department. With these two exceptions the work of this department is fairly self-contained.

In local stations the organization of news departments varies much more than in the networks. A generalized picture can be drawn which is reasonably accurate for most stations, but the amount of variation is still considerable. In the average local station there is no source for news other than that furnished by the wire services. The staff may consist of one person, or even one member of the announcing staff, who has some specialized interest in news, and who may take charge of the preparation of all such programs on the station as well as doing a certain amount of staff announcing work.

In some of the larger independent stations a very complete staff of editors and writers is maintained and operates in the same general way as the news and special events department of a network. This is true, for example, of station WLW in Cincinnati. Station WOW at Omaha and WHO at Des Moines, also maintain staffs of editors which work in the building of news programs in a manner similar to the networks. Some local stations also have reporters gathering local news which they incorporate in certain of their news broadcasts. All these things are, however, exceptional, and the average independent station draws nearly all its news from regular wire services. If they have any special writers working in the news department, thev are concerned with editing and rewriting copy for broadcasts.

Producing the News Program

There are three general types of news programs, and since they differ rather widely, the production procedure for each varies somewhat. They must, therefore, be considered separately. First, there is the regular news program which originates in a studio of the station. Second, there is the multiple-point news pickup, such as the world news roundup which most networks broadcast at least once daily. Finally, there is the on-the-spot news broadcast where the microphone is taken directly to the point of the happening for a play-by-play account of news as it happens. These three types of news programs will be discussed separately.

Let us first consider the regular studio news program. The first consideration must be the script or copy itself. In a network the copy for a news broadcast is a carefully edited and meticulously rewritten script which is all timed and furnished by the editors and rewrite men of the news department to the announcers for reading. The preparation of this script follows certain fairly clearly defined principles. Radio news writing differs considerably from regular newspaper news writing, and this is a lesson which every editor responsible for preparing radio copy must learn early.

In local stations practice varies widely, depending upon the size of the staff. In some small stations wire copy is used directly as it comes from the teletype machine, with no editing other than arrangement in some kind of logical order. In some local stations a complete rewrite of all incoming copy is made and a regular script assembled from the news sources available to the station. This latter practice is certainly to be preferred if the personnel of the station permits. Most radio newsmen agree that wire copy as it comes in is hardly ready for broadcast. However simple or elaborate the preparations may be, the first step is obviously the preparation of the script itself.

In local stations, even in a network station, a production director is not usually assigned to a broadcast if it is to appear only locally. As a matter of network policy, however, all network broadcasts are covered by a production director. This holds for news programs as well as for any other kind of program. In local stations, where there seldom is a production director of any kind (at least not people who are called production directors), news shows go on the air without benefit of so-called "production."

Two types of talent are involved in producing news programs. Some of the work is done by staff announcers and some by specialists, such as news analysts and commentators with specialized background. Not all regular staff announcers may be suited to news work. In local stations where staffs are small, most announcers take on news programs at some time or other during the week. In larger stations and in network operations there are usually a few specially fitted announcers who do the bulk of the news work. An announcer, to be a good newsman, should have certain qualifications. First, he should be interested in news and its developments. Second, he must have a considerable amount of background information. Third, he must be a man with a high degree of communicability. In other words, he must be able to say things and read copy in such a way that the audience immediately understands what he is talking about. The broadcasting of news demands that the announcer be clear, have a calm delivery, be able to pronounce foreign names, and have enough general information to know the meaning of what he is reading. To the layman it might seem that if the script is furnished, anyone could read it. As a matter of fact, an audience is very sensitive to unintelligent reading. No matter how smooth or how glib the reading may be, if it is not accompanied by a definite understanding of what is being read, this fact will show through clearly. Therefore, if an announcer reads a news program and is not familiar with what is going on in the news or is not cognizant of the significance of what he is reading, he cannot bring to an audience the degree of communicability necessary for a good news broadcast. For all these reasons, news announcing is a specialized job and is usually assigned to those members of the announcing staff who have special ability in this field.

On nearly every station of any size there is at least one person who styles himself a news commentator or news analyst. In the larger stations and in all networks this group of specialists in the field of news is growing both in size and in the excellence of their work.

Most news commentators and news analysts write their own scripts. Out of their own special background for their job they not only report the news as it happens, but they also make comments on it out of their own experience in the particular field under discussion. Their sources are the same as are available to the other men in news and special events. The commentators, however, take this copy and incoming news as a starting point and write scripts which are a mixture of reporting and editorial opinion.

Most news commentators or news analysts are usually successful and astute newspapermen with a long background of reporting or corresponding, or they are men with special information in a given area. They may be men with special background and information in military or agricultural or political affairs. They may be travelers who have a wide first-hand knowledge of the places currently important in the news. With the increased interest in news engendered by the war there has been a regular epidemic of people who feel "called" to the microphone to impart their special knowledge to the public. Among these there are naturally a great many incompetents, whose only claim to preparation for such a job is a wish to do the job. On the other hand, a great many fine news commentators have been uncovered by the interest in news and the need for it.

Any production director who is responsible for a news program must recognize that such a program tends to take on the style of the announcer. Some programs have a fixed style to which the announcer must conform. Others create a style out of the mannerisms and approach of the reader of the news. Whether it works one way or the other, it is certain that many programs do have a definite flavor or style and this must be preserved by the production director. The style may be chatty and informal, or highly departmentalized with special topics, such as foreign news, domestic news, local news, and sports news coming in a prescribed order. Or it may be analytical in nature with the personality of the analyst coloring the whole program. Still another style may be highly personalized and rather explosive. All these variations in style must be taken into consideration by the production director. If properly handled, they give individuality and flavor to a news broadcast. If improperly handled, they only get in the way of the news or comment which is the chief purpose of a news program.

Most of the mechanical details of producing a news program are matters of routine. The scheduling of announcers and studio engineers are handled in the usual manner. Only unusual occasions demand special bookings.

Most of the pre-broadcast preparation which, in other program types falls to the production director, become matters for the reader of the news in the news program. Usually the announcer or the news commentator will read through his copy to be sure he is familiar with all meanings and pronunciations of words. This is especially important where copy is prepared by the news staff and read by an announcer who does not see it until it is ready to broadcast. Any awkward sentences should be discovered and taken out at this point. Points to stress in any given sentence or paragraph may be marked. The announcer will look for "gag" or humorous stories which are usually put into newscasts to help lighten them up. He must know where these are in advance so that he can treat them properly. Most announcers seldom do more than read through the copy once. As they read it through, they may hold a stop watch on the copy and mark time elapsed at one-minute intervals. Finally, the announcer will look for paragraphs near the end of the copy which can be cut or stretched to adjust the program to time. The common procedure here is to furnish the announcer with a little more copy than he will be able to crowd into the time allotted. The last few paragraphs are written in more or less descending order of importance so that the broadcast can be closed at the end of any paragraph.

There is usually no rehearsal on a news program. A routine check on microphone position and level is always made, and these constitute the rehearsal on a news program.

On the air the production director has few worries in doing a news program. As a matter of fact, the production director is usually assigned to a news program on a network not so much to produce the program as to be on hand in case anything goes wrong. He is there as an insurance against trouble rather than as a director of the news program. If a director, however, is assigned to a news show, he takes care of the routine matters of putting the show on the air on time and taking it off on time. His only responsibility is to see that the pickup is good on the microphone and that the reading is intelligible. Beyond that, the responsibility lies with the announcer.

The Multiple Point Pickup Program

This is the type of news program where reporters or correspondents in several spots in the world report in during the same broadcast. This pattern of news program began in the early stages of the war in Europe and has been a standard item with most networks ever since. Because of the complexity of building such a program, it presents real production problems.

To begin with, one central point is always designated as the origination point for the program. No matter how many other studios or communication systems are involved, that point remains the center of the program. The staff at the origination point controls these things: the pattern for the program; the points and commentators to be included; the opening and closing continuity; emergency material to fill in if any pickup point is unintelligible; a timetable for all pickups; and the cue lines for the switchings. In some instances the staff also may provide part of the script for some of the remote points. The remote points normally supply the script for the time allotted to them, and are responsible for timing their part of the program. They also arrange for studio space and local facilities in which to work. The facilities to connect the remote pickup to the origination point are provided from that point.

In this kind of news program the production director is always assigned at the point of origination. In case the program involves other pickup points inside the United States, production directors are normally assigned to them also. Obviously, it is impossible to have a production director cover the remote points all over the world, but whenever it is possible, directors are assigned at them also.

The talent requirements for such a program as this becomes very specialized. Facile, quick-minded, and articulate men are needed at the origination points. Foreign pickups are always a gamble. One never knows when atmospheric conditions may make a pickup unintelligible. In these circumstances the man or men at the origination point who are to do the announcing must be flexible enough and sure enough of their procedures to fill in at a moment's notice. The talent at the remote points will consist of the best correspondent available on the spot. Usually he will be one of the regular foreign staff of the network.

The style of delivery on such a program is usually straightforward news delivery. It is not usual to have a commentator report from remote points. The reason for this is simple. Analysis or commentary ordinarily takes time, and time is a commodity that is very precious on such a program. Pickups from London or Algiers or Australia usually last less than three minutes and a great deal of information must be crowded into the report. Little time is left for opinions when there are so many facts to state.

One of the most interesting facets of the multiple-pickup news program is the facilities necessary to make such a program possible. By "facilities" we mean the land wires, transoceanic cable, and short-wave relays which bring together all of the pickup points on the program. All point-to-point broadcasting in this country is handled by land wire. Most transoceanic broadcasts are handled by short-wave radio telephone. Neither of these facilities is owned by the networks. The companies which own them serve other customers besides the networks, so it is always desirable to order facilities as far ahead of time as possible. Unfortunately, news being what it is, it is seldom possible to anticipate where the news will break very far in advance.

Normally, two circuits are required to each pickup point. A channel must be provided for the microphone line which brings the correspondent in to the central point, and usually a second channel is provided for a telephone conversation with the various pickup points preceding the program. These latter facilities are not often needed for regular pickups within this country, since most networks have their own private teletype system for communication between their various main points, but it is very necessary sometimes for foreign pickups. Therefore, the man in charge of building a multiple pickup-point news program commonly has two-way telephone conversation available with his correspondent or correspondents in whatever parts of the world they may be. When the time schedule for the program is finally determined, a cue sheet is sent to all the points involved in the broadcast. This will show to the minute and second when the various switches are anticipated and what the cue line will be which precedes each switch. Most such programs use a standard switching cue which does not change from day to day, and thus makes easier the anticipating of proper switches. The time schedule, however, and the points of pickup do change from day to day and sometimes from hour to hour, so cue sheets must always be sent out. To pickup points in this country they usually go out by teletype, telegram, or telephone. To foreign pickup points they go out over the telephone preceding the broadcast. Most readers are familiar with the line, "We return you now to the NBC news room in New York." In times when the news is breaking slowly, these cue sheets may come out five or six hours ahead of the broadcast. It is not an uncommon thing for pickup points to be switched while the actual program is on the air. In this case the production director at the point of origination communicates the change to all his various pickup points by telephone

This process is not quite as mysterious and difficult as it may sound, because when one pickup point is substituted for another, the eventuality has probably been foreseen and the new pickup already has timed copy. Very often several more pickup points will be made ready than there will be room for on the broadcast, and if the news from each of them is of more or less equal value, the ones will be used which have the clearest reception. This possible intelligibility of speech on a foreign pickup is still always a big question mark when one goes on the air with a news broadcast of this sort.

There is no such thing as a rehearsal on a multiple pickup-point news program. Each pickup point knows how much time it will have. Either the production director in charge at that point, or the correspondent if there is no production director, works out the copy and times it exactly. The whole program is a nicely calculated mathematical song, and the production director at the point of origination knows within a very few seconds what will happen during the entire broadcast. All this is possible without a complete rehearsal. In case a pickup has to be cut off because of atmospheric disturbances, the point of origination will come back in with emergency copy and fill until the next scheduling switching time, at which time the program will be put back on its original schedule. This means that the announcer at the point of origination must be nimble-witted. In spite of all these careful preparations, mistakes do occur. Not long ago, for example, on the Alka-Seltzer "News of the World" program one of the foreign correspondents made a mistake in switching. He was supposed to say as his cue line, "We take you now to the NBC news room in Washington." Instead, he absent-mindedly said, "We return you now to the NBC news room in New York." Since all segments of the broadcast are controlled from New York, the engineers naturally switched the program to New York at that point. John W. Vandercook, with great presence of mind, said, in effect, "I'm sorry, there seems to be a little confusion and we take you now to the NBC news room in Washington." The engineers then switched the program to Washington where it belonged and the program proceeded on schedule.

On the air this kind of program is comparatively simple, in spite of the complex facilities involved in its execution. Unless something goes wrong, production merely consists in following the switching schedule. Each point times itself and the program usually proceeds very smoothly. All cues must, of course, be clear and exact. All remote points must be monitored by each other and by the central point so that they can hear what is happening and know when the cue lines come up. The production director at the point of origination has the responsibility for taking any bad transmissions off the air. The normal practice is to leave such transmissions on the air for one minute unless they are beyond all possible intelligibility. Short-wave broadcasting is still a somewhat tricky business and a transmission which sounds hopelessly muddled in the first ten seconds often clears up as it progresses. In these cases the production director must use his judgment. A fairly flexible closing must be provided to allow for small variations in the time schedule. Most transmissions will vary from one to three seconds from their allotted time. Sometimes they vary as much as five or ten seconds. Usually these tend to average up and cancel each other. If all of the pickup points varied as much as four or five seconds and each one of them was on the over or under side, then the program might be seriously off time. If this should be the case, and it sometimes is, the slack must be taken up at the point of origination where the program closes. This is done by the simple process of providing several short items, of which as many can be included as is necessary to bring the program to its proper time termination.

Below is reprinted a typical cue sheet from the "News of the World" program which airs over NBC each evening at 7:15 Eastern War Time.

Control (2)
NBC Announcers
NBC Production — 1/10/44
News room — CUES
Eric Danielson

MILES LAB "NEWS OF THE WORLD" program, tonight

January 10, 6:15-6:30 PM opens & closes in New York with instant switches.

Switch to Chicago at appx. 6:15:45 on cue: "A WORD FROM CHARLES LYON."

Switch Chicago to New York at appx. 6:16:30 on cue: "THE NEWS OF THE WORLD."

Switch to Ankara appx. 6:20 on cue: "TO NBC IN ANKARA." (Noumea stand by. If used – 6 secs. switch via San Francisco on cue: "COMES BY WAY OF SAN FRANCISCO."

Switch Ankara to London appx. 6:23 on cue: "TO NBC IN LONDON."

Switch Washington to Chicago appx. 6:27:30 on cue: "THAT'S WHAT HAPPENED IN WASHINGTON TODAY."

Switch Chicago to New York at appx. 6:29:05 on cue: "NOW BACK TO THE NBC NEWS ROOM."

On-the-Spot News Programs

On-the-spot news programs are those in which radio, like the newspaper reporters, go to the scene of a news break and broadcast as it happens. Stations and networks were just beginning to perfect this kind of broadcasting when the war came along and stopped most of it. One of the most famous such broadcasts was the coverage of the burning of the Zeppelin *Hindenburg* at Lakehurst, New Jersey. Like all spot news, these programs are unpremeditated and are done on the spur of the moment. Seldom are they of sufficient significance to be worthy of network time. They are usually done on a local or regional basis.

There are no rules concerning this kind of broadcast because no two of them are alike. The only thing these programs have in common is that anything can and usually does happen. They are usually of short duration and may be taken in several different spots. One of the most spectacular jobs of this kind ever done was radio's coverage of the floods along the Ohio and Mississippi Rivers several years ago. With whole towns and communities being flooded, radio not only covered the big disaster story on the spot, but also helped to direct the rescue work over a period of days. On one occasion a local network was rigged up which not only furnished news of the disaster, but also acted as a clearing-house for all orders to Coast Guard crews and other rescue workers.

On-the-spot programs are usually done by short-wave relay. The station's portable transmitter, mounted on a truck, proceeds directly to the scene of the news and communicates by short wave back to the central station. Here the short wave is received and rebroadcast on standard waves by the regular station facilities. In addition, roving commentators with engineers carrying pack transmitters may be on the job.

These programs are usually partly or completely ad-libbed by the announcers on the spot. This is rough-and-tumble broadcasting of the old school and is a thorough test of the mettle of any announcer. It is seldom that a production director goes along on such an assignment as this. There is ordinarily not time, and the arrangements are usually simple because of the portable equipment. Only in rare instances where a story may last over a period of hours or days might a production director be dispatched to the spot to supervise a series of broadcasts as an event unfolds. The bulk of the work in covering an on-the-spot news broadcast falls on the shoulders of the announcers on the job and the engineers.

Sometimes multiple-point pickups are arranged and the story told from several different angles within the span of a single broadcast.

Producing the Special Events Show

There are two general types of special events programs which dominate all others in frequency of occurrence. These are talks programs coming from a remote point, and sports broadcasts. Since these two occur most frequently, they will be discussed in detail, the others only briefly. Regardless of what kind of special event is under consideration, the chances are that it will involve picking up one or more speakers. The production of talks programs has already been discussed, but when the production director moves outside the studio to pick up a speech or series of speeches on the scene of a happening, he encounters a great many special circumstances that are worth noting.

Production of a Remote Pickup of an Outside Speaker

In order to make this discussion specific, let us take a hypothetical case. The governor of the state is speaking at a national bankers' convention. The decision is made to broadcast the speech and a production director is assigned to the job.

In this kind of situation, the production director will have little concern with the manuscript. It will have been written by whoever writes the governor's speeches and submitted to the station well in advance of the broadcast. The continuity department will have checked it for policy and approximately for time, and so far as the production director is concerned, it is a finished product. The station will have made clear to the governor the time regulations, and men in such positions are usually anxious to conform to the time restrictions. The one thing which the production director will probably do with the script is to get an approximate timing. This must be known in order to plan on how the production will be handled.

There is some production analysis involved. It does not, as usual, concern itself so much with the content of the script as with the geography and personality of the situation itself. Since the script is a more or less finished product when the director gets it, and since he will not rehearse anyone so prominent as the governor of a state in how to deliver his speech, his main concern is with the manner of picking it up.

There are several things which the director must know because these factors will color most of his decisions. Where is the speech to be made? Most programs like this originate in the "grand ballroom" of some hotel. Is it a business session or a dinner meeting? Will there be a speaker's table? Who is to precede and follow the address? Who is chairmaning the meeting? Who is to introduce the speaker? What are the acoustical conditions in the room? Will the situation be complicated by the presence of a public address system? Does the speaker habitually stick to his script or is he famous for interpolating new material? What will be the physical disposition of tables, chairs, and other impedimenta? All these questions must be answered before the production director can chart his plan of action.

A general answer to these questions can be secured by talking with whoever is in charge of arrangements for the convention. This may involve getting in touch with several committee chairmen, the governor's office, and hotel officials. Whatever has to be done to get this information must be done. The seasoned production director, however, knows that such information is general, often inaccurate, and subject to change without notice. He soon learns to accept philosophically the fact that plans seldom go through completely as announced, that changes are usually not communicated to the broadcaster, and that whatever arrangements are made may not work out. He, therefore, proceeds, with a general picture of the situation in mind, to provide for operation under any of the possible situations which may evolve.

Let us suppose the situation to be this: This is a dinner meeting at which perhaps a thousand people are expected. They are to be seated at tables of eight all over the large banquet hall (which will be noisy and have considerable amount of echo, plus a typical hotel public address installation). The speaker's table will be a long one running lengthwise of the room, with some thirty-five people seated at it. The governor will sit approximately at the center of this table, flanked by appropriate dignitaries. The man who is to introduce him, however, is seated seven places to the right of the governor. His speech will be preceded by two preliminary speakers who are noted for long-winded addresses. This is a typical and fairly difficult situation in which to attempt a broadcast. With this picture in mind, the production director sets out to make a production analysis.

He must first decide on his staff. He must have a good engineer, and an announcer who has a good appearance and who can keep his head in difficult situations. Depending on specific circumstances, he may even decide to take along an assistant to do errands or run messages during the critical pre-broadcast period.

Next he must decide on his pickup. How many microphones will he need and how will he dispose them? In the situation outlined, he may decide to use four. He will need one for his announcer, one for the governor, a third for the man who is to make the introduction, and a fourth to pick up crowd noise and applause if that seems indicated. He may decide that only two are necessary — one for the speaker and one for the announcer. The situation will determine this decision. The director must decide where he is to station himself and where he will place his engineer and announcer.

He must decide how much time it will probably take to make the arrangements once on the ground, and plan accordingly. Incidentally, here is a safe place to be liberal. If not enough time has been allowed for a few things to go wrong, the production director is just asking for trouble.

He must decide on how much "atmosphere" he wants in the broadcast. Is this speech to be an end in itself or is the situation important? Is it wise to give the audience the "feel" of the occasion and stress the circumstances under which the address is to be given — or is it to be minimized? If the situation is to be stressed, both time on the air and facilities for pickup must be planned. Let us say in this instance that the setting seems important and we want to transmit some of that to the listener as well as the address itself. Therefore, the director will provide microphones to pick up the general crowd noises and time for the announcer to describe some of it.

Finally, provision must be made to handle time on the program. Arrangements must be made with the committee to see that the speech will definitely begin at a certain time. Wise planning here can save many headaches. If this is to be the only speech broadcast, it should be set apart from the rest of the program. Suppose, for example, the broadcast period is from 9:30 to 10:00 P.M. The dinner might be scheduled for

7:45, with plans made to dispose of the preliminary speakers before the dessert course. Then the audience could go ahead with their eating and talking and be happily occupied until time for the main address with no danger of a hitch in the schedule. If all the speeches were scheduled for after dinner, either the previous speeches might run overtime, with the embarrassing necessity for interrupting the speakers to get the governor on the air, or there will be an awkward wait for the main address with nothing for the audience to do. A little careful planning of the whole program, in which the production director can co-operate, will make for smooth operation.

Such a plan as this will guarantee the broadcast getting on the air with a minimum of confusion. There still remains the problem of getting it off smoothly. A stand-by program should be arranged in case the speech is short. What can be done if the speech is overtime? Probably the best arrangement is to have the closing announcement come from the station, rather than from the point of pickup. In this way, if the program runs overtime, the director can simply fade it out and the announcer back at the station can make appropriate apologies to the audience and do the closing announcement without embarrassing either the speaker, the audience, or the broadcast staff. In fact, the governor need not know he has been cut off until later. He can continue until he finishes. Meanwhile, the station continues its schedule, uninterrupted. If the program is on time or ahead of time, this arrangement is still completely satisfactory. If the timing is only a few seconds under, applause may be used to fill to the appropriate sign-off cue. If the decision is made to take the closing from the studio, it requires scheduling another announcer and another engineer back at the station on the same broadcast.

Thus might run the production analysis on the hypothetical program under discussion. Its completion might involve a good many long-distance telephone calls and telegrams, or it might be decided fairly simply, depending on the availability of people and the remoteness of the pickup point.

Scripts are now ordered duplicated, with enough extra copies for the press unless the governor's staff has already provided them. Opening and closing announcement should be written and duplicated. The announcer must be prepared, either with copy or with ad-lib information, to fill in if there is a delay in starting the speech. Information on the dignitaries present and the person who will introduce the governor must be obtained. Some of this may be included in the announcer's opening.

Next, the staff must be scheduled, with ample time allowance for transporting them to the point of pickup and return. Transportation for staff and equipment must be arranged. In war times this may turn out to be a major item. Equipment must also be requisitioned and delivered to the point of broadcast. On such a pickup, name-plates on microphones and banners with the name of the station or network are a standard part of the traveling pack and should not be forgotten.

Telephone lines must be ordered and installed. The proper kind of microphones should be ordered. Ordinarily the unidirectional cardioid or pressure-type is best, because it allows for maximum efficiency in the pickup of the speaker and reduces background and crowd noise. Tables, chairs, and other physical needs must be ordered from the hotel, as well as accommodations if it is to be an overnight affair. Dress for the occasion must be determined. At least the announcer and production director should try to conform here, even if the rest of the staff does not.

The press department should be notified and furnished all the ammunition available for press releases. In this instance the station will probably receive ample assistance from the governor's office and the newspapers. The station's or network's own angle of the program, however, should not be ignored. It might result in valuable linage.

In case there is a band or orchestra and music may be a part of the program, proper regulations must be checked and the music be cleared so that the director will not be guilty of broadcasting uncleared music.

A short conference between the traffic department head, the engineers, and announcers (both those who will handle the program at the station and those who will go on the remote) should be set up before the unit moves out. Cues in the script should be checked and all possible contingencies discussed and provided for.

It is advisable to do a "back-timing" on the script at this point. This is done by reading the last couple of pages of the script and the closing announcement as nearly as possible at the pace at which it will be read on the air, making time entries every fifteen seconds. Suppose this reading takes two minutes. There will be entries for :15, :30, :45 seconds and 1:00 minute, 1:15, 1:30, 1:45, and 2:00 minutes. Of this, perhaps the last forty-five seconds are the closing announcement. Suppose it is to be a fifteen-minute program and runs fourteen minutes and thirty seconds. By working backward from the end of the script, the director can enter timings thus: at the 2-minute point (or the end of the copy) he puts down 14:30; at the 1:45 spot he enters 14:15; continuing this way, he reaches the point at which the timing began and enters there 12:30. This means that the program should have been running twelve and a half minutes at that point. Then, if the program is ahead of or behind schedule, the director will know it and have time to plan on what he will do.

There is no rehearsal on a program of this kind. It has to be right the first time. Therefore, it is well for the entire unit to be on the ground well ahead of the broadcast. Time must be provided for checking everything – not before the broadcast, but before the dinner guests arrive. Last-minute setups in a broadcast of this sort are hazardous.

Once on the ground, the engineers go to work. When the production director, in conference with the committee on arrangements, has made his decision about the disposal of equipment, the setup is made. It is ideal if a small table can be provided behind the speaker's table at which the production director and engineer may work. If the layout of the room does not permit, they may set up wherever the director can clearly see the speakers and still be as much out of the way of the audience as possible. Sometimes a balcony overlooking the speaker's table works out well. Perhaps the equipment will be placed down at one end of the speaker's platform. However it is placed, it should provide easy visibility and access to the speaker's table and be as inconspicuous as possible.

While the engineer is setting up, checking telephone lines, testing microphones, and exploring the acoustics of the room, the production director will look up the chairman of the meeting and go into conference over details. The routine will be explained, cues determined, and the layout of equipment and personnel understood. Pronunciations of all names in the broadcast should be checked for the announcer. When all this is done, all is ready for the broadcast.

After the crowd has arrived, the production director and engineer can listen to various microphones and check their position and angling for proper pickup. Acoustics can be finally ascertained and any re-angling or placement of microphones can be made on the basis of the actual situation. The mikes are all tested and mixing levels determined roughly. Provision is always made by the engineer for a check of the telephone lines back to the studio well ahead of the broadcast. Incidentally, a pair of lines is usually ordered. One line carries the program and the other provides two-way communication direct from the station to the point of pickup. The production director and engineer can thus have direct telephonic communication with the station at all times.

At this point the program is ready to take the air. The director will usually check with the chairman of the meeting about five minutes ahead of time so that appropriate announcements can be made, waiters disposed of, dishes quieted, and the audience made ready for the occasion. Shortly before the broadcast, the director will synchronize his stop watch or clock with the station by telephone and then wait for the "go-ahead." This sign will come by telephone to the engineer, who relays it to the production director.

The director will then cue the announcer, who will tell the

radio audience something of the situation and introduce the introducer. Depending on the situation, the announcer may come up to the speaker's table to do this, or he may stay in the background with the director and engineer. When he is finished, a cue is thrown to the man who is to introduce the speaker. This will be followed by the main address.

During the actual broadcast, the production director has three specific tasks. First, he must follow the script and see whether or not the speaker sticks to his text. If he does not, the director tries his best to insert the interpolated remarks into his script. If these are very long or frequent, of course it is impossible to get them down, but at least he can indicate at what points the speaker departed from his script, and for how long. He must also be on the alert for any deviation from station policy which the speaker may cause by his spontaneous remarks. If such occur (and this would be unlikely in the case of the governor of a state), he must make an instantaneous decision as to whether or not he will cut the speaker off the air.[1] If he feels he must make a cut, he does that first and then decides what to do next. If it is only a remark or a sentence, he may return the program to the air, uninterrupted. If he cannot tell from the context of the remarks how long this ad-lib is likely to continue, he may call for the stand-by program and put it on until the speaker returns to the script and is on safe ground again.

The director's second task is to be on the alert for audience reactions and use them to highlight the broadcast whenever it seems desirable. If a microphone is placed to pick up audience reactions, he may open it when a pause in the speech or the turn of a phrase elicits some response from the audience. In a situation where there might be a heckler in the audience who breaks in with remarks that were not safe for broadcast, he must be sure that they are blocked out. That is a comparatively rare occurrence, but it does happen.

Finally, the director keeps track of the time. In making his own timing on the script, he noted, each thirty seconds, the

[1] For examples of policy which might be violated, see Chapter 14.

accumulated time. After the first two or three minutes, it will become apparent whether his timings are slow, fast, or about right. By rapidly calculating the difference in pace over three or four minutes, it is possible to forecast rather accurately whether or not the program will approximately fill the time. The announcer's timing on the reading of the closing continuity is, of course, a known quantity. By back-timing the close, the director will know exactly where the speech ought to end, in order to come out on time. As the speech progresses, he can tell whether it is likely to be over or under and can transmit this information back to the station on the spare telephone line. This gives the station time to prepare for whatever kind of close seems indicated. If the program is within thirty seconds of the estimated time, the director can always use applause as a time cushion. If it is long, he will simply fade it out at the right time and the announcer back at the station can do his closing; if it is short, the stand-by program has adequate warning.

Thus runs the routine in producing a remote talk. The speakers change, and the surroundings change, and the speeches change – but all surprisingly little. One situation is very like another and the same basic elements are common to most instances. Most speakers and audiences accept the stringencies of radio time and are good-natured about it. It is up to the production director to do his work as unobtrusively as possible and let the broadcast interfere as little as possible either with the speaker or the audience, and still deliver a good show to his listeners.

Producing the Sports Broadcast

Football, baseball, horse-racing, boxing, and hockey are all sports which enjoy a certain amount of broadcasting. Each of them demands specialized knowledge and presents certain different problems, but for purposes of explanation we will concentrate on only one.

In some ways football is the most complicated of all sports to broadcast, because there are so many players involved, because the action happens quickly and in close quarters, and because the observer must necessarily be some distance from the play. As an example of broadcasting sports programs, suppose we take a typical assignment which might be handed a production director, a play-by-play broadcast of a Big Ten football game.

The first step in this process is one for which the production director would not be responsible – that of arranging with the proper authorities for the broadcast of the game. Contact would have to be made with the university involved and provisions made for the accommodation of the representatives from the station or network.

The next task would be that of choosing the talent for the program. For a football broadcast there must be an announcer who is something of an authority in the field. A regular staff announcer is not qualified to do an adequate job of this kind, though the fact that he may be a staff announcer does not disqualify him for the job. The point is that whoever does it must have specialized knowledge. He must know football thoroughly and preferably be familiar with the major tactics of the two teams involved. This announcer must also be provided with two "spotters" who also know the game very well and one of whom is familiar with the entire personnel of each team. These spotters may be other members of the station's staff, but they are often furnished by the athletic departments of the respective universities.

Next comes the matter of script. The reporting of the game itself is, of course, ad-libbed as it happens. There is some script, however, involved in a football broadcast. The opening and closing of a broadcast is usually read from script because there are certain credits and announcements which must be made and also certain information which must be imparted to the audience which the announcer need not memorize. The broadcast will probably go more smoothly if as much of the program as possible is read from script. This prevents reaching for words and the rambling style which is characteristic of most ad-libbed work. By its very nature, however, the bulk of the broadcast will be a running description of what the announcer sees happening before his eyes, augmented by what his spotters tell him. In addition to the opening and closing, the announcer will come prepared with much script material to use during the times when nothing is happening on the field. There must be as little dead air as possible. To fill in these gaps during the time-outs, between the quarters, and at the half, the announcer comes prepared with a considerable amount of script material which he may insert into the broadcast at will. This material may include background information about the two universities, the two teams, personalities on the teams, statistics of previous games and similar information which is always of interest to sport fans. Also some human interest material can sometimes be prepared in advance which may fit nicely into a slow spot in the game. All this information is written out in script form and the announcer can fall back on it when he needs it.

The complete staff for such a broadcast will probably consist of a production director and an announcer, two spotters, and an engineer. The production director may ask for an additional announcer to relieve the regular announcer at the quarter and half time to add color to the broadcast and give it change of pace and to furnish a human interest commentary on what is going on.

The next step of the process is the ordering of facilities. Most large universities provide sound-proofed (or at least semi-sound-proofed) booths for broadcast purposes. Usually these are equipped with telephone and Western Union lines permanently connected into the local telephone office. Ordinarily two pairs of lines will be ordered, one for the broadcast and one for two-way communication back to the studio to discuss cues and any other technical matters which might come up. Very often arrangements are also made with Western Union to provide the scores of other games direct to the broadcasting booth so that the announcer can keep the listening audience abreast of the progress of other games while he is reporting the one in front of him.

A stand-by program must be prepared for this kind of broadcast. In a well-operated station, and certainly in a network, a stand-by program should be provided for every out-of-the-studio broadcast scheduled. Even though telephone lines are very dependable and things seldom go wrong, there is always the possibility, and the station should be ready. In scheduling something like a football game there is no way of knowing exactly how long the broadcast will take. Therefore, a fairly generous time allowance must be made. Several different circumstances in a game may cause this amount of total elapsed time to vary considerably from one game to another. Since the program director of the station has no way of knowing in advance how long a broadcast will run, he must provide for some sort of fill-in until the next regularly scheduled period comes up. The same group will ordinarily stand by during the entire game in case of a line failure. Along this same line a good program director will work out a tentative booking of programs following the game, to be used in case the game runs shorter or much longer than expected. Great confusion is often caused in stations when plans are not made in advance about what will be done in each eventuality. If the plans are made in advance and everyone knows exactly what those plans are, then, no matter what the elapsed time on the game may be, the condition is provided for.

The production director will next look over the ground and decide at what various points he wishes to make microphone pickups. He will almost certainly order at least two microphone placements; there will be a microphone in the booth itself for the announcer and one down in front of the stands to pick up crowd reactions and music. It is possible that the production director might want as many as six pickup points for such a broadcast. He might put a microphone on each side of the field to pick up the band music. He might want an additional one in front of the main cheering section on each side of the stand to get crowd reactions. If there is any kind of special ceremony between the halves, this may call for an extra microphone position either out on the field during the half or down along the sidelines. How many pickups seem desirable will depend on the game, on the festivities surrounding it, and on any special activities planned for the half. Whatever the plan of pickup may be, it should be determined in advance, and the information passed to the engineer so that he can bring the appropriate amount of equipment.

The next thing which the production director must do is to consult the conductors of the two university bands (if bands are involved) and find out what music they plan to play during the afternoon. A complete list of all the music that can possibly be played by both bands must be submitted to the broadcasters in order that it can be cleared for broadcasting. While the broadcasting station and network have nothing to do with this music and while they do not even control it, it still is being broadcast and according to their agreements with their licensing organizations, proper clears must be made for it. It is possible that some pieces may not be approved for broadcast and must be eliminated from the repertoire of the band. At any rate, a list of the numbers should be obtained and proper clears made.

All this procedure must be accomplished previous to the broadcast. This all comes under the heading of advanced preparation. In addition, the production director and his engineer should be on the ground at least two hours before the broadcast to see that everything is in proper order. If it is an out-of-town trip, this may mean leaving the station or network headquarters several hours or days in advance of the broadcast. A proper safety factor of time must be provided to allow for any possible circumstance. Early on the day of the broadcast the engineer will get his equipment ready to install and have ample time to hook it up, test it, and see that everything is working all right. The production director will normally use this time to check with the university officials and possibly with the coaches and members of the team to see what interesting information and background material he can get that might improve the broadcast. Time is always necessary to get familiar with between-the-half routines so that, if they are to be broadcast, arrangements can be made for picking them up. Once everything has been completely checked and double-checked and a report made to the station, the crew can relax until broadcast time. As a matter of fact, the crew seldom relax because they are usually busy getting information and holding interviews with the various coaches and team members (if possible) to garner fresh information which will be suitable to broadcast.

Once the program goes on the air, the production director has certain definite responsibilities. The announcer is a very busy man trying to see everything that is happening and framing it into words. He does not have time to worry about program details or even over-all impressions. He is usually concerned with the immediate. It is, therefore, up to the production director to keep as much objectivity and perspective as possible, and to see that the program makes interesting listening. He must strive constantly to get variety into the broadcast. This must not ever be done at the expense of the report of the game or of distorting it. There is plenty of opportunity, however, for providing variety in a football broadcast. The production director can at convenient times call for a pickup of crowd cheers or of the band. This gives the announcer a chance to rest momentarily and also to get caught up on his facts and to confer briefly and quickly with his spotters. It also gives the audience a rest and a change of pace in listening. Both the production director and the announcer have the very difficult job of translating a spectacle which is primarily visual into an oral medium. Words alone cannot always paint the picture of the color, the excitement, the thrill, the clash, of an important football game. Wherever the production director can use crowd noises or the bands playing or any other pickup to lend variety and to add color and authenticity and reality, he should do so.

The production director must constantly remember that people are tuning in late to the broadcast. It is up to him to remind the announcer to give the score frequently and to identify the game and the location. On a busy Saturday afternoon at the height of the season it is not unusual for every station and network in a given locality to be broadcasting a different game. The casual radio listener tuning in during the progress of the game has no means of knowing to what game he is listening or what the score is. Therefore, these facts must be repeated frequently. The announcer has enough to think of without having to worry about this. Therefore, the production director should keep check on these things as well as on such routine matters as announcing station breaks and station identification at stated intervals.

The production director can also be of considerable assistance in watching the game itself. Accuracy is one of the great virtues to be striven for, and the announcer, in his wish to get the play delivered to the audience as quickly as possible, may frequently be guilty of certain inaccuracies. The production director, watching the game also, but being free of the necessity of speaking, can sometimes help the announcer in calling difficult plays and complicated happenings on the field. All these things may be considered a legitimate part of his job as the production director of such a special events program.

Finally, the production director is responsible for seeing that a fast and accurate summary is made at the end of the half and at the end of the game. This should be correct, concise, and to the point. A football broadcast should not be stretched too far beyond the closing gun. Once the tension of the actual game itself is relieved, the major interest in it is finished and it should be wound up as quickly as possible. A good summary is a fine thing, but the broadcast should not go much beyond this point.

Other Sports

The same general problems present in the broadcast of a football game hold for most other sports. In some ways baseball is one of the easiest games to broadcast, since the progress of the game is fairly leisurely and the times when fast action is happening are comparatively infrequent. Also baseball is an open game where visibility is usually good and the reporter can see fairly clearly what is happening. Nevertheless, there is a specialized jargon connected with baseball as there is with all sports, and no broadcaster can be very successful unless he is reasonably familiar not only with the game but with the individual players about whom he is speaking.

Horse-racing, boxing, hockey, and basketball are all very difficult sports to broadcast because they involve a considerable amount of specialized knowledge. Also there are fewer experts in these sports than in baseball or football, and finding someone who can do a creditable broadcasting job of these sports is difficult. It is seldom that the announcing staff of a station boasts anyone who is capable of doing a really worthwhile job in any of these sports. Boxing and hockey are probably the two most difficult sports to report, because so much happens so fast. Broadcasting stations usually hire someone who has specialized in these sports to do the broadcasts for them. Even though listeners may not themselves know much about a sport, they are quick to detect ignorance in the announcer reporting it.

Other Special Events

In normal peacetimes all networks and many large independent stations cover a great variety of special events which, for one reason or another, seem to be desirable for broadcasting. It is impossible to be specific about such programs because no two of them are alike. If they were, they would not be "special" events. Under this general heading might come inaugurations, dedications, important political meetings, and conventions. Each program is a specialized set of problems for which specific solutions must be found. About the only thing such programs have in common is that they are all troublesome from a production point of view. Any broadcast becomes a problem when it moves outside the studio. Radio is surrounded with a great deal of mechanical gadgets, all of which are necessary and all of which are provided as a matter of course in the regular studio setup. When an event does not come to radio and radio has to go to the event, it is hampered by the large bulk of equipment which it must move to the scene of action. The very fact that radio has achieved such a high degree of technical efficiency means, by the same token, that a great deal of equipment is necessary to achieve that efficiency. Once a broadcast leaves its natural habitat, it is headed for difficulties.

It is true that most of these difficulties tend to run in a familiar pattern and once a production director has done several special events programs, he can begin to anticipate the kind of trouble he is likely to have. Like the leak in the dike, however, there is still no way of knowing where it will break out next. The director can only assume that it will break out and in an unexpected place, and govern himself accordingly. Of all the problems which are likely to occur in a special events broadcast, there are two which happen most often. One of them is the technical difficulty of getting the pickup back to the station or network, and the other is the matter of timing.

The author recently did a broadcast which will serve as an excellent example of the kind of thing which may happen. As a reward for winning a national wastepaper collection drive, a one-room country schoolhouse in Missouri was selected as the site of a broadcast of the "Truth and Consequences" program. The schoolhouse from which the broadcast was to take place was typical of a thousand like it in small communities all over the United States. This particular schoolhouse measured approximately twenty by thirty feet, of which a considerable area in the middle was taken up by a large coal stove. Twelve students ranging from the first to seventh grade occupied it during the school day. It was six miles from the nearest town and two miles from the nearest telephone. It was completely innocent of electricity and, at the time of the broadcast, was surrounded by a temperature of eight degrees above zero and eight inches of snow on the ground. In order to originate one half-hour program from that point, two miles of telephone line and three miles of electric power line had to be installed, a "control room" had to be built on the outside of the building butted up against one of the windows, electric heat had to be provided to keep the engineer's hands from freezing on the knobs, and a few other assorted odds and ends had to be arranged. Electric clocks could not be depended upon for accuracy within fifteen seconds variation in an hour because of variations in the power supply which came out to the school building over the new lines from the local power company. All of these difficulties, however, were overcome and a listener, hearing the program on the air, would never have guessed the amount of time and money that was necessary to make the broadcast possible. This kind of procedure is typical in the special events show which takes place outside the broadcast studio.

The other big difficulty which occurs with special events programs is the matter of time. Here radio is usually an eavesdropper on a program which is planned, not for a radio audience, but for an audience present at the event. The result is that radio cannot make the stringent time requirements which it can for studio broadcasts and because of this fact, special events programs create considerable difficulties. It is a tribute to the special events departments of all major networks that as many of these programs come off on schedule as do. Only ingenuity and very careful planning make such results possible in the face of conditions under which special events broadcasters normally have to work.

On top of these two standard difficulties which the production director will encounter, there will be specialized problems involved in almost every special events broadcast. Speakers will speak longer than they have been scheduled to speak. A whole meeting may be late in starting at a convention where one of the speeches is to be broadcast. The waiters may be in the midst of clearing the tables when the time comes for the broadcast of an important speech in a hotel ballroom. A chairman will decide at the last minute that someone other than the person scheduled should introduce the next speaker. All these things can, and do, happen as a matter of course in special events programs.

The production director who can remain calm in the face of

conditions like these is a rare person indeed. After having done several such programs, he finally reaches the point where he assumes that everything will go wrong that possibly can go wrong and proceed from there. Having once reached this point, he is in an ideal position to do a good job. Only by anticipating everything which could possibly happen and providing for it can broadcasts be possible under such conditions.

Broadcasting of special events has been seriously inhibited by the war and will probably be held to a minimum until the war is over. There is every reason to believe, however, that a heavy schedule of special events programs will be resumed as soon as it is possible to do so. In spite of all the problems involved, these broadcasts represent one of the important ways in which radio can operate in the interest, convenience, and necessity of the American public.

CHAPTER 12

THE DRAMATIC PROGRAM

Preliminary Steps

In the dramatic program alone does the total and final burden rest with the production director. In the talks program he can only offer help and make suggestions – he cannot turn a dud into a brilliant speaker. In a musical program the actual performance is in the hands of the artists or the musical conductor, and the director has only a remote control over the program. In a dramatic show the responsibility for the success or failure of the program rests directly on the production director. He works directly with all the elements of the program. For this reason, the dramatic directors are usually the envy of their brethren in other fields of production because they *do* have, not only the responsibility, but also the opportunity, of working first-hand with a program. This is a real challenge to any artist who wants honestly to do a good job.

The Program or Script Is Chosen

A dramatic script may originate in different places and ways. It may originate in the continuity department of the station or network, either as the work of a staff writer or as a purchase from a free-lance writer. It may come from the special events or the public service departments of the station or network. It might come from the outside from a non-commercial sponsor, such as a university or association of some kind. It might originate with the program director or program planning board, either from their own discussion or by purchase of a free-lance's script. Most frequently, it originates in an advertising agency, either written by staff writers or contracted for from free-lance writers.

Where and how a script originates is more the concern of a program department than of production. The real production process does not start until the program idea has been approved and a script written. Advertising agencies usually hire their own free-lance production directors to handle their programs. This also happens occasionally in the case of non-commercially sponsored programs such as might originate from a university. Nearly all other kinds of dramatic programs will be handled by the staff of dramatic production men on the station or network. The origination point of a program has little significance to the production director beyond dictating the people he will have to contact in the execution of his work.

A Production Director Is Assigned

In a network origination point there is usually a fairly large staff of dramatic production directors. The number, of course, varies with the amount of production traffic to be handled. Generally the staff is large enough to make some specialization possible. One director may be especially good with heavy dramatic material; another may have an excellent touch with comedy; still another may be particularly well equipped to handle certain kinds of public service programs, and so on. More often than not programs are assigned to production directors on the basis of traffic alone. The man who is free at the time the program is scheduled gets the assignment. Within these limits, however, and whenever possible, directors are assigned to programs on the basis of their special ability to handle the particular type of material involved.

In local stations, where production directors are infrequent and where dramatic programs are seldom done, such programs usually fall to the program director or to an experienced announcer. In spite of the fact that not many programs of a dramatic nature originate in stations outside of network centers, there is no valid reason why they cannot be done if staff members are interested, and willing to do the extra work.

Editing the Script

Director Meets Script

Despite the fact that a busy production director meets new

scripts every day — sometimes two or three in a day — he will, if he brings the right spark of imagination to his job, get a thrill as he first looks at the fresh pages. Most of the scripts are routine affairs that call only for the director's craftsmanship, not for his artistry. But each new one offers the chance that it may be the one that will challenge the best that is in him.

Most directors like to read a script through once hurriedly to get a general impression. This impression is likely to be somewhat close to the impression the audience will get on hearing the script. After the first reading the director should know whether he likes the script and whether it is acceptable from a production point of view. If he does not like the story, the important thing to find out is — why? Where has the author missed fire? Why does the story fail to "jell"? On rare occasions the production director may decide that everything is wrong and the whole script is useless, but this will indeed be rare because usually the script has passed through the continuity department and been accepted before it reaches him. That means that somebody saw possibilities in the show. The problem is how to get that something which continuity saw in the program into the foreground when the program goes on the air. The director must use critical analysis. He cannot say, "I don't like it," and let it go at that. He must be able to put his finger on the exact reasons for his opinion. This will mean several more readings of the script. During these readings, he will ask himself these specific questions: [1]

1. How is the opening? Is it fast? Is interest aroused at once? Does the story get under way at once?
2. Are the time, place, and characters clearly exposited in the opening scene?
3. Is the over-all structure of the script good? Does it proceed swiftly and surely from inciting action, through well-planned minor climaxes, to a major climax? Is this structure clear on examination?
4. Are all characters in the script well drawn and properly identified at all times?

[1] This list of questions is taken from the author's book on *Radio Writing.*

5. Are there any unproducible spots? Has the author written something in sound which is too complicated for an audience to get with sound alone? Are there scenes which could not be produced so that the audience would know what was going on? Is additional sound or dialogue needed to make clear certain situations?
6. Are the sound and music called for in the script adequate? Will it be necessary to add or subtract or change?
7. Are all the scenes necessary?
8. Are the scene transitions of the sort you want? Is there a silent transition which you would like to have made with music? Or do you wish to use a different transitional device?
9. Are the scenes properly blocked so that it is clear at all times where the audience is in the scene and where all the other characters are in relation to the audience?
10. Are all entrances and exits covered with lines or sound? (A character cannot fade out unless he has either a line or a sound effect to fade on.)
11. Is all the action (both dramatic and physical) properly motivated?
12. Are there lines which contain unconscious double meanings?
13. Are there lines which are so difficult to say that they may cause the actors to flub?
14. Are some of the speeches too long?
15. Are any of the characters unnecessary?
16. Is there enough sound indicated to exposit the action? Is the script cluttered with unnecessary sound?
17. Is the script approximately the right length? If it is too long, what can be cut out? If it is too short, where can it be stretched most effectively?

A good dramatic production director should be specific and constructive in criticism. He should be able to put his finger on what is wrong and suggest a remedy. Having found the answers to these questions, he then must decide whether he himself can make the desired changes. In general, any corrections which call for rewriting entire scenes or redrawing characters or tampering with the plot should be made by the writer. If the changes are merely matters of production detail, such as adding or subtracting sound, changing transitions, breaking up long speeches, and the like, they may be done more quickly and efficiently by the production director himself. If a rewrite is indicated, the production director should either confer directly with the writer, if this is possible, or make a detailed list of the changes he wishes, with reasons, so that the author will have the information he needs to do the rewrite.

Script Editing: An Example

To help the beginner to see specifically just what kind of changes need to be made, there is reproduced here a recent script which the author of this book produced on the NBC "Author's Playhouse" series. This script is reproduced photostatically exactly as it came to us. It was written by Dorothy Cheney Quinan and purchased by NBC because of the clever plot and crisp dialogue which seemed to make it an interesting play for this series. However, the author, at the time this script was written, had done very little writing for radio, and some repair work had to be done on the script to make it producible. Some of the corrections are only matters of taste in lines which are, after all, a matter of opinion. Other changes were necessary to furnish proper instructions to sound, actors, and music in the production of the script.

On first reading, the script seemed to be a simple, yet somewhat sophisticated comedy, with a clever situation; shallow, obvious but acceptable characterization; nice movement of plot; and dialogue which was alternately crisp and clever, and heavy and obvious. It was also apparent that its writer was unused to radio, since much necessary sound was omitted, and some sound routines called for were unnecessarily difficult. All these things had to be changed. Also the script was long; the first estimate seemed to indicate that at least two and a half minutes would have to be cut.

Having arrived at this general impression, the next step was to see whether a rewrite by the author was indicated or whether the production director should do the job. Since very little fundamental change was needed, and since most of the additions and corrections were of a production nature, it seemed easier and simpler not to ask the author to do it. What happened thereafter is reprinted here in photostat form so that the reader may see the changes in this script made in what is commonly called the editing process. It is only fair to say that rather more was done to this script than is normal, but because of this, it makes a better example.

Bearing in mind the fact that the script should open on a situation that is likely to catch the audience's fancy, we look at the first page. It seems good. The first line indicates trouble and conflict. A crowd is gathering. Something is going to happen. That is enough. There *is* something there to catch interest. We will let the opening dialogue stand.

(Obviously we need an opening to the program. This program has a regular opening format, and continuity will take care of that. We can forget it. That will come in the normal process.)

There are two things, however, that need to be done on this first page. First, the author has opened cold, with no scene set other than that indicated in the lines. If this scene is to take place in front of a church on Fifth Avenue, we must tell the audience that in sound as well as in lines. The lines tell us there is a crowd present — slightly amused, slightly unruly, mostly curious. So we write a sound scene set which will be heard as soon as the scene starts. Knowing that many sound recordings of traffic have streetcars on them (and knowing that there are no streetcars on Fifth Avenue), we note that in the sound routine.

There is one other fault on this page. There are two very long speeches. Those need to be broken up — especially since they come from a minor character and the leading man has little or nothing to say. We cannot cut these speeches, since they contain necessary exposition, so all we can do is break

PROFESSIONAL BRIDE

SOUND: CITY STREET NOISES - CURIOUS CROWD (NO STREET CARS) CONTINUES BEHIND SCENE

HANK WARING:	What seems to be the trouble, officer? What's the crowd?
IRISH COP:	As near as I c'n make out, the byooti-ful dame up there is gettin' the brush-off. She's been standin' there on them cathedral steps since a quarter past nine. ~~All dressed up in~~
HANK:	and in a ~~that fancy~~ wedding dress!
COP:	She counts the floors o' that buildin' acrosst the street — she counts 'em up and she counts 'em down again, then she looks up the street. I tell you, it's pathetic.
HANK:	Couldn't we do something — ?
IRISH COP:	I'm a married man, meself. But no kiddin', soldier, I'm just waitin' for this crowd to get a little bigger, and a little more unrooly, then bang, I'm goin' to crack down on 'em.
HANK:	Good idea!
COP:	(Thoughtfully) O' course, I could run the young lady in f'r causin' a riot —
HANK:	But she's so beautiful, you wouldn't meet with the sympathy of your fellow officers. Right?
IRISH COP:	Now you're cookin' wit' gas.
HANK:	I beg your pardon?
IRISH COP:	Now you're talkin' — Oh, I can see be the ribbons on your chest that you ain't been around these parts lately, and you ain't in the groove, so to speak.

them up by the simple and obvious device of having the other character break in. In doing this, we must be sure that the lines we give to Hank are in character and match the rest of his dialogue.

We must keep in mind that the script is approximately two and a half minutes long, so we must look for possible cuts. The first speech on page 2 is a possibility. It is too long, to begin with, and slightly out of key with modern idiom. Hence, we make the cut shown. The second speech is also too long and ought to be cut. When we try to cut it, though, it does not respond very well. Except for the first two lines, it is all one thought and difficult to split up. Also, we have to establish the fact that the soldier is a New Yorker and that he has been away. In order to introduce that subject, the author gave the cop that speech. In spite of the fact that it is too long, we will have to let it stand. Incidentally, it will give the cop a good character speech and keep him out of the strictly typed Irish New York cop.

Hank's second speech sounds effeminate. Perhaps this is because a woman wrote the script. At any rate, it is a little too fanciful for brisk, sophisticated comedy. We still need the exposition it contains. There is nothing to do but rewrite it, so we cut and patch. Not a brilliant change, perhaps, but passable. It sounds a little more masculine, anyway, and preserves the central idea of the speech. It does, however, ruin the cop's next line so that he cannot use the gag the writer put in. It must be made into a straight line.

With the cop's malapropism at the middle of the page, we pause again. This seems a good gag. We will leave it in. But the speech in which it occurs is too long. There is danger also of burying the gag. We will fix both problems at once by inserting a line for Hank which points the gag.

At the bottom of the page comes a voice from the crowd. We must indicate that it is off mike and, to point this fact, we will add a line for Hank *on mike* to help point up the perspective and keep the audience straight.

HANK: (Laughing) Maybe you're right. But I can still recognize a lady in distress. ~~That's a universal language.~~ ~~She's~~ Probably waiting for some young man whose leave has been cancelled and he couldn't let her know.

IRISH COP: Could be, Lieutenant. Could be. Well, we'll wait and see what happens next. You know, son, in New York, if you want to draw a crowd in fifty seconds flat, all you have to do is stand wit' you mouth open, lookin' up at the heavens, and first thing you know there are hundreds of fools doin' the same.

HANK: I'll let you in on a little secret. I was born here. I used to dream, about Fifth Avenue ~~on Guadalcanal, that~~ when I was out on Guadalcanal. ~~the Isle of Manhattan would float away before I could get back to it.~~

IRISH COP: Musta been lonesome ~~malaria.~~ You c'n imagine what this dame with that swell torso —

HANK: She has a pretty smooth figure, at that.

IRISH COP: Who said anything about her figure. I said her torso — the veil and the blossoms and the dress —.

HANK: Oh. I see.

COP: Well, anyhow, can you imagine what her standin' on those church steps is doing to my beat? Why, pretty soon traffic on Fifth Avenue will be standin' still.

HANK: What do you do then?

IRISH COP: I'm thinkin' about it right now.

VOICE: (CALLS OFF) Hey, lady, throw us yer boquet. We don't wanta be the old maid!

HANK: (CLOSE) Oh oh!

Earlier in this book it was stated that the convention of radio dictates that the audience is always with the nearest sound source. It is necessary to keep the audience informed at all times as to what is going on in a scene, where they are in it, and the relation of all other parts of the scene to their location. Such a problem presents itself here. The intent in the lines is clear. The Lieutenant leaves the policeman, walks through the gathering crowd, up the church steps, and speaks to the girl. He then takes her with him, through the crowd to his parked car. How can we tell the audience all this so they will not become confused? Some of it is, of course, obvious in the lines themselves. However, if we let the audience hear sounds which are contrary to this illusion, they will not know what to think. We must tell the audience, by the way we handle perspectives, what the action is. We do it as follows:

At the top of the page, the voice from the crowd we place off mike. Hank and the cop are on mike. The audience thus establishes the crowd as a little distance away. In the middle of the page we begin to bring the crowd closer to the microphone, which the audience will hear as their (and Hank's) moving into the crowd. General background crowd level will be brought up at this point, too. Hank's whispered line to the girl will be close on mike.

As the girl accepts and they start to push through the crowd, we establish that fact in the minds of the audience by having several of the crowd lines come in at varying distances from the mike to give an impression of a rather large crowd. There will also be general crowd noises. Hank's last speech on the page will be given very close to mike to create the impression that he is saying something to Hollis which he does not want the people close by to hear. This simple labeling of perspectives should, together with the lines, keep the scene clear to the audience.

VOICE: (OFF) Hey, sister, ya better go home. He ain't worth waitin' for!

IRISH COP: That settles it, soldier. I'm gonna go in there and break a few heads.

HANK: Wait. Let me handle it. Let me just go up to her, offer her the use of my car. It's right here. All she has to do is step in, and I'll let her out around the corner.

IRISH COP: No, that's still my beat. Let her out in the Fifties.

HANK: Wish me luck.

IRISH COP: A fine-lookin' lad like you don't need no luck. Just get in there and pitch.

VOICE: (FADING IN) So, here you are. Where you been, soldier? In the guardhouse?

VOICE: (Sings) "Here comes the groom."

HANK: (Low) What about making this mazurka mine? Once around the block until the crowd breaks up. Perhaps he'll be here by then.

HOLLIS WILCOX: Oh, thank you, Lieutenant. It is - lieutenant, isn't it? This is awfully kind of you.

HANK: Hang on to my arm.

VOICE: (SLIGHTLY OFF) Ain't they a handsome pair!

B.G. OF CHEERS

VOICE: (OFF) If you was any kind of a man, you wouldna' stood her up.

VOICE: (OFF) Waddayamean, insulting the uniform of the armed forces?

HANK: (VERY CLOSE) Let's make a run for the curb. And let them fight it out themselves.

SOUND: CROWD UP AS THEY PUSH THROUGH

The sound routine on the top of page 4, as originally written, is poorly done. All dialogue is stopped while this sound routine takes place. Such a routine would take ten or fifteen seconds. In the meantime the characters are lost in the sound. While the sounds called for are fairly easy to identify, it must be remembered that they will be heard against a background of an excited crowd and traffic noises. That is too much competition for a sound routine. We fix it by expanding the sound routine slightly and inserting the dialogue. This helps to exposit what is going on, it gives us a chance to keep perspectives fixed, and it makes the sound routine more real and natural.

The sound cue also fails to include the car shifting gears and pulling away from the curb. An alert sound man would put it in, but it might as well be in the script correctly as long as the page has to be redone anyway. It should also be indicated that when they get inside the car and close the doors, the level of the crowd and traffic drop somewhat. As they pull away, the crowd will fade altogether. Traffic can remain optional.

Hollis has two very long speeches on this page. One of them is necessary exposition, but the other has a couple of lines that can be cut without hurting the story at all. We cut them.

Meantime, it should be understood that behind this whole scene we hear the sound of a smooth-running motor as heard from the interior of the car. This, together with an occasional bit of traffic sound, will keep the locale of the scene established inside the car.

HANK This is it!
HANK: In you go!
SOUND EFFECT OF CAR DOOR BEING OPENED ~~AND~~ SHUT ~~TWICE~~, ENGINE BEING STARTED.
CAR DOOR OPENS, SHUTS
TRAFFIC AND CROWD DROP IN LEVEL

HANK: Whew! Wasn't that something!

SOUND: CAR PULLS AWAY. GEAR SHIFT. THEN HOLD MOTOR UNDER.

HOLLIS: I'm afraid they embarrassed you terribly.

HANK: Nothing to what you went through. Where to? Around the block a few times and wait again?

HOLLIS: No. I'd like to go home. I'm all right now. I was just going to call a cab and go home anyway.

HANK: I'd been there quite a while.

HOLLIS: Then you saw what happened? Paul always forgets something.

HANK: As a matter of fact, I didn't see --

HOLLIS: The ring -- or something equally important. I don't mind having to stand around and wait for him when I'm not wearing anything so conspicuous. But he's certainly left me waiting in some funny places. This time, I'm really angry.

HANK: I can't say that I blame you.

HOLLIS: But he promised to be right back. I was to go inside and wait, but the door was locked. He must have run into trouble. ~~Speeding, maybe. He thinks he's kind of a Barney Oldfield.~~ I'd like to make a 'phone call right away. Where --

HANK: Do you want to collect another crowd?

HOLLIS: I should find out what happened to Paul.

HANK: I live on the Drive. Why don't you make your

Hank's speech on the top of page 5 is too long and unnecessary. We leave in what is essential to tell the audience a little about him and cut the rest of it. It has no significance to the story. The cut also necessitates a change in Hollis's following line.

The author's original note, "Music to denote change of scene," is not helpful. The man [1] who will compose the original music for this spot does not have much to go on. Later, in conference, this cue and others will be discussed and the exact type of thing we want will be decided. However, we should indicate here whether the music is to start suddenly and loudly, or sneak in, whether it remains quiet or comes up in volume, and whether it stops abruptly or fades. Accordingly, we indicate this. The why of this decision will be discussed when we come to the subject of music and transitions.

From the lines, it is plain that in the following scene, Hollis calls Paul on the telephone while Hank retires to make coffee. That is plain in the lines, but it wouldn't be plain to the listener if it was produced exactly as written. All the normal sound which will help exposit the scene was omitted. Therefore, it has to be written in, and written in in logical sequence, allowing a believable time lapse between sounds. In other words, Hollis cannot pick up a telephone and say, "Hello, Paul." She has to call him first. She has to dial a number and wait for it to ring. Meantime, the show cannot stop. The normal practice is to cover this business with lines. Here, the lines are provided. All we need to do is space the sound properly.

We take care of Hank by having him fade on his last line. That sends him to the kitchen. We put Paul on a filter mike which is the conventional way of telling an audience we are hearing both ends of a telephone conversation, and there we are.

[1] In this case, Doctor Roy Shield, well-known NBC music director.

call from my apartment. I can't promise you my family will be there, but perhaps the doorman will recommend me.

HOLLIS: I really don't know a thing about you, except that you're very gallant.

HANK: Here's my pre-war card. My name is Hank Waring once of Willard, Choate and Waring, Engineers. ~~But I'm not the tail that wags the dog. They've cut the tail right off by my being in the army, and the firm survived.~~

HOLLIS: ~~You sound modest.~~ Sounds impressive! ~~And~~ But you don't look a bit dangerous.

HANK: (With pretended gloom) Kind of an indictment, isn't it?

(Laughter from both)

MUSIC ~~TO DENOTE CHANGE OF SCENE~~ LIGHT, RIPPLING MUSIC, STARTING LOW, THEN UP HIGH AND FADE FOR

HANK: There's the 'phone.

HOLLIS: Thanks

HANK: You do your stuff and I'll wrestle with the coffee-pot.

SOUND: PHONE OFF CRADLE HOLLIS: Let's see. DIAL TWO LETTERS, 5 DIGITS, PAUSE. RINGING AT FAR END OF THE LINE

HOLLIS: Do you mind if I —

HANK: (FADING) No, take off your — I was going to say — hat — that doo-dad.

HOLLIS: Veil. I will. With pleasure and relief.

SOUND: PHONE PICK-UP AT FAR END

HOLLIS: Hello, Paul?

PAUL: FILTER Hello, Hollis?

HOLLIS: Where were you? Whatever happened?

PAUL: I got there right after you left. Where are you now?

HOLLIS: I'm looking at some etchings.

PAUL: (Muted) I'm terribly sorry, Holly, for letting you down like that. You know that I would move heaven and earth to avoid such a —

Page 6 is fairly simple. There are two very long speeches by Hollis that we shall have to do something about. We still need cuts, so we could cut them. However, the whole point of the story hinges on the fact that as yet neither the audience nor Hank knows that Hollis is a model and Paul a photographer. We need to keep the double-meaning lines in enough to plant them. Therefore, it seems unwise to cut. Our only other alternative is to break them up. We do, as indicated.

Our next problem is to get Hank back from the kitchen. The author made no provision for this. It can be done simply by setting perspectives. We are with Hollis at the telephone as she hangs up (which, incidentally, we have to add to the script) and Hank is in the kitchen. We tell the audience that by having Hollis call as though he were at a distance and then having him answer from off mike, at a distance. So far, so good.

What follows is obviously an intimate scene. It would hardly be played shouting back and forth to each other. We can either bring Hank in or have her go to the kitchen, but we must get them together. Since on the next page she talks about the room, it is better to leave her where she is and bring Hank in. The only way we can do this is to "hear" him come in; that is, have him fade in on a line. However, there is no suitable line. The simplest solution is to give him an unimportant line to fade in on. It must be in character, but that is about the only requirement. Hence the added line.

HOLLIS: (Wearily) Just leave heaven and earth where they are. What you should do is move yourself -- a little faster and on time.

PAUL: But, darling. I told you I'm sorry

HOLLIS: Oh, you're always so contrite, Paul. Do you know I waited for hours? Well, almost an hour, then.

PAUL: Hollis, I did my best. I was looking for something, something very important.

HOLLIS: Yes, I know.

PAUL: (Pleading) Darling, what about this afternoon?

HOLLIS: Definitely not. I gave you the choice of the time and the place. You can wait on me now. ~~Perhaps indefinitely.~~

PAUL: But listen, Holly...

HOLLIS: I have other things to do besides waiting around for you in odd corners of New York. You're spoiled. You think any girl in New York ought to eat out of your hand.

PAUL: Now, Hollis, you over-estimate me. Tomorrow. Ten ---. Same place. Say yes.

HOLLIS: Let me think. Oh, I don't know, Paul. I'll have to let you know, later.

PAUL: But, Hollis --

HOLLIS: I'll call you. Good-bye.

SOUND: Phone HANG UP

(Pause) (Raises voice)

HOLLIS: (CALLS) How's the coffee coming?

HANK: (OFF) It won't boil because I look at it all the time.

HOLLIS: (CALLS) Then talk to me and don't look at it.

HANK: (FADING IN) A good idea! I'll buy it. Do you realize I don't know your name?

HOLLIS: Is it necessary?

HANK: (ON) You have no idea.

In the middle of page 7 there is one rather stilted line. It is interesting to note that most of these stilted lines are Hank's. This is often true of women writing men's dialogue. It is, of course, equally true of men writing dialogue for women. A slight change makes it passable.

An interesting omission develops on this page. The coffee is brewing. There was a single line referring to it in the middle of the page and nothing else. We should either do without the coffee or make provision for it in the whole production scheme. It is very unimportant and the audience will probably not notice it if the omission is done well. It seems best to keep the coffee-making in, since there is no other excuse for her staying there, and we have to keep her there long enough for them to get acquainted. The room she talks about also gives us additional hints about Hank's character and social status.

We fix the coffee business by inserting enough lines and sound to send him out to the kitchen, give him time to pick up the coffee and a tray of cups, and then bring him back in. We tell the audience what is going on mostly through having Hollis project while he is in the kitchen and placing those lines of Hank's off mike. In actual production, no point will be made of all this business. The actors will "throw it away." But if it were not included, it would leave gaps in the business which would call attention to themselves. Correctness of detail here is important only so that it will not call attention to the detail. It will also give the scene a little flavor of reality that it might not have if it were simply dialogue taking place in a vacuum, as so many such scenes are.

HOLLIS: I'm Hollis Wilcox.

HANK: (Slight pause) Oh. Hollis Wilcox. That's a very nice name.

HOLLIS: Thank you. I wish you'd tell me something about yourself. Are you coming or going?

HANK: I've been. Guadalcanal. Now I'm home for a rather long furlough, I guess. Training young men in the art of jungle fighting.

Teaching them the Jap tricks we learned by the trial and error method.

HOLLIS: New York must seem ~~This must be so~~ strange, after the fighting

HANK: It is. ~~It's so strange, this life, now, that~~ I can't get used to pressing a wall-switch. I can't get used to the feeling of the rug under my feet. Even the people I once knew seem changed. (Abruptly) Maybe it's me. (FADE) Let me see how ~~Let's try~~ the coffee's ~~now~~ coming.

HOLLIS: (PROJECTS SLIGHTLY) This is ~~Such~~ a beautiful room. Yet it's essentially a man's room.

HANK: (OFF) Thanks. Coffee's ready. I'll bring it in.

HOLLIS: You've been so very kind, Lieutenant Waring.

HANK: (FADE IN) Anyone would have done exactly what I did.

HOLLIS: (FADE IN) But not with such finesse.

SOUND: TRAY SET DOWN WITH RATTLE OF CUPS

I must bring this dress back to Monsieur Torlonia's. — I think that would be best.

HANK: I'll be glad to drive you there. But how about the ~~I hate~~ coffee first? ~~to see you go.~~

HOLLIS: All right.

HANK: It's nice having you here. You fit into the décor.

SOUND: CUPS, SAUCERS, SILVER AD LIBBED AS COFFEE IS POURED

HOLLIS: You know I really don't. You know, with this dress, I'm a jarring Eighteenth Century note

Nothing remarkable was done with page 8. The line change at the top merely completed the coffee business.

At the top of page 9, the author had the couple leave the apartment in mid-scene and descend in the apartment-house elevator to the street. Unfortunately, they never got to the street before the scene ended and there was no reason why they should. For that matter, there was no sound dramatic reason why they should leave the apartment. Therefore, the sound routine of the elevator business was simply cut and the scene played to its conclusion in the apartment. The elevator business is perfectly possible to produce, but since it has no real purpose in the script, there is no point in taking valuable rehearsal time to work it out. There is good reason why this sound should be cut, aside from its lack of meaning. The scene which is being played at the moment is important. Hollis is stating a philosophy which seems very odd indeed to Hank. The entire plot revolves around his misunderstanding of what she says in this scene. Because it is so important, it is essential not to distract the audience with movement or sound which is not important. Besides, the lines are of a nature that would scarcely be tossed off casually in an elevator.

The additions to the transition at the bottom of the page are twofold. The notes give the composer some idea of what kind of transition is desired, and the sound notes give the sound man a more definite idea of the pattern desired to help set the scene and back the dialogue which follows. The "Music and Laughter" indicated by the author is correct enough, but it is not complete enough. Incidentally, it is usually confusing to an audience to have transition music *segue* directly into scene background music. Hence, we will have sound cover momentarily before the dance music comes up as the scene starts. This will avoid possible confusion.

The change on the top of page 10 is purely a matter of taste. The original line seemed to make it appear as though Hollis was doing all the courting. We want to give the audience the impression that it is a completely mutual interest. Banter will do this better, with a little wisecrack to cover their mutual seriousness.

in the midst of this harmony of convex and concave shapes. But it's lovely here, I'll admit.

HANK: ~~Don't blame it on me.~~ One mug Java coming up!

HOLLIS: Thanks

HANK: I've often looked around this place and wondered if a woman — I mean, a wife, would balk at living in it.

HOLLIS: If I had a husband, I'd live in a pup tent, if necessary.

HANK: A romanticist!

HOLLIS: No. An opportunist.

HANK: If you're really an opportunist, instead of sitting and brooding about what happened this morning, you'll have a date with a fine, upstanding young man with incomparably superior wearing qualities.

HOLLIS: It wasn't as bad as that — I mean, I'm not going to sit and brood. I'm quite recovered from my little embarrassment.

HANK: Little embarrassment, you call it.

HOLLIS: Worse things than that have happened to me. Once I fell through a glass roof in the Royal Hawaiian Hotel in Honolulu. This is good coffee.

HANK: You mean you minded that more.

HOLLIS: Well, it hurt me physically more.

HANK: I must say you have an odd point of view.

HOLLIS: (Serenely) Not really. I have learned to take things as they come. Saves wear and tear on my disposition. I can take disappointments easier. ~~Shall we go?~~

HANK: ~~Er — yes, let's.~~ I suppose.

~~SOUND EFFECT: DOOR OPENING AND CLOSING.~~

HANK: Down!

SOUND OF ELEVATOR DOOR OPENING.

HOLLIS: I have to be so careful of this dress.

~~HANK: (Dryly) I should imagine.~~

HOLLIS: Why so quiet? Are you regretting your kind deed already?

HANK: I'm sorry. I guess I'm not quite able to grasp the philosophy women have taken unto themselves - shall we say -- since I've been gone from New York.

HOLLIS: (Equably) It's a workaday world philosophy. A cloak that women need. It wouldn't do nowadays for a girl to faint prettily on the church steps to rescue herself from an awkward situation.

HANK: I get it. What about the fine, upstanding young man I was telling you about a while back?

HOLLIS: If it's the one I think you mean -- you can call for me between eight.

HANK: Swell! Let's dress, and do the town, -- then tomorrow afternoon --

HOLLIS: Hold on, Lieutenant. You forget I'm a working girl.

HANK: Oh. (Pause) Sure. I -- of course. But, tonight, anyway!

~~SOUND EFFECT: MUSIC UP TO SHOW CHANGE OF SCENE. BACKGROUND OF MUSIC AND LAUGHTER.~~

MUSIC: STINGER CHORD INTO FAST, GAY, SOPHISTICATED BRIDGE WHICH BUILDS QUICKLY, THEN FADES ALMOST OUT FOR...

SOUND: LARGE DINNER CROWD IN FASHIONABLE HOTEL DINING ROOM UP AND UNDER

MUSIC: DANCE ORK IN AND COVERS CROWD SLIGHTLY AND HOLDS BG

HOLLIS: (CLOSE) I don't know when I've had so much fun, Hank. You're a smooth dancer, Lieutenant Waring — or has someone told you.

HANK: Hey! Stop it. Stick to the script. That's my line!

~~If anyone has — I'd still want to~~

HOLLIS: So sorry. (THEY LAUGH)

~~hear it again from you.~~

HANK: I thought I ~~had~~ forgotten how to dance. Have you really had fun?

HOLLIS: Um hum.

HANK: Forgotten all about this morning?

HOLLIS: You think about it more than I do. I haven't had even so much as a single cross thought for Paul.

HANK: Tell me about this - Paul. What sort of person is he?

HOLLIS: He's probably one of the three best in his line in the country. Terribly temperamental, though. And the girls are mad for him.

HANK: Doesn't — didn't that bother you?

HOLLIS: (Surprised) Why should it? I may not be the most beautiful of them all, but he seemed to want me more than the rest. I suppose because I'd do anything he asked me to. Hang by my toes in Grand Central Station, if that's what he wanted me to do.

HANK: Whew-e-ew-w!

HOLLIS: (Blandly) So far it hasn't been necessary. He always told me I was a good sport, and that's why I know he prefers me to some of the others, more beautiful, perhaps.

HANK: There couldn't be anyone more beautiful.

HOLLIS: I'm afraid you're not looking at me with the same detached, critical and jaundiced eye of Paul.

On page 11, one production change had to be made. If the orchestra – which was playing as the scene began – is to go into a waltz, we must have it stop playing and spot in the usual murmur of a dinner crowd. During the pause between orchestral numbers, the crowd in the background will be up slightly high, especially on the dance floor, where the scene is located. The scene could be played as the author wrote it, with the orchestra simply making a musical transition from a fox trot to a waltz. However, breaking the music slightly reinforces the setting and also gives more importance to the waltz music which is the motivation for the first kiss.

The orchestra leader's line near the bottom of page 11 creates a question. It must be done over a public-address system to make it believable. Is it worth the bother of setting up a P.A. system for one line? Since we want to make the blackout waltz impressive, to help create the atmosphere for the first kiss, we decide to leave it in. The sound crew will groan and ask if this is the Moscow Art Theatre, but we will stick by our guns.

The line changes on page 12 are calculated to keep Hank from sounding mid-Victorian. The cut also saves time by eliminating lines without omitting essential material.

The changes on page 13 were the most radical in the script, necessitating a retyping, but the actual change was trifling. Both versions of page 13 are reproduced. The general content is the same. The only change was the introduction of the voice at the other end of the telephone. This was done for three reasons. First, the scene must be left in because it is the first which gives the locale and atmosphere of a model agency office. Second, the long, one-sided conversation is too obvious because everything must be repeated for the audience's benefit. A one-end telephone conversation is all right for a short conversation, but when a lot of exposition must be given, the device becomes awkward. It is simpler to let the audience hear both ends of the conversation. Third, we have already accustomed the audience to hearing both ends of a telephone conversation on pages 5 and 6. It would be inconsistent to use it at one place and not another.

HANK: How can anyone be detached about you. Tonight you look like a city saint in that dress. An Angkor Vat princess. This morning you looked - a little vulnerable in that wedding dress. But I suppose all brides look a little vulnerable.

HOLLIS: They hope they do. I can see that being away from it all for months and months hasn't impaired your knack of making pretty speeches.

HANK: These aren't pretty speeches. They're digests. They're love words stripped of all parrying and excess verbiage. They're for those who must love as they run. I'm here today and gone to-morrow. I haven't time for the preliminaries.

MUSIC: FLOURISH TO NATURAL END

SOUND: SCATTERED APPLAUSE. CROWD UP SLIGHTLY

HOLLIS: I like this place. I like to come here. No one

~~SOUND EFFECT: THE ORCHESTRA SWINGS INTO A WALTZ.~~

has the faintest desire ever to analyze your handwriting, sell you a —

HANK: Don't try to change the subject.

HOLLIS: — a pink, stuffed dog, or read your palm.

MUSIC: DREAMY WALTZ STARTS. CONTINUES IN BG

HANK: Almost all the lights are out. Shall we dance again?

HOLLIS: And you can get a drink in a glass, instead of in pineapples or cocoanuts.

HANK: (Softly) Look at me!

ORCHESTRA LEADER: (OVER P.A. SYSTEM This is our blackout waltz; we hope you like it.

HANK: You're stalling. You can't get a drink in a cocoanut any more. You're just talking — what are you afraid of? Look at me! Hollis.

HOLLIS: Now, now Lieutenant. I'm not one of your men taking orders. I can shut my eyes tight if I want to.

HANK: But you won't.

HOLLIS: No. I rather like looking at you.

HANK: In a minute we'll hardly be able to see each other.

HOLLIS: But I'll know you're here.

HANK: I want to make sure of that.

(Pause) I shouldn't have done that. ~~Can you forgive me for -- that?~~

HOLLIS: Why not? ~~What is there to forgive?~~ I wanted you to kiss me, and you knew it. Why should I pretend? I'm for condensations, too.

HANK: Do you mean that, Hollis?

HOLLIS: (Simply) Yes.

HANK: I like Your being honest. ~~is swell.~~ ~~Once I worked on an engineering job with a man whose favorite expression was -- 'Time is of the essence'. It had a quaint flavor and used to make me smile whenever I heard it. I thought it was meaningless. But now -- 'time really is of the essence'.~~ I've got to make myself indispensable to you -- so you won't have time to think -- to think of -- anyone.

HOLLIS: Why, I haven't been thinking of anyone. Except one Hank-for Short Francis Henry Waring.

HANK: Really mean that? Not -- you mean -- May I see you tomorrow night? I mean, tonight, because this is already this morning.

HOLLIS: Stop. You're all mixed up. Of course I'll

see you. And now, I've got to get home. I've some early appointments.

MUSIC: WALTZ SEGUES INTO SPRIGHTLY CLIMAX AND ENDS.

SOUND: PHONE RINGS. RECEIVER LIFTED PROMPTLY.

MARY: Alfred Minor Hoyt Agency.

LEWIS: (Filter) Mary? Miss Lewis at Fashion Magazine.

MARY: Oh, hello, Miss Lewis.

LEWIS: Mary, can we have Hollis Wilcox at ten?

MARY: I'm sorry, Miss Lewis, but Hollis is tied up. She's doing a wedding picture this morning with Paul Haron and you know how fussy he is..

LEWIS: What about three this afternoon?

MARY: Just a minute. Let me look at her schedule....That's fine.

LEWIS: Good. Tell her to bring a riding habit.

MARY: (AS IF WRITING) Riding habit. Oh...will it be a color picture or black and white.

LEWIS: Color.

MARY: All right. Thank you, Miss Lewis.

LEWIS: Good-bye.

SOUND: PHONE RECEIVER IN CRADLE. DOOR OPENS...

HOLLIS: (OFF, FADING IN) Hi, Mary...

SOUND: DOOR CLOSES.

HOLLIS: What's on for today?

~~see you. And now, I must go home. I've~~

some early appointments.

MUSIC TO DENOTE CHANGE OF SCENE

MARY: Alfred Minor Hoyt Agency. Who's calling?... Fashion Magazine. No, Hollis Wilcox won't be available this morning, Miss Lewis. She's doing a wedding picture with Paul Haron, and you know how fussy he is....What time, then. 3? What do you want her to bring along, Miss Lewis? Riding habit. Let me check her schedule.........Okey, she's free at that time. Oh—will this be a color picture, or a black and white? Thank you.

SOUND EFFECT OF DOOR OPENING AND CLOSING

~~HOLLIS: Hi, Mary, what's on for today.~~

MARY: I have your schedule here, Hollis. You've got to be at Fashion Mag. at 3. Riding habit. It's a color picture, so watch your accessories.

HOLLIS: ~~I shall mount my steed at least by one. So~~ Rest easy, my lass. Anything else?

MARY: Pop Hoyt told me to tell you to get down to Torlonia's ~~salon~~ as soon as you can this morning. Torlonia's changed his mind again, and wants you to wear the taffeta wedding dress instead of the satin. Says it breaks up the sunlight better.

HOLLIS: Mary, I stood for hours day before yesterday while he fitted that dress just right. He's driving me stark, raving mad. And on top of that,

there had to be a last minute fitting yesterday morning. Then, Paul forgot some of his paraphernalia and left me standing on the Cathedral steps like a forgotten bride. In no time, there was a crowd, ~~and little me, embarrassed almost to tears~~. I hate these outdoor shots.

MARY: Sure. Either you stand at the feet of George Washington's horse the middle of August, wearing a dream of a mink coat, while the sun beats down on you and your makeup melts — or you stand in a cold March wind wearing a filmy dress and a cartwheel hat. ~~What do you think I installed myself behind these fourteen 'phones for~~? A model's life is not for me.

HOLLIS: Sometimes it has its compensations.

MARY: Meaning what?

HOLLIS: (Dreamily) Meaning I met a man yesterday.

MARY: You cover gals are always meeting men. Fat ones, thin ones, rich ones, poor ones. I wish you'd toss your leftovers my way.

HOLLIS: Have you ever heard me making with the love routine before?

MARY: Now that you mention it, I haven't.

SOUND EFFECT 'PHONE RINGS RECEIVER PICK UP

Alfred Minor Hoyt Agency....What's he got that the other brokers, playboys and Army men haven't? Hoyt Agency...Miss Rakham speaking....Miss Gallagher? I check with her

The remaining cuts on pages 13 and 14 sharpen the dialogue and take out lines that might miss fire, or which were meant to be funny and which might fail to get a chuckle. Some of these speeches are long, especially Mary's in the middle of page 14, but it is strong enough to play well; it adds local color and gives the audience a little peek behind the scenes which they seem to enjoy. Therefore, it was left in.

When we come to pages 15 and 16, the axe comes out. Here is the logical, easy, economical place to cut. Customers one and two are completely extraneous. They were put in originally, in all probability, to set the scene at Torlonia's and give a little build-up to Torlonia's character. This is unnecessary on both counts. In the first place, the dialogue on page 16 sets the scene sufficiently, with the few changes and additions made in the lines. Second, it is bad dramaturgy to build up to Torlonia's entrance because he is a minor character and has nothing to do with the plot. He merely furnishes the dresses in which Hollis poses. It is not Torlonia of whom Hank thinks he is jealous. Therefore, his appearance in the script is purely incidental and need not be planted so definitely. Finally, to cast the show properly might mean that at least one additional actress would have to be hired just for that little bit. It would be worth it if it were necessary. Since it is not, it is a good place to practice economy.

The line changes in the middle of page 16 merely reinforce the exposition eliminated in the cut. The line insertion at the bottom of the page helps a little to exposit the action there and break up Torlonia's long speech.

schedule.

HOLLIS: Nothing — and everything.

MARY: She's not free until twelve...Will that be all right?...Thank you....Good-bye. Wait until I write this down.......There. What's his name, Holly?

SOUND: RECEIVER REPLACED

MARY:

HOLLIS: Hank Waring. I think I'll wear the beige suit tonight.

MARY: It must be laa-ve. You've been saving that suit for weeks for that coffee ad. Get out of here and get down to Torlonia's or he'll change his mind again.

HOLLIS: I'm practically there now. Oh, — my hat-box!

MUSIC SHARP BEGINNING, FAST BUILD TO PEAK, THEN DESCEND AND FADE

~~SOUND EFFECT: MUSIC TO SHOW CHANGE OF SCENE.~~

~~CUSTOMER I: (With over-modulated voice) You know, Louisa,~~ when I went to Bonnie Torlonia in his Paris salon, I never had any idea what he looked like. He never came out of the workshop. When his young partner, M. D'Balencieville, was mobilized in France, Torlonia decided to come to America. Weren't we lucky? Something good came out of the war, Louisa.

CUSTOMER II: A very talented designer. Very talented. Have you ever seen him — here?

CUSTOMER I: I've seen him, and my dear, he's a short, ugly man with clever hands and the soul of an artist.

CUSTOMER II: They say he always cuts his stuff from the material right on the form.

CUSTOMER I: They say he's a little bit crazy.

~~CUSTOMER II: Wouldn't you know. Look at the lovely work he does.~~

CUSTOMER I: M-m-m. There goes Hollis Wilcox, the photographer's model. Look at that. She has entre to his workshop. Walks right in.

CUSTOMER II: Well, my dear, she can wear them, but she can't buy them.

CUSTOMER I: How right you are.

SOUND OF DOOR OPENING AND CLOSING

TORLONIA: Ah, Hollyhocks, I heard that you got the royal trounce yesterday.

HOLLIS: Bounce, Torlonia, bounce. You'll never be able to face the customers if you don't stop tearing the language apart. Your assaults on syntax are terrible.

TORLONIA: (Sighs) I know. But women buy my dresses - not my English ~~How well I know it.~~ Here put this on. Be hind there.

HOLLIS: (FADES SLIGHTLY) Changed your mind again, I see.

TORLONIA: Yes. ~~Well, I'm glad you got the royal flush because~~ After you left, I said to myself, Torlonia, that's not the right dress to have a full-page spread in Fashion Magazine with Flaubert jewelry. Now, that's the dress. A wedding dress to make the conversation. But not to talk out loud. My No. 76. And when I talk to myself, I listen.

HOLLIS: (Muffled) I rather liked the other.

TORLONIA: That's the dress for you. That piece has a good midriff.

HOLLIS: (OFF, STRUGGLING) It's also hard to get into.

TORLONIA: When I call up Pop Hoyt, I always say, 'Send me a girl who can do justice to my dress. I want a tall girl, not too short. A short girl, not too tall.' You are the one.

Pages 17 and 18 present a real problem. As the scene is written, it plays continuously from Hollis's entrance to the fitting room until Paul's cab arrives at the shooting location. There are not more than two minutes of dialogue provided to cover all this action. It will be a little difficult to make an audience believe that things could move so fast. During that two minutes Hollis comes in, gets into a dress, goes downstairs, gets into a cab, drives to a church and gets out, ready to make pictures. Too much happens in too little time. It must be fixed. The beginning of the solution is seen in the changes on page 17.

Obviously, the only way of getting out of this time dilemma is to insert a scene transition which will allow for a lapse of time. Since nothing is accomplished by having Hollis go down the elevator and get into the car, we cut that part of the script. The scene in the dress designer's shop is then played out to its finish right in the shop and ends in a musical bridge, which is shown here on the top of page 18.

The business of having Hollis get in the car with the photographer and his assistants is unnecessary and can be cut. There is only the dialogue on page 18 to let them get from Torlonia's to their destination, hardly enough time to shift gears on the car, to say nothing of getting somewhere in New York traffic! Certain liberties can be taken with time in a radio script, but this routine goes beyond the bounds. The simple solution is to start the scene with the whole party in the car and the car on its way. The audience can then happily assume that it has been traveling for some time and comes in on the scene as the car approaches its destination. An audience will gladly make such an assumption. The lapse of time provided by the transition cares for the whole problem nicely.

The cut at the bottom of page 18 saves some of the two and a half minutes. The speech is not important. The idea can be retained without so much dialogue and the cut takes a too-long speech away from an unimportant character. This is the kind of cut that is good to make. Nothing is lost and the dialogue will be speeded up. Probably it was a filler speech to begin with, the writer being aware that she needed more

HOLLIS: (OFF) There! (FADES ON) How does it look?

SOUND: RUSTLE OF TAFFETA AS SHE WALKS

TORLONIA: In all New York, that dress has no equals, no imitators. A twitch here. A twitch there. We don't allow no Fift' Columnists of fashion thieves in here. Hollis-wood, that piece has social significance.

HOLLIS: What's more to the point, Tortilla, does it conform to W.P.B. rulings?

TORLONIA: Ah, you Americans, so practical.

HOLLIS: You should say that. We must hurry. Paul doesn't like to be kept waiting.

TORLONIA: Ah, Paul, Paul! He is the master. Didn't he keep you waiting yesterday? You're the prima donna, not he.

HOLLIS: I let him think he is. He likes me for it.

TORLONIA: You're all ready. Now, out the back way. Be good to it.

HOLLIS: I will! ~~Harry, take me down to the street floor?~~

~~SOUND EFFECT OF ELEVATOR DOOR OPENING AND CLOSING, CREAKING OF OLD ELEVATOR.~~

TORLONIA: (~~Shouting~~) It's one of my children, that dress. It was not cut out thirty at a slash by a power-driven machine.

HOLLIS: (~~Shouting~~) Don't worry, Monsieur, I love it almost as much as I love you.

TORLONIA: It's not a Seventh Avenue dress!

HOLLIS: And I am no 7th avenue girl and Paul is no 7th avenue photographer. ~~Harry, sometimes I think he's a little crazy.~~ And he's waiting in the car with the boys downstairs. Goodbye ~~M-m-m. Crazy like a fox.~~

TORLONIA: Goodbye, beautiful. Be careful in that dirty elevator.

MUSIC: SHORT, DESCENDING RUN OF CHORDS TO SAY "GOING DOWN"

SOUND EFFECT OF ELEVATOR DOOR OPENING AND CLOSING.

SOUND EFFECT OF FEET RUNNING.

HOLLIS: Oh, Paul, I couldn't get out of there. You know how he is.

PAUL: After yesterday, I'm not complaining.

HOLLIS: Hello, boys, think you can make it today?

ASSISTANTS: You bet, Hollis. Climb in.

SOUND EFFECT OF CAR DOOR OPENING AND CLOSING.

SOUND EFFECT OF CAR MOTOR STARTING UP. RUNNING, INTERIOR PERSPECTIVE

PAUL: My blushing bride, you look wonderful.

HOLLIS: I actually did blush yesterday. What happened to him, boys?

ASSISTANT: He couldn't find a certain filter. It had to be a certain kind of a filter, and he knew just where it was in the studio. He could put his hand on it. He couldn't put his hand on it if it jumped up and bit him on the nose. It was in the third left-hand drawer in the cabinet where he keeps all the filters. So he said.

HOLLIS: Have you got everything today? I hope?

PAUL: Everything, my sweet.

HOLLIS: Please, Paul, stop kissing my ear. Every time I do a wedding picture for you, you begin to feel like a groom.

PAUL: It's that white dress. I feel a proposal coming on.

ASSISTANT: Well, keep it to yourself. You got a lawfully wedded wife already, and two suing you for back alimony.

time for the car to reach its destination. Failing in that purpose, it has no other.

Most of the changes on page 19 are self-explanatory. The author had implied accompanying sound in her dialogue, but had failed to include it in the script. Like many writers new to the field of radio, she failed to recognize that writing for radio is writing a score in sound. It must include dialogue, music, sound effects – all the elements of the program which go to make up a total meaningful pattern of listening. When the author fails to do this, it has to be supplied by the production director in the process of editing the script with which we are now concerned.

The cuts on page 20 are all to save time. This scene is not vital to the plot except as it provides a setup for Hank to see Hollis in a wedding dress again. All the rest of it is simply setting the scene for that one bit of action. It is not dramatically important otherwise. Therefore, although there are some good speeches on this page (especially the one at the bottom which is cut), time has to be saved somewhere, and here is another spot where it can come out without hurting the story. So, much as we hate to, we cut.

HOLLIS: Talk to him like a Dutch Uncle.
SOUND: CAR SLOWS, STOPS, MOTOR IDLES
PAUL: Saved! If this trip had been longer, my suit had been stronger.

HOLLIS: Oh, that's awful. You can do better than that.
SOUND: CAR DOOR OPENS
PAUL: There's a parking space, boys. You get the cameras out, boys, and I'll help Hollis and the dress out.

HOLLIS: Wait. Don't step on that train. Let me throw it over this arm - now, you take this one.
SOUND: FADE LIGHT BOULEVARD TRAFFIC B.G.
PAUL: Easy does it. There you are. Now, let's see. How about right up there. Against the background of that lovely old door.

HOLLIS: (Groans) Here we go again, boys.

PAUL: We can try a few poses until the boys are ready. Try another step up.
HOLLIS: (OFF SLIGHTLY) How's this?
PAUL: Fine. Now turn around a little. Turn your head and shoulders — not your body — now — smile at me. Look down — down — Hollis.

HOLLIS: Oh, wait a minute, Paul. There's someone I know. Hank!

PAUL: Well, stop waving at him. This is business, not pleasure.
HOLLIS: (CALLS) Hank!
PAUL: Pull your stomach in. Chest out. This way a little — we'll try that a couple of more times on that step, — we've got plenty of time before they're ready to set them up. Why, what's the matter?

HOLLIS: He didn't even smile, Paul. He just — he just looked away and stepped on the gas.

PAUL: New York is full of good-looking soldiers, ~~sailors and marines.~~ Why worry about that one?

HOLLIS: He's special.

PAUL: They're all special, to someone. Well, forget it for now, Hollis. Look soulful. Soulful, I said, not mournful.

HOLLIS: I'm trying.

PAUL: Turn your head a little this way. ~~Put your right hand out a little way.~~ Now -- lift your chin at about a forty-degree angle. The best model I have and you have to fall in love. Love's the bunk.

HOLLIS: You ought to know. You've been married three times.

PAUL: No cracks. I made you who you are today --

HOLLIS: I hope you're satisfied.

PAUL: Move 'em up, boys.

HOLLIS: (Kidding) ~~I made you what you are today, you mean.~~ How many models in New York would stand on the ~~top of a hill on a hot day in a ski suit and let you throw moth flakes in her hair and spray salt water in her face -- for a picture?~~

PAUL: You love it, sugar-puss. Now, retard the jaw motion -- we're going into action. No mistakes -- color pictures don't cost peanuts. Come on, now. Give me that great big smile! I said a smile!

An interesting problem presents itself on page 21. A new character is introduced. Legsy has no purpose in the script except to introduce the seed-pearl dress. She comes into the show, talks about the dress, and disappears. The dress is important to the dramatic action of the show because it provides the means for the next meeting between Hank and Hollis, which is our main concern. The question to decide is: Shall we cut the character of Legsy or leave her in? She is present for a very flimsy reason, since Mary could just as well introduce the subject of the dress. Shall we hire another actress and confuse the audience with another character just to get that dress in? Perhaps against our better judgment we decide to do so, since Legsy is rather interesting as a character. It might be hard to justify, but the lines are not bad; we follow the path of least resistance and leave Legsy in.

All the changes on page 22 are occasioned by a single decision. Many of the scenes in the script are short. Too many short scenes give a choppy, irregular effect which is disturbing to an audience. A director should remember that it takes an audience a few seconds to get adjusted to a new scene. Each time a scene opens, the audience must discover where it is taking place, with what characters, and why. Suppose this takes fifteen seconds. In a series of scenes which play less than a minute, a quarter of which time the audience spends orienting themselves, the over-all effect is confusing. There is danger of this in our script. We have already broken one scene into two and introduced an additional transition. The other one was permissible because it was a fairly long scene and could stand the division. Here we have two very short scenes and the only way to prevent choppiness is to fuse them if possible.

The scene which starts on page 22 has only one dramatic function: to tell the audience that Hollis has been assigned to wear the seed-pearl dress – the one introduced in the preceding scene. The two scenes can be joined simply by sending Legsy out and then having Mary break the news. So we take out the music transition near the top of the page, take out the repeated routine about Hank failing to call, and cover the news

MUSIC LIGHT COMEDY BRIDGE, FADE END
~~SOUND EFFECT: MUSIC UP TO DENOTE PASSAGE OF TIME~~

HOLLIS: (Reading) M-m-m. 9.00 - Hairdresser

11.00 - Weems Advertising Agency, bathing suit.

12.00 - Retake on cigarette picture.

Mary, you're sure no one by the name of Waring called?

MARY: Everything that came in for you is right down there, Hollis.

SOUND EFFECT OF DOOR OPENING ~~AND CLOSING.~~

HOLLIS: Hi, Legs-y.
SOUND: DOOR CLOSES
LEGS-Y: Hi, Hollis. Any inside dope on who's going to wear the dress?

HOLLIS: What dress?

LEGS-Y: Hollis, Honey, you been in a fog the last three days. The half-a-million dollar dress that's made en-tirely of seed pearls sewn on by hand. Some one of us gets to wear it Saturday night at the China Relief Fashion Show at the Ritz-Astoria roof.

HOLLIS (UNIMPRESSED): Do tell.

LEGS-Y: Whoever wears the dress gets two bodyguards to boot. I hope they're smooth.

HOLLIS: Oh, Legs-y, you're always thinking of men.

LEGS-Y: (Surprised) Honey, what else *is* there to think about?

HOLLIS: Maybe Betty McLain will wear it. She's the one who usually gets those plums. ~~She's just right for that sort of thing.~~

LEGS-Y: Well, at least she's hefty enough to carry it. The darn thing must weigh a ton.

HOLLIS: Now that doesn't sound a bit like you.

LEGS-Y: I know it. But little old Legs-y would just

love to get to wear that dress. All I ever do is stocking ads. Would my face stop a clock? Tell me, Hollis.

HOLLIS: Of course it wouldn't. And you know it.

MARY: Legs-y, don't be late for your appointment.

LEGS-Y: (FADE) I'm just going. Be seein' you.

SOUND EFFECT: DOOR OPENS - PAUSE - CLOSES ~~MUSIC TO DENOTE CHANGE OF SCENE.~~

HOLLIS: Gee, Mary, I wish that Waring man would call me! ~~'Morning, Mary. What's on my schedule?~~ Anything real good?

MARY: ~~I can tell you what isn't. A call from Hank Waring.~~ Maybe he'll call today

HOLLIS: No. ~~I expected you to say that. I wasn't going to ask you today. I gave him this number that night.~~ If he hasn't called by now, he's never going to call. ~~I don't know what I said or did, to offend him.~~

MARY: Maybe he's had his orders.

HOLLIS: No, he's been out, before. I don't think that's it.

MARY: I have some news for you that I ~~haven't had~~ didn't want to tell you while Legs-y was here. ~~a chance to put down on your schedule.~~ You're going to wear the seed-pearl dress Saturday night.

HOLLIS: I am? Oh, that's great.

MARY: Pop wants you to take it easy until then, because the dress is extremely tiring to wear, and he wants you to be fit as a fiddle.

HOLLIS: ~~I am? Oh, that's great!~~ What about my hair?

MARY: Pop says 'no jewelry'. Wear your hair parted in the middle with a low chignon at the back. ~~Very simply.~~ You'll be a knockout

HOLLIS: Maybe. But I haven't got my heart in my work

about the dress by the line inserted near the bottom of the page. Mary says that she did not want to break the news in front of Legsy to postpone disappointing her. By this simple process we have eliminated two short scenes and substituted one longer one which will play more smoothly.

On page 23 the reader will notice that the music of the dance orchestra was started after the scene opened instead of simultaneously with the beginning of the scene. This will keep the audience from being confused between transition music and scene background music.

The few changes on page 24 are only to prevent the hint of mid-Victorianism from creeping into the dialogue. They are not terribly important, but the line changes should bring some improvement.

On page 25 we encounter another elevator routine. Evidently the author believes in her ups and downs. It is true that most hotel ballrooms are on the mezzanine floor, and that apparently is the reason for the business. However, she puts the characters in the elevator and never takes them out. One speech later they are walking and Hollis is breathless. This is business which the author failed to think through, so we have to fix it. The simplest thing to do is to ignore the whole business and get them out as fast as possible, and into the car. If anything, we have erred a little in getting them out too fast. Probably in rehearsal, we will take them out of the ballroom about line 2 of page 25 to allow a little more time to cross the hotel lobby before they emerge on the street.

Most of the rest of the changes or corrections are self-explanatory. They are either the addition of necessary sound which the author has omitted, or they are line changes to keep the dialogue in character where we feel that she has deviated slightly from the pattern established. The student might do well to look at the remaining changes and determine why each of them was made. No changes were the result of idle fancy on the part of the production director. Each one eliminates some minor problem that might prevent the audience from getting the clearest possible impression of the story.

MUSIC: MINOR MELODY BUT NOT HEAVILY DRAMATIC FOR BRIDGE

~~SOUND EFFECT: MUSIC UP TO DENOTE CHANGE OF SCENE.~~

SOUND: BACKGROUND OF TALK, LAUGHTER, ~~MUSIC~~ AND CLAPPING.

HOLLIS: Mary, help me off with this coat of armor, will you, like a darling? I'm glad that's over - that ramp was so long, I thought I'd never get to the end of it.

MUSIC: DANCE MUSIC STARTS - OFF MIKE

MARY: No, you don't, Hollis. You go right out there in the ballroom and mingle with the cash customers.

HOLLIS: Oh, No!

MARY: They want to see the dress close to. If you see two sinister-looking men following you, those are the men from the detective agency.

HOLLIS: Throw me to the lions, then. See if I care.

SOUND: DOOR OPENS ON. CROWD UP.

~~MUSIC UP AS DOOR IS OPENED~~:

MUSIC: UP IN VOLUME

GEORGE: May I have this dance?

HOLLIS: I think so.

GEORGE: When I saw you just now in that fashion show, I said to myself, "George, how would it be to have your arms around a million dollar baby in a million dollar dress! Ha-ha-ha.

HOLLIS: I wish you wouldn't hold me quite so tight. The dress is so fragile -- I must be very careful of it.

GEORGE: No more fragile than you, baby. Why don't we slip outside? I want to talk to you. Come on --

HANK: (Coldly) May I cut in?

~~GEORGE:~~ ~~I haven't had more'n two words with this baby. What do you think!~~

HOLLIS: Oh, Hank, darling — later, George, we'll have our dance. ~~A — waltz. Something not so jumpy. Shall we?~~

GEORGE: But I just...

HOLLIS: later, George, we'll have our dance.

GEORGE: All right, then, don't forget. Cost me twenty-five dollars to get into this swar-ray — least I can do —

VOICE FADES OUT

HOLLIS: (Coldly) Destry rides again! Now that you've performed your tricks, why don't you slip off before you get yourself involved.

HANK: That's exactly what I intend to do. Would you like to have me take you to a neutral corner? ~~or should I turn you over to some other unsuspecting male.~~

HOLLIS: I don't know what you're talking about. And I think you owe me an explanation, Mr. Waring.

HANK: I owe *you* an explanation! You made a date with me you never intended to keep. ~~You're nothing but a heartless flirt.~~ You tell a man exactly what you think he wants to hear, while inside, you're laughing at him.

HOLLIS: ~~How dare~~ What makes you say such things? You were kind to me and in return, I was nice to you. I thought you were — special — but now I see how mistaken I was.

HANK: You were nice to me. You pulled my leg, that's what you did.

HOLLIS: I did no such thing.

HANK: You're coming with me, and you're going to do some tall and fast talking. You'll explain just what kind of a girl you are. You and your peculiar moral code.

HOLLIS: Let go of my wrist.

HANK: I will not.

HOLLIS: Don't you dare take me out of here. I won't go.

HANK: ~~DOWN!~~ Don't argue.

SOUND EFFECT: ~~ELEVATOR DOOR OPENING AND CLOSING.~~ CROWD AND MUSIC BEGIN TO RECEDE

HOLLIS: Why should I explain anything to you? I was the easy conquest. Waiting — like a — little schoolgirl — at the telephone.

HANK: We ~~get out here.~~ go out this way. Come on.

HOLLIS: (Breathlessly) You don't have to walk so fast. I'm — I'm tripping over this — this darn dress.

HANK: (Hurrying) Watch the door.

SOUND: DOOR OPENS, CLOSES, CUTTING OFF CROWD AND MUSIC. TRAFFIC IN.

HANK: Some man ought to take you over his knee and whale you. I hope that guy gets wise to himself before it's too late.

HOLLIS: Don't you even think of such a thing.

HANK: I ~~wish it were my privilege~~ can think, can't I? Here's my car.

SOUND: CAR DOOR OPENS

Get in!

HOLLIS: But — I can't.

HANK: Afraid Paul will see you?

HOLLIS: Paul! Paul! What's he got to do with us?

HANK: What's Paul got to — Say, you are a cool one. Get in.

HOLLIS: I'll get in — but I'm telling you that —

HANK: ~~I wish it were my privilege~~ Somebody ought to shake you

doubled-crossed
until your teeth rattle for every man you've
slip the lock on the other door.
~~misled with your beautiful face, your~~

SOUND: CAR DOOR CLOSES. STEPS. LOCK CLICKS. CAR DOOR OPENS.
~~lovely voice, and your charming and insincere~~
CLOSES. CUT TRAFFIC.

HANK: ~~ways.~~ You've got the face of a saint who does a little train-wrecking on the side.

<u>SOUND EFFECT OF CAR MOTOR STARTING UP</u>.

HOLLIS: I didn't deceive you. I told you who I was. You knew the sort of thing I did. Darn nice girls are doing the same thing all the time.

HANK: Sure. All our best people are doing it!

How was I to know you were so high-minded? <u>And</u> narrow-minded. Girls aren't sitting home doing fancy-work these days.

HANK: High-minded, you call it. ~~What a gag!~~ What a sense of humor you have. Making a date you never intended to keep. Probably laughing over it with Paul!

HOLLIS: I was doing the ~~one kept~~ waiting -- like a fool.

HANK: Waiting? ~~Am I to~~ Are you trying to make me believe that you were waiting for a date with another man on your wedding day?

HOLLIS: You're driving too ~~fast!~~ ~~I think someone's following us.~~ My WHAT?

~~HANK:~~ ~~Don't try to change the subject. I'm only going fifty.~~

HOLLIS: My wedding day. Ridiculous. Why I never --

HANK: I saw you. And I wasn't spying, either. I go by the Cathedral at least six days a week! ~~because it's the shortest distance between two points, my home and headquarters. NOTHING that happens five days a week can be-~~

~~called spying.~~

SOUND EFFECT OF POLICE SIREN.

HOLLIS: (Laughing uncontrollably) Oh, dear — Oh, Hank —

HANK: What's so funny!

HOLLIS: Please, Hank, I — think you'd better stop the car. The police — I —(LAUGHS AGAIN)

COP(SHOUTING) Pull over, you!

HANK: That's not funny.

SOUND: CAR SLOWS TO STOP. SIREN DIES

HOLLIS: But I'm not laughing at that. I'm laughing at you. You're the dumbest, funniest, blindest —

CAR DOOR OPENS. TRAFFIC UP SLIGHTLY

SOUND ~~EFFECT OF SCREECHING BRAKES~~

POLICEMAN: Hey, where do you think you're going with that girl?

HANK: Where do you think I'm going? For a ride.

POLICEMAN: Say, ain't I seen you before? Yah, I know — you're the ~~Lothario~~ guy that took the dame off the church steps. ~~What are you — a snatcher?~~

HOLLIS: And I'm the dame. (LAUGHS AGAIN)

POLICEMAN: The one with the torso! Well — by gorry. M-m-m. Why do you two have to make trouble on my beat? (CALLS OFF) Here's our man, O'Connor, and he's got the girl with him. She's all right, though.

HANK: (To Hollis) One of your husbands?

POLICEMAN: Look, lady, you're all right. Stop the crying! O'Connor had his eye on him the minute he took you out of the ballroom. He wouldn't hurt you, with us right on his tail.

HOLLIS: I'm not c-c-crying. I'm laughing!

HANK: Will somebody please tell me what goes on here?

HOLLIS: It's the dress, Hank. It's -- Officer, he's innocent. ~~He really doesn't know what the score is or who's carrying the ball~~. He doesn't know anything about the dress. I'm the one he's interested in. He doesn't know I'm a model. He thinks I'm sort of - of a professional bride. He wanted to fight with me about it.

HANK: Now - now wait a minute.

POLICEMAN: I don't get it, Miss.

HANK: I'm just beginning to. Stick around.

POLICEMAN: I'm just fulfilling my duties. These two Pinkertons were assigned to watch that dress. When they come running out of the hotel, trailing you two, they picked me up. Now they don't want to be explaining to no insurance company --

HANK: Why didn't you tell me you were modelling that day?

HOLLIS: I thought you knew.

POLICEMAN: ~~I think~~ Look. We'll have to take you two back with us.

HANK: ~~We'll~~ I'll make you a ~~bargain~~ proposition. We'll turn right around and go back to the Ball and you can trail us.

POLICEMAN: Okay.

HANK: But first - I've got a little "remodeling" to do ~~And how about giving us time for one little kiss?~~ Officer, would you mind looking at the skyline a moment

POLICEMAN: ~~Haven't you made enough of a fool of yourself for one night? She might slap your face. And,~~ You be careful, Lieutenant. She might say -- yes.

HANK: Now you're cooking with gas, officer.

POLICEMAN: I'll give you time out -- on wun condition --

HOLLIS: Name it.

POLICEMAN: That if you two get married -- you don't live on my beat.

MUSIC: IN FOR PAY-OFF

This has been a detailed and laborious exposition of the problem of editing a dramatic script for production. It is only fair to repeat that the author chose a script in which a great deal of editing had to be done. Most scripts are written by more experienced authors and require less editing. Few radio writers, however, have enough knowledge of production procedures to think of every possible problem and provide for it in the script. There is always some editing for the director to do. If he can do it on the original manuscript before it is duplicated, it will mean a much cleaner script from which to work once the show goes into rehearsal. If there are many changes and the author is available, it is simpler to call him in, talk the problems over, and have the author make the changes. If the author lives a thousand miles away, as is often the case, it is simpler to make the changes oneself.

The Production Analysis

By the time the production director has done a thorough job of editing a script, he has taken a long start toward the job of making a production analysis. Conscientious dramatic directors may do a step-by-step analysis such as is described here for the benefit of the beginner. Not a few production directors on daily serial programs walk into the rehearsal without having read the script. The entire directing job — if one can call it that — occurs during the hour in which the director and cast read through the script and rehearse it. Obviously this is not directing. It is only conducting rehearsals. Perhaps some of the criticism leveled at the "soap operas" is due to slipshod directing.

Aim of the Program

The first step in the production analysis is the decision about the aim of the program. This will be evident by the time the director has read the script and become acquainted with the show. The majority of dramatic programs have no other aim than to entertain the audience, though some are educational and some are propaganda pieces. However, this decision must be kept in mind because it will inevitably color the purpose. A program must sell goods or create good will for the sponsor. In dramatic programs this purpose can best be served by eliminating it from the program proper and giving the audience the highest entertainment value possible. If commercial considerations get involved in a dramatic show, both the sponsor and the production director are skating on thin ice. Under all normal circumstances the audience will respond best to a sponsor who gives them the best entertainment.

Dramatic Type

The director must next decide what type of drama he has at hand. This seems an obvious problem, but its very obviousness sometimes deceives directors into assumptions which are dangerous. It is important further because some kinds of scripts allow for several different treatments and the author himself may have been confused in purpose. In this case the production director is forced to make a decision and stick to it. Is the script drama or melodrama? Is it high comedy, low comedy, or farce? Is it a tragedy? The decision about this matter will color many subsequent decisions. In the script just discussed, there is a possible ambiguity in type. The characters are light-comedy characters. But the situation is based entirely on mistaken identity, one of the oldest farce devices. Most of the Shakespearean comedies become farces in modern handling because the mistaken identity situation is hardly as believable to contemporary audiences as it was to those in the Elizabethan theaters. Farce presupposes that the audience accepts a basically unbelievable situation for the sake of the fun which follows. In this script it is hard to conceive of a man's being deceived about the model's matrimonial intentions. It seems that he would guess the truth. But if he does, there is no story. If the audience can be made to accept the situation as real happening, we have a light comedy. If the audience cannot be made to accept it realistically, our only choice is to play it as broad farce. The difficulty is that the characters are not essentially farcical. Torlonia and Paul border on it. But the leads are not farce characters. Therefore, it will be necessary to play this script as high comedy and doctor the situation if necessary until it becomes realistically acceptable to the audience.

No final decision about the handling of characterizations can be made until the type of play is determined. In this instance care must be taken in the characterizations of the Irish cop, the dress designer, and the photographer, to see that they are not played too broadly for credibility. If it were farce, they should be played broadly – the broader the better.

The decision about the type of play will color very considerably the next decision: the manner in which the director will approach this work. This term "production approach" is another new term to indicate the general attitude or philosophy with which the director attacks the particular problem. For example, the script seems best suited to high comedy. That means the director will look at every problem in the script from the high-comedy point of view. What about pace? It must be quick, glib, easy. It will not be the breakneck pace of back-and-forth gag dialogue. It cannot be the snail pace of daytime serial drama. It cannot be the deliberate pace of a psychological drama. It must move quickly, smoothly, effortlessly, and with verve. What about characterization? It must be deft, light, easy. It dare not be studied, labored, heavily thoughtful. It must, on the other hand, not be so broad as to go into farce. It must be realistic. This is no fantasy. No trick effects will be used. And so it goes. Every possible aspect of the whole general approach to the play will be decided on the basis of this analysis.

Dramatic Structure

Next comes a study of the structure of the script. Every piece of good dramatic writing has a plan as definite as the blueprint for an airplane. The production director cannot do the best job of creating the program in sound unless he is familiar with the plan. If it is a play, it should have a definite conflict, with a protagonist and an antagonist. The conflict should become sharper and more complicated, finally emerging in a showdown in which either the protagonist or antagonist comes off victorious. In the first event, it is a comedy. In the latter case, it is a tragedy. In either case, you ought to know.

Having discovered the bare bones of the plot outline, the director then proceeds to plot the pacing, tempo, interpretation, and motivation of the whole script on that basis. The director must realize which scenes are merely expositional, telling the audience facts they need to know, and which ones are hand-to-hand struggles between the two elements of conflict in the story. It is from this study of structure that the director draws his conclusions about characterization and interpretation. It may influence his casting. It will certainly dictate the pacing of the show.

Interpretation

The study of the structure of the play leads directly to another consideration, interpretation. A good director, by the time he finishes his production analysis, will know exactly how he wants every line in the script read. If he does not know this, he is not ready to start rehearsals. What he finally uses on the air may not be what he originally had in mind, but this is no excuse for not having something in mind. Unless he understands the motivation for every line, he cannot possibly sit in judgment on an actor's reading, and this is one of the things he is called upon to do. A production director must do some of his most careful work here. If he finally arrives at the reading he wants by insisting that the actor imitate his reading, he will get a mechanical, emotionless performance. If he can make the actor understand what the character is thinking and feeling and how he is reacting, then the actor can give him a reading growing out of real emotional reaction.

Setting

Next, the director must look to the locale of the play For

every line of every scene in the script he must be able to answer these questions:

1. What is the exact locale of the scene?
2. What is the geography of the locale?
3. Where is the audience within that frame?
4. Where is each character in the scene with relation to the audience?
5. When the audience is moved either from one locale to another, or from one location to another within the same locale, how can it be accomplished to the complete satisfaction of the audience?

These are simple questions. It is an easy matter to find the answers, but this painstaking kind of preparation is not always done by the average production director. Sometimes it is enough to decide that the locale is a corner of a busy street in a large city. A careful director will probably go so far as to decide what corner of what street. It might make a difference. Perhaps any street corner would do so far as the plot of the play is concerned, but if the actors can visualize a specific spot, it helps them in the creation of the scene.

The exact lay-out of each scene should be decided upon. Perhaps the script indicates only a kitchen. The director needs to know how the kitchen is arranged in order to block his scenes. How can the audience get a clear picture of the scene if the director has never bothered to create one himself? Even when the locale is not of great importance, the knowledge of these details lends a sureness and a conciseness to the handling of scenes which will be apparent in the finished production.

It is of paramount importance that the director place his audience within the scene. If the scene is in a courtroom, the audience wants to know whether it is with the judge on the bench, in the juror's box, or out in the audience. This placement is achieved by perspective. If the scene were built so that the audience heard audience whispers close at hand while the official part of the courtroom procedure came from a slight distance, the listener would know that he was sitting in the audience. The use of sounds at various distances from the microphone will orient the listener in the surroundings of the scene because the audience places itself at the point of the closest sound.

Moving the audience about within a given locale or moving it from one locale to another is one of the most difficult jobs in radio production. It is difficult because it is primarily a visual problem and it must be done in a blind medium. The effect can always be managed if the director has a close sound source to work with and can then vary the perspectives of surrounding sounds. Take the courtroom scene again as an example. Suppose the audience is located with the spectators, sitting beside one of the important characters in the play. As the scene progresses, the audience hears whispers between the character and a friend and at the same time hears the business of the trial proceeding at a distance. Suddenly the bailiff calls (from a distance), "Will Miss Jones please come forward to the witness stand." Our character, next to whom we are sitting, makes an involuntary "Oh" very softly; there is a pause during which we hear the rustle of the spectators, and then, close to mike, our character stands up and, projecting, says, "Here I am." Then she says softly to the people sitting next to her, "Pardon me, please." There is a slight scuffle close to mike as she crowds across the knees of people seated in the same row. We hear the bailiff saying, "Please come forward, Miss Jones. Inside the rail here." As he says it he gets louder, giving us the effect of coming closer to him. At the same time the rustle of the audience fades slightly, giving us the effect of moving away from them. The bailiff says, "This way, Miss Jones," close to mike and quietly, so that he is obviously close to Miss Jones and hence to us, the audience. Now we hear the judge say, "Will you take the stand, Miss Jones." Whereas before we heard him from a distance, we now hear him comparatively close to us. This is followed by a suppressed giggle from the audience, this time some distance away. The gavel, which had been a distant sound before, now pounds close at hand to suppress the noise, and the trial proceeds. We have moved the audience from a seat among the spectators up to the witness stand.

In cases where there are not many sounds to use as reference, the director may have to fall back on footsteps to help transport the audience from place to place. If footsteps get louder, we assume someone is walking toward us. If they fade, we assume someone is walking away from us. If they do neither, we assume we are walking beside the person making the footsteps. Reinforcement of this idea in the dialogue helps to complete the illusion. It is in keeping the audience located that we can best make them understand what is going on in a scene and what it means to them. As Orson Welles [1] once said, "Of radio script shows there is only one that you will listen to: the kind you can follow."

Transitions

The director must decide what techniques he will use to transport his audience from one scene to another. The director has a choice of these means:

1. Music can be used.
2. Sound can be used.
3. Silence can be used.
4. An announcer may be used.
5. Any combination of the preceding four elements may be used.

The kind of transition chosen will depend first on what is available. Most daytime serials use the silent transition almost exclusively. Most elaborate nighttime dramatic shows use music almost exclusively. Part of this is because of the availability of music, part of it is habit. Daytime serials are, for the most part, hurriedly produced, and the silent transition is the simplest if not the best means of keeping two scenes apart. Ideally, each kind of transition has a particular application, and, if the director has a choice, he may use the technique

[1] Quoted in John S. Hayes and Horace J. Gardner, *Both Sides of the Microphone.* New York: J. P. Lippincott Company, 1938.

which does the most for the particular spot in the particular show under consideration.

The silent transition is probably most useful to cover a time lapse within a scene where neither characters nor scene changes. This tells the audience very well that the scene went right on and gives them the impression that what happened during the transition simply was not of importance at the moment.

Sound is sometimes useful to indicate a change of locale and also the means by which characters move from one scene to another. The conventionalized effects of trains, cars, and planes indicate not only a change of scene but the means by which the central character or characters proceed from one scene to another. This has been illustrated earlier.

The use of an announcer to change scenes is usually an admission on the part of the writer that he could think of no other way to change the scene. This is not always the case, but it often is. Announcer transitions are most useful in scripts where the announcer is the narrator on the program and, as such, a definite part of it. In such an instance, the transition becomes more than a mere interruption to change a scene. It is really a continuation of the scene in narrative form which may strengthen the over-all structure of the play rather than weaken it. This transitional device is most useful when the script involves a considerable amount of narration or exposition which can be more easily and economically handled by this means than by any other. The announcer transition should never be used in conjunction with too many other devices.

Music is probably the most often used transitional device; it is certainly one of the most flexible. Its uses are limited only by the skill and sensitivity of the composers and executors of the music. There is almost no dramatic transition assignment which cannot be handled by music.

Casting

The next consideration in the production analysis is talent. How many actors and actresses are needed, what kind, and finally, which specific ones? The first step in deciding on the talent problem is to clarify the picture of each of the characters. If the problem is a very simple one, it may not be necessary to spend much time on it. For the beginner, it is often helpful to sit down and write a twenty-five or fifty-word sketch of each character in the script. This does two important things. First, it clarifies the director's thinking. Nothing exposes vagueness and fuzziness in thinking so much as the necessity of putting thoughts on paper. Second, the sketches will be helpful to the actors later on when it is time to cast the show.

Here is the author's list of characterizations for the script reprinted earlier in this chapter. It is evident that no attempt is made at literary excellence. Its whole purpose is to state as definitely as possible the outstanding characteristics, habits of mind, and backgrounds of the character under consideration.

THE PROFESSIONAL BRIDE — AUTHOR'S PLAYHOUSE

Plot Synopsis

Lt. Hank Waring, home on leave, sees a bride left standing on the church steps. He rescues her from a curious crowd and falls in love with her, and she with him. She neglects to tell him she wasn't waiting to be married, but only to have her picture taken — she being a Powers girl. Love runs a rough road for 26 minutes. Ends in a burst of sunshine.

Characters

Lt. Hank Waring: An awfully nice sort of a guy — 28-32 years old, nice New York family. Knows what the score is, but not a smoothie. Has all the right instincts, but just a touch on the too serious side. There is a nice streak of naïveté in him too, or he'd tumble earlier to the gag. The key — dashing, quick-thinking-nice naïve.

Irish Cop: Not quite AFRA No. 16. I want him to be just a little pixilated. He's Irish, yes, and blustering, yes — but just a little plaintive. Everything that happens on 5th Ave. happens on his beat — and sometimes it's just too much!

Hollis Wilcox: This is the Powers model. She's strictly Powers as to chassis, but she's also a very nice girl — which is why she's the busiest model in the agency. All the photographers want her because she's a good sport with a sense of humor and not too many illusions about the glamour of her work. Sweet, smart, quick on the uptake, but no flirt. When she falls for Hank, she means it. Warm, friendly, rather calm. We've got to like her, right off, and keep liking her.

Paul, the Photographer: An absent-minded, middle-aged Don Juan who keeps forgetting he has a wife. Nice guy and a real artist whose only real concern is his color filters. He likes his models, but he seldom pursues them. Play him 40 years old, nice voice, straight with a ready laugh, and considerable objectivity on his own weaknesses.

Mary: Ex-model receptionist at the agency. She mothers the girls, sees that they keep their appointments, stalls off irate customers and difficult photographers, and in general keeps things in line. She is crisp, matter-of-fact, has a sharp tongue, a warm heart. She got tired of standing in a draft and gave up modeling while she still had a figure. She's 28, fast on the uptake, brittle, but warm.

Torlonia: French accent – thick. Dress designer who got out of Paris in time to land safely on upper Fifth Avenue in the right location. His name preceded him here, so he's doing fine. Always has several pages in *Vogue.* He is a genius who lives only for his creations. However, he has a kindness under his explosive temperament. Likes Hollis very much because she does the right things to his dresses.

Legsy: She is the model in the agency who always gets the stocking accounts. Her underpinnings are like that! The face is O.K. too, as well as the rest of the chassis, but mental development arrested itself at an early age. With her, it won't matter, though. She'll always get along. Some hardware dealer from Emporia, Ohio, will make her very happy some day.

George: He is the aforementioned hardware dealer from Emporia, Ohio. Hearty, Elk-toothy, extrovert, very unsubtle, and not exactly original in what he considers to be very snazzy repartee. 48 years old, unmarried and happy.

Having decided the kind of character needed for each part, the next step is to consider who, among the available actors, can do the best job. Names are jotted down for each part, to be used later when calls go out for casting. It is also wise to decide what parts can be doubled to save actors' fees. AFRA rules state that actors can play one double and one unnamed or unidentified voice and no more in any one program. There are one or two exceptions to this general rule, but it will do to go by under ordinary circumstances. If the station uses AFRA actors and there is any doubt about rulings, always make it a practice to consult with the legal adviser or whoever is responsible for making the AFRA contract. There is no artistic rule about doubling. Whether or not the director decides to use doubles, and how many, will depend entirely on the ability of his actors and the importance of the parts. It is never wise to try to double two large parts, but it is common practice to give an actor the maximum assignment in small bits. Often an important member of the cast can do one short double with little difficulty.

Talent problems sometimes solve themselves. Sometimes a part is so perfectly written for a certain actress that there seems little point in even holding auditions. It is just inevitable that a certain person will play a certain part. On the other hand, a director may find himself so handicapped for actors that there are only three or four really good people available and he knows in advance that he will have to use them. This latter case is seldom true of network origination points, where the pool of available acting talent is usually large and varied. There are always plenty of adequate actors. There are seldom enough really good ones.

The chances are the director cannot cast his whole show from "naturals." Some auditions will have to be held. A list should be made of several people who might possibly do each part, the number depending on the difficulty of the rôle. If it is extremely difficult, six or more actors might be called to read one part. If it is simple, the director may wish to decide between only two people. Whatever the problem, the production director makes out a list of all the people he wishes to hear.

Much time can be saved in casting if a little preliminary

work can be done now on routining the audition. It is a good practice to pick exact spots in the script for testing each character. If the part is difficult, with a wide range of flexibility, the director may pick three places: one passage that seems typical of the character at his average; another spot where the character is being funny; and a third where the character displays emotion. These examples are only hypothetical. Whatever the range of emotion the part calls for, extreme and average passages may be chosen for testing the actor's flexibility. The page and line should be noted in each case.

Scenes should also be chosen so that every possible character combination is represented in at least one bit. This is advisable because an actor must not only do his own part, but must also fit in with the other actors. Checking one casting against another should always be done, and the director should choose places in the script in advance which include all the combinations. Finally, the director will decide on the order of his casting. It is wise to cast the most difficult and important spots first, since the largest number of people will be called for these parts, and since, if changes have to be made for contrast, they can be made in the less difficult rôles.

The next step is to schedule a studio and an engineer at a convenient time when the most of the actors are likely to be available. The amount of time reserved will depend on the difficulty of the casting job and the number of people called. Ordinarily an hour will suffice, but the task should not be rushed. When the director knows the time and studio available, calls are made to all actors wanted for the audition.

Staff, Studio, and Special Effects

The director now turns to the problem of staff. He knows he will need an engineer, an announcer, probably a sound man or men, and music. Of course, on many programs the staff is constant. The same engineer, announcer, sound men, and musicians or musical director work the same program all the time. In this case there is no problem with staff, once it is set up. In many ways, this is the most satisfactory arrangement of all, because when people get used to working with each other, smoothness of teamwork is possible that cannot be achieved in any other way.

Next in the production analysis comes the consideration of studio needs. What kind of studio or studios are needed and for how long? Normally, the music on the program will govern the size of studio. If music is to be furnished by an electric organ and the sound is not complicated, a small studio may be desirable. If a concert orchestra is to furnish the music and the sound is complex and likely to take up considerable room, a large studio is indicated. Of course, if an audience is to be present (and it should not on a dramatic show), a studio that will accommodate an audience must be selected. The particular requirements of the program will make the answer to this question fairly obvious. It is not impossible that as many as four studios might be tied up in the production of one play. Whatever the needs may be, they should be decided during the production analysis.

Now the director considers setup of the studio, disposal of all the program elements, and the placement and angling of microphones. This problem never gets its final answer until after the first mike rehearsals, but the director should think out the problems involved and have a plan ready. If he is doubtful about its workability, he should also have an alternate plan.

The problems in deciding on a studio setup are simple and definite. They might be listed as follows:

1. Microphones must be placed so that each sound source can be picked up more or less independently of the rest.
2. Visibility must be easy and direct between all elements of the program and the director in the control room.
3. Cast, sound, and music should be so disposed as to avoid any confusion as to who is getting cues.
4. The pickups from each microphone should be acoustically satisfactory to both the engineer and the production director.

Suppose we have a fairly complicated program using an orchestra for music, two sound-effect microphones which must have independent levels simultaneously, a cast microphone (for a large cast), a filter microphone, and an echo effect which must occur alternately with another sound source on which there is no echo. Figure 21 indicates a possible solution to this

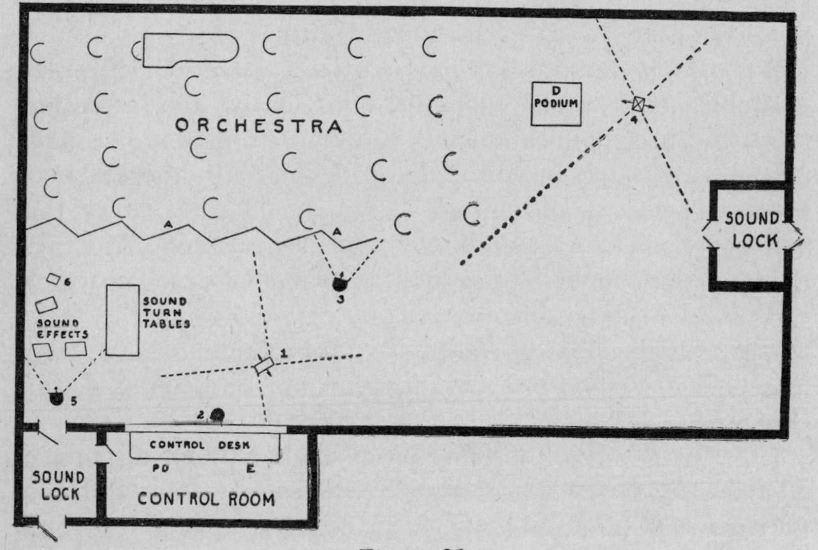

Figure 21

problem which should meet specifications as well as they can be met where a six-mike pickup is involved. The zigzag line indicated by *A* is a line of acoustical screens calculated to cut off the music of the orchestra from the cast and sound microphones. *PD* indicates the production director, *E* the engineer, *D* the music director. The cast microphone is 1 (a ribbon mike); 2 and 3 are the filter mike and echo mike respectively (both unidirectional mikes); 4 is a ribbon mike to pick up the orchestra; 5 is a unidirectional mike for general sound pickup; and 6 is a ribbon mike beamed vertically to the floor and ceiling for a special sound-effect pickup. The dotted lines indicate the general field of pickup of each microphone. None is shown for 6 because it is beamed vertically. Sound is well out toward the edge of the beam of the cast mike and considerable distance away. Both the filter mike and the cast mike are so placed and beamed that they are on the dead edge of the cast mike and, at the same time, their own beams are such as to pick up a minimum of sound from the actors on the cast mike. The cast mike is also dead-edged to the part of the studio from which a maximum amount of bounce from the music will come, and it is further protected from the orchestra by the acoustical screens. In spite of all these precautions there will be some cross-pickup between these various mikes, but it will be held to a minimum, and the difference in levels between various pickups will be enough to allow for adequate mixing of various sound sources.

Plate 30 shows the studio arrangement of Studio 3-A in Radio City New York, for a production of "The March of Time." Cast microphones are in the foreground, sound to the right, a special "dead booth" to the left (to give voices a very dead effect), and the orchestra on the stage. In a studio this large it is comparatively easy to set up to get a minimum cross-pickup between sound sources.

Every program presents its own peculiar problems, further complicated by studio acoustics. After working in any studio for a time, it becomes apparent that there are live spots and dead spots. They are not the same in any two studios, and their location will have to be discovered by the trial-and-error method or through the advice of the engineers. Sometimes shifting a microphone six inches will correct an unpleasant boominess or clear up the definition of a music pickup appreciably. One just has to hunt for the acoustic qualities of every studio.

If special effects are needed, they come up for consideration next in the production analysis. It is not possible to make generalizations about special effects; if it were, they would not be special. It is only possible to cite a few examples to indicate the kind of thing one may encounter. Perhaps it is a sound that is completely new to the sound men. In that case, you are in for experimentation, consultation, and a great deal of hard labor. Perhaps it is a problem that can be solved only with the aid of the engineering department. Whatever special effect is needed, now is the time to study it and decide exactly the effect desired. Then the director must try to find some possible way of achieving the effect. Later, in rehearsal, these various methods can be tried out and the most effective one chosen.

Rehearsals

Next on the production analysis check list is the estimate of rehearsal time. Most networks have no fixed policy regarding length of rehearsals. There is a usual average time for various kinds of programs, but there are no set limits. Some half-hour programs go on the air with four hours of rehearsal. Others have had thirty hours over a period of three weeks. Both of these are extreme cases. The average half-hour dramatic program over NBC rehearses about six hours. Few rehearse less than this. Many rehearse longer. Six hours is about the normal limit, although if there is special reason for longer rehearsal, there is no policy to prevent it.

The amount of rehearsal time needed for any dramatic program will depend on the amount of work to be done. A very simple-looking program may need a long time to rehearse because of complex interpretation and characterization. A very complex-looking program may be made up almost completely of routine effects which can be done almost without rehearsal. Only experience will tell the director what is really difficult and what is easy. In general, if there are many characters in a script, it takes a little longer to rehearse, since some time must be spent on each character. In general, also, the more sound and music involved, the more rehearsal time it will take. The minimum rehearsal time allowed by AFRA for a half-hour dramatic program is four hours. Unfortunately, too many stations make it a policy to allow only four hours of rehearsal as a base amount. Any time needed above this has to be arranged on a special basis. Four hours is simply not enough time to do a good job on a half-hour dramatic program where the entire program must be done from scratch. Possibly in a serial or episodic program. where characterizations are set and the major problems are sound, interpretation, and music, four hours might be sufficient. It is always better to have a little too much time than too little. A really good workman will be able to estimate the time needed very accurately.

Sound and Music

The next item in the production analysis is sound. The beginning director will usually err on the side of using too much sound. The experienced director may err in the use of too much conventional sound. Some directors, who have had a great deal of practical experience, show a tendency to become less and less critical of their sound routines. They have heard them so much, they begin to take them for granted and lose their keen analytical ear.

For specific guidance on the use of sound, the student should check back to the chapter on sound effects. No sound should be included in a dramatic program unless it has a definite justification under one of the headings listed there. Does it portray action? Does it set mood? Does it establish locale? If it has any of these or other legitimate functions, then and then only is it admissible.

Next comes music. The director should approach the problem of applying music to a dramatic show from an over-all point of view. Music may serve five distinct functions in a dramatic show. Each of these is subject to its own special rules, but if music is to be used, all of its uses must suit not only the individual spot at which it is used, but also conform to an over-all artistic approach. This can only be possible if the production director sees the whole pattern of music on his program in its proper relation to the rest of the play and at the same time keeps a critical eye on its application at any given point. This dual purpose is served only if the director can see both forest and trees, making sure that both are right.

What kind of music is used and how much will depend largely on two factors of budget and availability. The budget on a given program may make no provision for music at all, or it may provide for a full concert orchestra. And even though budget is provided for music, there is always the problem of whether or not the kind of musicians desired are available. Usually music is provided from a pool of staff musicians. Since union rules very strictly limit the number of hours per day and the number of days per week musicians may work, it is entirely possible to have a budget and no artists. Of course, if the budget is large enough it is always possible to either pay overtime or hire extra staff help for the show in question, but sometimes, no matter how much money is available, the right person or group just cannot be had for the program.

It is possible to have music on a dramatic program with no live talent at all if the director has access to a good library of recordings or transcriptions, and this is one thing that most stations can offer. Since many student production directors will not have an orchestra at their command for the study of music in dramatic programs, this point is worth some discussion. Most stations have some kind of transcription library [1] and most such libraries have a few records devoted to so-called "mood music." There will be perhaps six or seven large sixteen-inch recordings, on each of which are ten to twenty short bits of music specially designed for cue music and which may be classified under such headings as fanfares, lead-ins, conclusions, neutral bridges, dramatic bridges, etc. The catalogue of the transcriptions library may contain a listing of spots in regularly recorded compositions that may be suitable for various kinds of cue music. These may be listed under such headings as "impending doom," "chase music," "love motifs," and so on. Under each general heading may be listed several pieces of music and in some catalogues it is even indicated in approximately what part of the whole composition the spot occurs. If one has to work with recorded music, such listings can be very helpful. There is one serious drawback, however. If a director does many programs out of the same transcription library, he has soon used all the available cues and finds himself faced with the necessity for repetition. It is at this point that he begins to search through regular commercial recordings for suitable cue music.

[1] See page 159 in this volume.

A good record library, even in a small station, will contain a fairly large selection. The student production director would do well to spend a good many hours going through these recordings, just to become familiar with what is available. In general, the field of classical symphony music is a poor source of cue music for radio drama. Either the themes are too well known or it takes too long for them to develop to be useful. After all, in a dramatic program, the music must accomplish its purpose in a matter of seconds. Classical symphony themes develop in minutes, not seconds, for the most part, and are usually too long to be useful. This is not true of some of the modern symphony writers, who alter their patterns more abruptly and who are more spectacular in their sudden changes of emotion and instrumentation. There is little in any of the Beethoven symphonies, for example, usable as transition music. On the other hand, Shostakovitch is full of it. So is Debussy. Composers like Ferde Grofe, Jerome Kern, Richard Rogers, and Kurt Weil compose in a manner that makes their work admirable for dramatic scripts. Some of the music written for modern dance and ballet is highly descriptive and variable enough to furnish many useful passages. George Gershwin's music is ideal for the purpose except that most of it is so well known that bits are recognizable, even out of context. Highly descriptive music usually is the most useful. Compositions like Debussy's *L'Après Midi d'un Faun*, John Alden Carpenter's *Adventures in a Perambulator*, Richard Rogers's *Slaughter on Tenth Avenue*, Ferde Grofe's *Metropolis*, Gershwin's *An American in Paris*, and Dnieprostroi's *The Steel Foundry* – to name but a few examples – are all full of music which can be cued right out of the recordings and used for transitions in a dramatic show.

While recordings can be helpful to the student in the process of learning how to select dramatic music, they can also be used for actual broadcast work if it is carefully handled and well selected. Of course, this practice is not allowed on the networks, but stations can and often do use recordings in lieu of live music to dress up dramatic presentations. It is extremely useful to college and high-school radio workshops where no other source of music is available.

The cheapest and simplest live music is either organ or piano, organ being the more useful of the two simply because it is the more flexible. Most of the daytime serial programs use one or the other of these instruments because it is comparatively inexpensive and because the demands of a daytime serial program on music are usually not heavy. There are seldom more than one or two transitions in the nine or ten minutes of dialogue in a serial program, and these are usually silent transitions even though music is available. The chief use of music in these programs is to furnish the necessary time flexibility and theme music for identification. An organ or piano can do this nicely. An organ, in the hands of an organist with imagination and skill, can be very effective. Some outstanding nighttime network programs have used an organ for music very effectively.

For some kinds of programs a small string ensemble is the ideal solution. Such a combination cannot get the best heavy dramatic effects, but for light-comedy work or drama of a not-too-serious nature it is satisfactory.

If, as the expression goes, a production director could have his "druthers," he would rather have a full concert orchestra to furnish music for his program. This represents the most flexible music source possible; it also calls for the largest budget. Few programs are financed sufficiently to allow for such grandeur. A few of the outstanding nighttime programs are so staffed – and few others. However, if a production director is fortunate enough to have such a source for his music, all he can do is thank his lucky stars and use it to the best of his ability.

There are a few general rules for guiding the production director in his application of music to a dramatic show, regardless of what kind of music source he has available. These rules should be followed religiously until such time as the director has sufficiently developed his own sense of values to know when he may violate them safely. They should never be violated unless the director is very sure he will gain a desired effect which may offset the danger he incurs.

1. The music chosen for the entire program should have a certain homogeneity which is in harmony with both the script and the director's approach to the script. One would hardly choose broad-comedy music to weave into a tragedy. If the script is amusing and reminiscent, then the music should be of a similar nature. This simply conforms to the artistic law of unity.

2. Music should not be chosen by title except under very restricted conditions. This is probably the most common mistake beginners in the field of production directing make. It does not follow, because winter has passed and the next scene in a script takes place the following summer, that the appropriate selection would be "Summertime." There are several reasons for this rule. First, this procedure presupposes that the audience will know the title merely by hearing a fragment of the music. Most people will not. Second, if they do recognize the piece, there is a great temptation to start thinking about George Gershwin or *Porgy and Bess* and forget the play at hand. This is hardly to be desired. Third, the quality of the music chosen may not be "summertime-ish" at all. Or, if it is suggestive of summertime, it may suggest to the listener only summertime in Charleston, South Carolina, and not summertime in the place where the script is laid. The whole business is apt to catch the producer between two alternatives: either the audience will not recognize the title, in which case the point of choice is lost; or they will recognize it, and their train of thought will be distracted from the story. The only way to avoid this danger is not to choose music on the basis of titles.

There are a few special occasions in which choosing music by title may not only be permissible, but desirable. There are a few selections so well known that the director could be reasonably sure of their being recognized, and whose connotations are so universal that he could count on a similar reaction from his entire audience with comparative safety. Almost everyone recognizes "Taps," for instance, and almost everyone would connote with that tune either peace and sleep or death, depending on the circumstances. "There'll Be a Hot Time in the Old Town Tonight" would almost surely be recognized and a fairly universal connotation might be expected. In the field of obvious comedy, the use of titles sometimes gets a laugh. The musical pay-off on *Vic and Sade* five days a week is almost a national institution, and it is always built on the principle of getting a laugh out of music whose title makes a comment on what has happened in the preceding script. Of course, the music itself is always arranged so that it is in keeping with the show, but half the fun is missed unless the audience can spot the title. In cases like this, choosing music by title is not only permissible; it is funny. But in all ordinary circumstances, avoid it.

3. Choose music for the rightness of its emotional value, as applied to the specific place in the script. The emotional value of music is, of course, determined by the tone values and color values of the music as applied to time values. One would hardly choose a dirge-like piece whose melody was all in a minor key to end a scene in which the audience is told that "they live happily ever after." The music must say to the listener in its language what the lines say to the listener in their language. For a gay scene, the director will choose light, carefree music. For a heavy, highly dramatic scene, he will choose similar music. To climax a scene of rapid and violent physical action, he will choose music that is fast, tempestuous, chaotic.

4. Music is sometimes chosen for its expositional value. If a scene, for example, climaxed in an explosion, the explosion might be brought to the audience in music rather than in sound effects. In this way music would perform an expositional function in the broadcast. It can, and very well might, serve to highlight the emotional content of the scene at the same time, but its chief function would be expositional. Whenever music is used as a substitute for a sound effect, it is likely to have this function.

5. Music must be chosen which is appropriate for the instru-

ments used. It would be useless to choose a piece of exciting music that achieved its excitement by the use of tympani and percussion when it must be played by a string ensemble. Another piece of music might sound very eerie indeed when played on oboes and bassoons, but if there were nothing available but a piano, it would probably not be suitable.

6. If a large orchestra is available, music should be chosen which involves the appropriate instruments. Many directors seem to feel that, because they have a full concert orchestra of twenty-four pieces available, they must use every instrument on every cue. This is obviously foolish. Flexibility, and not volume, is the chief virtue of a concert orchestra. Perhaps the ideal music cue for a given scene might be a mournful melody played solo on a french horn. In another place, massed strings playing a melancholy wail might be infinitely more effective than the total effort of the whole orchestra.

7. The music must be the right length. The leeway which a production director can give to music is usually measured in seconds. The over-all pace of a program might allow for a thirty-second transition in one place and only six seconds in another. If this is the case, passages of these lengths must be found which will also meet all the other specifications. Sometimes a piece of music may be right in every detail except that it takes too long to develop. If this is the case, it is useless. Music, in a dramatic show, should never be long enough to call attention to itself. It must come in, do the dramatic job assigned to it, and get out. Otherwise the listener quits listening to a play and begins to listen to a concert.

Against this background of rules we may now discuss the uses of music in a dramatic program. The use of music as a signature or theme has already been discussed in the chapter on music and needs no elaboration here. The theme music of a dramatic program must conform to the same specifications and perform the same functions in a dramatic program as in any other.

Transitions have already been mentioned, but the use of

music as a transitional device needs amplification. To begin with, a transition should do several things for an audience: it should tell them that there is to be a change of scene; it may indicate a means of travel from one scene to another; it may indicate a time lapse; it may resolve the mood and emotion of a preceding scene; it may set the mood key for a following scene; or it may climax a scene. A successful music transition may do any one or all of these things. More often than not a music transition will perform at least three of these functions.

What the director needs to do with a transition will determine the kind of music used, the instrumentation (if there is a choice) and the way in which it is used. Suppose he has a situation in which the main difficulty is to get a scene ended properly. The scene which follows may present no problems and will start itself off very well by its own inherent interest. In that case music would be used to "pay off" the scene it follows only, with no reference to the following one. If the scene ending was not very abrupt or forceful and needed help to reach the desired climax, music might be faded in under the last bit of dialogue, finally topping it to conclude the scene. If the scene had an abrupt end with a fairly strong tag line, but needed still more reinforcement, music might be slammed in at a rather high level and carried on up to the desired climax. If the scene ended very strong, but quietly, the music might be held momentarily, and then brought in softly and developed slowly to a powerful climax. If the scene ended high and abruptly, the director might decide to bring in a sudden, single crashing chord to achieve a climax. All these suggestions are different ways of doing the same job — reinforcing the ending of a scene in climactic fashion. And this does not exhaust the possibilities by any means.

Suppose the problem is to end a powerful but quiet scene and then introduce a powerful, raucous scene. In this case the music would have to encompass two moods. A music cue would have to be chosen which had quietness and strength to lead out of the preceding scene and then develop into an appropriately strong and noisy kind of music to introduce the mood of the following scene.

For every transition there are a variety of ways in which the music can be handled. It may gradually overlay the dialogue in a cross-fade, build to a climax and then subside to cross-fade into a dialogue overlay. It could follow the same pattern except to start quietly at the end of the dialogue and end quietly just before the beginning of the following dialogue. It could start loudly and abruptly with the close of dialogue, build to a peak, and then drop to a quiet end for dialogue again. A whole transition conceivably could be a single screaming chord that crashed in right on top of the dialogue, held for four or five seconds, and abruptly stopped for dialogue to commence again. Between cross-fades and clean beginnings, high-volume takes and low-volume takes, there are a large number of combinations possible. Any one of them may be right in a given situation. Sometimes several different methods of handling seem equally effective. Usually, however, one particular combination seems to offer a better solution than any other, and that is the one which the production director should seek.

Music is very useful in putting together a montage scene, as has already been mentioned. The conventional method of building a montage scene is to play an appropriate musical introduction which ends on a chord that can be held tremolo or agitato fashion under the short dialogue of a quick scene, followed by another short burst of music ending on another tremolo chord, and so on through a series of vignette scenes which are finally resolved in music. There are many other ways of building a music montage, but this is the most common one and will serve for illustration. Montage scenes are most often used to present a mounting series of swift events which lead to some kind of climax. Music is very useful in creating this climactic effect. Often the music for such scenes is started low in pitch and slow in tempo, both increasing as the scene progresses. This does an excellent job of creating a feeling of mounting tension and suspense.

Music has the frequent function of supplying realistic background to a dramatic scene. Whenever a scene is laid in a night club or ballroom or wherever music would be expected, the production director must fill in the expected background. There are serious limitations on such scenes because the director may not have available the combination of instruments necessary for the scene. If program music is being furnished by an electric organ and the scene calls for a five-piece swing combination, the organist cannot hope to do the job. In a non-network situation where records are not banned, there is no problem. On a network, either musicians have to be provided or the script has to be rewritten. If the director is fortunate enough to have a fairly large orchestra to work with, there are few problems in scene-backing music with which he cannot cope.

Music may be used for its "melodramatic" effect on a program. The word melodrama is so much used in show business that it is easy to forget its origin. The French dramatists first used the term to designate that kind of drama backed by music, which they claimed, and rightly, was more powerful if properly done than straight drama. Using music melodramatically is nothing new in American theater. From the piano player of the old silent films down to the sound track of a modern movie, music is very much in evidence as a support for drama. Radio, where its use would seem to be a natural, has lagged far behind the movies in this respect, probably for economic reasons. The scoring of a whole program or any considerable part of it is a costly process, even using stock music. If an original score is used (and this is, of course, highly desirable), it is still more expensive. Because radio does so many programs each day, there are few that can afford the luxury of special music for only one broadcast. The few programs that consistently do use scene-backing music stand out for their dramatic excellence.

There are several conditions under which music can be used in this way. Sometimes a line or two can be added to the script to motivate the use of background music on a realistic basis. Suppose, for example, a soldier going off to war was saying good-bye to his sweetheart. Under ordinary circumstances, this might be a quiet, intense scene. If the director wished to highlight the fact that even a leavetaking could be marred by the world crowding in too much, he might back that scene with raucous music coming from a neighbor's radio. A completely different turn might be given by having the girl suggest playing their favorite record just once more, and use that as a motivation for backing the whole scene with quiet, moving, romantic music. The same scene, so far as lines are concerned, could be given two completely different slants by the manner in which background music was applied. In both cases it would be realistically motivated.

Fantasy lends itself delightfully to the use of melodramatic music. The simple fact that the story is a fantasy is reason enough for using music. Breaking the shackles of reality allows the imagination to run riot in the scoring of such a play. In Norman Corwin's delightful fantasy, "The Odyssey of Runyan Jones," music even took the place of some of the characters. In this story of a little boy who searched heaven for his pet, he encounters all sorts of fairylike creatures. When he talks to the Harpy, for instance, the thing which answers is a Harp. The score is so skillfully constructed that one can almost tell what the Harpy is supposed to be saying without the help of the little boy's interpretations. This is truly a creative use of music in radio drama.

Music can be used impressionistically in drama. Music can, in other words, be used to give the audience the feeling that unrealistic things are happening realistically. By backing a soliloquy speech with music, the audience will accept the fact that they are hearing a man's thoughts. When dead men speak and similar unrealistic things are made to happen in a script, the effects can often be made acceptable to the audience by the use of music. If the script contains a narrator who is acting in the capacity of storyteller, music can be used to back the narration to separate it from the realistic scenes and thus help the audience to keep things straight.

Music can be used as a substitute for a sound effect. This subject has been mentioned before, and it need only be said here that this use of music is possible only if the instruments available are numerous enough and flexible enough to permit it. Usually this will necessitate a special score also. At least, it means a special arrangement.

All these factors a production director considers when he plans the musical treatment of his script. He will go over it spot by spot and make an individual decision about each place. He will decide (*a*) whether music is to be used or not; (*b*) what kind of music; (*c*) what instrumentation if there is a choice; (*d*) how it is to come in and out; (*e*) how it is to be played; and (*f*) how long it should be. Armed with this information, the production director is ready to confer with the musical director and tell him exactly what he wants. If the musical director is temperamental or inexpert, the production director will do well to take a little prayer along, too. If he is both co-operative and expert, the music-planning session can be pure joy.

One last step in the production analysis still remains to be done. Provisional cuts must be made. This process is the same for a dramatic program as for any other kind.

By now the production director has finished his home work. If he has done a conscientious job, he is ready to talk about his show to anyone. Every decision has been made — at least tentatively. Everything that occurs from here on is simply putting into execution the plans formed in this session. Decisions may be changed. Emergencies may arise. But if the plans and decisions have been made wisely, there is little that can disturb the equanimity of the director now. He knows where he is going.

The Pre-Broadcast Period

Arrangements

The first step in the execution of the program is the duplication of scripts. It is usually the responsibility of the production director to indicate the number needed. Engineering, announcing, production, sound, and music will all get copies as a matter of routine. Scripts to go anywhere else should be ordered.

Next, the staff is requisitioned. Space and equipment must

also be requisitioned. The production director will first schedule a studio and an engineer for auditions and casting. At the same time he can ask for studio space for his full rehearsal schedule and broadcast. He should also give the studio assignment clerk a list of all the equipment he wants, and when he wants it. Special equipment, such as telephone filters or echo chambers, are ordered at the same time as studios and scheduled in master control. Once this is done, the whole elaborate machinery of production begins to turn.

Conferences

At the appropriate time the production director will set up as many conferences with the members of his staff as seem necessary. Normally he may talk to no one except the person in charge of music for the show and to the sound man.

With the music director the production director will go over the whole musical treatment of the program, explaining in detail exactly what he wants in each case. If the music director is an expert in his work, the production director may only tell him the effect he wishes to obtain and in general how it is to be handled, leaving the manner in which it is to be accomplished to the music director. If, on the other hand, the music director lacks imagination and originality, the production director may dictate what he wants in detail, even down to suggesting instrumentation. If stock music has to be used, the two may talk over possible selections to try.

If the original music is to be written, the discussion may take some time. The composer must completely understand everything the production director has thought about in reaching his conclusions in order to be able to compose the kind of music needed. After the composer has his work done – usually in the form of a piano lead sheet – he and the production director will get together, play it over, and discuss it. The production director may suggest some changes, accept it *in toto*, or reject it completely. This process is repeated until the score seems acceptable. If stock music is to be used, this second and succeeding conferences are usually omitted. The musical director will, instead, clear several numbers for each spot in the script and check them later.

Conferences with the engineer are necessary only in case some unusual acoustical effect is needed. Perhaps if the gain-riding routine was extremely complicated, rehearsal time might be saved if a short session is called for the engineer to mark up a script in advance.

A conference with the sound crew is wise if the routine is complex, if it does not all show in the script, or if there are unusual effects which need discussion. In the latter case a special rehearsal might be set up just to try the special effects in question and work out solutions to these problems outside of the regular rehearsal schedule.

Script Mark-Up

Having come to an agreement with the members of his staff, the production director is now ready to mark up his script. Theoretically, this could be done as soon as the production analysis is finished, but it is always a good idea to wait until after conferences, so that if any new ideas come up they can be incorporated in the mark-up. Also if any plans formed originally have to be abandoned for any reason, they can be left out of the mark-up and help to keep it neat.

Marking up the script for production has only one purpose. It is a putting down of visual cues which will remind the director of what he has planned to do with each spot in the script. The script mark-up is an individual affair and there are many different ways of doing it. Some directors make a neat series of signs, meticulously drawn in the margins. Others make hasty scrawls on the script at odd moments as ideas occur to them. Some directors have all sorts of trick symbols which mean "accent this," "swell volume here," "drop out sound at this point," and a hundred other instructions. Some make almost no markings on their scripts at all, priding themselves on being able to remember every little thing they planned to do.

A script mark-up should certainly not be so complete as to

become "reading matter." The whole purpose is to remind the director of the important or obscure things he intends to do at each spot. It should certainly not be so sketchy as to allow the director to forget to give an important cue. Somewhere in between these extremes probably lies the best method.

One system will be outlined here and it is recommended to beginners, especially if studying in a class, for the simple reason that, if all members of the class use the same markings, they will be able to interpret and work from each other's scripts. This is a real help in a class directing project and is recommended procedure. Mark all references to music in red. Mark all references to sound in green. Mark references to cast in blue. Mark references to engineering in black. All line cuts and write-ins should also be in black. For purposes of uniformity, it is recommended that students enter the following items in the script mark-up:

1. All cues to be given by the production director — cast, sound, and music.
2. All places where engineering changes must occur, such as
    - *a.* Introduction of sound mike.
    - *b.* Introduction of music mike.
    - *c.* Introduction of special effect mikes (filter or echo).
    - *d.* All fades and cross-fades.
    - *e.* All changes in balances between mikes.
3. All places where cast movement is involved.
4. All continuing background effects.
5. All changes in volume in any portion of the script other than cast.

Illustration of a method of marking up a script is shown in the following sample pages. Color cannot be indicated, but at least the markings are.

Title: THESE THINGS ARE TRUE

Cue

NARRATOR 1 This voice comes to you from a world in crisis!
DEEP VOICE
SLOW 2 This voice comes to you from a Democracy in that world.
DELIBERATE
RHYTHMIC 3 This voice comes to you from a city in that Democracy.

Build this!

Cue 4 ....And in that city is a University.

5 I speak to you from its campus.

6 This....(MUSIC CHORD..) is the voice of Northwestern University.

MUSIC CEASES TO SYNCHRONIZE HERE AND DROPS TO BACKGROUND

Cue 8 STRINGS, LIKE WIND ON THE KANSAS PLAINS

9 Rising out of a quiet college campus,

10 Stirring now with the first faint signs of summer,

11 This voice goes soaring out..

12 Over the lakes and rivers -

13 Over the long, flat country - and the mountains...

Cue 14 Out of this hemisphere - and into the next.

15 (ON LAST OF LINE 16 END IN SAME CHORD USED ON LINE 3)

16 Looking out on a world, framed in a campus gate,

17 It looks like this to us.

18 We see wars and the rumors of wars.

19 We see a Europe locked in deadly conflict, (MUSIC IN SYNCH. HERE)

20 State against state, raider against convoy,

Cue 21 Bomber against Bomber.

WARN FILTER MIKE 22 And on the sidelines stand the other nations,

23 Each cheering for one side or the other,

24 According to its lights, (VOICE AND MUSIC RISE) BREAK FOR

25 And the war goes on!

MUSIC 26 IN BACKGROUND

CUT COLD!

Title: THESE THINGS ARE TRUE

Cue BERLIN NEWSCASTER	1	(ON FILTER MIKE) A communique issued by the German High
	2	Command here in Berlin this evening said that German Panzer
	3	divisions have crossed the Polish frontier at 5 points.
Music sneak	4	German dive bombers attacked Warsaw in large numbers shortly
	5	after noon, Berlin time.
MUSIC	6	OVERLAPS A LITTLE, THEN GOES DOWN AND UNDER FOR...
Cue FOREIGN NEWSCASTER	7	German troop transports steamed into Oslo, Norway, this
	8	afternoon and unloaded troops without a sign of resistance.
	9	Before a surprised country knew what had happened, Norway
	10	had fallen.
MUSIC	11	UP AND UNDER FOR....
Cue LONDON NEWSCASTER	12	Fighting an amazing rear-guard action, The British Expeditionary
	13	Force is still evacuating Dunkirk in the midst of a hail of
	14	bombs raining down from the racks of the German Luftwaffe.
MUSIC	15	SWELLS TO COVER FADE, HOLDS AND FADES UNDER FOR......
Cue ALEXANDRIA NEWSCASTER	16	The British High Command in the Near East today reported a
	17	smashing victory over the Italian Army in Eastern Libya.
MUSIC	18	SWELLS UP AND UNDER FOR......
Cue ANKARA NEWSCASTER	19	The vanguard of the German Army of the Balkans tonight
	20	marched into Athens.
MUSIC	21	UP AND UNDER
Cue LONDON NEWSCASTER	22	London tonight got its worst bombing in two months as 500
	23	German planes roared in over the Channel.
MUSIC	24	UP AND UNDER
Cue PARIS NEWSCASTER	25	And in Paris, tonight (QUIETLY) children are hungry.
MUSIC	26	BUILDS QUICKLY AFTER LAST LINE TO CLIMAX IN MINOR KEY AND
	27	CUTS COLD. HOLD PAUSE

Title: THESE THINGS ARE TRUE

[CUE] NARRATOR	1	(PAUSE) And within the borders of America,	
	2	We see another picture, painted in movement.	
	3	We see a great Democracy, composed of many races,	
[WARN ECHO CHAMBER]	4	Faced with a question.	
	5	Out of a welter of diffuse opinion,	
	6	Out of doubt and indecision,	
	7	Out of the people, out of the Congress....	
	8	Comes a plan - an aim: Mobilize for defense!	
MUSIC	9	A CHORD TO PUNCTUATE THIS LINE. IT HOLDS AND FADES UNDER FOR....	
[CUE] VOICE [ECHO]	10	(CLERK READING BILL...) This bill will authorize the Congress	
	11	to purchase six new battleships, 4 airplane carriers, 48	
	12	destroyers, 7,000 ~~new~~ planes [FADE] (START FADE) and to increase.....	
[CUE] NARRATOR	13	That action threw the country into a turmoil of activity.	
MUSIC	14	PICKS UP THIS RHYTHM ON A MELODY OF	
VOICE	15	And the wheels start rolling.	c e e c a
	16	The wheels start rolling	c e e c a
VOICE	17	And men form lines at	d f f d b
	18	Employment windows	d f f d b
VOICE	19	And pink smoke belches	e g g e c
	20	From steel mill smoke stacks	e g g e c
VOICE	21	And freight cars rumble	f a a f d
	22	Through sleeping Kansas	f a a f d
VOICE	23	And lights start dotting	g b b g e
	24	The midnight skyline	g b b g e
	25	And then......	MAJOR 7TH CHORD
MUSIC	26	DOWN INTO BG [Cut cold]	

Title: THESE THINGS ARE TRUE

Cue

NARRATOR	1	The hurry caught up with us.
	2	We found out that we need more factories and skilled mechanics
	3	We need more nuts and bolts and washers,
	4	We need more time and understanding.
	5	But we don't have time - so we get confusion.
	6	And strikes are called and plants shut down....
	7	And production stops on assembly lines.
	8	Unions and managers can't allign.
	9	Their hours, and wages and over-time.
MUSIC	10	SWELLS UP A MOMENT THEN UNDER AND OUT FOR VOICES Crossfade
JOHNSON	11	You can't tell me, Mitchell, that your men are all behind
	12	this strike! They've been intimidated into it!
MITCHELL	13	That's not true, Johnson, and you know it.
JOHNSON	14	Blasted bunch of Reds are behind it. They're keeping
	15	trouble stirred up. They're stopping production, and
SOUND		POUND FIST ON TABLE TO PUNCTUATE LINES
	16	that's what they want!
MITCHELL	17	Your're the one that's stopping production. You know what
	18	our demands are. They're fair enough. Why don't you give
	19	in!
JOHNSON	20	I can't! I can't pay wages like that and still meet
	21	government prices.
MITCHELL	22	Maybe not, if you have to stack up an extra five million.
JOHNSON	23	And you won't call this thing off?
	24	We're standing pat.
HANLEY	25	Gentlemen. May I interrupt.
JOHNSON	26	Sure, Hanley. Maybe you can see a way out. I can't.

Casting

This brings us to the problem of casting, proper. The business of casting a dramatic program requires all the artistry, intelligence, and concentration that a director can muster. After all, the program stands or falls on choices made here. No matter how carefully the director has planned or how beautiful his conception of the play, it is the actors who actually read the lines. Unless a director gives himself the best cast possible, he cannot have the best show possible.

The director should be prompt at cast calls and expect his talent to follow suit. He will save time if he has prepared a typed synopsis of the story and an outline of the various characters. If he has not, then he must tell the assembled group of actors these things. In either case they ought to have time to digest this information and ask questions. Each auditionee should have a script and an instruction sheet. The director then tells each actor which part or parts to look at, and gives them all time to skim through the part of the script with which they are chiefly concerned.

The director is now ready to use the audition spots which were chosen and noted down while he was making his production analysis. This shows him the exact places in the script he can use to try out each character. Beginning with the most difficult part to cast, he can then work his way through the list of people until he has heard everyone. The most important parts should be chosen first so that the rest of the cast can be built around the voice and quality of the most difficult rôle (which may not always be the lead). Some directors prefer to keep all auditionees in the studio during tryouts. Others prefer to send everyone out and then call in the combinations of people, a group at a time. It should not be necessary to say that casting should be done by scenes in which two or more actors are reading lines to each other. A single actor should seldom be asked to read alone. After all, one of the things a director wants to know is how an actor can play to or against another actor.

Actors who obviously miss the part badly should be dismissed as soon as possible. Casting a difficult show might take two hours or more. If the director knows he cannot use a certain actor, there is no need of wasting the actor's time by having him wait until auditions are done. An actor's time is money and shouldn't be wasted. On the other hand, if a director is in any doubt at all, or thinks perhaps he might be able to use the actor in another part, he should not be hesitant about asking him to stay the full time.

Having heard everyone through the first time, the director can then dismiss all the impossibles. Perhaps he will want to hear the two or three leading candidates for a part again. Certainly, having chosen the main characters, he will want to check the minor characters against them to be certain that all possible voice combinations are workable.

A director, sitting in a control room listening to auditions, sometimes feels as though he is wandering alone in a forest full of tall trees which confuse him so that he has no notion where he is going. On a difficult play, where no actor seems to be doing what the director hoped someone would do, decisions begin to become oppressive. The director knows that a bad choice at this point may throw his whole show. Most oppressive of all is the acute awareness that there is no one to help him. He sits alone with his engineer (who, after the manner of engineers, is probably reading a mystery story) and listens. When he has finished listening, he must decide. If things are going well and the actors are giving him what he wants, he may feel elated and impatient to get to work with these wonderful people. Just as often, however, nothing sounds exactly as he had hoped it would. He seems forced to make a choice between the lesser of many evils, and there is no one to advise him or no one to share his disgrace if he makes a bad guess. This feeling is acute enough with the experienced director. With the beginner, it is even worse.

To aid the director who is facing control-room loneliness for the first times, here are a few rules which may help in making decisions:

1. Always cast on mike. All the program will be heard that way by the audience; it should start that way.
2. The director must cast by ear alone. It is wise to listen only and not even look at actors as they read. This will help to avoid the danger of casting people who look like the part. It also keeps off the air pretty girls who cannot act.
3. Cast to voice type. The director has to cast a voice which is natural to the actor and right for the part. Competent actors, who may have several "natural" voices, are exceptions to this rule.
4. Cast as closely to age as possible. Normally, a sixty-year-old actress will sound more like sixty than a thirty-year-old actress. The obvious exceptions to this rule are very small children. If the story calls for a two-year-old, you will probably choose for the part an adult actress who specializes in such things.
5. Cast for variety and contrast. If the script calls for three women of approximately the same age and same general social background, care must be taken to see that the voices are sharply contrasting.
6. In general, medium or low pitches should predominate. High pitches are often irritating, and too many high-pitched voices used together makes a bad impression on the audience.
7. Retain an open mind about your characters. Your own conception of how a character can be achieved may be less good than that of the auditionee. Retain enough flexibility to recognize a good job when you hear it, even if it is not exactly what you had in mind. If it will work, use it.

There are many things a director must take into consideration when he is casting. The prime consideration is, of course, how well the actor reads and how closely he delivers what is called for. There are additional factors, however. There are people who are "directors' actors." This is the kind of talent that every director dreams about – and finds just often enough to keep him in show business. There are several attributes which mark an actor with this special star. One of these is the ability to take direction. There are some actors who have the ability to make themselves clay in the director's hands. Their minds, their emotions, even their sense of timing can be influenced by the capable director. Artistically, the actor gives himself up to the shaping of the director. Some actors, for instance, can take direction, mull it over, digest it, and then give a performance; it will be a good piece of work, but they must not be molested in the performance of that work. Other actors seem not to need the independence of the digesting stage, nor do they need to be let alone in performance. From the start, they become sensitive reflectors of the will of the director. Even in performance, the director can – almost as if by willing it – lift that actor through a scene exactly as he wants it done. When the director can find people like this, he is in luck. They are "directors' actors."

The director wants to cast actors who are willing to work and able to grow. Two or three months in almost any location is enough time for a director to find out who these actors are. There are never a large number of them, but they are always busy. The director will learn to watch actors leave a rehearsal. Some of them – most of them – will toss their scripts on a chair and walk out. A few always take their scripts with them. Over the luncheon table, in the hall between calls, overnight, even in a corner of the studio while the rehearsal is in progress, these actors are working on their parts. They are going over lines, studying reactions, planning motivations, trying out interpretations – in short, acting.

A director listens for and watches for other little cues during an audition. He will watch for sensitivity to lines. He will watch for quickness of reaction and span of attention. Some actors will habitually gossip in the corner of the studio while important instructions are being issued. Others will hold up proceedings while they find the place, which all the other actors got on the first announcement. The director will see which actors watch control for signs or cues. Some actors seem always accessible when it is necessary to give them a cue. Others seem completely oblivious. Ease and rapidity of reading and flexibility are also good traits, and the director keeps an eagle eye out for them.

A word should be said here about specialists. In every large center of broadcasting there seem to converge people who do the most amazing variety of things for a living which usually flies under the occupational banner of acting. There are nearly always one or two girls who specialize in baby cries, men who imitate animals, and ingenues who can double as three-year-olds. If the script calls for a talking horse or the lilting love song of the African whiffle bird, there is probably some actor who makes a specialty of just that thing. Directors soon become acquainted with the specialists and learn to lean on them. They can save directors many grueling hours of rehearsal on some outsized effect or characterization just because they have done it before.

Specialization also applies to much more normal demands than that. In dialects, for example, every city boasts a few actors who not only have authentic dialects, but are able to speak the language involved. Actors tend to specialize in such common types as ingenues, leads, second business, the "menace," the "other woman," toughs, and juveniles, to mention only a few. It seems foolish for a director to waste valuable rehearsal time making a second-business actress into a lead when there are plenty of good leads available. On the other hand, it is equally shortsighted to ignore an actress on an audition simply because you never heard her do anything else but, say, second business. For the particular lead at hand, she may do a better job than any of the stock leading ladies. The principle is to use specialists wherever it saves time, but never fall into the lazy habit of assuming that an actor or actress can do only one thing.

It is sometimes embarrassing to a director to announce the cast after an audition, while all the actors are assembled. The director may want extra time to think it over and weigh judgment anyway. For this reason it is a practice at NBC to conclude auditions by announcing that they are done. The director then goes back to his office and makes up his mind. Once he has made his selections, these are turned over to the casting clerk and the actors chosen are called and told when to report for rehearsals. An actor assumes that he has not been cast until he receives a call from the casting clerk. This practice is sometimes a little cumbersome, especially if the schedule is close, but it does save embarrassment all the way around. Directors do not have to tell actors they are not wanted. Actors do not have to be told that in the presence of their brethren. To a casting clerk, calling an actor over the telephone, the whole thing is impersonal and much easier to handle.

Once your cast has been announced, the casting clerk should recheck the rehearsal schedule to be sure it is understood by each actor. If there is to be a studio audience so that the actor's dress is important, this should be announced also at the time of the call.

The final caution to beginning directors is this: be hard to satisfy. If a director will accept nothing less than the best, it is surprising how often he will get it. Do not make compromises if it can possibly be avoided. There are enough second-bests that cannot be helped. Be hard to please, and be kind, and actors will work their hearts out for you.

Final Checking of Sound and Music

The next step is the final selection of sound. If there are special effects to check, now is the time to check them. This may mean a rehearsal or an experimental period with the sound crew.

There still remains the final selection and checking of the music. If it is simple and there is little of it, it may be delayed until the final rehearsal period and chosen then. If it is complex and if there is very much of it, a special session may be required to choose the music and get it into shape. This is almost a necessity where an orchestra is involved or where an original score is used. In either case the music should, by all means, be checked and rehearsed before the regular rehearsal sessions begin. This is the only way in which time may be allowed for making radical changes should they prove necessary.

The production director, up to this point, may have heard only the piano lead sheet of the music, or nothing at all. Let us suppose, to be specific, that the music for a half-hour dramatic show is to be furnished by a concert orchestra, using original music. The session will be scheduled, and at the appointed time members of the orchestra, the conductor, and the production director meet to go to work. The simplest procedure is to start right through the script, taking each music cue as it occurs. The conductor will take a few moments to work it out with the orchestra and rehearse it. Then it will be played for the production director, who listens to it and times it. If it suits exactly, it is run over again a couple of times to set it in the musicians' minds, and the group proceeds to the next cue.

Suppose the production director is not satisfied. The cue is good, but too long. He will indicate by how much it is too long, and the conductor will go to work. He will eliminate as many bars of music as is necessary to meet the criticism. It is then run over and listened to again by the director, who will order it set that way. Suppose the cue is impossible. The tempo is wrong, the mood is wrong, the attack is wrong, the end is wrong. This may not necessarily mean that the cue in question must be abandoned. Music is, after all, subject to interpretation. Let us suppose the attack is not sharp enough. The conductor may suggest changing the pickup from strings to brasses and horns, fortissimo. It is tried and the director accepts it. Perhaps one passage is too slow. The director will change quarter notes to sixteenths and ask for a glissando playing. Another objection is removed. In another spot the melody may be taken away from brass and given to strings and woodwinds and another objection is met. By this process the same piece of music undergoes a radical change which more nearly checks with what the production director wants. This kind of musical skulduggery seems like black magic to an outsider, but to a production director and conductor who know their business, it is routine work. Once in a while, no amount of doctoring will make the selection meet the director's desires. In that case the conductor falls back on alternate numbers which he has cleared against this emergency, and they are rehearsed and tried until one is accepted.

This process is repeated for every cue in the script. By the time this rehearsal is over, these things should have been accomplished:

1. All the music is chosen.
2. Any missing scores or wrong notes have been noted.
3. The cuts in music are indicated and any change in playing marked.
4. All alternate numbers or discarded numbers are removed from the folders.
5. Each cue is rehearsed with the orchestra until they understand it.
6. Each cue is timed.
7. The music for each spot is noted in both the music conductor's and the director's scripts.
8. The director has memorized, if not all, at least the end of each cue so that he will know when to cue in whatever follows the music or comes in during music.

This session seldom lasts more than an hour. Sometimes it is cramped into a half-hour. This is not much time to accomplish all that has to be done. It does not allow for dawdling or indecision on the part of the director. He must know what he wants when he hears it, and what is wrong with what he does not like. Only in this way can his wishes be met. He must also concentrate in order to memorize the music quickly and surely because he may hear it not more than three or four times. With this done, the director is now ready for his rehearsal schedule.

Rehearsals

Rehearsal procedures vary widely, depending on a number of circumstances. The routine described here is a very elaborate one. Under many circumstances some of these steps are either eliminated or condensed and combined. Notes on these different practices will be made later. In general, the rehearsal period breaks down into four parts, with a definite set of tasks to be accomplished in each part.

1. Table or reading rehearsal.
2. First microphone rehearsal.
3. Cue rehearsal.
4. Dress rehearsal.

When the procedure is condensed, it is usually the first and third steps that are eliminated, or merged with the two others.

Table Rehearsal

At the table rehearsal several definite objectives should be accomplished. First, the detailing of the script should be transmitted to the cast. All line changes, cues to be taken, business to be done, and general pace and treatment should be given the cast. This should be done to get the mechanical details out of the way before starting on the more creative process. Second, the director and the cast come to an understanding about every single point in the script. This can be done in a variety of ways. The director may read the script to the cast, using his own interpretation of each line and follow this with a detailed discussion. He may have the cast read the script, interrupting constantly to clear up all matters of interpretation and motivation as the reading progresses. Still another method is to have the cast read through the script aloud and uninterrupted. If they have not seen the script before or read it completely, this gives them the whole general picture. Then, with the complete reading as a background, the director can go back and discuss the script scene by scene and point by point. If necessary, it can be taken line by line on the more important scenes. By this process director and actors reach a definite understanding so that the cast knows exactly what is expected of them at every point in the script. It only remains then to get it.

The next step in the table rehearsal is the discussion of and setting of all characterizations. By now, the actors know what the director wants. Between them, they now proceed to get it. Lines are read and re-read. Different approaches may be tried. The director will experiment with voice changes, pace changes, coloring, until the character begins to emerge. Sometimes it will stand out clear and correct on the second reading. Sometimes a great deal of trial and error is involved in making a character come to life.

How does a director work with an actor to make him act? What can he do? How can he draw from inside another man or woman the imaginative response he wants? Anyone who can answer these questions to his own satisfaction is a good director. Anyone who can answer them for someone else is a good teacher besides. There are stock answers, of course, and routine procedures. But if a characterization is difficult, stock answers are not enough. An actor is a sensitive human being. And every actor is a different human being. Much of a director's success may lie in his ability to analyze an actor and then devise a method of approach which will work in the special case. No reputable director likes to give an actor a line reading. No one who does not feel an interpretation can repeat someone else's interpretation except in a parrot fashion. The timing and inflecting of a line is such a delicate thing that it cannot be easily imitated. In hopeless cases, however, this is the director's only recourse. He can only say to the actor, "Read it this way," and illustrate. A director might get a line reading in that fashion, but he certainly could not help an actor to build a whole character by that means. The answer, in every case, lies in finding some means of making the picture of the character clear to the actor. Once that is done, if he is a capable workman and the casting has been wise, the actor can usually deliver.

Ordinarily the director needs only to explain the character, talking about it, and illustrating his ideas with incidents, examples. Sometimes making up a suitable background for the character will do the trick. Suppose, for example, that you are trying to help an actor to create the character of a stern, uncompromising old New England whaling captain. The whole point of the story may turn on his inability to forgive his daughter for some act of disobedience, for which the audience sympathizes with the daughter. Perhaps, unconsciously, the actor is also sympathizing with the daughter, and this underlying reaction comes through in his characterization and prevents his being the stern, uncompromising old man he needs to be. Perhaps the director can explain to the actor that the old man has had obedience ground into him all his life until he became a ship's master, and then he spent many more years grinding it into others. Obedience is one of the first laws of the sea because sailors work as a team in sailing a ship and there must be a captain for that team to tell it what to do. Often the lives of an entire crew and the ship itself may depend on prompt obedience to commands, no matter how much out of line they may appear. Obedience, in these instances, is a matter of life and death. The old man knows that. He has insisted on it from his men. Then, when he is faced by disobedience from his own daughter, he reacts true to form and refuses to consider it anything but mutiny. His whole habit of mind is built around another idea — that of obedience. With his background, it is impossible to understand how disobedience could be a forgivable crime. If an actor could be made to see that background, he might be better able to create the real feel of the character.

Sometimes a characterization can be created by indirect methods. A character seems, let us say, too serious. The director asks the actor to lighten it up a bit and add a little good humor to the character. The actor fails to do so. Sometimes the director can stop working on the play and begin to work on the actor. He will tease him, cajole him, get the actor to telling stories, loosen him up, and then, when he has achieved that mood, return him to the script. The carry-over may do the trick. There have been cases where a director deliberately set about to make an actor angry. Pick a quarrel with the actor. Criticize his acting, his judgment. Get him irritated -- and then make him read the lines in question. Often the irritation will carry over into the reading of the line and the character comes into focus. As soon as this is achieved, point out to the actor what he has done. See if he can analyze how he got the effect in terms of reading, and when the spot comes up again, the actor will know how he achieved the desired effect. Such a method of working with an actor is dangerous and can be used only by a very skillful and understanding director. But in extreme cases it may work. Once the actor hits on what is wanted, the director can nurse it along, build it, help the actor analyze it and finally make it his own.

Once an actor understands a character, the biggest battle is won. This understanding can best be given him by example. The director always has to build on the actor's previous experience. He must therefore keep hunting around with examples until he finds one that strikes fire with the actor's imagination or arouses a response out of his past experience. Five examples in a row may fail to make an impression and an accidental sixth one may do the trick. The actor's eyes will light up and he will say, "Oh! I see what you mean!" and the point is won. I was once trying to get an actor to show that the character "saw the light" or had a sudden inspiration. I gave him every possible example and he would still sound labored, or did not light up, or missed his timing. Finally, I happened to think of how the comic-strip cartoonists express the idea that a person has just had a brilliant idea. Remember how the electric light is drawn in over the character's head? I cited that example to the actor – with gestures – and got the right reading on the next try. I had finally found an example that meant something to him.

Sometimes having the actor paraphrase lines helps. Perhaps the actor misses a characterization or interpretation because the lines seem completely stiff and unnatural to him. Ask the actor to put the same idea and emotional content of the lines into his own words. Let him ad-lib a part of a scene. Once he has mastered the emotion, the feel, the timing of the scene in this manner, have him return to the author's lines and try to achieve the same thing.

Sometimes physical movement and posture are the key to a characterization. After all, a character is a whole person, and while the radio audience hears only the voice, the voice is influenced by the entire tonicity of the body. Sometimes a posture built around a caved-in chest and drooping shoulders can make an actor feel defeat more than anything else in his own mind and at the same time influence the tone of his voice to achieve the same effect. If you want an actor to portray a domineering personality, make him stand up, make him use strong, vigorous movements and gestures. All this will have an effect on his handling of lines.

One time I was directing a very delicate love scene into which we could not get a feeling of intimacy. In spite of an apparently adequate reading of lines, the scene still lacked warmth and human flow of emotion. The man and woman playing the scene on opposite sides of the microphone kept unconsciously reaching for each other as the scene progressed. Finally, I asked them both to work on the same side of the microphone where they could be close together, put their arms around each other. The scene "jelled" at once. The actors had to have the close physical contact to make it come alive in the scene. The sense of intimacy was there right away.

Sometimes a director can get a proper characterization or line reading from an actor by building a mood for him. He can paint a word picture of the scene or the character, doing a little acting himself to help the actor along. Here is where an articulate director can use his histrionic ability and vocabulary to good advantage. For example, let us assume that a director is working with an ingenue on a rôle which is causing trouble. The actress is supposed to portray a naïve, unsophisticated, frightened little girl from Iowa on her first night alone in Chicago. She knows no one, she is not used to the city, and she is feeling that aloneness which one can only feel in the midst of a lot of strangers. But our little actress, being an habituée of the showier eating places on North Rush Street, cannot somehow capture that desperate feeling of aloneness. She reads the lines with surface rightness, but the ache is not there. She is feeling nothing underneath, because she is not frightened and cannot feel so. The director might talk to the actress and try to create the feeling for her. He might say something like this:

"It's quiet where you live. After supper, people sit on their front porches, or sprinkle their lawns a little . . . maybe read the evening paper 'til it gets too dark . . . then they just sit. Some of the high-school kids drive around a little bit on their A coupons. The long whistle of the nine-o'clock train can be heard clear out at Parsons Corner – it's that quiet. The radio you hear playing quietly down the block is old Mrs. Anderson listening to 'The Contented Hour.' You know the habits of the town so well that you don't realize you know them. But . . . now you're in Chicago. And you don't know anything. You stand on the corner of Adams and Wabash and wonder whether you dare go into the Palmer House or not and how much it costs. Every time the 'L' trains turn the corner with their high-pitched screech, you jump. People push past you, going every which way. You don't know what to do with your suitcase. And you're lonely and there's an edge of panic creeping up on you."

Perhaps such a monologue would be a waste of time. It *might* give the actress a glimmer of the feeling you want to create in her. Maybe all of it will be wasted but one line – and that one may do the trick. One never knows. One can only keep working until somewhere an illustration, a phrase, will strike a response.

There is no standard device or procedure for working with an actor in the creation of a character. The director can only watch the actor and try to figure out what kind of person he is and reach back to some experience in the actor's past which will have meaning for him in the present situation. Each problem is a new one, each actor requires a different handling. Even the same actor may have to be handled differently to achieve different characterizations. It is the challenging character of this work that makes directing such a fascinating profession.

Right along with characterization comes interpretation or line reading. Once the actor thoroughly understands his character, he can usually decide how that character would react in any given situation. Even though the director and actor may have the same idea as to how a line should be interpreted, they may differ on the method of creating the interpretation. There is no one right way to read a line. There are often many ways of reading it to achieve an identical effect. Again, it is dangerous to dictate line readings. Perfect intonation, inflection, and timing can only come from within the actor himself as a result of perfect understanding of the character and the situation. Most misinterpretations are a result of misunderstanding. Once the actor understands the character's attitude toward other characters or to a situation, the interpretation problem has been solved. And solved it must be during the table rehearsal.

The director will discuss timing and tempo of individual scenes and the general pace of the show and set that during the table rehearsal. It is wise for him to discuss with the cast each scene in the play, what it is supposed to accomplish, and how it stands in relation to the whole play structure. General tempo should be set for each scene and for the show as a whole.

Sometime during the reading rehearsal, the director will put the watch on the show to see what the preliminary timing amounts to. If it is badly over, in spite of all his precautions in the editing process, the provisional cuts are called into play, but made only tentatively until after the dress rehearsal. If the timing is badly under, the director can send out an SOS for the author or, failing this, figure it out for himself. This reading rehearsal, incidentally, need not involve an engineer. This is work around a table where the director sits right with his cast and talks to them, works with them.

First Microphone Rehearsal

At the first mike rehearsal there are five specific goals to accomplish. First, all matters of characterization and interpretation are completed and polished. This is a completion of the work started at the table rehearsal. Second, all business is built into the show. ("Business" is used in the stage sense here to mean any action which is called for, either by the actors, or simulated by the actors, and executed by sound.) If the script calls for an actor to get up out of a chair, cross the room, sock a man on the jaw, heave a hand grenade, blow his nose, or anything else, this is rehearsed and set. The third objective of the mike rehearsal is to set all perspectives. The distance of every character and sound from the microphone and the angle of incidence to the microphone must be set for every line of the play. Most lines are played "on mike," which means facing the live sides of the microphone at a distance of from one and a half to two and a half feet. Some lines may be "off mike," which may mean that they are said ten feet away from the microphone, but facing into the live side of it. The whole purpose of perspective is to give the audience a sound picture of the relative position of people and sounds.

Let us take an example. In a recent story broadcast of Author's Playhouse, the scene opened in a little piano practice room off the main room of a large night club at eleven o'clock in the morning. As the scene opened, a pianist was practicing idly. The door was closed. Suddenly the door opened, we heard the confusion of waiters and cleaners getting ready for the afternoon cocktail hour out in the big room, and the voice of the man who opened the door. Then the door closed and the man who entered came into the room. The scene had to be set in this manner: The musician who was playing the piano to simulate the practicing was given a mike of his own and it was up full. The sound-effects microphone was cut down to half volume so that when the door opened it would sound as though it were across the room. Several members of the cast were instructed to ad-lib lines in the far corner of the studio away from all microphones to simulate the crowd of waiters setting up the tables. The actor who entered the room was placed about ten feet from the cast microphone facing the live side. When the piano player spoke, he was at a normal distance from the cast microphone. When the door closed, the ad-libbing in the background was cut, footsteps started on the sound mike which were faded up to full volume, and the actor at the door walked into normal position on the cast mike.

Next comes the matter of balance. Every speaker has a slightly different volume level. One character may have a loud, piercing voice and has to play a scene with a very gentle, soft-spoken character. In this case the soft voice would have to work closer and the loud voice farther away than normal from the mike to compensate for the difference in volume. Once these balances are discovered, the actors take a good look at the distance and do it that way thereafter.

Finally, in the first microphone rehearsal, sound is added to the script. The quality of the sound is checked for accuracy. The perspective is set for sound in the same manner as for actors. Every sound in a scene has a relationship to the center of the scene. A proper level for each sound is found and noted. Dial readings on all volume controls are made and recorded on the script so that the sounds can thereafter be duplicated. Manual sounds are handled in the same way the cast is managed. Distance from and angle to the beam of the microphone are determined for each sound, and the sound man makes a note of the volume he uses so that it can be accurately duplicated in succeeding rehearsals and on the air. Finally, difficult sound routines are rehearsed until they are right and smooth. This means rehearsing the sound and cast together so that they interlock properly. Sometimes ten lines of script incorporating one sound routine will take up half an hour of rehearsal. On the other hand, many routine sound effects come right the first time, and several pages may go by with no other direction than to set sound the way it is delivered on the first try. In some shows this business of setting and balancing sound takes longer than it does to get the cast ready. This is not usually the case.

however. At the end of the first microphone rehearsal, the show begins to take shape. Routines may not be smooth on everything yet, but at least everyone knows what he is supposed to do, when and how.

Cue Rehearsal

This brings matters to the cue-rehearsal stage. The cue rehearsal is designed for the express purpose of gearing the music into the program. It is conducted usually by having the cast and announcer read the half-dozen lines immediately preceding each music cue and having the music come in. When the music cue is finished, the first few lines of the new scene are run so that the director can see exactly how he is going into music and how he is coming out in each instance. This process may necessitate some music changes. If the music seems too loud in comparison with the scenes preceding and following, it may have to be toned down. If the director had planned a scene to open with a stinger cue and it seems wrong when he hears it with dialogue and sound, the music may have to be reworked so that there is less volume on the attack. This may be a matter of softening down volume. In the case of an orchestra, it might mean pulling a certain theme out of the brass section and giving it to strings. Whatever has to be done to make it right is done.

In cases where music plays under dialogue and has to time exactly with dialogue or synchronize with sound, considerable rehearsal may be needed. It may mean cutting dialogue or music to achieve perfect timing. Where music and lines occur simultaneously, balances must be achieved between music and cast. In some heavily scored programs, this cue rehearsal may take a lot of time, since it may mean rehearsing most of the script. If only theme and transition music are involved, the whole job may be done in less than half an hour. Whatever time is needed, by the time the rehearsal is done, the music should be geared into the show in the same way sound was in the previous step. The addition of music sometimes necessitates the changing of sound or cast balances. If changes must be made, they should also be made at this time.

Dress Rehearsal

This brings us to the critical point in the rehearsal routine — the dress rehearsal. A dress rehearsal should not be interrupted. The purpose of the dress rehearsal is to put all the little perfected bits together and see if they fit. This should give the cast a sense of the continuity of the program. In the dress rehearsal the director must divorce himself from as much responsibility as possible and get a very complete idea of the over-all effect of the program. He will usually make copious notes during this run. Anything which needs further rehearsal, change, or simply smoothing, is noted for spotting. Also a final timing is taken of the show, with cumulative entries being made in the script every thirty seconds.

If the general pace of the program in the dress rehearsal pleased the director, he will then make time adjustments in the script. If it is a little short, he may stretch the show with music, or add a few lines. If it is too long, he will use some of the provisional cuts — whatever is needed to bring the show to time. These cuts must be passed on to the entire company and should be rehearsed just to be sure that everyone understands what is being cut and how it will affect cues.

The director, after his dress, should have a quick conference with his entire staff and point out what was wrong and why. If the mistake was simple, it may only need to be mentioned. If it is a serious and complicated error, it may have to be eliminated by more rehearsal. This procedure is usually called "spotting." Only those sets of lines which encompass difficulties are rehearsed. It is good practice to work such a spot until it is perfect, and once that is achieved, go over it two or three times to establish firmly the right way of handling it.

On rare occasions time may be allowed for a second dress rehearsal. It is seldom that such a luxury can be afforded, although it nearly always results in a smoother show with more finesse and sureness of touch. Whether there is a second dress or not, time should be allowed in the schedule to let the cast have a little rest before the program goes on the air. Acting is difficult. It depends on delicate timing, sure reactions, and on the actor being free of everything except the important job of acting. If the director flusters him with a hundred last-minute details and gives him no chance to get himself mentally and emotionally set for the program, he is giving him a decided handicap. Even good directors sometimes have the circumstances pile up against them – circumstances over which they may personally have no control. To watch a really good cast go to work to help a director out of a corner like this is a beautiful sight to see. They will stretch, squeeze, sharpen, drag, make cuts, make up lines out of thin air . . . they can and will do the most amazing variety of things to make the show come right on the air. No good director will count on a cast to do this for him as a matter of routine; if a cast is pulling a director out of a hole, it cannot possibly do its best job of acting. But when the pinch does come, it is comforting to know that a cast can, and will, go to bat for a director they like, and do seemingly impossible things.

Plan your rehearsal time. The director knows in advance exactly how much time there is available and how much has to be done. C. L. Menser [1] often says: "In radio there are always fifty things to do and only time enough to do twenty-five of them. The good radio person is the one who recognizes this and does the *right* twenty-five." If rehearsal time is planned in advance, the director can keep himself on schedule and save valuable time.

Encourage the members of your staff to contribute ideas. They may have good ones. It builds their interest and it may help your show. But insist that these suggestions be made outside of rehearsal times!

Allow your cast little breathing spells in long rehearsals. A director may be sitting down in the control room and forget that he is keeping his leads standing for three hours at a stretch. The attention span shortens as fatigue sets in. The director who works fifty minutes and allows a ten-minute break will

[1] Vice-President in charge of programs for the National Broadcasting Company.

probably accomplish more than the director who works straight through. Be considerate.

When you rehearse — rehearse! Don't doodle and waste time. Work hard while you do work and take the time saved to give your cast little breathing spells. Don't allow time-stealing horse play from your company and don't indulge in it yourself.

At the same time the director must watch for signs of over-tension in a company. Too many fluffs in lines, too many missed cues, a sudden attack of the giggles — all these things may be indications that tension is too high or that fatigue has set in. When those signs show themselves, take a short break in rehearsals. It will help.

Watching and nursing the emotional tension of a company is an interesting problem in applied psychology. A good director will have his finger on the emotional pulse of his company all the time. A little tension is a good thing. It keeps a company on the alert. When tension predominates, however, it is usually harmful. Sometimes companies need to be jerked to attention. Sometimes they need to be calmed. Whatever they need for their own emotional welfare and for the "feel" of the show must be instilled into them by the director during the final stages of rehearsals.

A good director should demand and expect just a little more from his company than they can give him. If it is too much, they rebel. If it is too little, they do not care and will not work. But if the director can ask just a little more always than they are giving him — he nearly always gets better results. Actors react to a challenge in the same way everyone else does.

On the Air

Between rehearsal and the broadcast period, the director has little time to rest and relax. There are often twenty or thirty little details to attend to. He should recheck his script to be sure that he himself has all the last-minute changes properly noted. If there is to be a studio audience, they should be ushered into the studio as soon as the dress rehearsal is over in order to give them plenty of time to get seated, settled, and quiet. The director will make a final check with his conductor or musician, his sound crew and his engineer. Perhaps there is a new member in the cast who is shaky. He must take a minute to calm and reassure that actor. If one of the more seasoned members of the cast is too lackadaisical, the director may have to take a moment out to wind that person up.

By two minutes before air time, everything should be set. The musicians should be in their places and seated. The cast should be in the studio and the announcer in his place. Sound and engineer are set and ready. The control room should be cleared of all persons whom the production director does not want there. The fewer guests in the control room, the better, and no one should be allowed to talk, no matter who he is.

On the air the director meets the final test of his skill. There are several routine jobs for which he is responsible. These must be done meticulously, but automatically. In addition, he must watch all balances to see that no sound – music, sound, or line – is too close or too far away. He must see that levels do not get out of hand. And he must do all of these things automatically, without thinking. They must be accurate, subconscious activity. All the director's conscious concentration should be on the program itself. He must somehow, amidst all the hurly-burly of activity in the studio and control room, listen objectively to this product of his work and evaluate it. If anything displeases him, he must know what, why, and how to fix it, and proceed to do so at once.

Perhaps it may help the beginning director to remember this fact. Someone has spent a great deal of time and money to provide him with a room that is sealed away from the rest of the world. Nothing comes into that room except sound which he himself has planned. All this effort and expense have been provided to give him sound to play with and an ideal place in which to hear that sound. In return for all this, it is up to him to handle that sound and mold it into patterns that will make exciting radio listening for many thousands of people who can also hear what is happening in this sealed room. Not until he can look on all this and make it his own and feel that he has mastery of it does he become a production director.

In a broadcast, the beginning director is seldom the master of the situation. He is a slave to it. He is subject to the performance which he has drilled into his company. He spends most of his time worrying about whether he will remember to do everything he is supposed to do. He will, perhaps, get fascinated with the clock and time and the necessity for recording it on his script and suddenly discover that he has not heard fifteen whole lines of dialogue. He may have no remote notion of what happened. He has, in other words, become embroiled in the details of his job and is consequently not on top of his main task. The reason is simple and the solution difficult. He gets embroiled in details simply because they are unfamiliar to him and he has to concentrate in order to do them. In so doing, he loses his main objective. Only after he has done these details until they are automatic, until he can do them without thinking – in other words, until he has done a hundred programs – will he be able to reach that state of detachment where he can manage details automatically and leave his mind free for artistic evaluation and control. The principle involved is the same as that of driving a car. To pilot a car through fast-moving traffic on a city boulevard requires a high degree of manual skill, an excellent sense of timing, and the mastery of a complex set of motor movements. A driver may know exactly what to do in every case, but if he has to stop to think about it before he does it, he gets a mashed fender. Suppose a driver wishes to pass a car. He does not stop and think, "Can I make it before I meet a car coming the other way? Yes. Then, I must depress the accelerator, turn my steering wheel gently counter-clockwise, making sure that these two movements are so synchronized that I will not catch up with the car ahead before I have turned sufficiently far to the left. Then I turn the steering wheel clockwise to a neutral position . . . " and so on. If a driver had to go through with all that conscious thought process, he would never get through traffic. An experienced driver may make only one conscious decision – "Can I make it past that car?" He decides he can and everything that happens from then on is pure reflex motor activity. This same kind of management of details must be achieved by the production director on the air. Normal work is handled automatically, and attention is riveted on the end result — the program as it comes out of the loud-speaker.

During a broadcast, the director's eyes watch the details of his program as a driver watches the shifting pattern of traffic. He sees the sound crew, the musical conductor, his actors, his engineer, and gives them cues, signs, approvals, or corrections, and he does this with the same detachment that a driver adjusts to the changing picture of traffic framed within his windshield.

Having achieved this much-sought-after detachment, what does the director do with it? He listens to the program. He listens as nearly as possible as a listener would. He must not listen to see whether he hears footsteps at a certain place. He must listen to the story which the sound is telling him. If the story is not clear in a certain place, he knows, because of his work, that it lacks footsteps and he gives the proper cues to correct it. This is the kind of process with which the director must be concerned. He listens to line reading and sees that it follows the pattern rehearsed. He listens to the delicate shift of pace and tempo in the scene and sees that it is right. He listens for balances and perspectives and corrects whatever has shifted slightly out of place. In other words, he *conducts* the program exactly the same way that a symphony conductor conducts, and he is after the same results. The only difference is that a dramatic director has a more complex task. He must not only control music, but also sound and a cast of actors and mold them all into a moving, meaningful pattern. That is the production director's job while on the air.

There is comparatively little for the production director to do in the post-broadcast period. However, what there is to do should be done. If the company has done a good job, the director ought to tell them so. He is working with human beings and they respond to nothing so promptly and so positively as praise. If it is due, give it to them. If it was a poor performance, the immediate post-broadcast period is no time for a critical hash-session. Everyone is too tired, too nervously exhausted, too close to the work to make it of any value. Next day is time enough for that. A pat on the back to cast, sound crew, musicians, and engineer, if deserved, should be given by the production director. A pay check is one thing, but a kind word, an appreciation of a job well done, is something else additional and should not be overlooked. The director should never forget that his success depends directly on what he is able to get out of *people.* And people like praise if it is deserved. Actors will work for a director who treats them like human beings. And from a combination of spirits like this — occasionally great drama occurs.

Routine paper work must be completed and it is often easiest to do directly after the broadcast. Any signatures that have to be put on the master script or any other routine work should be done as soon as possible.

The routine work in striking the studio is not usually a part of the production director's responsibility. However, it is well to see that all this is done. Sound effects have to be put away. Microphones are taken down and returned to their proper places. Scripts sometimes have to be collected and filed. Chairs and tables must be removed or replaced. All this, in a good organization, happens as a matter of course. If it does not, the director should check it.

The Production of Dramatic Serials

Because such a large segment of the drama which is broadcast every day comes to the listeners in the form of serial dramas, and because the routines for handling such programs are somewhat different from ordinary routines, special mention should be made of the problems of handling serial dramas.

By far the most serials on the air are fifteen minutes long and are broadcast five days a week. The story is continuous and concerns the same general set of characters all the way through the series, with many additions and subtractions in the less important rôles in the story. In general, the same actors play the same parts week in and week out. The same director handles the show every day and, more often than not, the same sound man and engineer are assigned. The program is even broadcast from the same studio. In other words, there is a considerable amount of continuity to many factors in the program.

Because all these things are true, the methods used in the production of a daytime serial program are considerably different from those employed in building a one-time program, or even a regular program where there is a complete story each broadcast. The whole production procedure need not be gone through again, but the points at which procedures differ will be discussed.

To begin with, the program, the production director, and the writer are all constants. The director will have to do infinitely less with the script than is usually the case because the writer is usually a highly skilled craftsman who knows the medium intimately. The common errors which show up in scripts brought on the free-lance market are for the most part absent from serial scripts. The writer has created the characters over a period of weeks, months, or years and is thoroughly familiar with them. He is also familiar with the format of the show, which is usually fairly constant and unchanging. In addition, because nearly all such programs are agency-produced, the radio executives in the agency have gone over the scripts fairly carefully in advance. Therefore, nearly all the editing that normally has to be done in other kinds of programs is eliminated here. The main concern is time. If the writer is careless on this score, cuts may have to be made or inserts called for or written to bring the program to time. Even this is usually no problem, since a day-to-day check on any given set of characters can tell the writer very accurately exactly how much dialogue will be needed.

The aim of the program, the production approach, the type of material are all matters which are set from the inception of the program and are a part of the production director's background as he picks up each new script. He must make a study of the structure of the show, since this will change from day to day — but very little. One read-through is usually enough to make this evident.

Talent becomes a problem only under two circumstances. If the client or the agency becomes dissatisfied with the way a part is being played or an actor behaving, it may be necessary to recast. Even though it happens infrequently, it is a major operation when it does happen because so much depends on it. Sometimes a prominent rôle will be the subject of hearings and auditions for weeks before a final decision is made. Because the listening audience to the daytime serial is so large and so loyal, they are quick to make known their dislike either of a story turn or an actor they do not like. And because the sponsor has so much money invested in the program, he can seldom afford to ignore such reactions. Therefore, when, for any reason, an important part in a serial program has to be recast, it is usually done with considerable thoroughness and only after due deliberation. Unfortunately, this is not always a process in which the production director has a free hand. The account executive of the advertising agency and the sponsor may also dabble in directing.

In addition to this kind of major talent problem, directors have minor casting problems all the time. New characters are introduced into the story from time to time and have to be cast. Sometimes programs use dramatized commercials frequently and actors must be found for these spots. These are seldom major problems, however, since a large part of the cast is constant and there is no problem of casting from scratch before each performance.

Staff needs, studio needs, and studio layout are almost as constant as the cast. And since the same people work the same programs every day, there is a chance to build up a mutual understanding and a teamwork which makes the whole process infinitely simpler. Special effects are few and simple. Rehearsal time is nearly always the same each day because the basic problems are the same. Sound is held to a minimum and consists usually in the very simplest of obvious effects. Music is usually confined to opening and closing theme, which is standard, and possibly an occasional bridge. There are a few serial programs on the air which use much background music, but they are few, indeed.

There is an obvious reason for keeping serial programs as simple as possible in production. The whole idea of the daytime serial is predicated on the knowledge that listeners cannot attend to them exclusively. Housewives, who form the majority of the listeners to such programs, have work to do. They cannot sit all day doing nothing but listen to the radio. The radio, therefore, designs a type of dramatic fare that they can listen to, even while they are doing something else. This simple concept is back of almost everything that is done on a serial program. A complicated fast-moving plot would not do, because that would demand undivided attention from the listener. So would complex sound and elaborate use of music. These programs are paced very slowly and the story development moves at glacier speed. As one of the engineers once remarked, a lamp which falls off a table on Monday has not hit the floor by Friday of the following week. Because of this slowness of movement and simplicity of structure and production, neither sound nor music is ever very complex.

Ordering of scripts, scheduling of staff, space, and equipment, and staff conferences are all routine. In most cases they are standing orders which are made when the program goes on the air, and are seldom if ever altered. Certainly, they do not have to be specially scheduled for each program.

Marking up the script must be done the same as in any other kind of dramatic program, except that it is an infinitely simpler process. A five-minute session is usually enough to mark up a serial script — a process which could run anywhere from one to three hours on a more complex program.

What casting has to be done should be done in the same way that casting for any other kind of a program is handled. One warning is in order. When a new character is cast, the other characters already cast who are likely to have to play scenes with the new character should be on hand just to check for contrast.

In the matter of rehearsals the serial program differs more widely from other kinds of dramatic programs than in any other phase of the work. The reasons are, of course, the same ones already stated. About seventy per cent of the work that has to be done during rehearsals in other kinds of programs is not necessary in the serial. Sound and music, which are held at a minimum, are usually of such a nature as to be done almost without rehearsal. They consist mostly of doors and telephones and such simple sound as any sound man can do ad lib. The cast is never large. The characters are all set. The business is never complicated and transitions are usually silent ones. In other words, the major jobs are timing and interpretation. Once these two things are under control, the most of the rehearsal problem has been taken care of.

The time allowed for the total rehearsal of a fifteen-minute serial program is seldom more than an hour and a half. Usually it is just an hour. The actual playing time of the dialogue is commonly about nine to ten minutes, and the rest of the program is taken up by the announcer, the commercials, and music. The ordinary procedure is to have the cast read through the script once in order to get the content of the script and the idea of the day's development. This is usually done on mike and the table rehearsal eliminated completely. What sound is used on the program goes on at the same time. Also during this first read-through, the director will make a timing of the show.

After the first read-through, during which the director will make as many notes as necessary to remind him of the corrections he wants to make and the places he wants to spot, these corrections are given to the cast in discussion. If they seem complicated, these places may be rehearsed and set. This process may take the first half-hour of the rehearsal period. The program is also brought to time by cuts or inserts after this first reading.

Then the program is dressed by a second read-through that will include only the dialogue. Usually it will be an uninterrupted reading of the show. Again corrections are noted. By this time the program is ordinarily on time. Most of the corrections will consist in little changes in business or in interpretation. Perhaps some minor adjustment may be made in sound.

During the last fifteen minutes before the program goes on the air, the opening and closing by the announcer are read and the commercials read and checked. If there is any music, other than theme, it is also selected during this fifteen-minute period. This process may take anywhere from five to twelve minutes, depending on the music. Perhaps a little time may be spent on rehearsal if there is a dramatized commercial to be done. This leaves the remainder of the time free until the program goes on the air.

Because, by comparison, there is so little to do on a serial program, there is sometimes a real danger of not doing what little should be done. Interpretation, which always has to be worked on, sometimes gets little more than a lick and a promise. Sound may be treated very cavalierly and music is almost taken for granted. If the program's only music is the theme, it is seldom even rehearsed. If there are a couple of bridges to be chosen, the director listens to the choice which the organist or pianist has cleared and indicates which one he wants. If there is time, he may even rehearse it once. Sometimes even the commercials are not rehearsed. This is sloppy operation and should not be allowed, but it happens all the time. Directors feel that there is no need to rehearse an announcer in the same commercial which he has been reading five days out of seven for six months. It is true that the copy does change some from day to day, but the essential message is nearly always the same. It is easy to relax and let things come as they will. And in this likelihood to relax is the greatest danger and the most difficulty in directing such programs.

Given only a great director and a conscientious one and this particular form of drama has some chances for greatness. Here, as in few other forms of theater, is a chance to develop a completely evolved character. Here is a chance to develop teamwork between writer and director; and between actors, announcer, sound, music, director, and engineer that can build into a oneness of concept possible in few other dramatic media. This could, in turn, make very real drama. The fact that so much of the daytime fare is mediocre says more clearly than could anything else that directors are not doing the best job of which they are capable.

The extremely slow pace at which this kind of drama must be played and the absence of many other problems give the director a chance to concentrate on interpretation in a way that is possible in few other programs. With characters set and growing, with plot moving as slowly as it does and helping as much as it does in the day-to-day development of the story, there is an excellent chance for the director to work for a quality of interpretation which should – and often does – outshine almost every other kind of acting on the air. And a daytime serial which does not excel in interpretation shows very clearly that it is being badly directed. Most of them manage an amazing quality of characterization.

CHAPTER 13

PRODUCING THE VARIETY PROGRAM

RADIO VARIETY PROGRAMS are to contemporary entertainment what the old vaudeville, music hall, and Broadway revue were to American theater-goers of fifteen years ago. They constitute the most popular form of entertainment on the air. Such programs nearly always get the choice nighttime spots because they represent the maximum entertainment value for all ages and classes of people.

Because such programs are so popular, a great deal of money is spent on them. This includes the budget for direction. Variety programs are usually the plums among directing jobs. They are also the most difficult of all to direct and demand a higher degree of skill and more diverse background than any other kind of program. The work requires a director with a sharp sense of comedy and the ability to work with gag dialogue, one who knows music well, and, above all, one who has the keen sense of showmanship that can appeal to all classes and ages of people. With such a set of requirements it is only logical that the law of supply and demand should be at work.

It has been previously stated that directing staffs in the networks are usually divided into dramatic and musical directors. The variety program should be directed by a person qualified in both fields. Most variety programs are agency-produced, and the directors are most often men who have been network-trained in both branches of the work. If variety programs are built by the station or network instead of by an agency, then a director who has shown special interest and aptitude in both musical and dramatic production is usually chosen.

Variety programs are a severe challenge to directors, not only because they employ both drama and music, but because of the wide variety of material and talent used. Music will run the whole gamut from hallelujahs to hoedowns and from symphony to swing. Guest artists may be experts on the piano or the musical saw. Aside from music, the director may have to deal with speakers, comedians, Shakespearean actors, celebrities, and movie stars.

To further complicate an already complex pattern, the show is seldom the same for any two programs. The whole structure of the variety program depends — oddly enough — on variety. Every week there is a different combination of elements to weld into a unified program. Every week different guest stars, with different talent to offer, will appear, and these may cause basic changes in the setup of the program.

Another difficulty which the director of a variety program faces is the shifting pattern of the limits of his authority. This varies widely from program to program and agency to agency. In some cases the director is given a more or less free hand. In other cases the director has little voice in the choice of talent or content of the program and is responsible only for getting it on the air. In all cases, where so much money is at stake and where so much depends on the program, the director is usually subject to all kinds of pressure, which may vary from suggestion to arbitrary demands. Sometimes the production director has a voice in the choice of writers and talent. He is nearly always consulted, but seldom has the final decision. No matter how the authority is distributed, the director is seldom the free, unhampered agent he may be when doing less pretentious programs.

Production Problems

Against this background of program complexity and uncertain authority, coupled with high pay and unlimited budget, let us examine some of the problems of production. One of the most difficult problems is that of script, about which the director may have little to say, but with which he is forced to work. Comedy is an elusive thing. Writers who can write comedy are few. What is more, the measure of the success of comedy writing can only be taken after it is put in rehearsal

Whereas in other program types the director can more or less start where the writer leaves off, in comedy routines and gag programs the director must work with the writer and the comedians until something funny comes out. It means trial and error, write and rewrite, and while this is primarily a problem of the writer, it is something in which the director is inevitably embroiled.

Casting is always a problem on the variety program. Good comedians and masters of ceremonies are very hard to find indeed. Sometimes weeks and months go into the building of the basic talent around which a variety program is built. Ordinarily, the director has little or nothing to say about this. The heads of advertising agencies and network executives concern themselves with decisions as important as this. However, after they have made their decisions, it is the director who has to work with the talent chosen and get something out of the people. Not only the basic talent, but weekly guests and other stars who appear on the program must be found and rehearsed. Some of this work will usually fall to the director. Again procedures vary.

Possibly the greatest difficulty connected with directing a variety program is accepting the responsibility for its success. When a sponsor is paying as high as a thousand dollars a minute, he wants results. A program becomes important in direct ratio to the amount of money spent on it and the size of the possible audience it can reach. Since most such programs go into the choice night spots, both these elements — audience and expenditure — are high. The resultant pressure on the production director is tremendous. It is even more difficult when one considers that in many cases the director's authority is rather severely limited to the actual conducting of rehearsals. If he has little voice in the choice of talent and script — which is often the case — he is indeed in a peculiar position.

Thus far all of the difficulties of the variety program have been stressed. There are, of course, many compensations which make directing in this area one of the most exciting and challenging jobs in radio. The director often has a chance to work with the very best talent available. Budgets are generous. Audiences are tremendous, the problems are always new and usually interesting. In other words, if a director is interested in playing for high stakes, here is a program type that is made to order. And, of course, it is the highest paid of all directing work.

The Format

Variety programs, as their name indicates, come in many shapes and sizes. However, there is a certain over-all pattern which is common among most programs. Music is usually the backbone of the program and the high lights will be a comedy act or acts. In addition, as spice for the program, there will be specialty numbers or guest stars. These elements are put together in a number of ways, depending on the ingenuity of the writing and production staff and the diversity of available talent.

The music is usually furnished by a full concert orchestra or a "name" band. There may be one or more soloists and a musical guest artist. A variety show must have stars. These are sometimes vocalists and sometimes comedians. On rare occasions they may be both. Top billing on the program will usually go to the person who acts as master of ceremonies and chief comedian. There is, for example, no question about who is the star of the Bob Hope show. The combining of chief comedian and master of ceremonies into a single duty is often done. Ordinarily variety shows have at least one guest on each program and sometimes several. The guest artist may be anyone from the leading tenor at the Metropolitan Opera to a singing mouse. It may be the leading man in the current production of *Macbeth* or a private, home on furlough from the war. Whatever kind of guest will have human interest for the public or talent which is worthy of inclusion may be used.

The routine of a variety show will vary considerably, of course, but it tends to follow a certain structure which alternates music, comedy, and drama. Here, for example, is the routine followed on a recent edition of the Kraft Music Hall program starring Bing Crosby. The program opened with the announcer announcing in fanfare fashion the name of the program, its personnel and the guest for the day. Then, without any introduction, the orchestra plunged into the first number with Bing Crosby singing "There's Gonna Be a Great Day," supported by the chorus. Out of the applause following the number came an OWI plug by Crosby, making an appeal to limit travel. This announcement blended smoothly, with no apparent change of pace, into a combination interview and gag routine with Miss Maxwell, guest soloist on the program, which involved two other members of the regular company before it was finished. This gag routine lasted a little over three minutes and terminated in an introduction to the next musical number, "Stormy Weather," done in a special arrangement by the Charioteers, featuring Wilford Williams, soloist. Out of the applause following this number came the first commercial. Immediately after the commercial, and with no verbal introduction, Bing Crosby sang "Take It Easy," supported by the orchestra. Following this number, Crosby introduced the guest of honor for the day, the movie star who played the title rôle in *See Here, Private Hargrove.* He had just returned from a USO trip in the South Pacific theater of war and the combination interview and gag routine centered around this trip. This lasted for about five minutes and terminated with Bing singing a parody on "The San Fernando Valley." This number was followed by Heraldry from the orchestra introducing a regular feature of the program — "'Way Back When." The introduction to this feature is in the nature of a gag routine and took place between Crosby and Marilyn Maxwell and terminated in Bing's singing "Dearly Beloved." This number was followed by the second commercial, after which Crosby sang his last number of the program, a very elaborate number in which Miss Maxwell also sang. This number was followed by the "tease" or announcement of what the next show was to feature. This was followed by signature music, over the last thirty seconds of which the announcer read a hitch-hike commercial. Boiled down to a production director's outline, the program might look like this:

Announcer	Opening Fanfare announcement	:30
Crosby & Orchestra	"There's Gonna Be a Great Day"	2:15
Crosby, Maxwell, Ukey	Gag routine	5:30
Charioteers & Williams	"Stormy Weather"	8:30
Announcer	First Commercial	9:25
Crosby & Orchestra	"Take It Easy"	11:05
Crosby & Wynn	Gag routine with guest	17:45
Crosby	"San Fernando Valley"	19:35
Orchestra	Heraldry	19:50
Crosby & Maxwell	"Time Marches Backward" gag routine	22:40
Crosby	"Dearly Beloved"	25:15
Announcer	Second Commercial	26:40
Crosby	Finale number	28:20
Crosby	Tease for next week	29:00
Orchestra	Signature music	29:05
Announcer	Hitch-hike announcement over closing music	29:30

Notice how talk is alternated with music. Between each musical number there is a gag routine or a commercial. Notice that there are no two musical numbers following each other immediately. Notice the difference in musical numbers. The first one is definitely a show tune which plainly indicates its musical-comedy origin. The next number is one of the evergreens of modern music — a modern classic. "Take It Easy" is a currently popular tune that may not last three months, but which, as this is being written, is having wide acceptance. "San Fernando Valley" is also a popular tune of the moment, but remember that this number was a parody, which made it a change of pace from the preceding number. "Dearly Beloved" is an out-and-out ballad of the sentimental type and, again, a complete change of pace. The finale number was an elaborate, colorfully arranged musical climax to the show.

This program is not to be taken as a paragon of variety programming. It is cited here as being typical in conformance to the basic requisites of change of pace, variety of material, and advantageous arrangement of talent. The whole philosophy behind this type of program is that of including something in the program which will appeal to all kinds of people. It must have something for every member of the family.

Production Analysis

The production procedure in the variety program differs

from any other kind of program so far discussed. One of the reasons for this difference is that talent is the beginning point of production. Nearly every variety program has certain talent which is permanently a part of the program. With this as the starting point, the next step is to choose the guest artists. These are usually picked by the agency executives responsible for the program, generally in consultation with the director.

From this point on, the director's responsibility and authority increase. The next step is that of selecting suitable music for the program. This cannot be done until the talent is chosen. If the guest star were to be Iturbi, one kind of music would be appropriate; if Harpo Marx were the guest, it would require another kind. While account executives are likely to make suggestions at any point in the routine, this task is normally considered a part of the director's work.

The next step is the choosing of the script material. Again this will depend on the guests for the program and the general occasion, and so usually follows the choosing of both talent and music. Script writers will consult with either the account executive or the production director (depending on who is charged with this responsibility) and an outline will be blocked. After a rough draft is written, it is submitted to the director for approval. After it is acceptable, it becomes at least the basis for the program, although it may be worked over and doctored right up to broadcast time. This will be true particularly of the gag routines and comedy sequences.

The next step in the process is the production analysis. First, a routine must be made out. Whereas in the dramatic show the director studies the structure of the script, in the variety show the director creates the structure in the making of his routine. Suppose the talent for a variety program consisted of an orchestra, a vocalist-comedian, a girl vocalist, a mixed trio, a comedian-stooge, and a guest who is a concert violinist. Any combination of these various elements may be used on the program. It remains only to decide in what order they will be used and in what combination. The director might decide to open with a very flashy musical number which would use a special arrangement featuring the vocalist-comedian, the girl vocalist, the trio, and the orchestra, all working together. This might be followed by a routine between vocalist and stooge in which the guest is introduced but does not perform. The next number might feature the trio. The production director would go right through the remainder of the program, planning how and what to use, where and when.

The staff for such a program is usually the same each week. The usual engineer, announcer, and perhaps sound men will be needed. Special requirements of specific programs may call for additional help.

Next, the studio layout is determined. If no audience is present, a setup similar to the one sketched for a dramatic program may be suitable. However, when a studio audience is used, the director feels some obligation to "dress the stage" somewhat toward the studio audience. That means the orchestra will probably face the audience, while the conductor faces them and the control room. The cast will at least try to play to the audience, although they must watch control also. Sound is usually disposed of as unobtrusively as possible, but the sound men must also be able to see the control room. Since music is involved, much of the concern over setup will have to do with the orchestra and getting a proper balance between it and the vocal talent. Diagrams or suggested studio layouts are useless here, because every program presents its own problems and solutions are valid only in the presence of known requirements. However, there are certain over-all requirements which are constant to all such programs.

1. The entire show should be directed at the studio audience.
2. The orchestra conductor must be able to see control and the vocalists who sing with the orchestra.
3. Dramatic and comedy talent should be able to see control.
4. Sound should be able to see control and also hear dialogue on the cast microphone.
5. Provision must be made for all musical specialty numbers.
6. All placements should be arranged to provide proper musical balance.

7. All elements must be placed advantageously for the best acoustical results in a given studio.

Finally, a rehearsal schedule must be worked out. Unlike other rehearsals, the variety program rehearsal is usually segmental. Each element of the program can be worked up a bit at a time and the entire program may never be put together until rather late in the routine. Comedians, vocalists, announcers, and solo musicians who are regularly featured on the program are usually paid enough to have first call on their time. They may even be the exclusive property of a given program. The orchestra, on the other hand, may be made up from the network pool of musicians and may be available for rehearsal only at stated times, which often remain the same from week to week. Depending on how much music has to be learned, the orchestra may be called for from three to ten hours of rehearsal. The first half of this time may be devoted to learning the numbers and working out interpretation. This work is done by the conductor and his orchestra with the production director listening and making suggestions wherever he can. The last half of the time may be spent in balancing the orchestra and timing the numbers, as well as smoothing out their performance. Then the orchestra is ready for dress rehearsal, or preliminary rehearsal with vocalists, depending on specific circumstances. Aside from the orchestra, each separate element of the program can be rehearsed independently of other segments. Using the talent list previously suggested, a rehearsal schedule might run something like this:

Monday	10:00 – 12:00 A.M.	Rehearsal of trio with piano
Tuesday	10:00 – 12:00 A.M.	Rehearse gag routines
	1:30 – 4:00 P.M.	Rewrite and doctor script
	4:00 – 5:00 P.M.	Rehearse revised script
Wednesday	12:00 – 3:00 P.M.	Rehearse orchestra
	4:00 – 5:00 P.M.	Second orchestra rehearsal
	5:00 – 7:00 P.M.	Dress rehearsal
	8:00 P.M.	Broadcast

In addition to the basic schedule above, additional times may have to be set aside for the rehearsal of the guest star, for the rehearsal of dramatic episodes, and for any other parts of the program which may demand special attention.

The last step in the production analysis is the making of provisional cuts. This process is particularly important in the variety program because it is not always possible to get an accurate idea of the program timing from the dress rehearsals. The musical portions of the program can be timed exactly. Gag routines can only be estimated and not accurately known from rehearsal. Therefore, the production director must provide sufficient cushion to allow for these variations. The usual solution is to provide a very flexible closing music number which may use one chorus, two choruses, or chorus, verse, chorus, depending on how much time is needed.

Rehearsals

From this point on in the production procedure, the variety show follows the pattern already discussed up to the point of rehearsals. Even here, most of the procedure is the same. Musical numbers are handled exactly as they are in a music program. Dramatic bits are handled in the same way as they would be in a dramatic program. However, the rehearsal of gag routines and comedy material departs from any pattern so far discussed.

Rehearsing comedy material is essentially a process of trial and error. Even experienced production directors, gag writers, and comedians can be fooled by comedy material. Something that seems rather dull and commonplace on paper may turn out to be very funny. Conversely, a routine that may seem very funny on reading fails to "jell," once it goes into rehearsal. The only sure way to test such material is to rehearse it and see what happens.

Rehearsal of comedy material has for its first purpose the polishing of the script itself. Sometimes mildly funny lines can be altered slightly in wording, timed differently, inflected differently, and made much funnier. This whole process of rewriting and rewording is the first concern of the rehearsal. If the material is not basically funny after concentrated rehearsal, the writers must be called in to furnish new material or do a radical rewrite on the original material. If it needs only rewording, or minor change, it is done by the production director. In either case, whatever is done happens as a result of his decisions during the early rehearsal period. This process of rewording and of eliminating unfunny material in favor of new lines continues all during the early part of the rehearsal period.

Once the script is set for the comedy portions of the show, intensive rehearsals are held to perfect the timing and pacing of lines, the inflection and pointing of interpretation, and the over-all smoothness that makes comedy seem funny to an audience. All comedy material is funniest if it seems completely spontaneous. This feeling of spontaneity is seldom achieved, however, except by hours of careful rehearsal, paradoxical as this may seem.

Somewhere late in the rehearsal process the guest artist is rehearsed and that portion of the program smoothed into the whole show. There is one danger here which is insidious because the director may be only partly aware of its existence. It is easy for a director to stand so in awe of his guest that he will not give that guest the benefit of his direction. He may think, "Who am I to tell the great so-and-so how to perform!" This is a false assumption. If the artist is good, he will have learned to depend on the help of a capable director. He will want help and expect it. After all, any guest wants to make a good appearance and it is a part of the director's job to help him do his best work.

A guest may not be familiar with radio technique to begin with. A great actor before the footlights can fail miserably before the microphone unless he can learn the technique of the microphone. A movie star may not become automatically a radio star. A violinist who is used to working on a concert stage may have to make some adjustment to working on a microphone. Making this adjustment to a new medium is part of the variety director's job, and he must not pull his punches in helping a guest to make this adaptation. Fortunately, most people who can qualify as guest artists these days are becoming familiar with radio technique through repeated appearances, and the director's job is less difficult now than it used to be.

Stage actors must be constantly watched for overprojection. They are accustomed to reaching the fifty-cent seats with their voices. On the air they often feel that they have to reach Kansas direct with their voices. The director will have to help them to get the feel of the intimacy of radio, which nearly always means using less voice and a more personal approach to lines. Movie stars are used to working on microphones, since that is how sound tracks are recorded, but they are also used to depending on body movement and visual cues to get their meaning across. The variety director must help them to put all their effort on lines. These are the kinds of things that a director can do to help guest artists who are not familiar with the techniques of radio.

This brings us up to the dress rehearsal. It is a good idea to have a small test audience in the studio during the dress rehearsal if it can be arranged. After all, the audience is one of the elements with which the director must work. That element, then, should be present in the dress. An audience at the dress will tell the comedians and the director where the laughs are going to come and how big they are likely to be. They will tell the director what lines are weak and need final polishing. They will tell the actors where they are missing their timing and pointing, and in general furnish the best possible index to the success of the gag portions of the program.

In the dress rehearsal the production director is primarily concerned with the over-all effect of his program. He must take care of routine matters like timing, music balance, and the marking of places for spotting rehearsal and so on, but his main concern is for the over-all effect of his program. One of the secrets of a successful variety show is pace. It must move. It must sparkle. It must create the pattern of variety to which the program is dedicated. The effectiveness of this pattern can only be determined as the whole program goes together. Each separate item in the program may be perfect, but in the dress rehearsal these separate items are smoothed together, made to fit, and welded into an effective whole.

If possible, the director ought to allow for two dress rehearsals. The first one can be devoted to putting all the parts together and noting where the glaring errors are. The first run-through will tell the director what to do with pace, where transition difficulties are likely to occur, which routines need extra work, and how the music works with the rest of the show. Following the first dress, solutions to all these problems can be worked out and then tried in the second dress, which will more closely approximate what the actual broadcast should be like. Because of the complexity and diversity of material in the variety program, a second dress is recommended.

On the Air

By now the program is ready to go on the air. The director will make the usual prebroadcast checks which are routine for any kind of program. Incidentally, dress rehearsals must be ended well ahead of air time. On many occasions the cast will have to dress for the program. Certainly time must be provided for getting the audience into the studio and seated well ahead of air time. The usual procedure is to open the studio to the audience thirty to forty-five minutes ahead of the air time and close the doors at least ten minutes before.

This brings us to a procedure which has not yet been discussed — the audience warm-up. Such a process is nearly always included in any program involving a studio audience, but it is particularly important in the variety program, because the audience is, after all, an element of the program. The production director has the standard job of presenting a program to a live audience and pleasing them, and he has the additional job of making that audience a part of the program which he presents to the larger, more important air audience. So the people in the studio represent not only immediate customers but also program talent. They must be taken into the director's confidence and made a part of the show. The warm-up period, therefore, must do these things:

1. Create good will for the station or network and sponsor by treating them as valued guests.
2. Polarize the audience so they are ready to respond to the program in a satisfactory manner.
3. Familiarize them with the part they are to play in the program.
4. Start them to responding, so that when the program hits the air, they are already "warmed-up."

There is no set procedure for conducting a warm-up, but most programs use some variation on the following pattern. The station or network announcer will come out and welcome the audience on behalf of the network and the program. Using a line of patter which has been audience-tested for reaction, he will introduce the orchestra and the talent on the program in climactic order, usually ending with the star of the program, the master of ceremonies, or chief comedian. The M.C. will then take over. In the few minutes preceding the broadcast, he will tell the audience to have a good time, laugh all they want to and enjoy the program. If there are any times when they must remain quiet, he will warn them about it and indicate how they will know those times. Then the M.C., either alone or with the co-operation of other members of the company, will tell a few stories, work a few gags, and in general get the audience loosened up and in a laughing mood.

This whole warm-up should not be left to chance or be ad-libbed. It should be just as carefully rehearsed as the air program. After all, it is very important that the audience be in a mood to laugh when the program goes on the air. The warm-up routine need not be different for every broadcast. It is often the same for show after show, but it must be well done Finally, the warm-up should continue right up to the moment the program goes on the air. If elaborate quiet is required ahead of the program, it may dampen the spirits of the audience so that they will be afraid to react when the time comes. That is why most variety show openings are noisy and allow for audience reaction the moment the program goes on the air.

If the audience can be carried right over from the warm-up into the program without too much time delay, they are in the mood and react much more quickly.

All the theatrical tricks of the trade can be used in the warm-up. Studio lights may be only three quarters on when the audience is admitted. Just before the warm-up starts, full lights can be flashed on. Or, if the program is given in a theater or theater studio, perhaps house lights can be dimmed out and spots and stage lights brought up. The band can help out with little fanfares and other musical tricks. The cast can make "entrances" as they are introduced. All of the time-tried theatrical devices can be called into play to give the audience a sense of important things happening. Showmanship is important in getting a studio audience ready for the broadcast.

Out of this welter of planned activity, the program takes the air. The director's work on the actual broadcast includes all the routine matters that attend other kinds of broadcasts. He must check time, balances, throw cues, and in general supervise the program. In the variety show specifically, there are two problems which he will give special attention. The first of these is timing. Even though a trial audience may have been present at the dress rehearsal, it may not be a perfect index of how the audience will react on the air. They may be in a laughing mood and tend to slow the program up. Or they may be in a not-so-happy mood and let it run faster than anticipated. This means that the director must keep very close track of time and make adjustments accordingly. He must not only get off the air on time, but he must not let the pace of the program suffer. If a studio audience wants to laugh too much and too often, thus slowing down the pace of the show, the director will have to cue the cast in more quickly and make them work over the laughter to keep the show from losing pace. Or, if there is not enough response, he may ask the cast to work on the audience in the studio a little harder in order to encourage laughs. These messages can be transmitted to the cast during musical numbers.

The other unknown in the equation is the cast's reaction to

the audience. Sometimes, if an audience is particularly responsive, comedians will go completely overboard in playing to it. They may even depart from the script into an ad-libbed routine that seems appropriate at the moment. Comedians are like that. They cannot resist a responsive audience. The director must decide whether they are right or not and act accordingly. If the comedians are taking too much time or milking a scene too far, he must signal them to get back to the script and speed up. He may even have to go out on the studio floor during a musical number and talk to the cast.

Managing all these things, and still keeping track of the dozens of details which are his responsibility during the airing of a program, makes of the production director a very busy man. He must maintain a degree of concentration which is nerve-wracking in order to cover all the facets of his job. Only long practice and many productions will make the director able to manage all of these details at once.

The student of production may wonder how he can ever hope to learn all of the complex skills which go into the creation of a variety program. He may assume that practice in handling such programs is not possible, since he cannot often have at his command a full orchestra, gag writers, and skilled comedians with which to work. This is true — but only to a limited degree. In the first place, it must be remembered that the musical and dramatic portions of a variety program differ very little from any other kind of program. The only new elements to contend with are the comedy routines and the over-all structure of this kind of program.

The beginner who is interested in this kind of directing will do well to concentrate on handling gag routines. Listen to several on the air. Time them with a stop watch. See how long such routines run. How long is spent on each gag? How many people are used? How is sound handled? How realistically are scenes handled? What makes them funny?

Having listened to several such programs, make contact with student writers and work out some comedy scripts and put them in rehearsal with the talent you have available. It may not be the most skilled comedy talent possible, but even from amateurs it is possible for a director to learn much about handling comedy. Practice on reworking lines to get the most fun out of them. Try different pacings of routines. Work with broad comedy characterizations until you have an idea of what these can add to comedy routines. Having worked in this way, get together a cast of people and some appropriate recordings and build a variety show, using student or staff talent and recorded music. Rehearse such a program and record it. A study of the playback will tell you much about the problems of production on a variety program.

CHAPTER 14

WHAT EVERY PRODUCTION DIRECTOR SHOULD KNOW

Several years of radio experience is usually required of an applicant before he is acceptable as a candidate for a position as a network production director. This requirement is made, among other reasons, because a network production director must be thoroughly familiar with the general business of radio. There are many rules and practices with which he must be familiar. And, until recently, there was no place where the neophyte could learn them except by the trial-and-error process of learning through doing. This chapter will attempt to codify some of the general information about broadcasting which a production director should know.

The Communications Act

A production director should know the federal regulations governing broadcasting which are pertinent to his job. All government regulation of radio, from a federal point of view, rests upon the Communications Act of 1934, which was passed by the Seventy-Third Congress and approved on June 19 of that year. This act is long and involved and much of it does not concern the production director. What follows is a digest of the pertinent sections which have direct bearing on the production director's job.

Section 3, paragraph C, defines "Licensee" as the holder of a radio station license granted or continued in force under the authority of this act. Paragraph O defines "Broadcasting" as the dissemination of radio communications intended to be received by the public directly or by the intermediary of relay stations. Paragraph T states that "Chain broadcasting" means simultaneous broadcasting of an identical program by two or more connecting stations.

Section 301 stipulates that licenses will be granted by the Commission for broadcasting and that no persons shall use or operate

> an apparatus for the transmission of energy or communications or signals by radio . . . [under any condition] . . . except under and in accordance with this act and with a license in that behalf granted under the provisions of this act.

Section 315 states:

> If any licensee shall permit any person who is a legally qualified candidate for any public office to use a broadcasting station, he shall afford equal opportunities to all other such candidates for that office the use of such broadcasting station, and the Commission shall make rules and regulations to carry this provision into effect: provided, that such licensees shall have no power of censorship over the material broadcast under the provisions of this section. No obligation is hereby imposed upon any licensee to allow the use of this station by any such candidate.

Section 316 says:

> No person shall broadcast by means of any radio station for which a license is required by any law of the United States, and no person operating any such station shall knowingly permit the broadcasting of, any advertisement of or information concerning any lottery, gift enterprise, or similar scheme, offering prizes dependent in whole or in part upon lot or chance, or any list of the prizes drawn or awarded by means of any such lottery, gift enterprise, or scheme, whether said list contains any part or all of such prizes. Any person violating any provision of this section shall, upon conviction thereof, be fined not more than $1000 or imprisoned not more than one year, or both, for each and every day during which such offense occurs.

Section 317 states:

> All matter broadcast by any radio station for which service, money, or any other valuable consideration is directly or indirectly paid, or promised to or charged or accepted by, the station so broadcasting, from any person shall, at the time the same is so broadcast, be announced as paid for or furnished, as the case may be, by such person.

Section 325 states:

> (*a*) No person within the jurisdiction of the United States shall knowingly utter or transmit, or cause to be uttered or transmitted, any false or fraudulent signal of distress or communication relating thereto, nor shall any broadcasting station rebroadcast the program of any other or any part thereof of another broadcasting station without the express authority of the originating station.

Section 326 says:

> Nothing in this act shall be understood or construed to give the Commission a power of censorship over the radio communications or signals transmitted by any radio station, and no regulation or condition shall be promulgated or fixed by the Commission which shall interfere with the right of free speech by means of radio communication. No person within the jurisdiction of the United States shall utter any obscene, indecent, or profane language by means of radio communication.

FCC Regulations Governing Standard Broadcast Services

Sub-part J, paragraph 3.24, states:

> An authorization for a new standard broadcast station . . . will be issued only after a satisfactory showing has been made in regard to the following, among others: . . . (*g*) that the public interest, convenience, and necessity will be served through the operation under the proposed assignment.

This is one of the most quoted of the government regulations because it is the generalized statement which sets forth the major function of all private broadcasting. When a station applies for a new license or for a renewal, it must demonstrate to the Commission that it has been "operating in the public interest, convenience, and necessity."

Paragraph 3.404 reads as follows:

> *Log.* The licensee of each broadcast station shall maintain program and operating logs and shall require entries to be made as follows: (*a*) In a program log: (1) An entry of the time each station identification announcement (call letters and location) is made. (2) An entry of the time the program begins and ends. An indication of the type of program, such

as, "Music," "Drama," "Speech," and so forth, together with the name or title thereof and the sponsor's name, with the time of the beginning and ending of the complete program. If a mechanical record is used, the entries will show the exact nature thereof, such as "Records," "Transcriptions," and so forth, and the name and time it is announced as a mechanical record. If a speech is made by a political candidate, the name and political affiliation of such speaker shall be entered. (3) An entry showing that each sponsored program broadcast has been announced as sponsored, paid for, or furnished by the sponsor.

Paragraph 3.405. *Logs, Retention of.*

Logs of standard or high frequency broadcast stations shall be retained by the licensee for a period of two years, except when required to be retained for a longer period in accordance with the provisions of Section 2.54.

Paragraph 3.406. *Station identification*:

(*a*) A licensee of a standard or high frequency broadcasting station shall make a station identification announcement (call letters and location) at the beginning and ending of each time of operation and during operation (1) on the hour (2) either on the half hour or the quarter hour following the hour and at the quarter hour preceding the next hour: provided, (*b*) such identification announcement need not be made on the hour when to make such an announcement would interrupt a single consecutive speech, play, religious service, symphony concert, or operatic production of longer duration than thirty minutes. In such cases the identification announcement shall be made at the beginning of the program, at the first interruption of the entertainment continuity, and at the conclusion of the program.

(*c*) Such identification announcement need not be made on the half hour or quarter hours when to make such announcement would interrupt a single consecutive speech, play, religious service, symphony concert, or operatic production. In such cases an identification announcement shall be made at the first interruption of the entertainment and at the conclusion of the program: provided, that an announcement within five minutes of the time specified in paragraph (*a*) (2) of this Section will satisfy the requirements of identification announcements.

(*d*) In the case of variety show programs, baseball game broadcasts, or similar programs of longer duration than thirty minutes, the identification announcement shall be made within five minutes of the hour and of the time specified in paragraph (*a*) (2) of this Section.

(*e*) In the case of all other programs the identification announcement shall be made within two minutes of the hour and of times specified in paragraph (*a*) (2) of this Section.

(*f*) In making the identification announcement the call letters shall be given only for the channel of the station identified thereby.

Paragraph 3.407. *Mechanical records.*

Each broadcast program consisting of a mechanical record or a series of mechanical records shall be announced in the manner and to the extent set out below:

(*a*) A mechanical record or a series thereof, of longer duration than thirty minutes, shall be identified by appropriate announcement at the beginning of the program, at each thirty-minute interval, and at the conclusion of the program: provided, however, that the identifying announcement at each thirty-minute interval is not required in case of a mechanical record consisting of a single, continuous, uninterrupted speech, play, religious service, symphony concert, or operatic production of longer duration than thirty minutes.

(*b*) A mechanical record, or a series thereof, of a longer duration than five minutes, and not in excess of thirty minutes, shall be identified by an appropriate announcement at the beginning and end of the program.

(*c*) A single mechanical record of a duration not in excess of five minutes shall be identified by an appropriate announcement immediately preceding the use thereof.

(*d*) In case a mechanical record is used for background music, sound effects, station identification, program identification (scene music or of short duration), or identification of the sponsorship of the program proper, no announcement of the mechanical record is required.

(*e*) The identifying announcement shall accurately describe the type of mechanical record used; i.e., where an electrical transcription is used, it shall be announced as a "transcription" or an "electrical transcription," or as "transcribed" or "electrically transcribed"; where a phonograph record is used, it shall be announced as a "record."

There are a great many other sections in the Communications Act and in the Regulations of the Federal Communications Commission, but the ones set forth here are those which have direct bearing on the work of the production director. It is strongly recommended that anyone working in the field of radio should become fairly familiar with both these sets of documents. Quite naturally, much of the Communications Act and many of the regulations of the Commission have to do with the licensing of stations and their technical operation. These considerations need not be of concern to the production director, but it is always well to be cognizant of the general regulatory measures governing the medium.

Code of Wartime Practices for American Broadcasters

This Code was issued by the Office of Censorship in revised form on February 1, 1943. Since that time changes have been made in the provisions as the progress of the war seemed to indicate, but it essentially remains in force. The first section has to do with news broadcasts and commentaries. It says:

> Broadcasters should edit all news in the light of this Code's suggestions and of their own specialized knowledge, regardless of the medium or means through which such news is obtained.

Special attention is directed to the fact that all the requests in this Code are modified by a proviso that the information listed may properly be broadcast when authorized by appropriate authority. News on all these subjects will become available usually from government sources; but in war, timeliness is an important factor and the government unquestionably is in the best position to decide when disclosure is timely.

It is requested that news in any of the following classifications be kept off the air unless released or authorized for release by appropriate authorities:

Weather. All weather data, either forecasts, summaries,

recapitulations, or any details of weather conditions. [This restriction has since been relaxed and stations are now permitted to broadcast local weather conditions. Local station practice should be checked here.]

Armed Forces. The type and movements of United States Army, Navy, and Marine Corp units, within or without Continental United States, including information concerning location, identity, exact composition, equipment, strength, destination, route, schedules, assembly for embarkation, prospective embarkation, or actual embarkation. Such information regarding troops of friendly nations on American soil is also censored. [There are certain exceptions with which the production director should be familiar, as stated in the Code.]

Ships and Convoys. Types and movements of United States Navy, or merchant vessels, or transports, of convoys, of neutral vessels, or of vessels of nations opposing the Axis powers in any waters, including information concerning identity, location, port of arrival, time of arrival, prospect of arrival, port of departure, ports of call, nature of cargo, assembly, or personnel. The same general restrictions hold for enemy naval or merchant vessels in any waters. Information concerning instructions about sea defenses or ships in construction or advance information on dates of ship launchings or commissionings are all to be kept off the air.

Damage by Enemy Land or Sea Attacks. Information on damage to military objectives in Continental United States or possessions must be kept off the air.

Action at Sea. Information about the sinking or damaging from war causes of war or merchant vessels in any waters must not be broadcast except on the appropriate authority.

Enemy Air Attack. Estimate of numbers of planes involved, number of bombs dropped, and damages of any sort should be kept off the air. It is presumed in the event of such an attack that the release of information through the proper authorities would be made when it was safe.

Accredited Military and Naval Correspondents. No provisions in this Code modify obligations assumed by accredited correspondents who accompany Army and Navy forces or are given special accrediting by the War and Navy Departments to visit restricted areas of the United States. These commitments under War and Navy Department practice pledge such correspondents to submit to censorship anything they write in zones of combat or restriction or what they may write at a later date as a result of their observation in these zones. The military department concerned is the censorship agency for all such material.

Planes. All information concerning air units, military air defenses, and those of the United Nations, including disposition, missions, movements, new characteristics or strength. Information concerning new military aircraft and related items of equipment or detailed information on performance, construction, and armament are all to be withheld until properly released.

Fortifications of Air Installations. The location and descriptions of such fortifications of all sorts should not be broadcast.

Sabotage. Specifications which saboteurs could use to damage war production plants, transportation lines, public utilities, or other military objectives or any information indicating sabotage to them should be withheld from broadcast.

Production. All collected data on a nation-wide scale disclosing production progress or capacity in connection with ordnance, planes, war vehicles, or other munitions must be withheld until released through the proper sources. This same restriction applies to secret designs for war plants and statistics of production.

Unconfirmed Reports, Rumors. The spread of rumors in such a way that they will be accepted as facts will render aid and comfort to the enemy. The same is true of enemy propaganda or material calculated by the enemy to bring about division among the United Nations. Enemy claims of ship sinkings or of other damage to our forces should be weighed carefully and the sources carefully identified if broadcast.

Combat Zone Interviews and Letters. Interviews with service men or civilians from combat zones (including accounts of escapes from foreign territory) should be submitted for a review before broadcast either to the Office of Censorship or the appropriate Army and Navy Public Relations Officer. Letters from service men in combat zones are censored at the source for home and family consumption only. When used on the air, broadcasters should measure the contents of such letters in the light of the provision of this Code.

War Prisoners, Internees, Civilian Prisoners. Information as to arrival, movements, confinements, escapes, or identity of military prisoners from war zones and all other information about this class of people should be withheld from broadcast.

Military Intelligence. Information concerning operations, methods, or equipment of war intelligence or counter-intelligence to the United States or its allies; information concerning available or captured enemy codes or ciphers; or that gained from the interception of enemy messages; or information concerning new secret chemicals or detection of these should be withheld from broadcast.

War News Coming into the United States. War information originating outside United States territory may be broadcast if its origination is made plain.

General. Casualties and casualty lists should not be made available until publication by the War or Navy Departments. Information disclosing the new location of national archives or of public or private art treasures, art objects, or historical data should not be disclosed.

Diplomatic information about the movements of the President of the United States, including advance notice of the place from which he will broadcast; information of official military and diplomatic missions to the United States or of any other nation opposing the Axis powers and all such routes, schedules, and destinations should be withheld.

Restrictions on Programs

Request Programs. No telephone or telegraph requests for musical selections should be accepted. No requests for musical selections made by word of mouth at the origin of broadcast, whether studio or remote, should be honored. No telephone or telegraph requests for service announcements should be honored except as hereinafter qualified. The same precaution should be observed in accepting classified advertisements for broadcasting. No telephone, telegraph, or word-of-mouth dedications or program features or segments thereof should be broadcast. All requests subject to the above qualifications may be honored when submitted by mail or otherwise in writing, if they are held for an unspecified length of time and if the broadcaster staggers the order in which these requests are honored, rewriting any text which may be broadcast.

Quiz Programs. It is requested that all audience-participation type quiz programs originating from remote points, either by wire, transcription, or short wave, should not be broadcast, except as qualified hereinafter. Any program which permits the public access to an open microphone is dangerous and should be carefully supervised. Because of the nature of quiz programs, in which the public is not only permitted access to the microphone but encouraged to speak into it, the danger of usurpation by the enemy is enhanced. The greatest danger here lies in the informal interview conducted in a small group — ten to twenty-five people. In larger groups, where participants are selected from a theater audience, for example, the danger is not so great. Generally speaking, any quiz program originating remotely, wherein the group is small, wherein no arrangement exists for investigating the background of participants and wherein extraneous background noises cannot be eliminated at the discretion of the broadcaster, should not be broadcast.

Forums in Interviews. During forums in which the general public is permitted extemporaneous comment, in which more than two persons participate, and interviews conducted by authorized employees of the broadcasting company, broadcasters should devise methods guaranteeing against release of any information which might aid the enemy as described in Section 1 of the Code. If there is doubt concerning the acceptability of material to be used in interviews, a complete script should be submitted to the Office of Censorship for a review.

Special Events Reporting. Special events reporters should study carefully the restrictions suggested in Section 1 of the Code, especially those referring to interviews and descriptions following enemy offensive action. Reporters and commentators should guard against the use of descriptive material which might be employed by the enemy in plotting an area for attack.

Commercial Continuity. Broadcasters should be alert to prevent the transmission of subversive or restricted information through the use of commercial continuity in programs or in announcements. In this connection, the continuity editor should regard his responsibility as equal to that of the news editor.

Foreign-Language Broadcasts

Personnel. The Office of Censorship, by direction of the President, is charged with the responsibility of removing from the air all those engaged in foreign-language broadcasting who, in the judgment of appointed authorities in the Office of Censorship, endanger the war effort of the United States by their connection, direct or indirect, with the medium.

Scripts. Station managements are requested to require all persons who broadcast in a foreign language to submit to the management in advance of broadcast complete scripts or transcriptions of such material with an English translation. It is further requested that this material be checked "on the air" against the approved script and that no deviation be permitted.

These points are the chief ones to be concentrated on in the broadcasting of war information. The general rule to remember is this: anything can be broadcast which has been released by a proper government authority. In case of doubt, the proper procedure is to get in touch with the local Office of War Information and check the material. Through the organization of regional offices of OWI, this procedure has been greatly facilitated.

The Postal Regulations

While the Post Office Department has no direct control over broadcasting, there is a way in which indirect control is exercised. Whenever broadcasters or listeners use the mails for any reason that is connected with broadcasting, the material sent through the mail must conform to the postal regulations. This means that any broadcast which has a "mail pull" in it must not ask listeners to write in or send in something which is contrary to postal regulations. Whenever a broadcast sponsors any kind of prize contest or competition, the chances are it will involve mailing in answers or entries from listeners, and when this occurs, the broadcaster becomes subject to postal regulations. It is always wise, therefore, to have all proposed contest material checked by the legal authority in the station to be sure that it does not run afoul of postal regulations.

State Laws

It is, of course, impossible to generalize on the subject of state laws as they pertain to broadcasting. The only safe procedure for any production director is to make himself familiar with local state laws which may affect broadcasting. Most broadcasting stations and networks are protected by legal advisers whose business it is to be familiar with these laws. The production director will do well to consult the legal adviser in any case that seems at all doubtful.

Some states regulate the kind of product which can be accepted for advertising and may place restrictions on such things as insurance, hard liquors, beer, cigarettes, or certain medicinal preparations. Some states have laws regarding the conducting of contests. Some regulate the impersonation of an individual, and in at least one state no impersonation can be made without the written consent of the person impersonated.

One of the most widespread problems is that of preventing the making of defamatory statements. Obviously, no broadcaster wants to involve himself in expensive lawsuits for defaming the character of a listener. It is seldom done consciously. In spite of very careful supervision, however, speakers will occasionally say things which may be defamatory and which were not in the script submitted to the station in advance. Under these circumstances the station, as well as the individual making the statement, is usually held responsible. These laws vary widely from state to state and the production director should be familiar with them. If a questionable statement is made on any program, the production director should report it to his superiors immediately, so that proper steps can be taken to protect the station or to make reparation if that is indicated.

No production director can assume that the law is a static thing. It changes from time to time and he must keep himself posted on changes either in federal or state regulations. In any efficiently operated organization it should be the duties of the legal advisers of the station or network to advise production directors as well as others of the changes as they occur, so that the station may conform to the new regulations.

The NAB Code

Radio has done an excellent job of policing itself. Conscious of its public-service nature from the beginning, radio has always been acutely sensitive to its obligations to the public. Early in the history of organized broadcasting, steps were taken toward self-regulation. The recognized organization for the expression of these regulations is the National Association of Broadcasters.

Because the NAB Code is so widely recognized as the base standard of ethical operations, it should be known in its entirety by every production director. Nearly all stations and networks have their own policies on local matters, but many, especially local stations, use the NAB Code as their policy book and note any exceptions which they may make to the regular Code. Since it is such a widely accepted document in the industry, it is reprinted here in its entirety.

The Text of the NAB Code

Adopted by the Atlantic City Convention, July 11, 1939

Recognizing the importance of radio broadcasting in the national life and believing that broadcasters now have had sufficient experience with the social side of the industry to formulate basic standards for the guidance of all, the National Association of Broadcasters hereby formulates and publishes the following revised Code:

Children's Programs. Programs designed specifically for children reach impressionable minds and influence social attitudes, aptitudes, and approaches, and, therefore, they require the closest supervision of broadcasters in the selection and control of material, characterization, and plot.

This does not mean that the vigor and vitality common to a child's imagination and love of adventure should be removed. It does mean that programs should be based upon sound social concepts and presented with a superior degree of craftsmanship; that these programs should reflect respect for parents, adult authority, law and order, clean living, high morals, fair play, and honorable behavior. Such programs must not contain sequences involving horror or torture or use of the supernatural or superstitious or any other material which might reasonably be regarded as likely to overstimulate the child listener, or be prejudicial to sound character development. No advertising appeal which would encourage activities of a dangerous social nature will be permitted.

To establish acceptable and improving standards for children's programs, the National Association of Broadcasters will continuously engage in studies and consultations with parent and child study groups. The results of these studies will be made available for application to all children's programs.

Controversial Public Issues. As part of their public service, networks and stations shall provide time for the presentation of public questions including those of controversial nature. Such time shall be allotted with due regard to all the other elements of balanced program schedules and to the degree of public interest in the questions to be presented. Broadcasters shall use their best efforts to allot such time with fairness to all elements in a given controversy.

Time for the presentation of controversial issues shall not be sold, except for political broadcasts. There are three fundamental reasons for this refusal to sell time for public discussions and, in its stead, providing time for it without charge. First, it is a public duty of broadcasters to bring such discussion to the radio audience regardless of the willingness of others to pay for it. Second, should time be sold for the discussion of controversial issues, it would have to be sold, in fairness, to all with the ability and desire to buy at any given time. Consequently, all possibility of regulating the amount of discussion on the air in proportion to other elements of properly balanced programming or of allotting the available periods with due regard to listener interest in the topics to be discussed would be surrendered. Third, and by far the most important, should time be sold for the discussion of controversial public issues and for the propagation of the views of individuals or groups, a powerful forum would inevitably gravitate almost wholly into the hands of those with the greater means to buy it.

The political broadcasts excepted above are any broadcasts in connection with a political campaign in behalf of or against the candidacy of a legally qualified candidate for nomination or election to public office, or in behalf of or against a public proposal which is subject to ballot. This exception is made because at certain times the contending parties want to use and are entitled to use more time than broadcasters could possibly afford to give away.

Nothing in the prohibition against selling time for the presentation of controversial public issues shall be interpreted as barring sponsorship of the public forum type of program when such a program is regularly presented as a series of fairsided discussions of public issues and when control of the fairness of the program rests wholly with the broadcasting station or network.

Educational Broadcasting. While all radio programs possess some educative values, broadcasters nevertheless desire to be of assistance in helping toward more specific educational efforts, and will continue to use their time and facilities to that end and, in co-operation with appropriate groups, will continue their search for improving applications of radio as an educational adjunct.

News. News shall be presented with fairness and accuracy and the broadcasting station or network shall satisfy itself that the arrangements made for obtaining news insure this result. Since the number of broadcasting channels is limited, news broadcasts shall not be editorial. This means that news shall not be selected for the purpose of furthering or hindering either side of any controversial public issue nor shall it be colored by the opinions or desires of the station or network management, the editor or others engaged in its preparation, or the person actually delivering it over the air, or, in the case of sponsored news broadcasts, the advertiser.

The fundamental purpose of news dissemination in a democracy is to enable people to know what is happening and to understand the meaning of events so that they may form their own conclusions, and, therefore, nothing in the foregoing shall be understood as preventing news broadcasters from analyzing and elucidating news so long as such analysis and elucidation are free of bias.

News commentators as well as all other newscasters shall be governed by these provisions.

Religious Broadcasts. Radio, which reaches men of all creeds and races simultaneously, may not be used to convey attacks upon another's race or religion. Rather it should be the purpose of the religious broadcast to promote the spiritual harmony and understanding of mankind and to administer broadly to the varied religious needs of the community.

Commercial Programs and Length of Commercial Copy. Acceptance of programs and announcements shall be limited to products and services offered by individuals and firms engaged in legitimate commerce; whose products, services, radio advertising, testimonials, and other statements comply with pertinent legal requirements, fair trade practices, and accepted standards of good taste.

Brief handling of commercial copy is recommended procedure at all times.

Member stations shall hold the length of commercial copy, including that devoted to contests and offers, to the following number of minutes and seconds:

Daytime

Fifteen-minute programs 3:15
Thirty-minute programs 4:30
Sixty-minute programs 9:00

Nighttime

Fifteen-minute programs 2:30
Thirty-minute programs 3:00
Sixty-minute programs 6:00

Exceptions:

The above limitations do not apply to participation programs, announcement programs, "musical clocks," shoppers' guides, and local programs falling within these general classifications.

Because of the varying economic and social conditions throughout the United States, members of the NAB shall have the right to present to the NAB for special ruling local situations which in the opinion of the member may justify exceptions to the above prescribed limitations.

TYPES OF UNACCEPTABLE ADVERTISING

Resolution of Program Standards Committee Adopted by Convention

To clarify the phrase "Accepted Standards of Good Taste" and the canons of good practice set forth in the NAB Code, therefore be it resolved, that member stations shall not accept for advertising:

1. Any spirituous or "hard" liquor.
2. Any remedy or other product the sale of which or the method of sale of which constitutes a violation of law.
3. Any fortune-telling, mind-reading, or character-reading, by handwriting, numerology, palm-reading, or astrology, or advertising related thereto.
4. Schools that offer questionable or untrue promises of employment as inducements for enrollment.
5. Matrimonial agencies.
6. Offers of "homework" except by firms of unquestioned responsibility.
7. Any "dopester," tip-sheet, or race-track publications.
8. All forms of speculative finance. Before member stations may accept any financial advertising, it shall be fully ascertained that such advertising and such advertised services comply with all pertinent federal, state, and local laws.
9. Cures and products claiming to cure.
10. Advertising statements or claims member stations know to be false, deceptive, or grossly exaggerated.
11. Continuity which describes, repellently, any functions of symptomatic results of disturbances, or relief granted such disturbances through use of any product.
12. Unfair attacks upon competitors, competing products, or upon other industries, professions, or institutions.
13. Misleading statements of price or value, or misleading comparisons of price or value.

The Code Committee of the National Association of Broadcasters is a continuing and active committee which issues interpretations on the basic code from time to time as exigencies arise which are of industry-wide importance. Production directors should become familiar with the rulings of this policy committee as they come out. Since most stations have an active participation in the NAB, it is quite simple to follow its proceedings and keep up to date on its decisions.

Network and Station Policies

Nearly every station and all networks have some kind of policy book for the guidance of its staff and particularly of its production directors. No two of these policy books are alike, since even major networks do not always agree on certain issues. Therefore, in this chapter it will be impossible to lay down any policies with which a production director should be familiar. At best it can only outline those points on which there is almost certain to be a policy ruling. These may serve to indicate to the uninitiated the kind of information that will be expected of them in the performance of their duties.

Relations with Artists

In most large broadcasting centers actors are organized in their own union, as was mentioned previously. The radio actors' union is called AFRA, the American Federation of Radio Artists, an affiliate of the American Federation of Labor. AFRA operates under a guild shop arrangement. This is not a closed shop, since AFRA agrees to accept as a member any actor or singer whom a broadcasting station wishes to employ except those who are not eligible because of suspension or expulsion from any organization in the Associated Actors and Artists of America. In other words, anyone that the station or network wishes to use may be used, provided he becomes a member of AFRA. AFRA agrees to accept him upon the payment of the entrance fees. The production director should obviously be familiar with the local rules under which AFRA members operate and also the salient points in the contract between AFRA and the station or network. Sound-effects men, singers, and announcers are also organized in AFRA.

If the station is not operating on an AFRA contract, the production director must know the craft scale of payment in effect and the general station policy regarding the use of actors.

Auditions

Holding auditions of all kinds is a regular part of the duties of a production director. He must hold auditions for acting and vocal talent. He may hold auditions for musical groups. He will have to conduct auditions for "house hearings" and also client auditions. "House hearings" are auditions prepared for the program director or program board of a station or network, whereas client auditions are primarily for the benefit of a sales department which is trying to sell a program. Who pays for these auditions, how they are set up, under what conditions they may be made, and the rules for their conduct, are usually subject to the policy of the station.

Continuity

The manner in which continuity is to be handled and the relationship between the production director and the continuity department, so far as routine and special handling of script is concerned, will usually be outlined in the station policy book. In addition to the continuity department, some networks have a continuity acceptance department, which is responsible for the inspection of all commercial copy to see that it conforms to network standards. What part of the continuity work is in the hands of the continuity department and what in continuity acceptance is again a matter of policy and should be known by the production director. Most stations and networks require that all continuity be passed on by one or the other of these departments, and a production director should never broadcast any material which has not had their okay. In emergencies, where it is impossible to submit material to these departments for inspection, the policy book will state the procedure which the production director should follow.

The policy book will undoubtedly contain a great many special rulings regarding continuity which will differ from station to station and network to network, and with which the production director should be familiar. Some of these are matters of network policy. Others are stipulated by the FCC rulings. Still others are, at least currently, in effect because of war conditions.

Music and Musicians

Nearly all musicians who work for broadcasters are members of the American Federation of Musicians, and the same general practices pertain for them as for members of AFRA. There will be a contract between the station or network and the AF of M stipulating minimum pay for all kinds of work, and working conditions, hours, and so forth. In nearly every case there is one person on the station staff designated as the contract man between the station and the union and in any matter requiring special decisions, the contract man should be consulted.

Music is really property just as much as is a house or lot. Whenever a piece of music, which is subject to copyright, is played on the air, it must be played only if permission has been granted to use it and payment made. Nearly all broadcasting stations and networks have some kind of contractual arrangements with certain music licensing organizations, such as the American Society of Composers, Authors, and Publishers, commonly known as ASCAP, and Broadcast Music, Incorporated, BMI. There are also several other licensing organizations. Each station will have some routine for clearing music for use on the air, and the production director must be familiar with these routines and also the procedure in unusual cases. If the station has a music library or a librarian, he will usually be in charge of clearing all music. In the case of networks, there is ordinarily one central point where all music must be cleared. In the National Broadcasting Company all music must be cleared through the Music Rights Division in New York. Only by having a central clearing-house can duplication and confusion be avoided.

Whatever the contractual relations and whatever the contract the station has, these must be known and general policies regarding music and musicians must be completely familiar to the production director. With music, as with other factors in the broadcast picture, emergencies will arise from time to time which are apparently not covered by the policy book. In all such cases the production director should know to what member of the staff he should turn for information and help.

Policies on Political Broadcasts

Political broadcasts are usually a thorn in the flesh of broadcast stations. They fall outside of the regular business arrangements of most commercial broadcasts and therefore have to have special policy arrangements. Most stations and networks protect themselves by a preceding and closing announcement stating that the speaker takes full responsibility for what he says and that the station or network does not in any way endorse any candidate, and then let him say what he will. Policy varies widely, however, and the local practice should be one of the things thoroughly understood by the production director. In case of any doubt, it is always wise to consult with the production manager or program director and shift responsibility to his shoulders. Radio has, so far, remained remarkably clear of political control and most station managers fight to keep it that way. To that end the policy book will probably make fairly definite statements regarding political programs.

Recordings

Stations usually have a strict policy governing the making and playing of recordings and transcriptions on the air. This business is all tied up, not only with the Federal Communications Commission, but with contracts with the AF of M, and needs to be handled carefully. Most stations are equipped with recording equipment, and many programs, which cannot be carried locally at the time they are offered on networks, are recorded for rebroadcast in local schedules at a convenient time. In most network operations this involves getting special permission. In any matter concerning commercial recordings or transcriptions, or transcriptions cut by the station or network itself, there will be policy rulings governing procedure.

Remotes

The handling of remote broadcasts in a local station may not be much of a problem. Most local stations do not use many remote pickups, or, if they do, they tend to be regular features on the station schedule and routines are clearly outlined. In network operation, however, many remote pickups are scheduled in every day's broadcasting. Networks pick up many different points during a day, which means that a production director and an appropriate staff must go out to the point of origination of the program and see that it is properly sent back to a central division point for distribution to the network. Whenever a broadcast originates outside a studio where regular facilities are provided for broadcasting, dangers of misunderstandings and mishaps increase. Therefore, policy books are usually very specific about the method of handling a remote program. Whatever the local rulings may be where the production director is working, they should be strictly adhered to.

Sales Policies

A station's policies regarding commercial programs are often the most complicated and stringent of all policy matters. These will have to do with such things as program acceptance, courtesy announcements, cross-reference announcements, rules for contests, prize offers to be made over the air, audience mail, guest artists, the introduction of controversial subjects, and the reference by clients to legislation or pending legislation. Policy statements are sometimes also made regarding the use of studios, the setting-up of advertising displays in the studio by the client, the provision and use of client observation and audition rooms, and so forth. All these, and many other matters having to do with commercial programs and the relationship between stations, advertising agencies, and clients, will be the subject of statements in the policy book of the station.

News Policies

Many stations have no policies regarding news other than those set forth in the NAB Code and such policies as may be dictated by rulings of the Federal Communications Commission or currently by the War Censorship Committee. Others, however, have a fairly detailed set of policies to which they insist that all news programs adhere. In general, during the war, there has been a tightening of the control of news programs by stations and networks. Sponsors and clients have been more definitely told what they can and cannot do with a news program and few exceptions are being made. This is in line with the public's interest in the war news and the terrific responsibility which a broadcasting station assumes in the dissemination of news.

The most common provision in such policy statements is that there shall be a distinct separation between news copy and commercial copy on the program. Any writing of commercial copy which tends to give it a news flavor is usually discouraged. Also copy which tends to blend news into commercials is discouraged by most stations. Many stations insist on a strictly hands-off policy so far as the client is concerned in all matters except his commercials. In other words, the client shall have no jurisdiction at all over the news part of the program; this remains the responsibility of the station and network. There are many other more specific rulings in effect in nearly all networks and in most stations. The production director, of course, should be familiar with these restrictions and rules and see that they are obeyed in programs which come under his direction.

Finally, nearly every broadcasting organization will have a set of general policies which govern the kind of material which is acceptable and the kind which is not. Policy statements will also be made regarding office and studio routines, pay for employees, working hours and conditions, and so on. A policy may even be set forth regarding relations with studio visitors and guests and with their appearance on programs.

One final warning should be made to all beginning production directors in regard to policies. They are fluid things. No production director can read through the station policy book and assume that he knows all there is to know about them. They change in details from week to week and month to month. Certainly, it is the duty of the production manager or program manager to see that all production directors are informed of changes of policy or the addition of new statements to the policy book. It is easy, however, for the production director, in the press of his work, to assume that things are now the way they were last week or last month or last year, when executive orders may have been issued in the meantime which either alter policy or add new policy statements. The production director should constantly be on the alert for such changes and new additions.

General Information

Aside from the stringent rules and regulations which broadcasting is heir to, there is much generalized information which every production director should know. He should know, among other things, of the basic principles upon which his station or network operates. There are many tricks in the operation of a large network and these all affect network affiliated stations. The production director should be thoroughly familiar with all the routines both of production and engineering which may affect the programs for which he is responsible.

A good production director should have considerable knowledge of the organization and function of other departments with which he must work. If he knows something about radio writing and the problems involved in writing continuity and dramatic script, he will be not only more sympathetic and understanding with the continuity department's problems, but he can also be directly helpful to them and to himself. This same thing holds true for every other department in the station or network. If he understands the functions and problems of the press department, he can be of considerable help in boosting the station's publicity. If he understands the engineering problems involved in daily operation, he can be much more helpful here. And so it is with each department with which he may work. The more he knows, the more useful he can be and the better he can do his job.

CHAPTER 15

PRODUCTION DIRECTING AS A CAREER

THIS BOOK has been designed primarily for the student and the reader who has a serious interest in directing in the field of radio. Long before this, the question will have arisen in the reader's mind, "Where does such work go on?" Even more pertinent may be the question, "How can I get a job doing production directing?" And as one begins to think in vocational terms, many other questions crowd in. How many people are needed in this field? What is the chance for new blood? What is the road in? How much does it pay? What kind of life does it involve? What is likely to be the future of this profession? All these and a dozen more are pertinent questions which the student may well ask. An answer to all these questions will be attempted here.

Vocational Opportunities

The first obvious question is, "Who uses production directors?" The answer to that will be determined by how stringently one wishes to define the term "production director." If one chooses to be very strict in the interpretation of the term, there are only two kinds of organizations that hire production directors – the networks and the advertising agencies. If one rephrases the question to read, "Where does production directing go on?" the field opens up much more. No really complete answer can be given which will thoroughly represent the professional production director unless it is made to include all the places where production directing occurs, rather than just those places where people are hired with the title of production director.

All the network programs originating in the United States among the four major networks are produced by less than a hundred and seventy men. In other words, that figure represents the approximate number of professional network radio production directors. It seems, at first glance, like a very small number indeed. It makes the directing fraternity a very exclusive one. On the other hand, that figure represents more people than are actively engaged in producing and directing plays on Broadway. When one considers the stringent requirements of a production director and the years it takes to make a good one, that is not so small a number as it seems. When one considers the vast number of network programs which are broadcast every day, however, it does appear to be a great deal of work to be supervised by such a small body of men.

Advertising agencies, of which there are some hundred and twenty-five in this country with radio accounts, need and use production directors. There are more production directors working for advertising agencies than for networks. The reason for this is that directors seldom work on more than one or two programs when they are in the employment of an advertising agency. It is understood, of course, that advertising agencies build within their own offices nearly all the commercial radio programs that air over the network; that is to say, the advertising agency engages a director, hires a cast, a writer, and an announcer. The network furnishes directing supervision, studios, facilities, sound effects, and engineering. For this reason advertising agencies employ a great many production directors and this is the ultimate goal which many production directors seek — a job on a big commercial program with an advertising agency.

Although no exact figures are available, it has been estimated that there are some four hundred production directors in the employment of advertising agencies, either directly on the payroll or on a free-lance basis.

Only in the networks, the regional networks, and the advertising agencies does one find the peculiar job which is described as radio production directing. A great deal of production directing, however, goes on in many other branches of radio. It may be done by an announcer, by a program director, or a college professor, but it is still production directing. If the term is used broadly enough, it is safe to say that production directing occurs wherever radio occurs and even in some places where broadcasting itself does not occur.[1] Certainly a considerable amount of direction goes on in local stations. This is often of a somewhat amateur sort and is usually done by the announcing staff or some other member of the station personnel. Nevertheless, on almost any program except, possibly, a program which is all transcribed, some production directing goes on. The larger the station and the larger the station's staff, the more nearly this work approaches what is more commonly thought of as production directing in network terms. A few large clear-channel stations even maintain people on their staff whose primary business it is to direct and produce radio programs. It is still, alas, almost a nonexistent occupation in low-power local stations.

With the increase in interest in the subject of radio in high schools, colleges, and universities throughout the United States, and with the increasing number of school broadcasts, there has been a correspondingly increasing amount of production directing going on in schools and colleges. Much of this is purely amateur work which is done either for the love of it or as a part of university or college programs in adult education and public relations. In some isolated instances the work is a definite part of the operation of an educational station and is truly professional in its approach.

There are a surprising number of amateur groups around the United States who engage in the business of broadcasting. Some of these groups have their own directors who do very creditable work. Others turn to the station for help, and members of the station staff, still on an amateur basis, co-operate with the groups and furnish direction for their efforts and activities. Many cities have very active "little theater" groups who broadcast frequently on their local station. Many other cities have a program of public-service broadcasting where such

[1] This is true of making transcriptions, audition records, and several other types of work.

groups as the Community Chest, the Boy Scouts, the YMCA and others do regular programs on the air which require supervision. In all these places production directing is going on, on an amateur basis.

There is one final place where the production director functions. There are a few specialized sponsors and groups who hire a director individually to be responsible for a program in which that individual sponsor or group may be interested. In some cases they simply pay a stipend to a member of a local station staff to do the job. In other cases they may pay quite a large fee to a successful professional director to handle their program for them.

In all these places, then, production directing goes on. In some instances it is work done for the fun of it; in others, it is highly paid professional work. Naturally, everyone who has an interest in production directing as a profession hopes some day to do professional work and to earn his living that way. It is only natural that this should be so. This does not, however, prevent those people in less highly paid jobs and even in nonprofessional positions from gaining a great deal of pleasure out of the work they do and making a real contribution to radio.

How many paid jobs are there? This question can be answered only with an estimate, since most of the surveys that have been made cover only stations and networks, leaving out one of the very important sources of employment, the advertising agency. They also leave out jobs in all the other categories mentioned. The stations and networks employ about seven hundred people who are concerned with the business of producing programs. There are possibly two thousand people in the United States who have some more or less legitimate claim to the title of production director in the field of radio. This does not, certainly, represent a vocation that is very attractive in terms of the number of jobs available. Many small manufacturing plants will employ that many people under one roof. Whether the number of opportunities in this field will greatly increase or decrease in the future, no one has any way of knowing. The best minds in the industry seem to feel that radio is in for a considerable period of expansion during the next fifteen years. If this estimate proves to be true, then certainly there will be increased opportunities for production directors. More jobs will be available, and if more people are not ready to fill those jobs, the salaries will inevitably go up, following the law of supply and demand.

Certainly anyone interested in radio production directing as a profession should recognize the cold hard fact that there are not a great number of jobs available. It must also be recognized that there are very few trained production directors in the United States to take the jobs, and as more people are needed, the need for production directors will become more acute. Although over six hundred colleges and universities offer some radio courses, very few of them offer a course in production directing, and still fewer can offer practical experience which might result in turning out students who are at least ready for an apprenticeship in the job of directing radio programs. The result is that even though there are very few jobs in the field in comparison with many other businesses and industries, there is at the present a shortage of good production directors. This should be very encouraging to the student who is interested in this field of work.

What are the opportunities for new people coming into this field? Only a generalized answer is possible. It seems fairly safe to say that excellent opportunities are available for new people coming into the field of production directing. This is especially true right now because of the tremendous dislocation which radio personnel has suffered from war depletion. This situation, however, cannot be considered in a long-term view because it is an abnormal one created by the times. It is also a situation which is shared by every other kind of business and industry. A sponsor looking for a director would naturally prefer to use someone who has already made a reputation for himself. This is only right and natural. Since the demand, however, does now exceed the supply, there is good opportunity for young people coming in.

One thing is very encouraging in the situation from the

vocational point of view. Age is not considered important. There is no reason why a comparatively young man may not be considered for a responsible position. Nor, conversely, is advanced age considered a serious handicap.

Training

The reader will now probably ask himself, "How do I become a production director? What previous experience is required? What is the road in?" Unfortunately, there is no answer. If this question were to be asked of executives of the production or program department of a network or of the radio director of an advertising agency, the answer would probably come back, "We don't know. What have you done?" The fact that no hard-and-fast specifications have as yet been set down, for the apprenticeship to the job is both a help and a hindrance to the neophyte. It means that a prospective employer may not necessarily say no to him because he has had no specific background or preparation, and on the other hand, it gives him very little notion of where to go or how to set about gaining the experience and background which would make him eligible.

The one requisite which seems to be more common than any other is station experience. As has already been pointed out in this book, very little production directing which is called that goes on in the local or even in the regional station. Therefore, at first glance it seems a little odd that station experience should be required as a prerequisite to production directing. The reader, however, who has read the chapter outlining the general information which the production director should have, can see some good reasons for a background of experience. Though working in a local station may not give the candidate actual experience in production directing of the kind which he may encounter in a network and advertising agency, it does at least give him a thorough grounding in the fundamentals of broadcast operations. The smaller the station, the more catholic will be the experience which the beginner gets. Large organizations tend to be departmentalized. Small organizations are much more fluid and flexible and every member of the staff is required to double in brass. This process of doing everything from writing continuity to selling time is as good preparation as possible for more advanced and specialized work. Any specialist who is worth his salt should build his specialization on a broad and firm foundation of basic principles in his craft.

Having made the one stipulation of station experience, the people who hire production directors will from that time on look at what an applicant has done rather than at specific qualifications. Because there is yet no training ground for the preparation of production directors, networks and advertising agencies try to find their people where they can. They have in the past taken directors out of the theater. A few directors have come to radio from Hollywood and motion pictures. Others have come from the ranks of the announcing or sound-effects staff of a station or network. Many have come in through music. There are many directors who have simply stumbled in and cannot now tell you how or why they were first admitted to the fraternity.

Since prospective employers are seldom willing to commit themselves on the kind of training they would prefer in applicants for production jobs, the person planning to enter that field must depend chiefly on self-education. Chapter 2 deals in considerable detail with the characteristics and backgrounds desirable for a production director. Failing to find the place where this kind of background and training is offered in the form of courses given for credit, the only thing which remains is to prepare oneself for the job. This is, of course, the hardest kind of education to obtain, because what the student more often lacks than any other thing is the self-discipline necessary to keep going along a given line.

In spite of the fact that networks and advertising agencies have a great need for directors and no ready source of supply, they have done nothing about creating a training ground for them. They have been so busy with the day-to-day process of creating programs and getting them on the air that they have failed to provide a source for new talent. They are now beginning to realize that talent must be sought and trained. As this realization grows, the industry will begin to formulate certain standards of requirements and to co-operate more fully in the training of people to meet their personnel and talent needs.

As the situation now stands, a student wishing to enter the field of radio production direction should, if possible, do these three things:

1. Get as good and as broad a general college education as possible.
2. Take advantage of whatever professional courses are offered in the field.
3. Spend at least two years working in local and regional stations at whatever kinds of jobs are available for which the student has any talent at all.

The more kinds of station situations in which the student can project himself and the more kinds of jobs he can do, the better will be his preparation. If the student will add to all this a rigid self-training program in the development of those characteristics and skills which were discussed in Chapter 2 of this book, he will have given himself the best preparation which it is now possible to have for the business he hopes to enter.

Earning Expectancy

Those interested in any field of work want to know how much it pays. They wish to know, and rightly so, what their earning expectancy may be in that field. Naturally, like any other work the compensation for directing work varies considerably. Beginning production directors may expect to command a salary of about fifty to sixty-five dollars a week. The ceiling for successful production directors who have arrived and are safely ensconced in good agency jobs may be up to thirty thousand dollars a year. Obviously both of these amounts represent extremes. The average production director can probably have a salary expectancy of between six and ten thousand dollars per year. These are only the vaguest estimates, but since there is such a variation in the earnings of production directors, as there will always be among all artists, this is as close an approximation as can be attempted.

Compensation for production directing is very fairly commensurate with the pay in similar professional fields. Production directors rarely achieve the fabulous salary figures that seem to be bandied about in Hollywood. On the other hand, very few competent production directors are ever out of work or fall much below the minimum figures mentioned here. It seems fair to say that the pay is good for this kind of work. Certainly it is considerably above the average national income!

Working Conditions

What kind of life is it? This question may seem very unimportant, indeed, to the young person looking at the glamorous business of radio broadcasting. Stardust and artistic ideals get all mixed up in the aspirations of the person approaching radio for the first time and very often the hard practical questions of day-to-day existence seem comparatively unimportant. The beginner may feel that no price is too great to pay for success in his chosen work. This is an attitude which wears thin with the passing of time. After one has worked in radio for a time, the hard practical questions of living and working conditions come to the fore. Just what are these living and working conditions for the production director in radio?

Compared to many kinds of theatrical life, the way of life for a production director may be easy indeed. To begin with, he will usually have a job. Contrasted with the free-lance actor who is dependent on day-to-day calls for his income, the production director ordinarily works either on a salary or on a contract which runs over a fairly long period. His times "at liberty" are generally few and far between. In spite of the rather high turnover in jobs in the field, there is still a considerable amount of security. Most of the turnovers in the field are due to advancements and promotions rather than to people being let out completely from their work. It is commonly possible to work at the job of production directing and lead a normal, fairly orderly home life while doing it. Compared with the actor who must follow the jobs wherever they are, the production director can lead a comparatively normal and stationary existence if he chooses. It is true that programs do shift around and it is often desirable for a production director to follow a program if it has to be shifted. There is always a certain amount of shuffling around between Chicago and New York and Hollywood, but this is much less in extent than may appear on the surface. It is also true that there are certain programs which travel around the country and which put the production director in the position of working on "road show." These are fairly infrequent, however, and for the most part the production director can "settle down" if he so desires.

Working conditions are usually good. The hours are not long as compared with many kinds of work. It is true that the production director is very unlikely to draw a conventional "nine-to-five" schedule which he can count on day after day. After all, broadcasting begins early in the morning, and it ends late at night. A typical broadcast day runs from six-thirty in the morning until one o'clock the following morning. The production director may and probably will draw a program anywhere within this time range. It is not unusual that a director may have a late night show on Monday and an early breakfast show on Tuesday morning. His schedule will almost certainly be irregular and often unpleasantly bunched together. There is no need, however, for him to work a large total of hours per week. Because of the nature of broadcast schedules, he will spend a comparatively small part of his day actually working. The times and the split hours between programs mean that, although a working day may be long, the working hours are comparatively short.

Much of the work of production directing is routine. There is a great deal more of it which is very exacting indeed. It is a job that inevitably demands the expenditure of a considerable amount of nervous energy, because the production director is, after all, in a position of high responsibility. No matter how calm an individual may be, this sense of responsibility is wearing on the nerves. The necessity for working at high speed under great pressure when the production director actually is working calls for a tremendous expenditure of nervous energy, and the working day is not easy. But if he likes his work, the time flies quickly. It is possible to do much less really hard work in a week than the beginner might suppose. Because of the expenditure of nervous energy and because of the fact that in broadcasting no excuses are made for fatigue, a director must be physically and mentally fresh to do his best work. It is impossible to maintain this freshness if he tries to do too much. A two-hour rehearsal at a given time may be a hard and full day's work. On other kinds of programs the director may be able to do five programs in a day and end up comparatively fresh. How hard the work actually turns out to be depends entirely on the type of program and the intensity with which the production director works.

The Future of the Profession

What about the future of the profession? Is it likely to grow in importance or decrease? Again we enter the field of pure conjecture where one person's guess is as good as another's. No one quite knows what the future holds for radio, primarily because of the great looming question mark of television. Certainly it is safe to say that, if we think of television as a part of the business of broadcasting, the place of the production director is secure in the immediate future at least. It is the author's personal conviction that the two most important people in a broadcast are the author of the material and the director who sees that it gets on the air properly. Neither of these two is being given his full degree of importance in present-day radio. Emphasis still seems to remain on the stars and individual performers. No one can deny the importance of talent in broadcasting. If the singers, the actors, the comedians, the masters of ceremonies, are not capable workmen and good artists, radio will suffer severely. It is the author's conviction, however, that radio could more easily do without good performance talent than it could without good writers and directors. Where there is a creative artist who has something to say, either in words or in music, and a director who is interested in taking that material and delivering it in an effective way to the public, there will always be talent available to make that delivery possible. As long as good scripts are written and good scores put on paper, the miracle of translation into the magic of sound will somehow be effected, and that is the job of the production director.

If these premises are sound, there will inevitably be a growing recognition of the importance of writers and directors, and as this recognition grows, their lot will improve. And as it improves, the future of the profession of radio production directing will be assured.

So far production directors have been covered with a blanket of anonymity. Networks and advertising agencies alike seem to feel that the director is a workman instead of an artist. The author believes firmly that radio will never achieve its ultimate importance until the business of radio looks upon the director as a creative artist and allows him the freedom which he needs to do his best work. Most of the distinguished work which radio can boast to date has been the result of a happy meeting between an excellent creative writer and a good director on the same program. This statement is not meant in any way to detract from the magnificent job which radio talent has done in the past and will continue to do in the future. It simply means that this talent, no matter how fine it may be, is an incomplete entity until it is given something worth while to do and direction which allows it to do its best job. Talent has always been the featured part of show business. It probably will always continue to be, so far as the public is concerned. But behind the scenes the author predicts that there will be increased recognition of the important place which the director fills in the radio scheme of things. If this recognition comes about, the future for the profession is indeed a bright one. Never in the world was there such a magnificent opportunity.

Here, then, is radio. and this book has been dedicated to

the men who direct its programs and to the future generations of new directors. They will start from the point at which we have now arrived and go on from there to new methods and new levels of artistic achievement of which we can now only dream.

APPENDIX

STUDENT PROBLEMS AND PROJECTS

Chapter IV

1. Using an oscillator to generate pure sound, run a test on the microphones in your studio. See if you can discover a difference in frequency response range among the various types of microphones available.

2. By moving the sound source around in relation to the beam of the microphones, make a rough pattern of the directional qualities of the microphones available in your studios.

3. Examine the treatment of your studios for sound isolation and write an estimate of its effectiveness. Does sound come through the walls, the ceiling, the floors or windows? How are the doors treated to exclude exterior sound?

4. Test the effectiveness of the sound absorption in the studio. Are there "boomy" spots. Are there very dead spots? As a result of your tests, write recommendations for improving the sound absorption characteristics of your studio.

5. Examine your control room so that you are able to locate the mixer panels, pre-amplifiers, line amplifiers, monitor amplifiers patch block.

6. Learn all the possible combinations of connections available on the patch block. If there are normals in the connections, learn these.

7. Work with the mixer panel until you are proficient at "riding gain."

8. Examine the available turntables. If they are dual speed tables, learn how to change them from one speed to another. Use the tables and practice cueing in recordings until you can play records with no noise and no time lags between cues.

9. Examine the recording equipment and learn how to use it. Make test recordings under the supervision of the teacher.

10. Make a studio set-up and actually test all the microphones necessary for:

a. A program of recorded music, with announcer.

b. A dramatic program needing a cast microphone, a sound microphone, and recorded sound and music.

Chapter V

1. Examine and list all the manual sound effects available in your studios.

2. Examine and list all the recorded sound effects available in your record library.

3. Work out and execute a sound routine to tell an audience:

a. That a man walks across a sidewalk, up wooden steps, across a porch, and opens a screen door.

b. That two people cross the sidewalk, get into a car, and drive away.

4. Work out and execute a background sound pattern that will establish the locale of:

a. Times Square in New York.

b. The inside of a busy grocery store.

c. The interior of a large transport plane in flight.

5. Work out and execute the background sound for a horror story which would set the locale as inside the laboratory of a sinister scientist.

6. Create a scene backing sound effect for a fantasy program that will give an audience the impression that the entire scene is taking place under water.

7. Take a script assigned by the instructor and work out the complete sound handling for the entire program.

Chapter VI

Find in the recording or transcription library of music a fifteen second passage of music suitable for:

1. Theme on a program to be called "Adventures in Science" sponsored by a large university.

2. A ten-second spot that could be used for a transition cue

between two exciting, action-paced scenes in a dramatic program.

3. A ten second spot in which music is imitating a train.

4. Find a short cue that might be "placid water" music.

5. Find a good ten second fanfare that would "pay off" a comedy sequence in a variety program.

Chapter IX

In producing and listening to class assignments, two facts should always be kept in mind. First, every assignment should be approached from a completely professional point of view. No "make-believe" should be permitted. Every assignment should be regarded as a potential program for actual broadcast. Second, class critics should always watch for production aspects of the assignment as much as possible and ignore the other factors that might influence the quality of the programs.

1. Design and produce a talk from your school that will interest the local station. Aim it at a night audience of adults, men and women. Here are some suggestions:

Find a student who has an unusual background of personal experience or who has done an unusual job. Get that student to write a thirteen minute speech. Produce it in your studio and record it. Play it back, listen for flaws and rework it. Try to place it on your local station.

Select a current topic on which the general public might be interested in a student's point of view. Find a speaker and produce the program.

Find a capable student to review one of the new books. Produce it.

2. Arrange to produce one speech from the next debate on the schedule. Arrange for the debate to take place close to your studios so you can run lines to it, but do not do it in the studios. Make this a remote job. Perhaps you can use the portable public address system amplifier to pipe it to your studios, or arrange to hold the debate in a neighboring classroom or auditorium from which you can run lines direct.

The problem here, in addition to producing a good speech,

is to do it outside of the studios and make your broadcast fit into the framework of an already scheduled event. Your problem is to start the program exactly at the scheduled program time, to present an opening and the first speaker, do a close, and return the program to the studio exactly at a prearranged time.

3. Work out a design for a series of talks that conforms to these requirements:

a. A series in which you can vouch for the contents.

b. For which talent is available in your school situation. (No make-believe here. Make it a realistic situation.)

c. Subject matter that might be of interest to the general public as well as to students in your school. Make it have actual broadcast possibilities.

d. Outline subject and general content of the first six programs.

e. Pick six possible speakers and justify your choice.

f. Work out and produce number one in the series. Record it and submit it for class criticism.

g. Revise it after the play-back and see if you can place it on the air.

4. Arrange an interview program with some member of the faculty or student body on a subject that would have interest to the general public listening on Saturday afternoon or Sunday. Work out the program and transcribe it.

5. Arrange an interview with some member of the team or with one of the coaches of whatever sport is in season. Arrange all production details and make a transcription of your program for class criticism.

6. Arrange a man-on-the-street program using students. Query them on a subject in which there might be general interest in the student body.

7. Using the members of your class as audience and talent, design and produce either a quiz program or a spelling bee, thirty minutes long. Reserve a few members of the class to stay out of the studio and ask them to listen objectively as audience.

8. Design and produce an amateur show from your production class, using whatever acts are available. Several of the same acts may be used by different student production directors, because the emphasis of interest is in production. Make ample arrangements and plans, but no rehearsal (since this assignment is designed to train the student to meet emergencies) and produce and record the program.

Some members of the class may act as studio audience. Others should be reserved as listeners who hear the program objectively, as broadcast.

9. Design and produce a studio party in which you call on a studio audience to amuse itself and the listeners by playing games, doing stunts. Again use some of the class for studio audience. Reserve part of the class to listen objectively and record the results.

10. Set up a round table program out of available talent in your school around a topic in which you think the general public will be interested in the student point of view. Produce and record it for class criticism. See if you can interest the local station in the program.

Talks Programs
Production Check Sheet

1. Evaluation of the content (Script)

a. Did the topic interest you very much .. mildly .. not at all ..

b. Would the topic interest the audience for which it was designed .. very much .. mildly .. not at all ..

c. Was the topic well stated .. passably stated .. poorly stated ..

d. Was there any violation of station policy? Yes .. No ..

e. Were all terms and ideas clearly defined? Yes .. No ..

f. Was a suitable opening and close provided? Yes .. No ..

2. Evaluation of the Production Analysis

a. Did the program seem to have a definite purpose? Yes .. No ..

b. Was there unity to the material? Yes .. No ..

c. Was there evidence that the production director had complete mastery of his materials? Yes .. No .. Some ..

3. Evaluation of the talent

a. Were the guests well chosen? Yes .. No .. Fairly ..

b. Were voices of speakers good? Yes .. No .. Average ..

c. Could speakers be understood easily? Yes .. No .. Average ..

d. Was there good contrast between speaker's voices? Yes .. No .. Fair ..

e. Were balances properly maintained? Yes .. No .. Most of the time ..

f. Was the staff well chosen? Yes .. No .. Fairly ..

4. Estimate of the rehearsal period

a. Did the program flow smoothly? Yes .. No .. Fairly ..

b. Was it stale from over-rehearsal? Yes .. No .. Slightly ..

c. Had technical details been completely settled? Yes .. No..

5. Evaluation of the handling of the broadcast

a. Was talent held to the subject? Yes .. No .. Fairly well ..

b. Did the program run smoothly, without apparent flaws? Yes .. No .. If no, what were the errors?......

c. Was timing properly controlled? Yes .. No ..

d. Was the pick-up good? Yes .. No ..

e. Was the studio arrangement good .. Poor ..

f. Were there technical difficulties? Yes .. No .. What? ..

g. Were there dead spots in the program? Yes .. No ..

h. Did speakers or participants seem at ease? Yes - No ..

i. Was there a summary? Yes .. No ..

j. Were relationships with guests well managed? Yes .. No ..

k. Were emergencies handled smoothly? Yes .. No .. None occurred ..

6. Over-all considerations

a. How much of the content did you remember after the broadcast? Most .. Some .. Little .. None ..

b. Would the intended audience have listened? Yes .. No .. In spots ..

c. General impression left by the program. Well done .. Adequately done .. Poorly done ..

d. What grade would you give to the program? ....

Chapter X

1. Design and build a program of recorded music to the following specifications:

a. Fifteen minutes in length

b. Slant it to a high school popular-music-loving audience.

c. Use music by the same orchestra, throughout, including theme.

The student should choose the music, spot all recordings, supervise the writing of the script by a member of the script writing class if one is in session, or write the script himself. He will select a staff consisting of a turntable operator and an engineer from the production class and an announcer from the class in announcing and actually produce the program.

2. Design, build and produce a program of recorded music to the following specifications:

a. Thirty minutes in length

b. Slant it to an evening all-age audience.

c. Build it around the great musical comedy favorites of all times.

Follow the procedure outlined above and actually produce the program. Fellow members of the production class, not engaged in helping with the program, will listen and make critical comments on the basis of the check sheet at the end of this chapter.

3. Design, build and produce a recorded music program meeting the following specifications:

 a. Fifteen minutes in length
 b. Designed for an audience of older people.
 c. Suitable for broadcast at 10.00 P.M.
 d. Of a quiet, reminiscent nature.

Follow the procedure outlined above.

4. Build a program featuring the campus or school dance band. Confer with whatever local dance band group is available. Lay out a routine, plan to rehearse it in a regular manner. Call the band into the studios and carry through the regular procedure of building a live-music program. See if you can get an outlet on the local station.

5. Build a program featuring the campus or school choir or glee club. Follow the procedure outlined above.

6. Enlist the cooperation of the music school or music department and plan to make a pick-up of the full symphony orchestra. Spend all the time possible in balancing the orchestra for a proper pick-up in the surroundings available, whatever they may be. Again, see if you can arrange an outlet for such a program over the local station.

Other assignments of a similar nature may be made, depending on the talent available in the local situation. Two aims should always be kept in mind. Nothing should be approached as a class exercise. In each case, *plan the program for air!* Evaluate it on the basis of actual broadcast. Excuse nothing because it is a "class exercise." No good can be accomplished. Second, try to place as many of the programs thus built on the local station as possible. Union restrictions and all other kinds of difficulties may be encountered, but try for it anyway. Students learn best by doing. Each of these assignments will have to be repeated for each student in the production class, some of them several times. Keep thinking up new program ideas and slants so that class interest does not lag before everyone in the class has had a chance at each kind of program. After all, students' success will finally be measured in their ability to come up with something interesting and different. Here is a good place to begin.

A Critical Check Sheet of Music Programs

1. Will the program appeal to the audience for which it was designed? Yes .. No .. Why?
2. Was the selection of music
   a. Appropriate? Yes .. No ..
   b. Homogeneous? Yes .. No ..
   c. Varied? Yes .. No ..
   d. Was the order right? Yes .. No ..
3. Was the continuity good?
   a. Was it original? Yes .. No ..
   b. Was it suitable? Yes .. No ..
   c. Was it consistent? Yes .. No ..
4. Was the production smooth? Yes .. No ..
5. Were the balances good? *a.* Between voice and music? Yes .. No .. (In case of live music) *b.* Between various parts of the group? Yes .. No ..
6. Were cues clean and understandable? Yes .. No ..
7. Were levels satisfactory? Yes .. No ..
8. Was the program on time? Yes .. No ..
9. Was the over-all pace good? Yes .. No ..
10. Did the director get the most out of his talent? Yes .. No ..

Suggestions for changes:..............................

....

....

....

Chapter XI

1. Build and produce a fifteen minute news program slanted toward the students of your school. Use the editorial staff of

the school newspaper as your source of copy. Select your announcer, time the copy and produce the program.

2. Lay out all the plans for broadcasting a sporting event of your school. Prepare all copy for filler and background material. Get all the necessary information ready in advance. Select announcers, assistants, spotters, etc. Plan the location and use of all equipment including lines and engineering help needed. If equipment — even public address equipment — is available, carry out and produce the assignment.

Chapter XII

1. Edit an original script for production.

The best possible kind of script to use for this assignment is one written in the radio writing class in your own school. If there is no such class, perhaps scripts can be obtained from your local radio station. Failing this, use scripts from some of the anthologies of scripts available. The instructor will confer with the student on these assignments and make comments. This assignment should be repeated until the student is able to make a producible script out of the material given him.

2. Write out a complete production analysis on this same script. This analysis should include all of the following items:

a. The aim or end result desired from the show.

b. What type of drama is it?

c. Indicate the production approach.

d. Outline the structure.

e. Indicate the kind of talent needed.

f. Select try-out places in the script.

g. Decide on staff needed.

h. Draw a rough sketch of the studio showing disposition of equipment and personnel.

i. Indicate in the sketch mike placement, type and angling.

j. Estimate rehearsal time needed and work out a work schedule for every minute of the rehearsal time.

k. Make a complete line-by-line description of the sound treatment.

l. Write out a complete description of every music cue wanted and how it is to be used. Indicate type of music and length.

m. Indicate an appropriate number of provisional cuts.

3. Make a mark-up of the same script and submit it for criticism.

4. Cast this script from the available acting talent. Write out a report indicating why each actor was called for casting and a justification of the final selection.

5. Select and spot the music needed for this script from the available music library.

6. Rehearse and record this same script, using other members of the production class and of acting classes for cast and company. This should be followed by a play-back of the recorded program for criticism by the instructor and the class. The following procedure is recommended for critical playbacks. Play the program five or six times with the attention focused on different items each time.

First playing will give the class a general impression and over-all effect.

Second playing, concentrate on production alone.

Third playing, listen for acting and interpretation only.

Fourth playing, listen to the musical treatment only.

Fifth playing, listen to the sound only.

Sixth playing, listen for scenes that had special production problems.

This assignment routine can be repeated many times, beginning with very simple programs and proceeding to more complex programs encompassing increasingly difficult production problems until the student develops a sureness of touch in handling this kind of material.

Chapter XIII

Design, build, and produce a variety program, using school talent. If a school orchestra is available, use live music, and handle it as an actual broadcast. If an orchestra is not available, use recorded music, but do the rest of the program in the normal variety pattern. Select the acts from the available talent in school. Audition and select the master of ceremonies, comedians and other talent required. Have the writing class furnish the script for the program. Rehearse and produce it and make a recording for analysis and criticism.

DB46

INDEX